Contents

The appendices to this report are available in a separate document.

Pensions: Challenges and Choices

The First Report of the Pensions Commission

Copies of this report and accompanying documents are available at: www.pensionscommission.org.uk or from The Stationery Office.

Foreword: The purpose and style of this report and most useful response to it

The Pensions Commission was appointed in December 2002 with the remit of keeping under review the adequacy of private pension saving in the UK, and advising on appropriate policy changes, including on whether there is a need to "move beyond the voluntary approach."

In June 2003 we published our work plan, setting out the analysis we would conduct in the period before our First Report. We made it clear that the First Report would focus on a detailed description of the present position, but would not make policy recommendations.

We deliberately chose this approach because it is essential that the problems facing Britain's pension system are analysed comprehensively, looking at how all the different facets of the system relate to one another. Pension reform in the UK has too often in the past proceeded on the basis of analysis of specific isolated issues.

We are now presenting that First Report.

The **purpose** of the report is to stimulate debate and to ensure that the debate is fact-based and well-structured. We therefore set out not only our analysis of the facts, and what will happen if policies and behaviours do not change, but also, in Chapter 7, the logical set of alternative policy responses which could address the undoubted problems. In presenting these alternatives, however, we make it clear that we have not concluded in favour of any one approach, and we point out the disadvantages and difficulties entailed in any of the proposed solutions, as well as the apparent benefits.

The **style** of the report is detailed and fact-based. There is a large number of exhibits, footnotes and appendices. This is deliberate. We want to make clear the facts on which our analysis is based, enabling experts and interested parties to point out where we are wrong, or where we have missed key issues. We also make explicit the deficiencies of the data sources available, and the extent to which we have had to make judgments. And where, particularly in our modelling, we have had to make assumptions on variables such as rates of return or costs, we have made these explicit, enabling people to judge how far different assumptions would lead to different conclusions.

The **most useful response** to this report by politicians of both government and opposition and by other interested parties would not entail immediate conclusions. There are no easy answers to the problems we face. It would therefore be unfortunate if initial debate on this report, particularly in a pre-election period, led to any options being ruled out. We are not making specific recommendations, but we know already that it is impossible to deal with the challenges facing us without making difficult choices. The problems of the British pension system today reflect the cumulative impact of decisions and commitments made, and of policies rejected, often with unintended consequences, by governments over several decades. We need to develop an approach which can command consensus across parties, and which can be sustained across parliaments and governments.

We are now launching the consultation phase of our work, details of which are set out in Chapter 9. We would like to receive written submissions by the end of January 2005. In about a year we will produce a Second Report, which will include specific policy recommendations.

Some people will ask whether the problems of Britain's pension system do not require more rapid resolution. Our response to that question is twofold:

- First, while there are short as well as long-term problems in the UK pension system, the Commission's focus, responding to our remit, is on the long-term. Our primary focus is not therefore the current standard of living of existing pensioners, nor is it the immediate problems created by failures in the inherited system (e.g. by the distressing insolvency of some existing pension schemes). These are important issues, but they are not ones which we have been asked to consider. Our focus is instead on what society and individuals need to do to ensure a sound pension system looking forward over the next several decades.

- Second, given this focus, it is more important to arrive at policy recommendations which are well founded, comprehensive, and sustainable, than to develop those recommendations this year rather than next.

Finally in this Foreword all three members of the Commission would like to thank the Commission's secretariat for the enormous amount of work which has gone into producing this First Report.

Members of the Pensions Commission

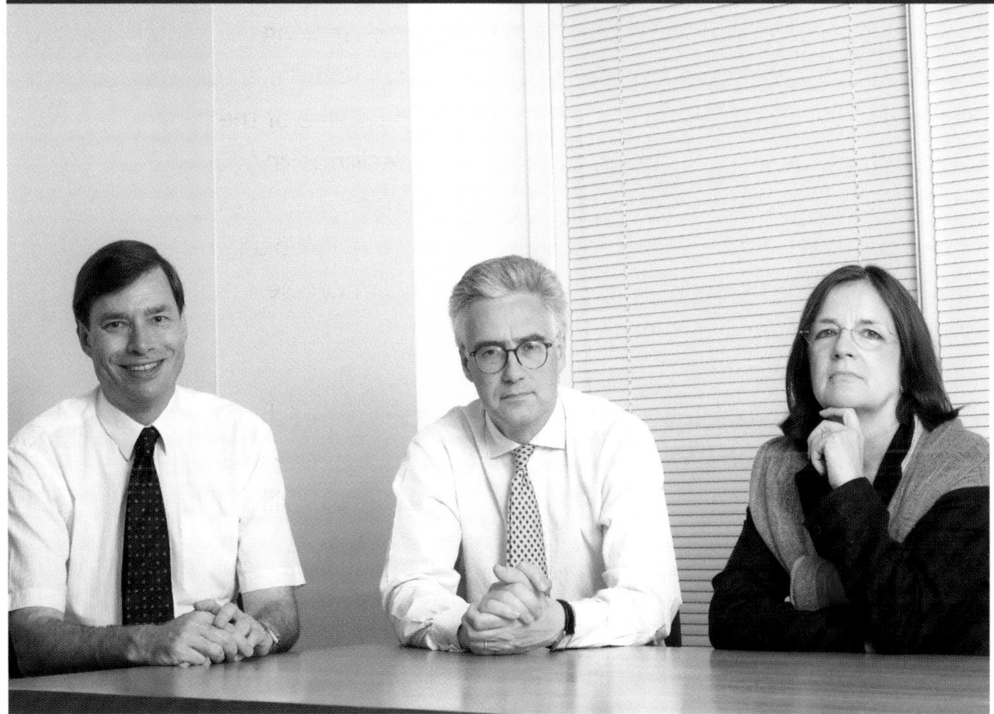

Left to right: John Hills, Adair Turner and Jeannie Drake

Adair Turner (Chairman)

Adair Turner is currently Vice Chairman of Merrill Lynch Europe, a director of United Business Media plc and chair of the UK Low Pay Commission.

Jeannie Drake

Jeannie Drake is the Deputy General Secretary for the Communication Workers Union and President of the Trades Union Congress.

John Hills

John Hills is Professor of Social Policy and Director of the ESRC Research Centre for Analysis of Social Exclusion (CASE) at the London School of Economics.

Executive Summary

Introduction

This document is a summary of the First Report of the Pensions Commission. The Commission is an independent body which was established by the Government following the pensions Green Paper in December 2002. Its remit, set out in the Green Paper is, in summary:

> *"to keep under review the regime for UK private pensions and long-term savings, and to make recommendations to the Secretary of State for Work and Pensions on whether there is a case for moving beyond the current voluntarist approach."*

This report presents the findings of an analysis of the UK pensions and retirement savings system. It describes in detail the present situation, the trends in place, and the challenges which need to be met. It does not make specific recommendations on pensions policy: these will be set out in our Second Report, planned for Autumn 2005, and will follow a consultation process. It does, however make recommendations relating specifically to improvements in official data sources: these are discussed in Appendix A and listed at the end of the main report.

The key conclusions from our eight analytical chapters are set out below, along with a summary of Chapter 9, which describes the consultation process.

Chapter 1: The demographic challenge and unavoidable choices

Life expectancy is increasing rapidly and will continue to do so. This is good news. But combined with a forecast low birth rate this will produce a near doubling in the percentage of the population aged 65 years and over between now and 2050, with further increase thereafter. The baby boom has delayed the effect of underlying long-term trends, but will now produce 30 years of very rapid increase in the dependency ratio. We must now make adjustments to public policy and/or individual behaviour which ideally should have been started in the last 20-30 years.

Faced with the increasing proportion of the population aged over 65, society and individuals must choose between four options. Either:

(i) pensioners will become poorer relative to the rest of society; or

(ii) taxes/National Insurance contributions devoted to pensions must rise; or

(iii) savings must rise; or

(iv) average retirement ages must rise.

But the first option (poorer pensioners) appears unattractive; and there are significant barriers to solving the problem through any one of the other three options alone. Some mix of higher taxes/National Insurance contributions, higher savings and later average retirement is required.

Chapter 2: Average retirement ages: Past and possible future trends

Our response to the demographic challenge should include a rise in the average age of retirement. Healthy ageing for many people makes this possible; and an increase in employment rates among older people is now occurring. But the increase needed to make later retirement a sufficient solution alone looks very large; and significant inequalities in life expectancy and health across socio-economic groups may limit the scope for across the board increases. Increases either in taxes/National Insurance contributions and/or in private savings will therefore also be needed to meet the demographic challenge.

Chapter 3: The UK pensions system: Position and trends

The UK pensions system appeared in the past to work well because one of the least generous state pension systems in the developed world was complemented by the most developed system of voluntary private funded pensions. This rosy picture always hid multiple inadequacies relating to specific groups of people, but on average the system worked, with the percentage of GDP transferred to pensioners comparable to other countries. But the state plans to provide decreasing support for many people in order to control expenditure in the face of an ageing population and the private system is not developing to offset the state's retreating role. Instead it is in significant decline.

The underlying trend in private sector employer pension contributions has been downwards since the early 1980s, and the total level of funded pension saving is significantly less than official estimates have suggested. But irrational equity markets and delayed appreciation of life expectancy increases enabled many Defined Benefit (DB) schemes to avoid necessary adjustments until the late 1990s. As the fool's paradise has come to an end, schemes have been closed to new members, and a shift to less generous Defined Contribution (DC) schemes has followed. The underlying level of funded pension saving is falling rather than rising to meet the demographic challenge, pension right accrual is becoming still more unequal, and risk is being shifted to individuals sometimes ill-equipped to deal with it.

Chapter 4: Looking forward: Pension adequacy if trends unchanged

Given present trends many people will face "inadequate" pensions in retirement, unless they have large non-pension assets or are intending to retire much later than current retirees.

Current government plans and private savings levels imply that total pension income flowing to normal age retirees will rise from today's 9.1% of GDP to a mid-point estimate of 10.8% by 2050, and that there will be no significant shift in the balance of provision from state to private sources. This level of transfer in turn implies either poorer pensioners relative to average earnings or significantly higher average retirement ages.

The burden of adjustment will however be very unequally distributed. We estimate that at least 75% of all DC scheme members have contribution rates below the level likely to be required to provide adequate pensions. Our estimates suggest that around 9 million people may be under-saving, some by a small amount, some severely. But the significant minority of people in still open private sector DB schemes will enjoy more than adequate pensions and most public sector employees will be well provided for, as will some higher paid employees in Senior Executive schemes. The present level of pension right accrual is both deficient in total and increasingly unequal.

The implications of this for pensioner income will be more serious in 20-25 years time than in the next 10. And over that long time span many adjustments, for instance to savings rates and retirement ages, may naturally occur. A muddle-through option does therefore exist. But it is highly likely that the muddle-through option will produce outcomes both less socially equitable and less economically efficient than we could achieve with a consciously planned response to the problems we face.

Chapter 5: Non-pension savings and housing

In addition to occupational and personal pension funds worth £1,300 billion and unfunded public sector pension rights worth about £500 billion, the personal sector owns about £1,150 billion of non-pension financial assets, some of which could also provide resources for retirement income. But the ownership of these assets is very unequally distributed, and for the majority of people they can only provide a modest contribution to their standard of living in retirement.

Housing assets are more significant both because they are much bigger (£2,250 billion net of mortgage debt) and their ownership is more equally distributed. While the liquidation of housing assets during retirement will likely remain limited in scope, the inheritance of housing assets by people who already own a house may play an increasing role in retirement provision for many people. But house ownership does not provide a sufficient solution to the problem of pension provision given (i) uncertainty over future house prices; (ii) other potential claims on housing wealth such as long-term care; and (iii) the fact that housing wealth is not significantly higher among those with least pension rights.

Business assets, meanwhile, are important stores of wealth and potential sources of retirement provision, but for only a small minority of people. The fact that pension saving among the self-employed is not increasing therefore remains concerning.

Chapter 6: Barriers to a voluntarist solution

The present level of pension right accrual, private and state combined, will leave many with inadequate pensions. And there are likely to be limits to solving the problem solely via increased retirement ages. If state system plans are taken as given, a higher level of private saving is required.

There are however big barriers to the success of a voluntary pension saving system, some inherent to any pension system, some specific to the UK. Most people do not make rational decisions about long-term savings without encouragement and advice. But the cost of advice, and of regulating to ensure that it is good advice, in itself significantly reduces the return on saving, particularly for low earners. Reductions in Yield arising from providers' charges can absorb 20-30% of an individual's pension saving, even though they have fallen to a level where provision to lower income groups is unprofitable. This poses a fundamental question: in principle can a voluntary market for pensions work for low income, low premium customers?

But both the behavioural barriers to savings and the costs of provision have been made worse by the bewildering complexity of the UK pension system, state and private combined. This complexity reflects the impact of multiple decisions made over the last several decades, each of which appeared to make sense at the time, but the cumulative effect of which has been to create confusion and mistrust. Means-testing within the state system both increases complexity and reduces, and in some cases reverses, the incentives to save via pensions which the tax system creates. The scope of this means-testing would grow over time if current indexation approaches were continued indefinitely.

Unless new government initiatives can make a major difference to behaviours it is unlikely that the present voluntary private system combined with the present state system will solve the problem of inadequate pension savings.

Chapter 7. Revitalised voluntarism, changes to the state system, or increased compulsion?

To achieve adequacy there are three possible ways forward:

(i) a major revitalisation of the voluntary system and/or;

(ii) significant changes to the state system; and/or

(iii) an increased level of compulsory private pension saving beyond that already implicit within the UK system.

This chapter considers possible change along these three dimensions, and the issues to be considered in choosing between them. Its purpose is solely to stimulate debate and to highlight the difficulties, as well as the advantages, of any way forward. Analysis of these issues, discussed only in outline here, will be the key focus of the Pensions Commission between now and the publication of the Second Report in Autumn 2005

Chapter 8. Women and pensions

Women pensioners in the UK today are significantly poorer than men. This reflects both labour market features (lower employment rates, lower average earnings, and more part-time work) and specific features of the UK's state pension system. These state system features have in the past entailed most women gaining pension income through their husband, and reflected assumptions about family structure which have ceased to be valid. An effective pension system for the future must be one in which the vast majority of women accrue pension entitlements, both state and private, in their own right.

Some progress towards that aim is now occurring, with some labour market trends favourable to women, and some changes in the state system which benefit women. But important issues remain relating to overall equality in the workforce, to state system design, and to low levels of pension provision and take-up in some service sectors in which women's employment is concentrated.

Chapter 9. Issues and consultation process

In its deliberations over the next year, the Commission would like to hear the views of interested and informed parties, and to get their reactions to this First descriptive report. It would be helpful if in setting out those reactions, organisations or individuals could separately and explicitly identify:

(i) Any areas where they believe that we have the facts wrong or where we overlooked available sources of information.

(ii) Whether they believe the judgements we have had to make about future trends are over-optimistic or over-pessimistic.

(iii) What the organisation or individual believes should be the appropriate responsibility of the state in ensuring adequate pension provision.

Specific issues on which we would welcome views are mentioned at various points in the report, and are then pulled together in Chapter 9.

The Commission would like to receive written submission on these issues by end-January 2005. The arrangements for making submissions are set out at the end of Chapter 9.

List of figures

List of tables

The demographic challenge and unavoidable choices

1

Life expectancy is increasing rapidly and will continue to do so. This is good news. But combined with a forecast low birth rate this will produce a near doubling in the percentage of the population aged 65 years and over between now and 2050, with further increase thereafter. The baby boom has delayed the effect of underlying long-term trends, but will now produce 30 years of very rapid increase in the dependency ratio. We must now make adjustments to public policy and/or individual behaviour which ideally should have been started in the last 20-30 years.

Faced with the increasing proportion of the population aged over 65, society and individuals must choose between four options. Either:

(i) pensioners will become poorer relative to the rest of society; or
(ii) taxes/National Insurance contributions devoted to pensions must rise; or
(iii) the savings rate must rise; or
(iv) average retirement ages must rise.

But the first option (poorer pensioners) appears unattractive; and there are significant barriers to solving the problem through any one of the other three options alone. Some mix of higher taxes/National Insurance contributions, higher savings and later average retirement is required.

This chapter covers five points:

1 Increased life expectancy and low fertility will lead to a major rise in dependency ratios over the next 50 years, which could be higher than official projections suggest.

2 The effect of the baby boom has been to concentrate the impact of long-term changes into the next 30 years.

3 Society and/or individuals face an unavoidable choice: poorer pensioners, higher taxes/NI contributions, higher savings or later retirement.

4 The current combination of choices and assumptions being made is unsustainable.

5 A wide-ranging public debate is required to ensure that conscious and well-informed choices are made both by society and by individuals.

1. Demographic trends and dependency ratios

Increasing longevity and a low birth rate mean that the percentage of the adult population over the age of 65 will increase dramatically in the next 50 years. The Government Actuary's Department (GAD) projects that the ratio of 65+ year olds to 20-64 years olds will increase from 27% to 48% by 2050, but even this assumes a dramatic slow-down in the rate of increase in longevity. A considerably larger increase is possible.[1]

- Estimating future trends in life expectancy is an uncertain science. But it is clear that life expectancy, both at birth and at 65, has increased dramatically and will continue to rise. Average male life expectancy at 65 has grown from 12.0 years in 1950 to an estimated 19.0 today, and is projected to rise to 21.0 by 2030 and to 21.7 by 2050.[2] Female life expectancy is higher and also increasing, though at a slightly slower rate. But it is important to realise that past official projections have significantly understated subsequent developments. In 1981 GAD projected that by 2004 male life expectancy at 65 would be 14.8 years: today it is believed to be 19.0. Looking forward the official projections assume a major decrease in the rate of improvement from now on, and a very slow pace of increase after 2027. If instead life expectancy at 65 keeps rising in line with the past 50 years' trend, average male life expectancy will reach 24.4 years by 2050: if it rises in line with the 1980-2000 trend, it will reach 27.7 [Figures 1.1 and 1.2].

[1]Note: In this report we have taken GAD's 2002-based projections as our base case assumptions, and considered variants about these to highlight the degree of uncertainty. We do not consider whether policy can affect the demographic outcome, whether in respect to immigration or to birth rates.

[2]Note: It is also worth nothing that life expectancy at 45, particularly for men, has been increasing with lower late middle age mortality rates (GAD, 1980-2000). This also swells the number of pensioners as more people are surviving to retirement ages.

Figure 1.1 Cohort Life Expectancy for Men and Women at 65: England and Wales, historic and G.A.D. principal projection

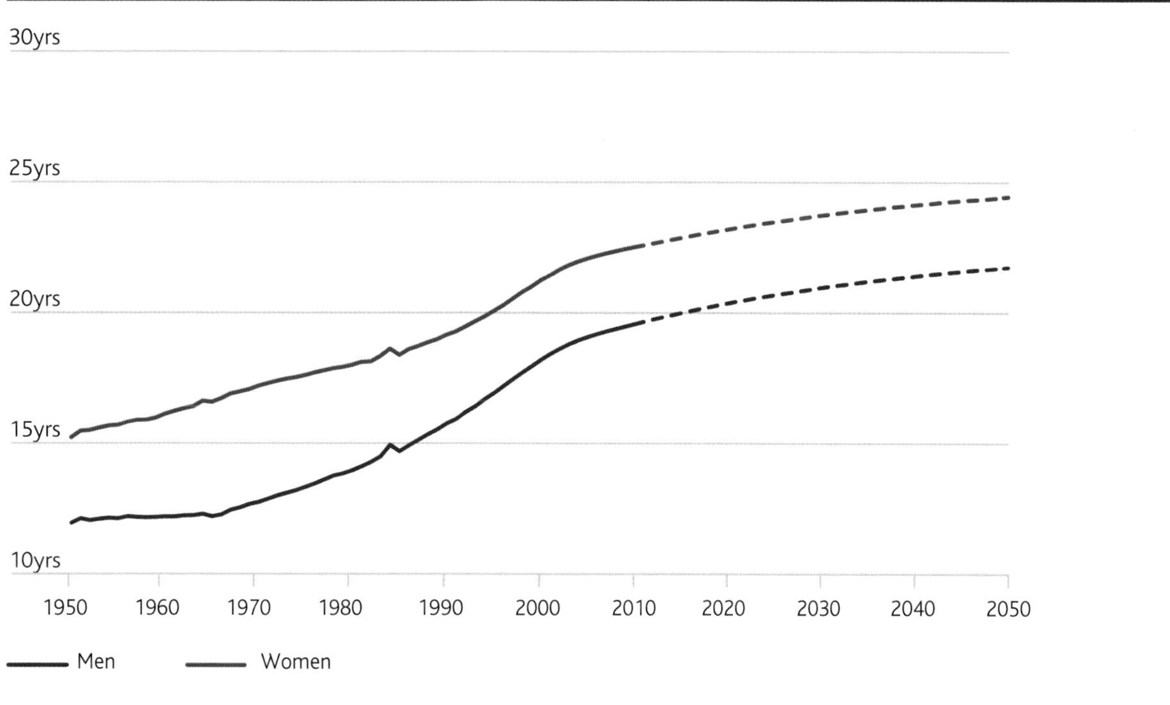

Source: GAD Historical data to 2002, England and Wales
GAD 2002-based principal population projection from 2003 onwards, England and Wales

Note: See Appendix E for the definition of "Cohort life expectancy" which is a better measure of true life expectancy at a particular age than the frequently cited "Period life expectancy".

Figure 1.2 Cohort Life Expectancy for Men at 65: UK

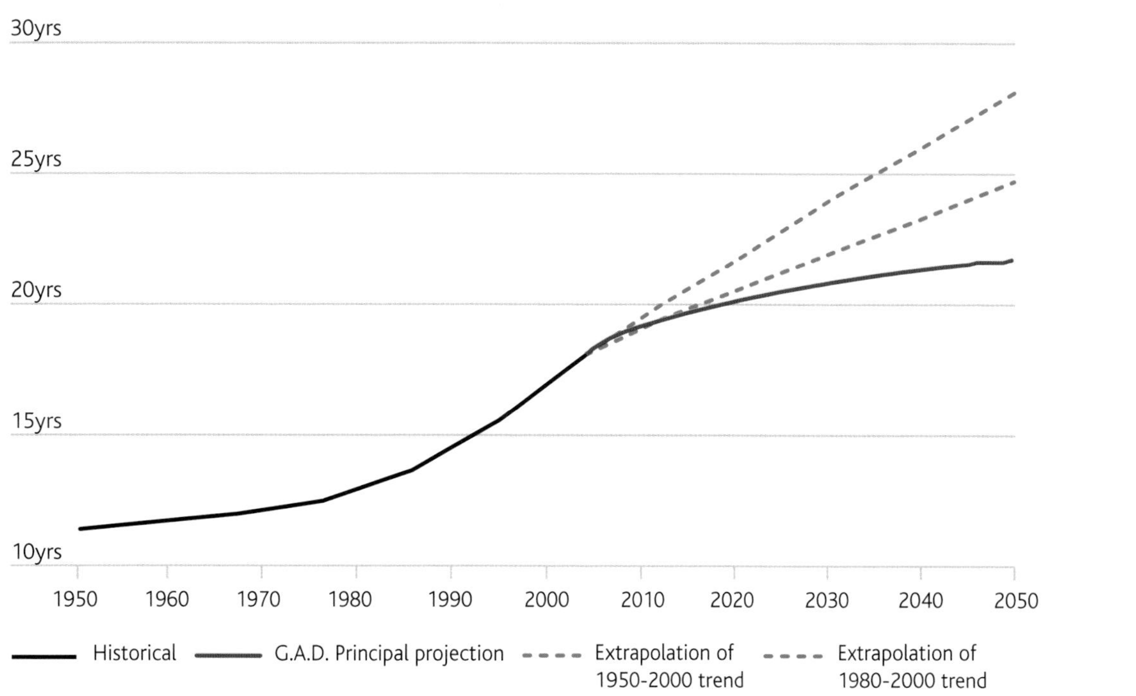

Source: Pensions Commission analysis 1950-1970 based on GAD historical data, England and Wales
GAD historical data 1980-2002, UK
GAD 2002-based principal population projection, UK, from 2003 onwards

- Forecasting future birth rates is also uncertain but in the UK, as in most developed economies, the birth rate has fallen below the replacement level. The total fertility rate in England and Wales is now about 1.7 children per woman, and despite a slight increase in 2003, shows no signs of sustained and significant recovery [Figure 1.3]. While the rise in birth rates after the Second World War might suggest that a recovery is possible, no significant increase has been observed in any developed economy since birth rates came down in the 1970s and 80s, and the most reasonable assumption is that only a small recovery will occur. GAD project a small rise in the UK total fertility rate over the next 18 years levelling off at 1.75 after 2022.

- The combined effect of these trends in longevity and fertility is that the shape of the UK's demographic structure will change dramatically over the next 50 years, with only a negligible increase in the number of 20-64 years olds, but a 78% increase in the number of 65+ year olds [Figures 1.4 and 1.5]. As a result the ratio of 65+ year olds to 20-64 year olds will increase (on GAD's principal projections) from 27% today to 48% in 2050, with almost all of the increase concentrated in the next 30 years. This marks a major break from the very slow increase in the last 20 years [Figure 1.6].

- Moreover, the last 20 years have seen a significant fall in the ratio of children to working age people. As a result the total dependency ratio (i.e. the number of those either below 20 or above 65 divided by the number of 20-64 year olds) has actually fallen, and is now at the lowest level for over 40 years [Figure 1.7]. The working population in 2004 supports a historically very low burden of non-working pensioners and children. The size of that burden, if average retirement ages remain unchanged, will now rise significantly.[3]

[3]Note: The ratio between workers and non-workers will also be affected by (i) whether the numbers of years of youth dependency is changing – its recent trend has been to increase with greater higher education participation; and (ii) the number of non-working people below retirement age. This Report does not consider the first issue. The second issue is considered in Chapter 2.

Figure 1.3 Total Fertility Rate 1900-2050: England and Wales

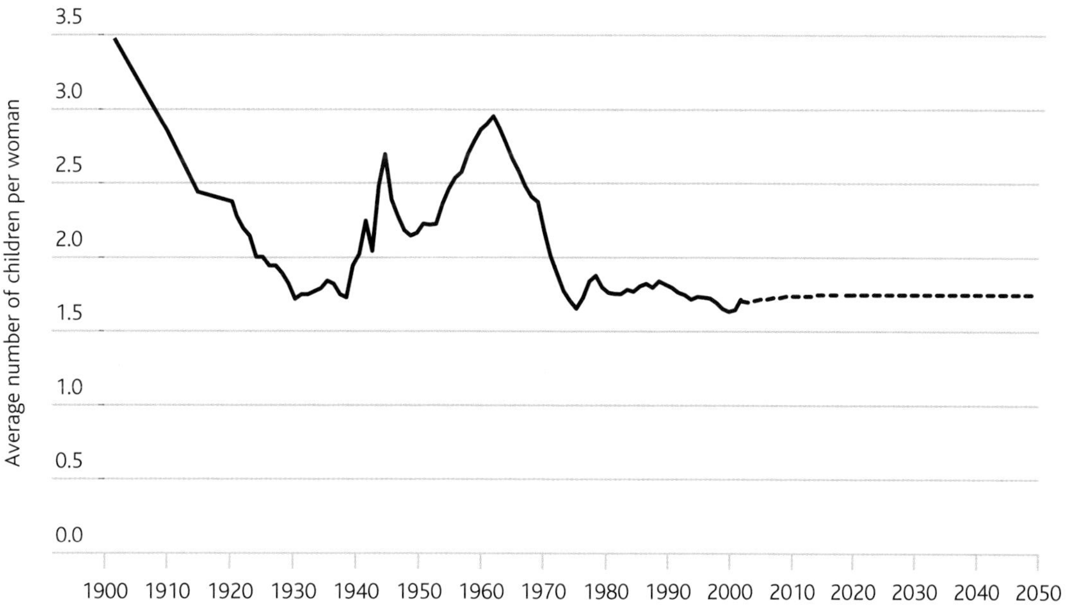

Source: ONS Birth Statistics Series FM1

Note: The definition of Total Fertility Rate, and the way in which it is influenced both by completed family size births and by decisions as to the timing of births is explained in Appendix E, which also sets out the argument for believing that a repeat of the 1945-1965 reversal of the downward trend is unlikely.

Data from birth registration on age of mother at birth is only available from 1938. Figures for the years prior to 1938 are ONS estimates.

Figure 1.4 Distribution of the UK population, by age: 2002

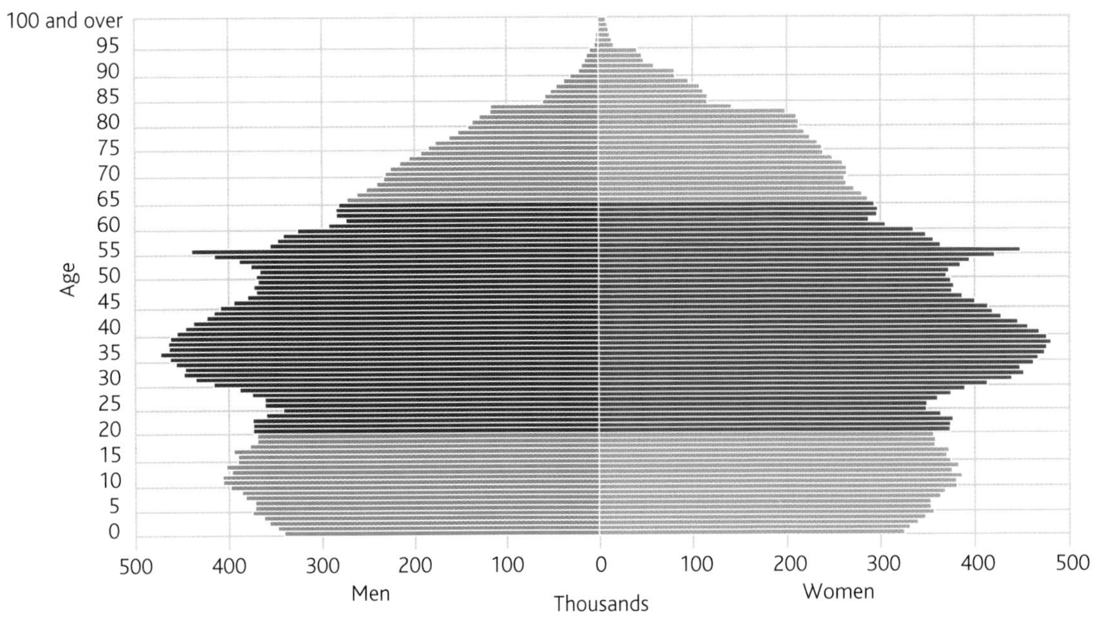

Source: GAD 2002-based principal population projection, UK
Pensions Commission analysis

Note: A smoothing assumption for the population groups aged 90-94 and 95-99 years has been made by applying the distribution of the 85-89 year cohorts five and ten years previously. The darker area highlights those aged 20-64.

Figure 1.5 Distribution of the UK population, by age: 2050

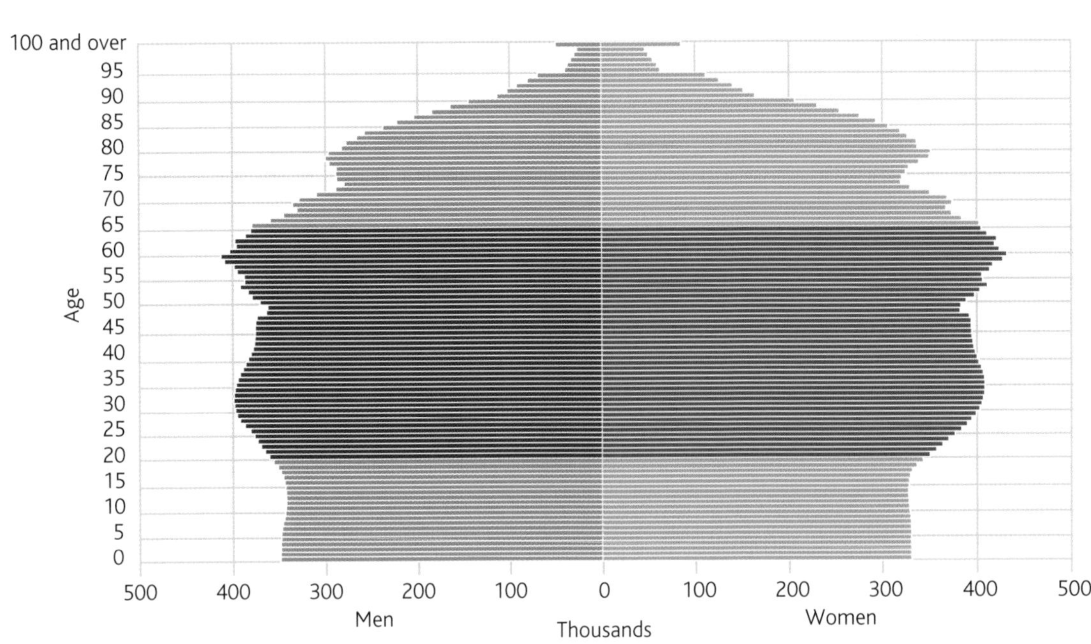

Source: GAD 2002-based principal population projection, UK
Pensions Commission analysis

Note: A smoothing assumption for the population groups aged 90-94 and 95-99 years has been made by applying the distribution of the 85-89 year cohorts five and ten years previously. The darker area highlights those aged 20-64.

Figure 1.6 Old-Age Dependency Ratio: All 65+: 20-64, UK

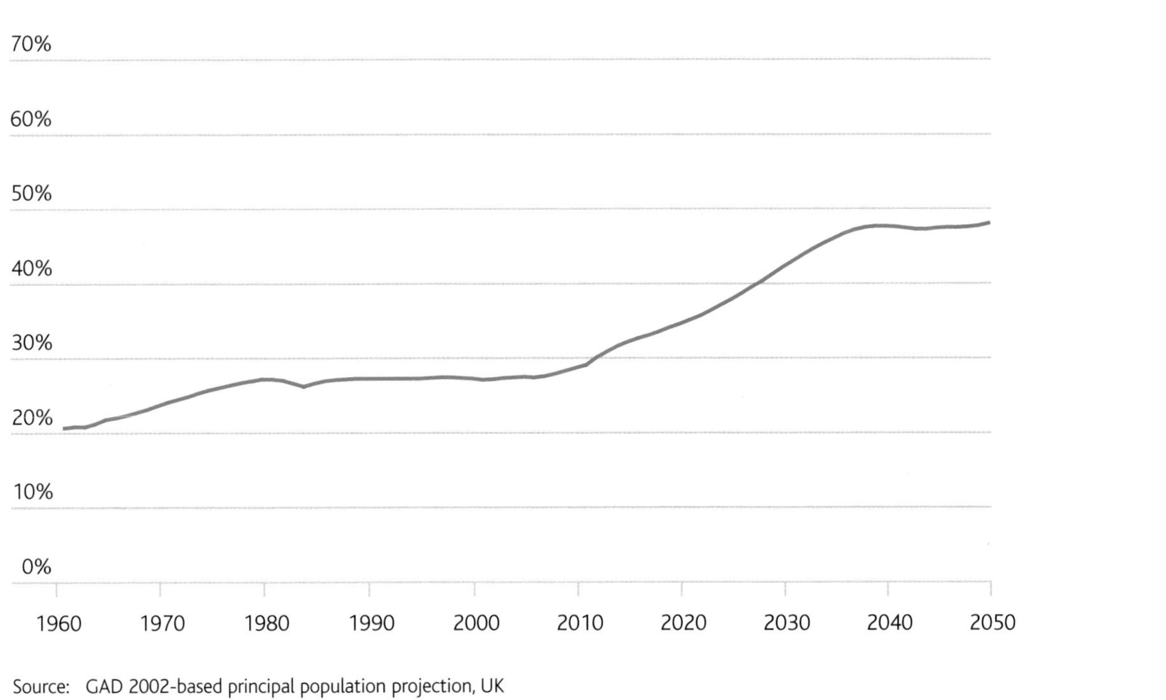

Source: GAD 2002-based principal population projection, UK
ONS Population estimates unit, UK

Figure 1.7 Old-Age, Youth and Total Dependency Ratios

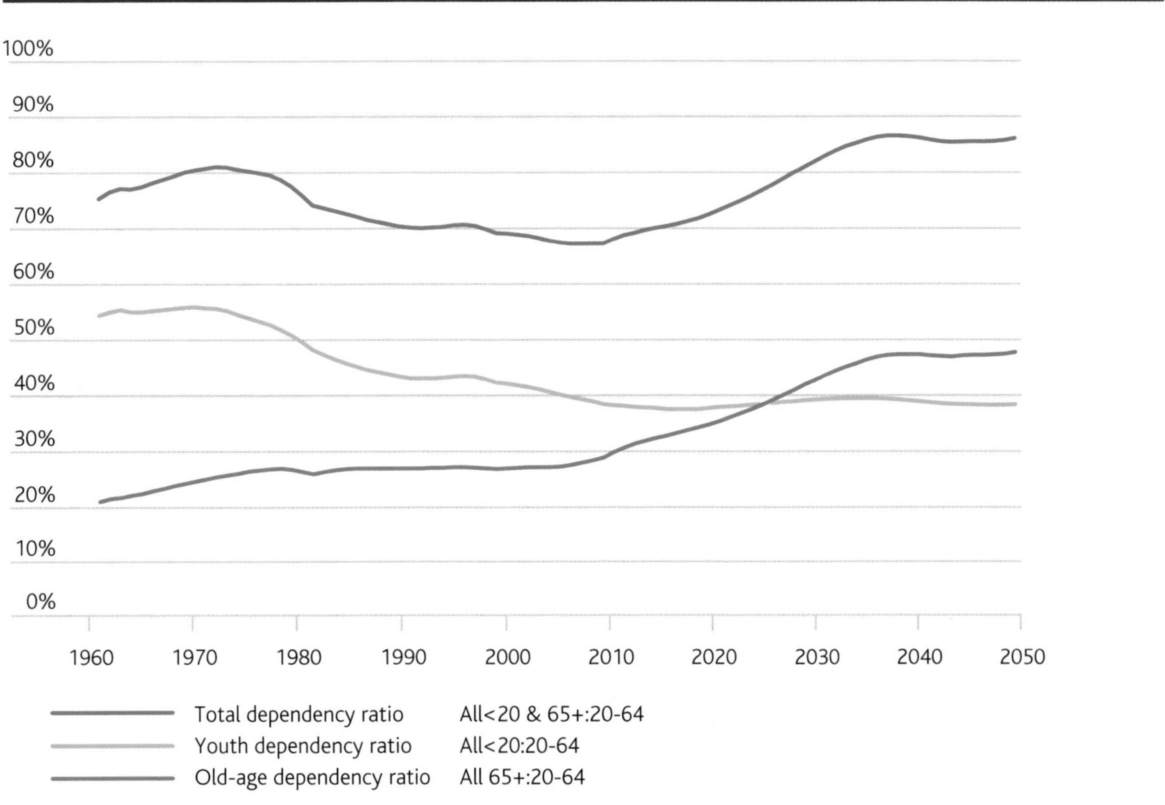

Source: GAD 2002-based principal population projection, UK
ONS Population estimates unit, UK

- Alternative scenarios around the principal projection are more likely to produce still higher dependency ratios than lower, at least over the next 40-50 years.

  - If the projected slowdown in longevity increase does not occur, but instead mortality rates continue to decline in line with recent trends, the old-age dependency ratio will rise to 54% in 2050 versus 48% in the principal projection, and will continue to increase thereafter [Figure 1.8]

  - Poor lifestyle trends such as increasing obesity among young adults and children may in the long-term reduce the increase in life expectancy, but over the next 30 years they could make the burden on the working population worse, since they may reduce the number of healthy working-age people more than they reduce the number of elderly pensioners.

  - An increase in the birth rate meanwhile will have no impact on the number of 20-64 year olds until 2025, and any feasible pace of increase from current levels will have only a minimal impact on the size of the working population in 2040. GAD's "high fertility" projection only pulls down the projected 2040 old-age dependency ratio from 47.3% to 45.9%, though the impact would gradually increase thereafter. In fact until 2030, a rise in the birth rate would produce a **rise** in the **total** dependency ratio, with the increase in the number of dependent children offsetting the rise in the ratio of workers to pensioners.

  - Only high immigration can produce more than a trivial reduction in the projected dependency ratio over the next 50 years. Net inward migration at +300,000 per year could bring the 2040 old-age dependency ratio down from 47.3% to 42.1%. But it is important to realise that this would only be a temporary effect unless still higher levels of immigration continued in later years, or unless immigrants maintained a higher birth rate than the existing population, since immigrants themselves grow old and become pensioners who need workers to support them.

On any reasonable assumptions therefore, the UK faces a big increase in the old-age dependency ratio, as measured by the ratio of 65+ year olds to 20-64 year olds; and this increase will be particularly dramatic over the next 30 years.

Figure 1.8 Effect of alternative GAD Scenarios on the All 65+ : 20-64 Dependency Ratio

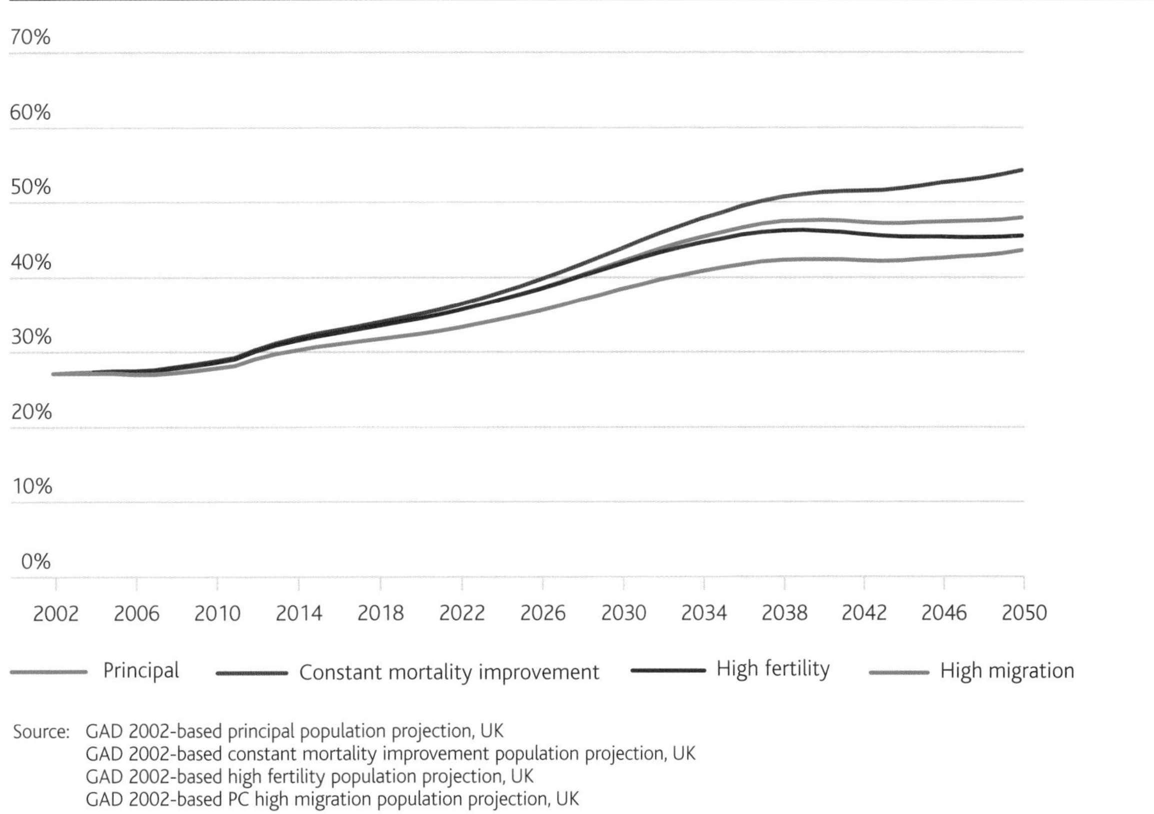

Source: GAD 2002-based principal population projection, UK
GAD 2002-based constant mortality improvement population projection, UK
GAD 2002-based high fertility population projection, UK
GAD 2002-based PC high migration population projection, UK

Note: The GAD "constant mortality improvement" scenario assumes an annual fall in the mortality rate of around 2% in line with recent trends. This is equivalent to cohort male life expectancy at 65 of 29.6 years in 2050.

The GAD "high fertility" scenario applies a fertility rate of 1.94 throughout the projection period i.e. from 2002-03 onwards.

The GAD "Pension Commission high migration scenario" assumes from 2003-04 onwards an annual net migration of +300,000, versus +130,000 in the principal projection.

2. The impact of the baby boom: postponing necessary adjustments

It is useful to understand the balance of longevity and fertility effects in driving this increase, and in driving the acceleration which we now face. Over the long-term, increasing longevity has been and will be the key factor, but past fluctuations in the fertility rate have concentrated the change in the next 30 years.

- Over the whole period 1960-2050, increasing longevity is the predominant driver. The size of the 1960's working population was largely determined by interwar fertility rates, which were similar to those of today and those forecast for 2050. Over the 90 years from 1960-2050 therefore, fertility rate decline is not the key factor driving the increase in the old-age dependency ratio. Instead, the increase in life expectancy at 65 from 12.2 years (for men) in 1960 to a forecast 21.7 in 2050 explains almost 80% of the increase in the dependency ratio over that period. [See Appendix E for detailed analysis of this breakdown.] And if fertility does not fall below current levels, any further increases in the dependency ratio after 2050 will be entirely driven by further increases in longevity.

- The impact of the baby boom, however, has been to concentrate this long-term longevity-driven rise in the dependency ratio into a 30 year period. The post-war baby boom resulted in a temporary increase in the fertility rate, lasting from the mid 1940s to the mid 1960s. This increase had no effect on the old-age dependency ratio in 1960 and will have no impact on the 2050 ratio, but between about 1970 and 2030 it has depressed the ratio below its long-term trend [Figure1.9].

The baby boom is not therefore the cause of the high dependency ratio from 2030 onwards. Instead the baby boom has depressed the ratio for 30 years and thus enabled society to ignore the long-term trend. Because the baby boom allowed us to ignore long-term realities, we must now in the next 30 years make adjustments to public policy and to private retirement and savings behaviour which we should ideally have started to make over the last several decades.

Figure 1.9 Impact of the 1940s-1960s Baby Boom on the Old-Age Dependency Ratio

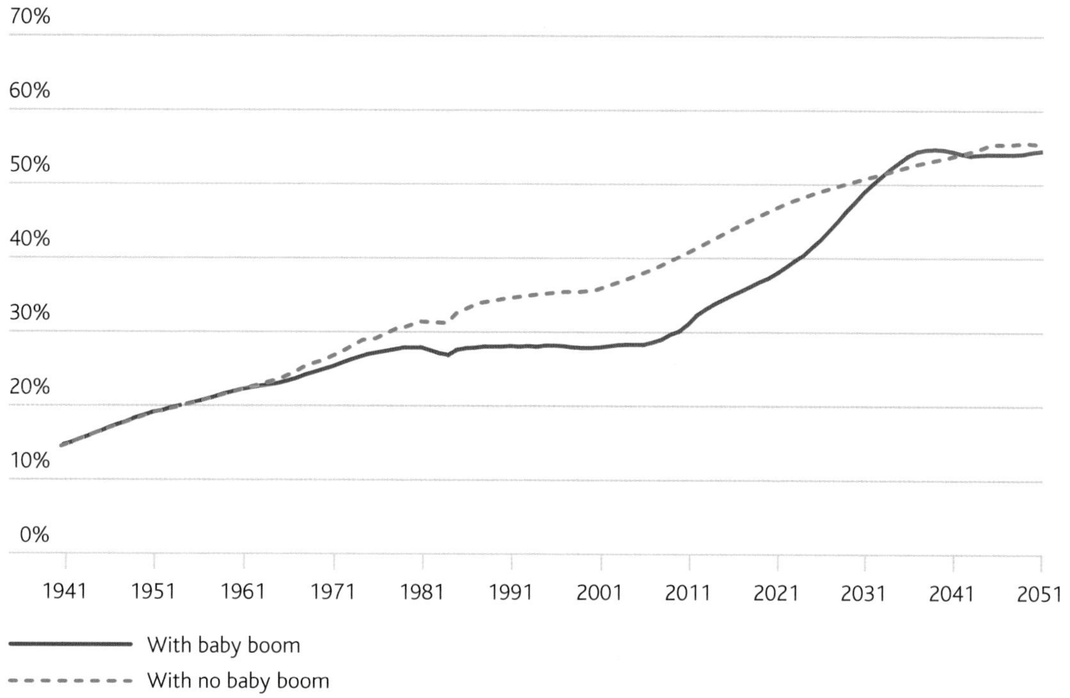

Source: Pensions Commission analysis based on a synthetic model of the England and Wales population.

Note: See Appendix E for explanation of assumptions made.

3. Unavoidable choices

An increase in the old-age dependency ratio puts strain on any pension system, whether Pay As You Go (PAYG) or funded. Appendix B explains the macroeconomics of pensions. It makes the point that in any pension system the current generation of pensioners is dependent on a resource transfer from the current generation of workers. In a PAYG system the current working generation pays taxes/National Insurance (NI) contributions which are used to pay pensions to retirees. In funded systems the working generation saves, consuming less than it produces, and thereby makes available goods and services which pensioners can consume. Pensioners pay for these goods and services with pensions financed by selling their own accumulated assets to the next generation. Some important differences between funded and PAYG systems do exist: these are outlined in Appendix B. But the fundamental fact that at the aggregate level pensioners are reliant on output produced by workers is unchanged by the choice between funded and PAYG systems. It is a delusion to believe that funding pensions magically reduces the challenge of an ageing society.[4]

Given these fundamental facts, some combination of four things must happen when the population ages. Either:

1. Future pensioners will on average be poorer relative to average net incomes than today; or

2. Taxes/NI contributions will have to rise to pay for pensions or other public spending be cut to make room for pensions; or

3. Each generation will have to save more, and will be reliant on the next generation also choosing to save more and therefore buying the larger stock of assets accumulated by the prior generation; or

4. Average retirement ages will have to rise.[5]

There are no alternatives to these four choices. And the scale of the challenge can be illustrated by considering how much we would have to change along any one dimension, if that were the only response available.

- If we do not raise tax rates, savings rates or average retirement ages, pensioners will on average suffer about a 30% decline in their incomes relative to average incomes between now and 2035.

[4]Note: One of the important differences is that in a funded system there exists the option of saving and then investing overseas, thus making future UK pensioners partly reliant on the output and the savings behaviour of future workers in other countries who may not be ageing as fast. For reasons explained in Appendix B this does not produce a complete escape route from the demographic challenge, but it is a useful flexibility, at least for a transitional period.

[5]Note: An increase in average retirement ages can occur without any increase in the State Pension Age (SPA) as Chapter 2 discusses.

- If we want pensioners to be on average as well off as today, but keep retirement ages totally unchanged (i.e. not even allowing for the equalisation of male and female state pension ages already planned), the percentage of GDP transferred to normal retirement age pensioners would have to rise from 9.9% today to 17.5% in 2050.[6] Part of this required income may be offset by the effect of the rise in the female State Pension Age (SPA) from 60 to 65 between 2010 and 2020. This increase will give the UK another ten years in which the ratio of people above SPA to those below does not rise [Figure 1.10]. It will therefore reduce the increase in the required percentage of GDP to be transferred (from 17.5% to 15.1%) if (but only if) it produces an actual increase in average female retirement ages. But even after allowing for the potential knock-on consequences of the equalisation of SPA, the percentage of GDP transferred would have to rise from 9.9% to 15.1% [Figure 1.11].

Figure 1.10 Effect on the Dependency Ratio of the Planned Increase in the Women's State Pension Age

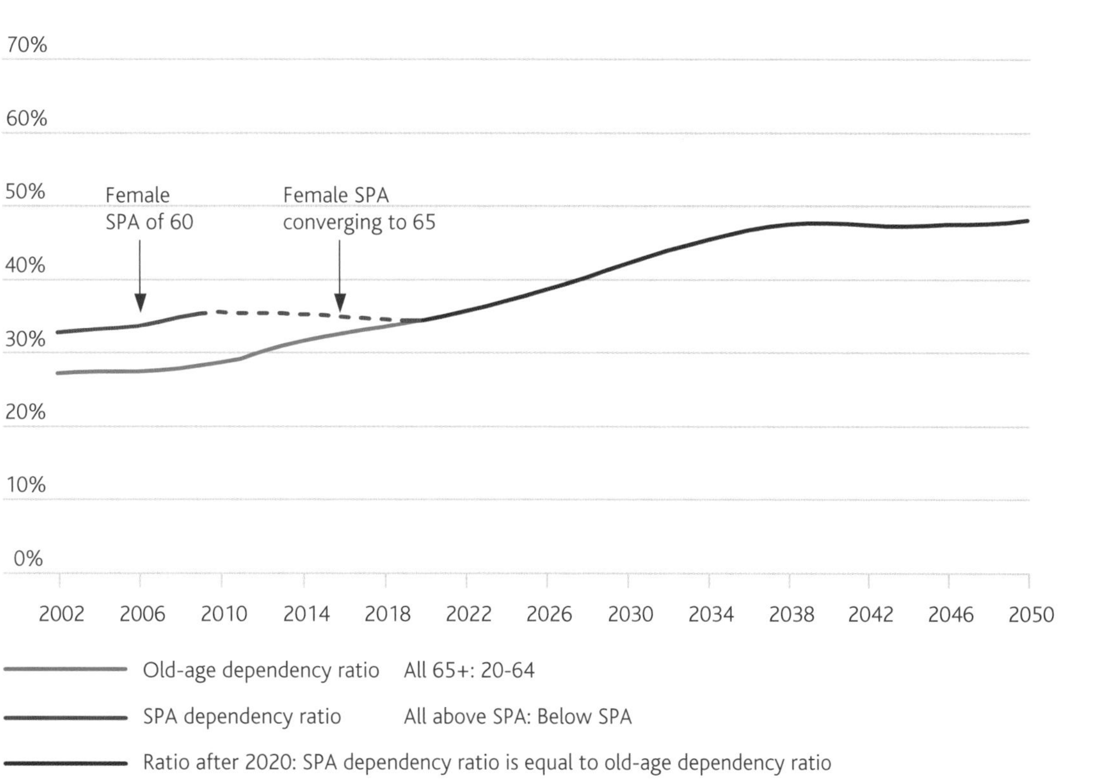

Source: GAD 2002-based principal population projection, UK

[6]Note: See the panel "Pensions and pensioner income as a percentage of GDP" at the end of the chapter for the different possible definitions of the percentage of GDP transferred to pensioners, and the important distinction between normal retirement age pensions and retirees below state pension age, who at present receive a surprisingly large 40% of all private pension incomes.

- Achieving this increase in the percentage of GDP transferred would require either:

  - State spending on pensioners rising from 6.1% to 11.3% of GDP, with taxes/NI contributions rising by £57 billion in current day terms; or

  - Private funded pensions received by pensioners above the SPA rising from 2.2% to 7.4% of GDP. Even if the proportion of funded pensions flowing to early retirees (who currently receive 40% of all funded pension income) fell drastically, this would require a doubling of the stock of capital held in pension funds. [See the panel at the end of the chapter for the various different possible definitions of public pension expenditure and private pension income.]

- Finally, if we want to keep pensioners as well off relative to average net incomes as today but we do not increase taxes or savings rates, the **average** age of retirement would have to rise from the current male average of 63.8 to 69.8, in addition to the current female average of 61.6 rising to equal the male level.[7] This would enable pensioners' relative living standards to be maintained without increasing the percentage of GDP transferred to pensioners [Figure 1.11].

[7]Note: An increase in the average age of retirement could come either from fewer people becoming economically inactive before the current SPA of 65, and/or from an increasing number working beyond 65. The possible balance of these effects is discussed in Chapter 2.

Figure 1.11 Percentage of GDP Transferred to Pensioners required in 2050 to preserve Pensioner Living Standards relative to Average Income

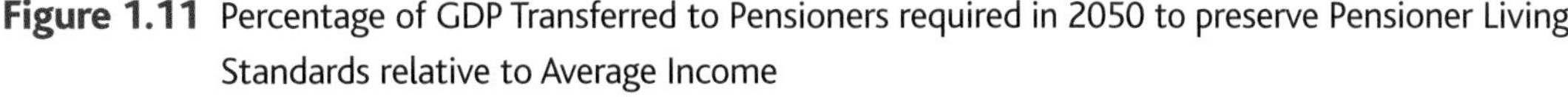

	State pension	Public sector unfunded pension	Funded pension	Investment income excluding lump sums	Total
Current position 2002	6.1	0.8	2.2	0.8	9.9
Required in 2050 to preserve pensioner living standards relative to average earnings:					
– If no change in retirement ages	16.1			1.4	17.5
– If female average retirement age rises from 61.6 to current male level of 63.8 after SPA equalisation by 2020	13.9			1.2	15.1
If both male and female retirement ages rise further to 64	13.7			1.2	14.9
65	12.8			1.1	13.9
66	12.0			1.1	13.1
67	11.2			1.0	12.2
68	10.4			0.9	11.3
69	9.7			0.9	10.6
69.8	9.1			0.8	9.9

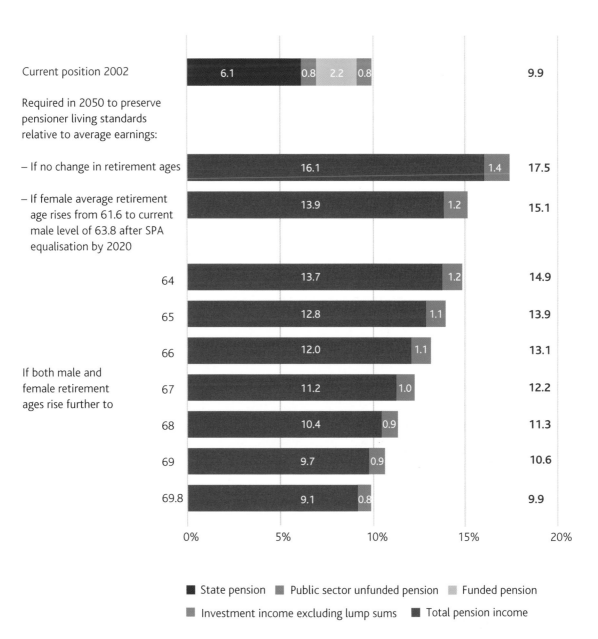

Source: Pensions Commission analysis

Note: In Figure 1.11 we include an estimate of non-pension investment income. We have not exactly modelled future scenarios for this element of income, but assume that it will vary proportionately with the number of pensioners. In Figure 1.12 we then look solely at pension incomes. The conclusions drawn from Figure 1.12 are not changed by the assumed changes in investment income.

4. Current combination of choices and assumptions unsustainable

Major changes along one or more of these four choice dimensions are therefore required. The current combination of the explicit choices and implicit assumptions being made is unsustainable.

- Current plans for the state system assume expenditure rising only from 6.1%-6.9% of GDP between now and 2050. The underlying level of funded pension saving, meanwhile, is likely to produce future pensions of 3.4%-4.2%.[8] The implications of this for the resource transfer to pensioners over 65 depends on how much of this income flows not to over 65 years olds but to early retirees [Figure 1.12].

  – If the proportion of funded pension income flowing to early retirees continues at the current 40%, funded pension income reaching over 65 year olds in 2050 will be only 2.1%-2.6%, similar to the current 2.2%, and the total resource transfer via pensions would be 9.8%-10.3% versus 9.1% today.

  – If all future funded pension income flowed to over 65 year olds, the total resource transfer via pensions would be 11.1%-11.9%.

- Taking the mid-point of this range of estimates suggests a total resource transfer via pension of 10.85%. This implies one of the combinations of reduced pensions or increased average retirement ages shown in Figure 1.12.

  – With no increase in average retirement ages, relative pensioner income would fall by about 21%.

  – To achieve no fall in relative pension income would require an increase in the average age of retirement to over 67.

[8]Note: See Chapter 4 and Annex B for the modelling of the relationship between current savings levels and future pensioner incomes.

Figure 1.12 The Implications of Current Plans and Savings Behaviour for the Percentage of GDP Transferred to Pensioners

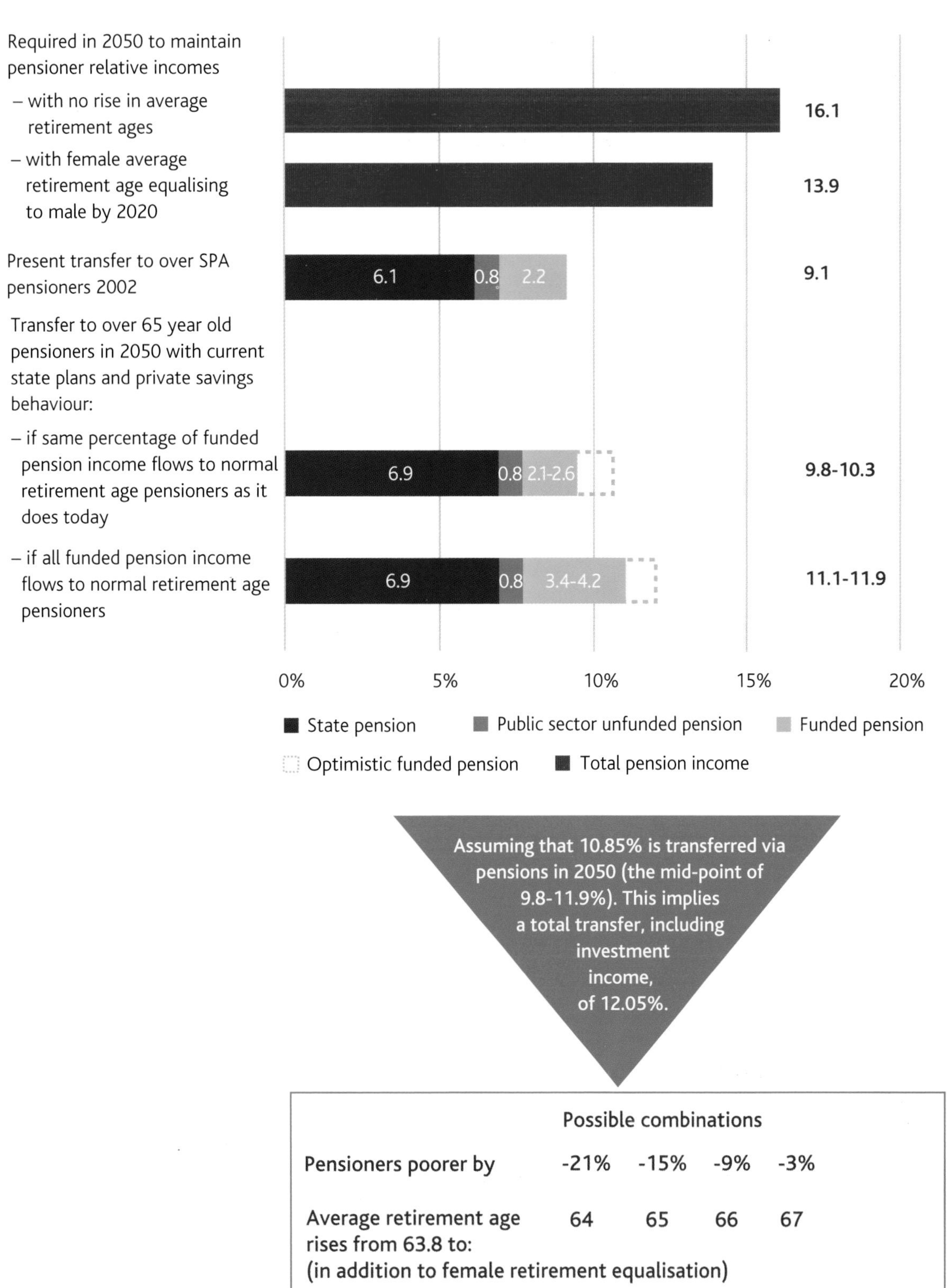

Source: Pensions Commission analysis

- But there is little evidence to suggest that people know that this result is inevitable or have consciously chosen it as desirable.

  - There is for instance no sign that younger people expect to have to retire later than their parents. The *Pensions 2002* survey responses suggest that people below the age of 55 expect to retire earlier than workers about to reach retirement ages, and that women have not adjusted retirement age expectations in the light of the forthcoming equalisation of the SPA [Figures 1.13 and 1.14]. This may in part reflect the fact that many people do not realise by how much life expectancy has increased [Figure 1.15].

  - However, survey evidence does not suggest that people either expect or accept as desirable that future pensioners should be less well off relative to average incomes than pensioners today.

Figure 1.13 Percentage of Men Expecting to Retire Before 65

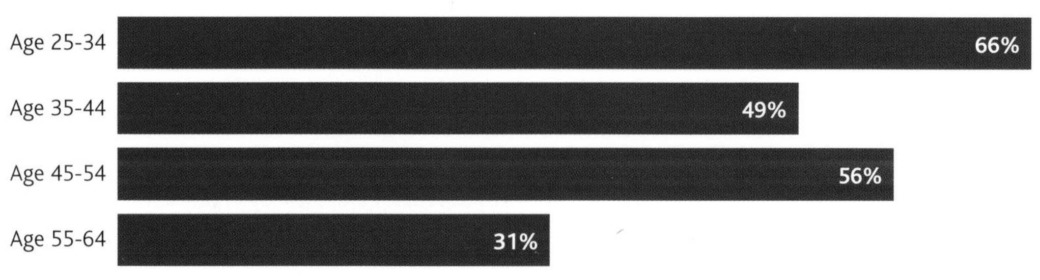

Source: Pensions 2002: Public Attitudes to Pensions and Saving for Retirement, Victoria Mayhew

Figure 1.14 Percentage of Women Expecting to Retire at 60 or Earlier

Source: Pensions 2002: Public Attitudes to Pensions and Saving for Retirement, Victoria Mayhew

Note: Those who have responded "don't know" have been excluded.

Figure 1.15 Perceived and Officially Projected Chances of Living to Age 75, by Sex: Current Age 50-54

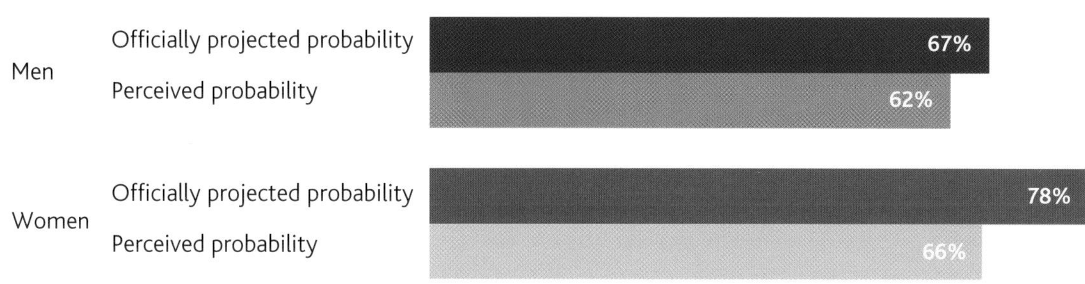

Source: ELSA, produced by IFS for Seven Ages of Man and Woman, ESRC (2004

Note: The offically projected probability could itself be an underestimate. See Figure 1.2

5. Conscious and informed choice required

A conscious and well-informed choice needs to be made between the four options. That choice will carry implications for the division of the economic burden between current and future generations of workers.

- Options 1 and 4 (poorer future pensioners or a later average retirement age) place the burden on the current generation of workers.
- Option 2 places the burden on future taxpayers, i.e. on future generations of workers.
- Option 3 places the burden essentially on current workers (who have to save more) but, as Appendix B explains, the effectiveness of this choice is also to a degree dependent on the next generation also choosing to save more.

These choices need to be considered both by society as a whole and by individuals.

- Choices need to be made collectively, i.e. at the level of government policy, in respect to the generosity of the state pension, the level of taxes/NI contributions and the SPA.
- But some choices will be made individually, with individuals making their own trade-offs between their savings rate, their standard of living in retirement and their age of retirement.
- Meanwhile if compulsory private savings were extended, a combination of social and individual choices would be implied. Compulsory private savings would involve society deciding what increase in the savings rate was desirable; but would still leave it to the individual to decide the trade-off between income in retirement and retirement age.

A key purpose of this First Report is to stimulate a wide-ranging public debate on these choices. We do not therefore in this First Report set out a recommendation for the precise balance to be struck between the four options; nor do we reach a conclusion on how far the government should make the choice versus leaving it to individuals and concentrating only on ensuring that choice is well-informed.

But the Commission's current judgement is that Option 1 is unattractive in respect to the vast majority of pensioners, while a **sole** reliance on one of Options 2, 3 or 4 is unlikely to be feasible.

- Option 1 (poorer pensioners relative to average earnings) is unlikely to be attractive. Our argument for this proposition is set out in detail in Chapter 4, where we consider the definition of "adequate" pension income. There are two key points: one relating to current pensioner incomes, the other to desirable future growth.

  - Current pensioner incomes: A minority of current UK pensioners may be better off relative to their lifetime income than is in some sense necessary, optimal, or sustainable. But average UK pensioner incomes relative to workers' incomes are slightly lower than in comparable European countries [Figure 1.16].

  - Future growth: Even given the scenarios for state and private pension income presented in Figure 1.12, average pensioner incomes are likely to grow at least in line with prices, i.e. to rise somewhat in real terms. But they will fall relative to average earnings. Our judgement is that most people would desire pensioner incomes (if appropriate to start with) to grow over the long-term in line with average incomes, to ensure that pensioners can participate fully in society.

- The feasibility and desirability of Option 2 (higher taxes/NI contributions) can be debated. Some people would support greater tax-financed generosity to current and future pensioners, arguing that the UK tax ratio is currently lower than some comparable countries. Others would argue that it is unreasonable for the current generation of workers to impose an increasing tax burden on the next generation. But whatever the resolution of this philosophical debate, the scope for higher taxes to finance a more generous state pension system would need to be considered in the context of other pressures on public expenditure arising from an ageing population, in health and in social care.

- Option 3 (increased private savings) will almost certainly have to be an element in the response, whether chosen voluntarily by individuals or required by compulsion. But it is unlikely that the doubling of the pension savings rate required to meet the challenge via increased savings alone will be either feasible or desirable, both because many people are likely to prefer later retirement to such a higher level of savings, and because a savings increase on this scale might produce a fall in rates of return. The possibility that a "savings only" response to the challenge will produce offsetting macroeconomic effects is discussed in Appendix B.

- Some increase in the average age of retirement (Option 4) will also have to be part of the solution. It is possible because much of the increased life expectancy being enjoyed is healthy and average retirement ages have been on an upward trend over the last ten years. But the increase in the average retirement age needed to make later retirement the only solution looks very large; and there are significant differences in life expectancy by socio-economic class, which may limit the feasibility and equity of increased retirement ages among some specific groups of people. These issues are discussed in Chapter 2.

We therefore believe that the best policy for society to choose, and the one which is likely to reflect well-informed individual preferences, would involve some mix of Options 2, 3, and 4. A survey by the Association of British Insurers (ABI) suggests that when people are forced to choose between the four options, very few people favour a fall in pensioners' relative living standards, and the two most favoured responses are an increase in the average retirement age and a higher rate of saving [Figure 1.17].

The Commission will conduct more research into people's attitudes and preferences over the coming year.

The next chapter considers the feasibility of increasing average retirement ages and the limits to this response being a sufficient answer alone.

Figure 1.16 Median Income of People Aged 65+ as a Percentage of median income of people aged less than 65: 2001

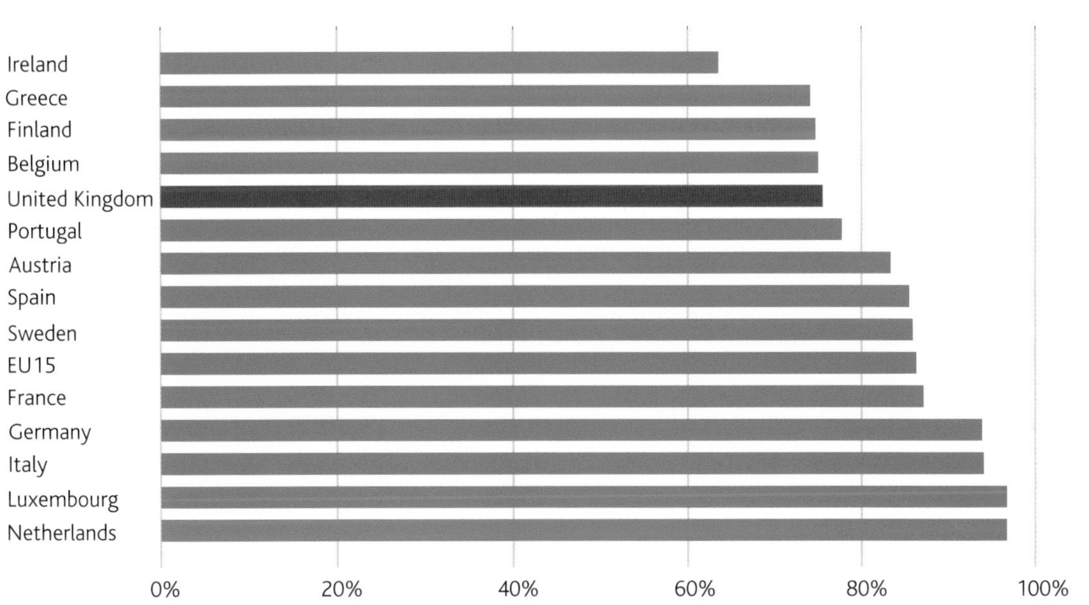

Source: Eurostat, ECHP-UDB, version July 2003

Note: The data for Sweden only includes people aged less than 85.

Figure 1.17 Preferred Responses to the Demographic Challenge

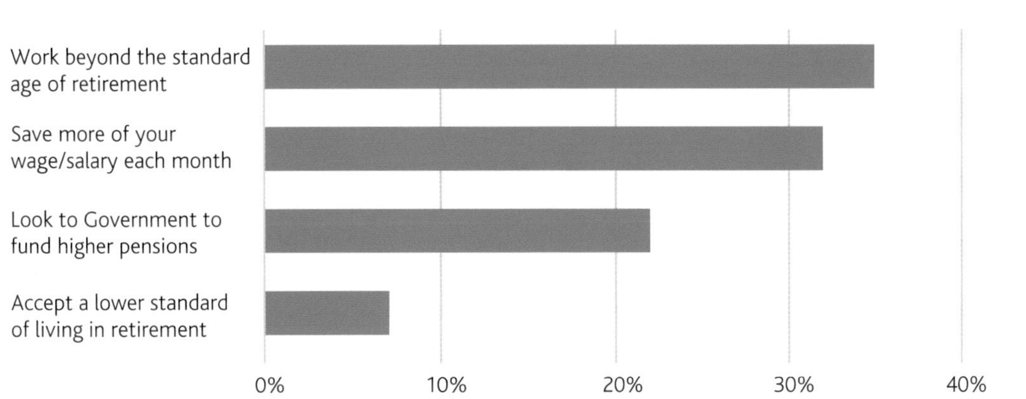

Source: Pensions and Savings Index, Survey 1 (Sept 2003) by YouGov for the ABI

Note: Response to the question "Most people can expect to live longer and spend more time in retirement than their parents and grandparents. Bearing this in mind, and if you had to choose one of the following options which are you personally most likely to do?"

Base: working age population. Excludes those who answered "don't know".

Pensions and Pensioner Incomes as a percentage of GDP: different definitions

At different points in this report we refer to pensions or to pensioner incomes as percentage of GDP. We also draw distinctions between public expenditure and private income sources, and between funded and unfunded pensions. Different measures and distinctions are relevant depending on what question is being asked. It is therefore important to be clear about the numerous different ways to define pensions and pensioners income.

The different measures are set out in Table 1.1. Key points to note are:

- A distinction needs to be made between incomes received by normal age and early retirees, where a normal age retiree is someone who retires at SPA. Estimating the numbers of such normal age retirees is complicated by the fact that within a couple who are receiving pension income one member may be above and the other below SPA, which differs for men and women. We use the Pensioners Benefit Unit (PBU) definition as used by the DWP to define normal age retirees.

- State pension expenditure at 4.8% of GDP is less than state expenditure on normal age pensioners (6.1%), which includes that element of Housing Benefit, Council Tax Benefit and Disability Benefit which is paid to pensioners.

- Total public expenditure on pensioners should include unfunded public sector pensions. These however count as occupational and personal pensions rather than state pensions in assessments of which people are accumulating private (non-state) pension rights.

- It is a striking fact that of the 3.4% of funded pensions in payment (excluding lump sums) 1.4% (i.e. 36% of the total) are being paid to non-PBUs, i.e. to early retirees. The same is true for public sector unfunded pensions. This is explained by the existence of occupational pension schemes with retirement ages pre-SPA and by the large number of early retirements (often paid for out of pension fund surpluses) which occurred during the 1990s.

- Non-pension investment income received by normal age pensioners is significant, at 1%, but heavily concentrated – a small minority of pensioners receive most of this income.

- Funded occupational pensions include the funded element of the public sector (mainly local authorities) which we estimate account for about 17% of the total. As a result, while occupational and personal pensions split – in the total column – between 3.8% funded and 1.5% unfunded, the private sector/public sector split is 3.4% private and 1.9% public.

Table 1.1 Pensioner Incomes and Pensions as a Percentage of GDP: 2002

	Incomes received by normal age retirees	Pensions received by Early retirees	Lump sums received	Total
State pensions and benefits				
- BSP	3.6			
- SERPS/S2P	0.6			
- Minimum Income Guarantee	0.4			
- Other pension benefits	0.2			
State Pension Expenditure	4.8	State expenditure on early retirees (e.g. Incapacity Benefit) not included in this analysis		4.8
Housing and council tax benefit	0.6			0.6
Disability benefits	0.6			0.6
State expenditure on pensioners	6.1	n.a		6.1
Unfunded public sector pensions	0.8	0.5	0.2	1.5
Total public expenditure	6.9	0.5	0.2	7.6
Funded occupational and personal pensions	2.0	1.4	0.4	3.8
Non-pension investment income		Non-pension income of early retirees not considered in this analysis		
- Deriving from lump sums	0.2			
- Other	0.8			
Earnings from employment	0.9			
Total Income	10.8	1.8	0.6	n.a
Total occupational and personal pension (including unfunded public)	2.8	1.9	0.6	5.3
Of which				
Public sector unfunded	0.8	0.5	0.2	1.5
Public sector funded	0.3	0.1	0.1	0.5
Private sector	1.7	1.3	0.4	3.4

The figure of 2.2% used as funded pension income in Figure 1.12 is 2.0% funded occupational and personal pensions plus 0.2% investment income deriving from pension lump sums.

Notes: State pension and benefit expenditure from DWP for financial year 2002/03.
Pension income for normal age retirees and early age retirees based on Pensions Commission estimates from the Family Resources Survey and the Blue Book.
Some rows and colums do not sum precisely due to rounding.

2 Average retirement ages: past and possible future trends

Our response to the demographic challenge should include a rise in the average age of retirement. Healthy ageing for many people makes this possible; and an increase in employment rates among older people is now occurring. But the increase needed to make later retirement a sufficient solution alone looks very large; and significant inequalities in life expectancy and health across socio-economic groups may limit the scope for across the board increases. Increases either in taxes/National Insurance contributions and/or in private savings will therefore also be needed to meet the demographic challenge.

It is important to start with a distinction. An increase in the average retirement age carries no necessary implications for State Pension Age (SPA).[1] The average retirement age can rise if employment rates pre-SPA (e.g. among 50-64 year olds) rise. And it can rise if more people choose to work beyond the SPA, receiving income from employment in addition to their state pension. In general, pension policy should aim to dispel the idea that there are normal or required ages of retirement; and it is likely that a rise in the average retirement age will be combined with more flexible approaches to retirement (e.g. people gradually stepping down from full-time to part-time work over a period of several years).

This chapter therefore considers the feasibility and possible barriers to an increase in the average age of retirement.

The key points are:

1 Healthy ageing suggests that on average later retirement is possible.

2 Employment rates pre-SPA are now rising and could rise significantly more.

3 But a realistic increase in employment rates for age groups below the current SPA could only make a moderate difference to dependency ratios. Removing barriers to working post-SPA is therefore also important.

4 However, the increase in average retirement ages required to be in itself a sufficient solution to the demographic challenge looks very large, and may not be what most individuals will choose.

5 Major inequalities in life expectancy and health between socio-economic groups may make across the board increases in retirement ages infeasible and inequitable, unless those differences erode over time.

1. Healthy ageing and later retirement?

The feasibility and desirability of later retirement depends upon whether longer life expectancy is associated with greater health in old age, i.e. whether people living 20 years beyond 65 rather than 15 are enjoying five more years of healthy active life, or facing five more years of ill health and impaired capability. Analysis on this issue is frustratingly incomplete, but the best judgment from available evidence is that for many people ageing is healthy.

[1]Note: This chapter does not consider the separate issue of whether a rise in the SPA could be desirable in order to make possible a more generous state pension within a constrained public expenditure limit. Chapter 7 explores this issue further.

■ One piece of evidence sometimes cited to suggest that ageing is not associated with greater health is the trend in self-reported sickness. This shows no decline in the proportion of people reporting that they suffer from a limiting longstanding illness [Figure 2.1]. But these data are almost certainly distorted by the impact of rising expectations. As people get healthier, it is likely that their measures of what constitutes health and sickness are changing. Frequently cited measures of "healthy life expectancy", which has increased but not as much as total life expectancy, are also based on these self-reported measures of health, and therefore suffer from the same methodological bias. From these data we simply do not know what the truth is.

Figure 2.1 Trend in Self-reported Sickness, by Age: Percentage with a Limiting Longstanding Illness

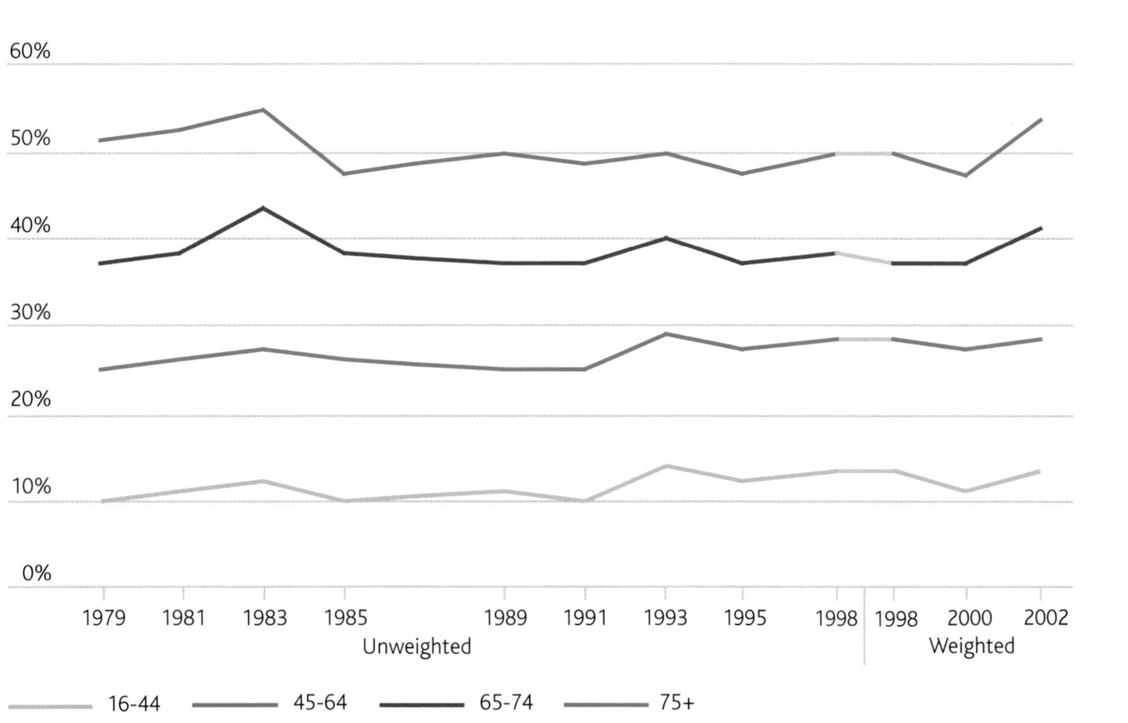

Source: Living in Britain, 1996 and 2002, GB

Note: Data shows the percentage who reported suffering from limiting longstanding illness. Data not available for 1997 and 1999. Data smoothed between 1985-1989 as well as between1995-1998.

Figure shows unweighted and weighted figures for 1998 to give an indication of the effect of weighting.

- Measures over time of precise physical and cognitive capabilities are therefore required, but few are yet available. Those which are, however, all tend to suggest that ageing is on balance healthy. The most comprehensive US study (Fries, 2002) finds an increasing percentage of over 65 year olds to be free of any disability and a decreasing percentage suffering from immobility [Figure 2.2]. UK figures from *Living in Britain* found substantial falls in the number of people aged over 80 facing difficulties with mobility [Figure 2.3].

- International comparisons also suggest support for the healthy ageing hypothesis. A detailed comparison of mortality and the health of those living in Sweden and Russia found that not only do Swedes live longer, but also that a higher proportion of those who live to 70-74 have disability free lives [Figure 2.4]. While we cannot assume that this international cross-sectional comparison necessarily implies a longitudinal trend within any one nation, it is significant evidence against the alternative pessimistic hypothesis that greater survival into old age will be associated with greater disability.

Figure 2.2 Health Status of US over 65 Population

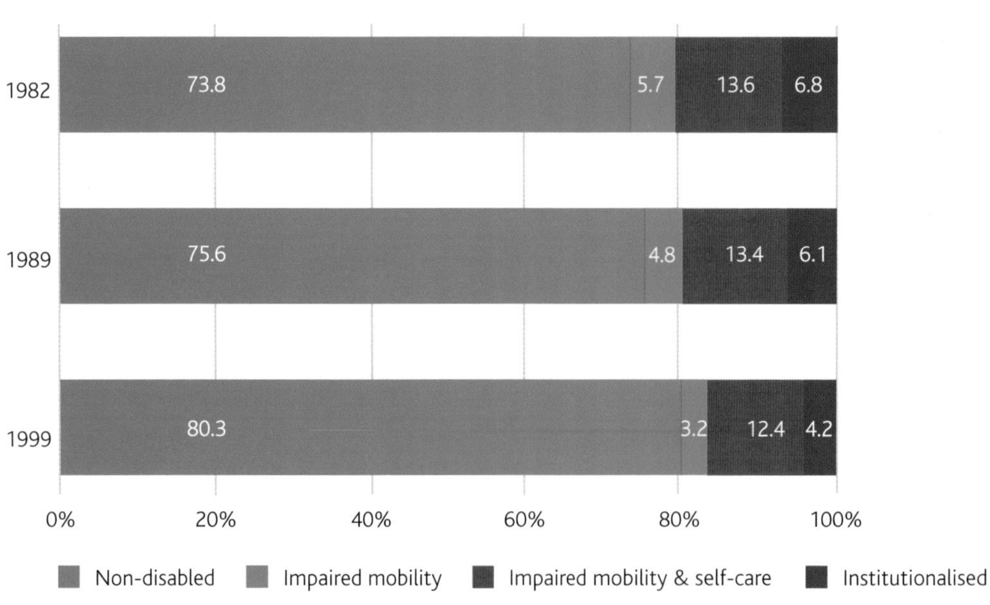

Source: National Long Term Care Surveys, 1982-1999, US. Manton and Gu (2001), Copyright 2001 National Academy of Sciences, USA.

Note: Impaired mobility includes difficulty with shopping, laundry, shopping, etc. Impaired mobility and self-care includes difficulty with bathing, dressing, getting to the toilet, etc.

Figure 2.3 Trends in Immobility, by Age

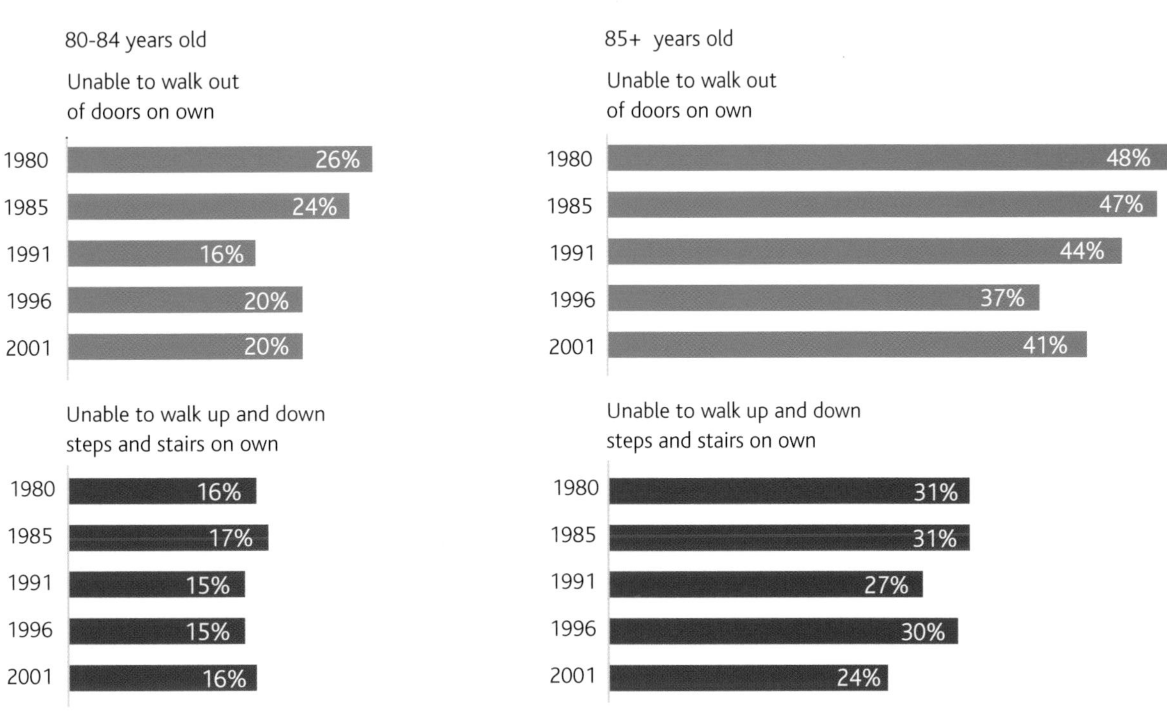

Source: Living in Britain, 1996 and 2001, GB

Figure 2.4 Likelihood of Total and Disability-Free Survival to Age 70-74 among Healthy 45-49 year old Men: Russia and Sweden

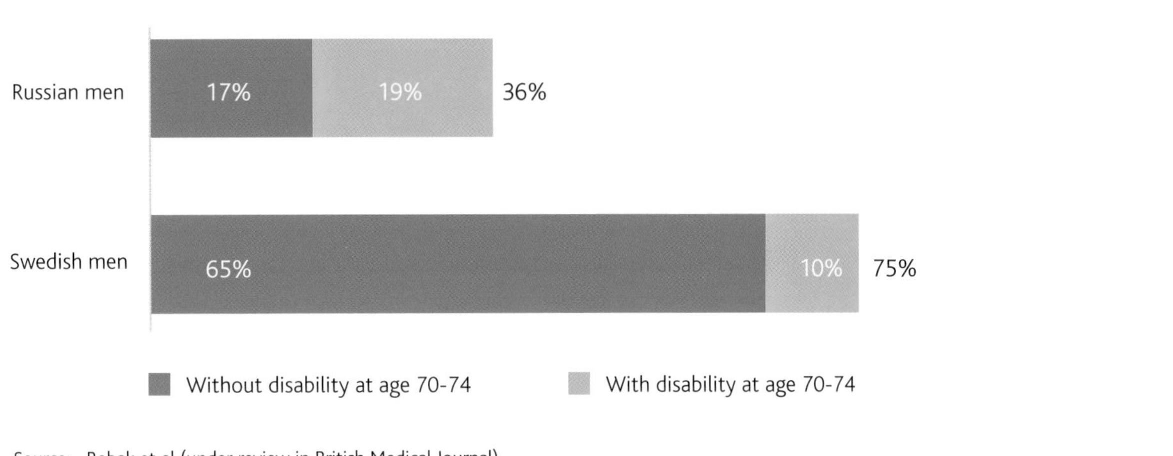

Source: Bobak et al (under review in British Medical Journal)

The recently launched English Longitudinal Study of Ageing (ELSA) will provide a far better evidence base on the impact of ageing, but unfortunately not for many years. Further work on these issues should be a priority for medical and social science research and the Commission would like to hear of any evidence or views on this issue during the consultation period and on the related issue of whether increases in the length of working life would themselves have any impact on health, either positive or negative.[2]

But our present judgment from available evidence is that at least for many people increasing life expectancy is associated with an increase in the number of years of healthy active life. This implies that an increase in average retirement ages is feasible.

2. Employment rates pre-SPA: trends and prospects

Chapter 1 illustrated how the old-age dependency ratio could rise over the next 50 years. It defined the ratio as the number of over 65 year olds divided by 20-64 year olds. But the economic cost of the retired population on workers can be still higher than this ratio suggests, since not all 20-64 year olds are working. An alternative dependency ratio can be calculated which uses workers aged 20+ (20+ year olds in employment) as the denominator [Figure 2.5]. This ratio is higher than the simple old-age dependency ratio and if employment rates do not change, it will increase by a similar proportion. But the fact that it is higher illustrates the theoretical possibility of meeting the economic cost of an increasing number of older people by increasing the employment rate in the working age population.

This could take the form of increasing employment rates at all ages but the scope for increase in employment rates above 50 years old is greater than in the 25-49 year age group. Employment rates for men aged 25-49 are about 90%, though still below historic highs. For women they are at the highest level ever [Figure 2.6].[3] Many women moreover, though classified as inactive in labour market statistics, are working as carers for children and for older relatives. And any market economy has a level of frictional unemployment as people move between jobs. Further rises in the employment rate of 25-49 year olds are possible. Female employment rates could rise further with better childcare. But it seems unlikely that increases in employment rates from present levels for 25-49 year olds will play the major role in meeting the demographic challenge.[4]

[2]Note: It is possible for the impact of longer working lives to be either negative for long-term health (via stress, physical work etc) or positive, given the importance of social interaction to health.

[3]Note: We focus here on 25-49 year olds, rather than 20-49 years olds because employment rates among 20-24 year olds are significantly influenced by increasing participation in higher education. There is therefore an issue about the average age of full-time entry into the workforce which is different from the issue of employment rates in the 25-49 age group.

[4]Note: At some point increases in employment rates among 25-49 years olds could indeed have counter-productive long-term effects. If for instance they were at the expense of maternity and paternity leave breaks, or longer periods of caring for children, they could drive long-term birth rate trends still lower.

Figure 2.5 Alternative Measures of the Dependency Ratio

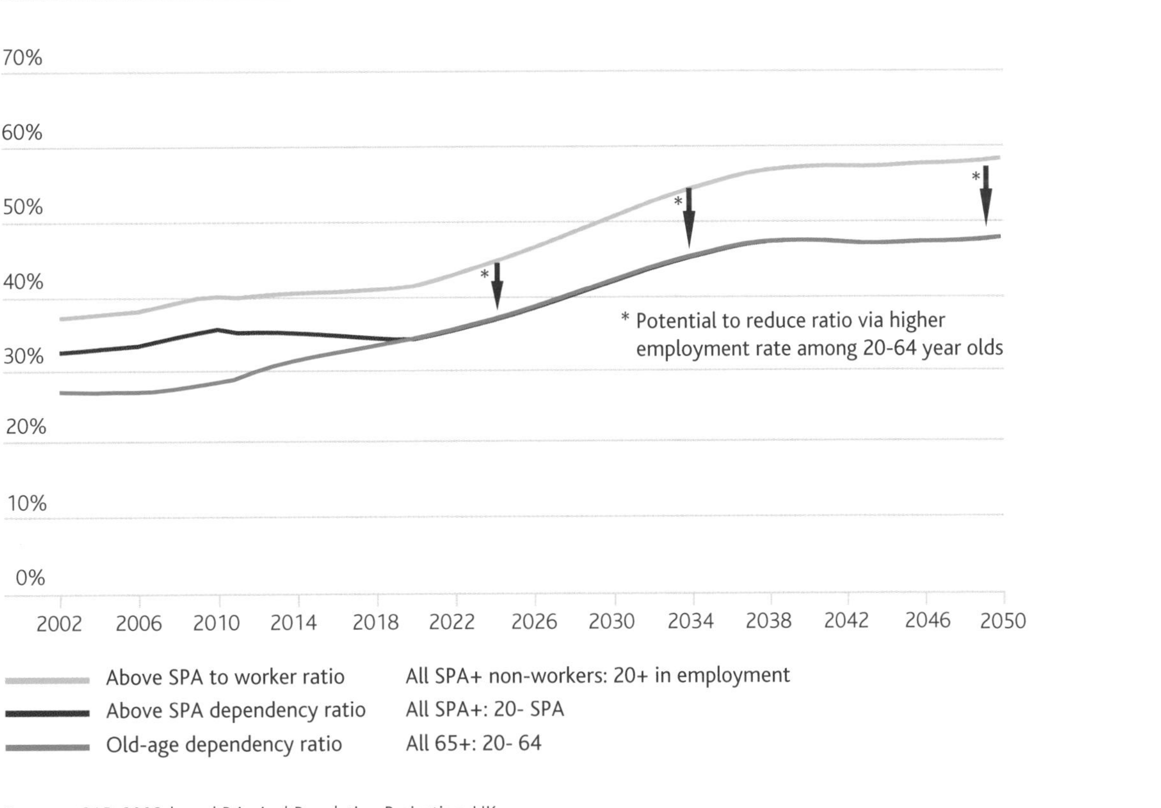

Source: GAD 2002-based Principal Population Projection, UK,
LFS, Q1 2004,UK.

Figure 2.6 Employment Rates for Men and Women aged 25-49

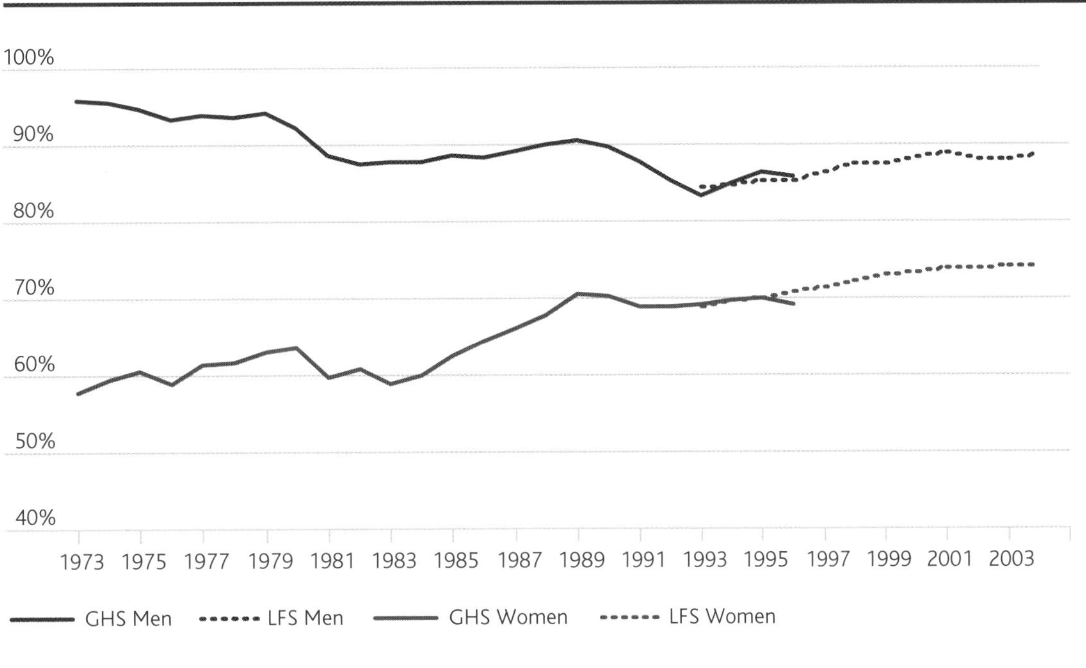

Source: GHS, GB
LFS, UK

The potential for increases in employment rates above 50 appears considerably greater. While people sometimes talk of 60 or 65 as being the retirement age, in fact only 53% of women remain in employment by age 59 and only 42% of men are employed at age 64 [Figure 2.7]. Conversely 21% of men are still working at 66. The average age of exit from the labour market for those men who were economically active at 50 is now 63.8 and for women 61.6. [See the panel at the end of this chapter for the complexities in defining the "average" retirement age.]

The average retirement age has fallen significantly over the last 50 years, but is now increasing slowly and could increase further even without a rise in the number of people working post SPA.

- The average male retirement age fell from 67.2 in 1950 to 63.1 in 1995. At the same time life expectancy rose significantly. The combined result has been a major increase in the percentage of the average adult male life spent in retirement, with most of the increase occurring after 1970 [Figure 2.8].

- During the 1950s and 1960s the key driver of this falling average retirement age was a fall in the percentage of men aged 65-69 in employment, from 48% in 1952 to 30% in 1971. But from the mid-1970s to the mid-1990s, the dominant factor was a large fall in the employment rate of men aged from 50-64 [Figure 2.9]. This fell from 88% in 1973 to 63% in 1995, with the decline concentrated in two periods. First the early 1980s, which saw a major reduction in the number of male manufacturing workers, many of whom never re-entered the workforce. Second the early 1990s, when there were further manufacturing job losses, but also a significant wave of redundancies and early retirements in white collar jobs, sometimes facilitated by generous early retirement packages from pension funds which were then in significant surplus, enabling companies to make over 50 year olds redundant at no accounting cost.

- These different drivers of early exit from the labour force are reflected in today's figures. Early inactivity for men aged 55-59 is concentrated in the lowest two and the highest wealth quintiles, with a large percentage of the lowest two quintiles describing themselves as sick or unemployed, while most of the richest quintile of earners who have left the labour force pre-SPA describe themselves as retired. There is a broadly similar picture for women aged 55-59, but with higher levels of inactivity across all wealth quintiles [Figures 2.10 and 2.11].

Figure 2.7 Employment Rates for Men and Women Aged 50-70: 2004

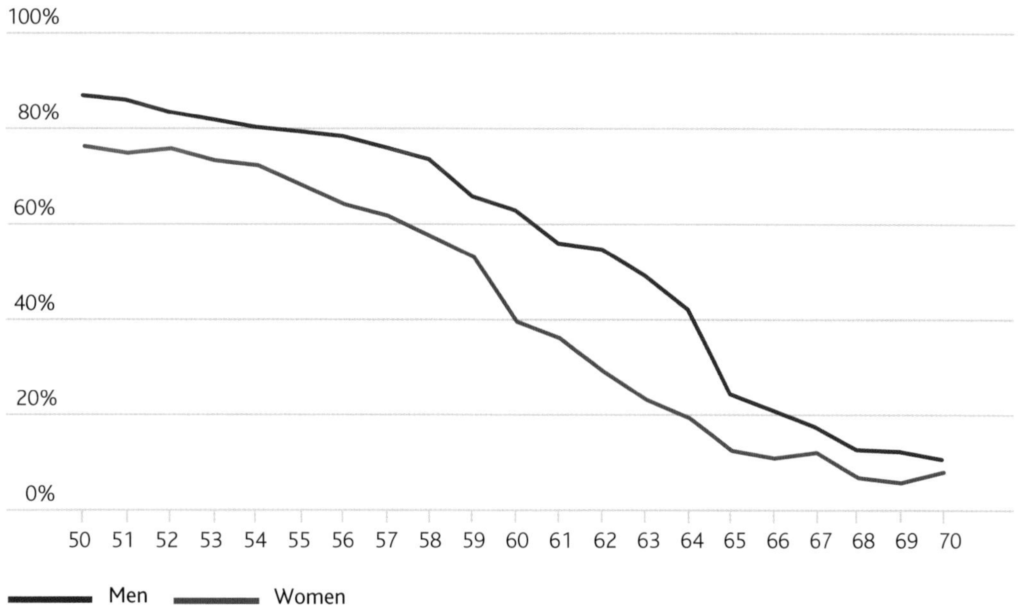

Source: LFS, Spring 2004, UK.

Figure 2.8 Percentage of adult male life spent in retirement

	Average age of exit from workforce	Life expectancy at age of exit from workforce	Percentage of adult life spent in retirement
1950	67.2	10.8	18.0
1960	66.2	11.5	19.3
1970	65.4	12.5	20.9
1980	64.6	14.2	23.4
1990	63.5	17.2	27.4
1995	63.1	18.7	29.4
2000	63.3	19.8	30.5
2004	63.8	20.1	30.5

Source: Blöndal and Scarpetta (1999)
Pensions Commission estimates from 1990 onwards.

Note: Percentage of adult life spent in retirement is given by life expectancy at retirement/(retirement age plus life expectancy at retirement minus 18). Life expectancy is calculated on a cohort basis.

Figure 2.9 Employment Rates for Men and Women aged 50 – SPA: 1973-1995

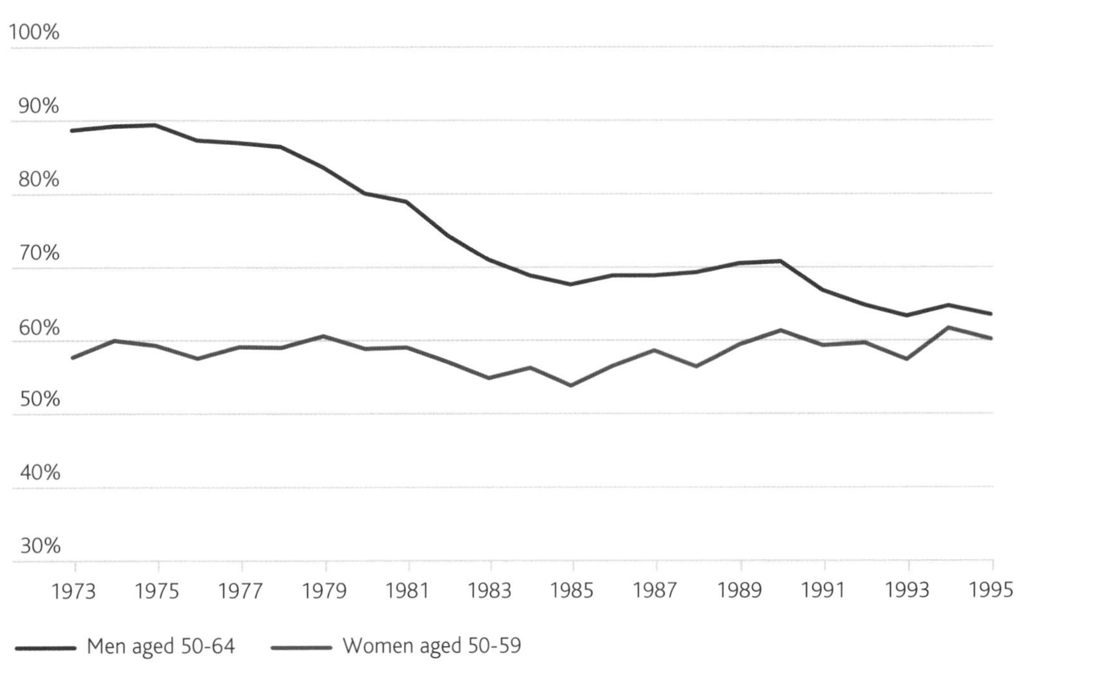

Source: GHS, GB

Figure 2.10 Inactivity by Wealth Quintile: Men Aged 55-59

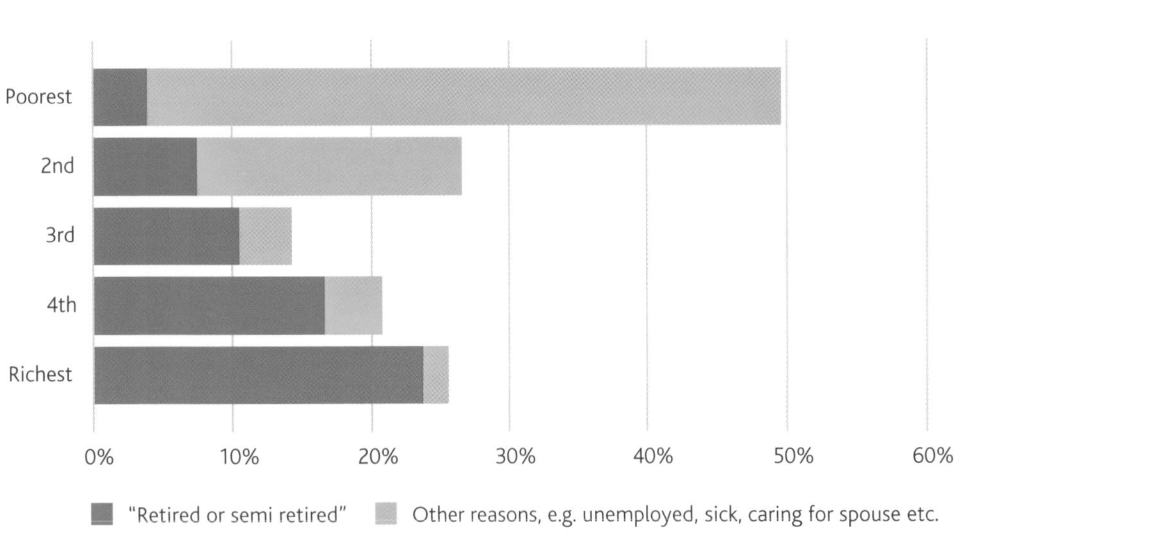

Source: ELSA, 2002, England

Figure 2.11 Inactivity by Wealth Quintile: Women Aged 55-59

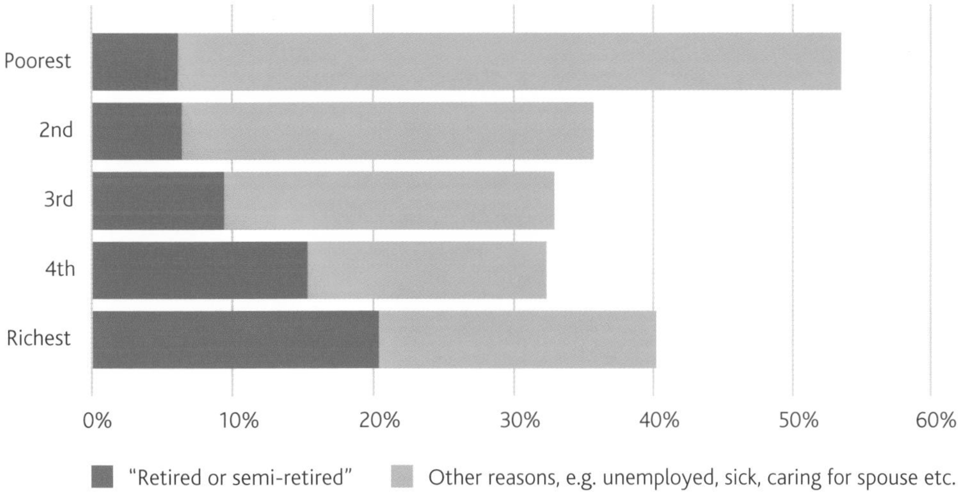

Poorest
2nd
3rd
4th
Richest

0% 10% 20% 30% 40% 50% 60%

"Retired or semi-retired" Other reasons, e.g. unemployed, sick, caring for spouse etc.

Source: ELSA, 2002, England

Figure 2.12 Employment Rates for Men and Women aged 50-SPA: 1993-2004

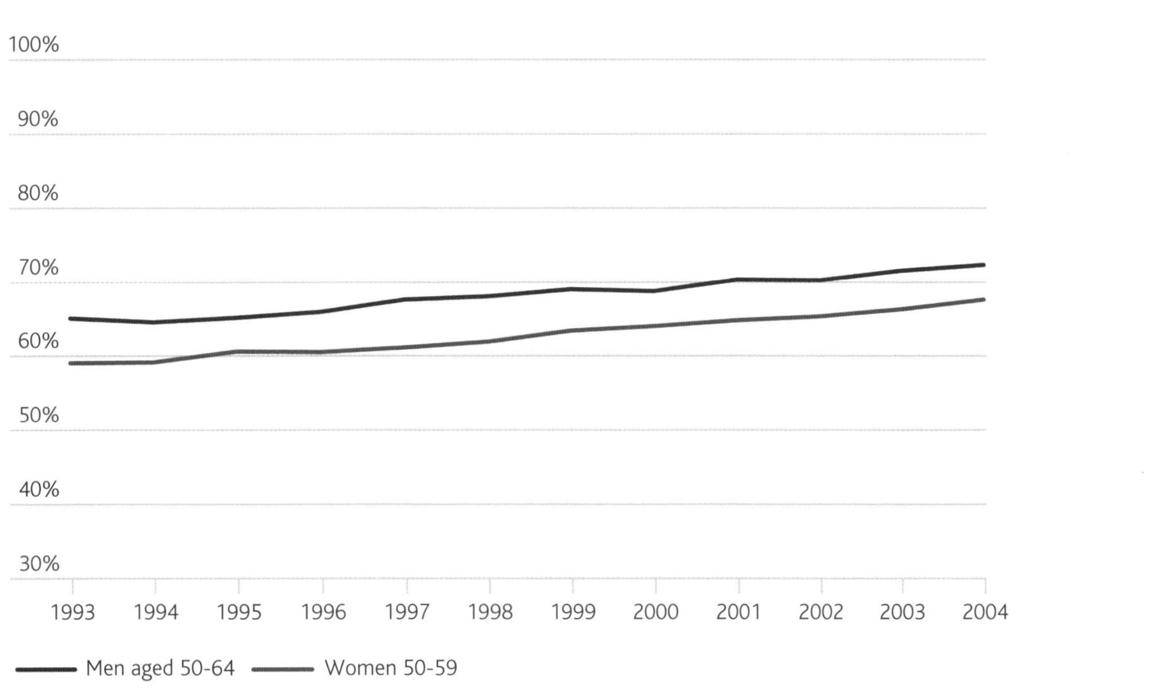

Source: LFS, UK.

- Since about 1993, however, employment rates among those aged between 50 and SPA have been on a gradual upward path [Figure 2.12]. This seems to reflect four effects:

  1. The absence of major macroeconomic shocks comparable to the recessions of the early 1980s and early 1990s has meant that fewer workers in their fifties have been made redundant; while for those who have faced redundancy, the general tightness of the labour market has made re-entry into the labour market easier.

  2. Over the last three years, economic incentives have probably been at work. We know that people with Defined Contribution (DC) pension schemes tend to work longer than people who are in Defined Benefit (DB) pension schemes, since they can gain higher annuity rates by delaying retirement [Figure 2.13]. It is therefore likely that the retirement behaviour of people in DC pension schemes is also influenced by equity market movements and by the overall trend in annuity rates. The fall in equity markets, and thus in the size of individual pension funds since 2000 and the significant reduction in overall annuity rates since 1998, are likely to have encouraged a significant number of people in DC pension schemes to delay retirement.[5]

  3. Companies are far less willing to provide generous early retirement packages now that pension fund surpluses have disappeared and been replaced, in many cases, by significant deficits.

  4. Government policies to encourage people off incapacity related benefits and into work have been increasingly effective among older workers (though not among younger) [Figures 2.14 and 2.15]. This could reflect a cohort effect, as male manual workers from heavy manufacturing industries who became redundant and sick in the 1980s reach 65 and move from Incapacity Benefit to formal retirement. It also reflects the tightening of Incapacity Benefit criteria. Other active labour market policies, e.g. the New Deal 50 Plus for older workers, and the tightening of benefit conditions have probably had an impact.

Looking ahead, there are good reasons for believing that pre-SPA employment rates could continue to increase given (i) continuation of sound macroeconomic policy; (ii) the increasing shift from DB to DC pension provision; (iii) continued focus on Incapacity Benefit reform; (iv) active labour-market policies to encourage search for work at all ages; and (v) the forthcoming introduction of age discrimination legislation.

[5] Note: While this financial incentive effect is a socially beneficial consequence of the move to DC schemes, that shift also has disadvantages since it exposes individuals to significant investment return risk. The issue of risk-sharing between pension scheme providers and members is discussed in Chapter 3.

Figure 2.13 Distribution of Labour Market Activity, by Pension Type: Men aged 60-64

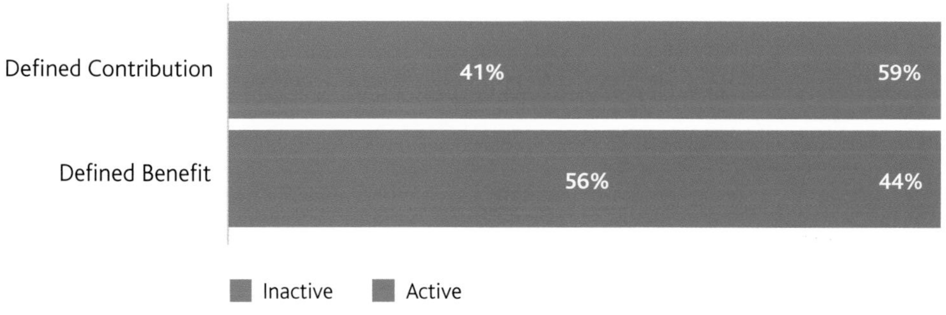

Source: ELSA, 2002, England

Figure 2.14 Percentage of Men in receipt of Incapacity Related Benefits, by Age

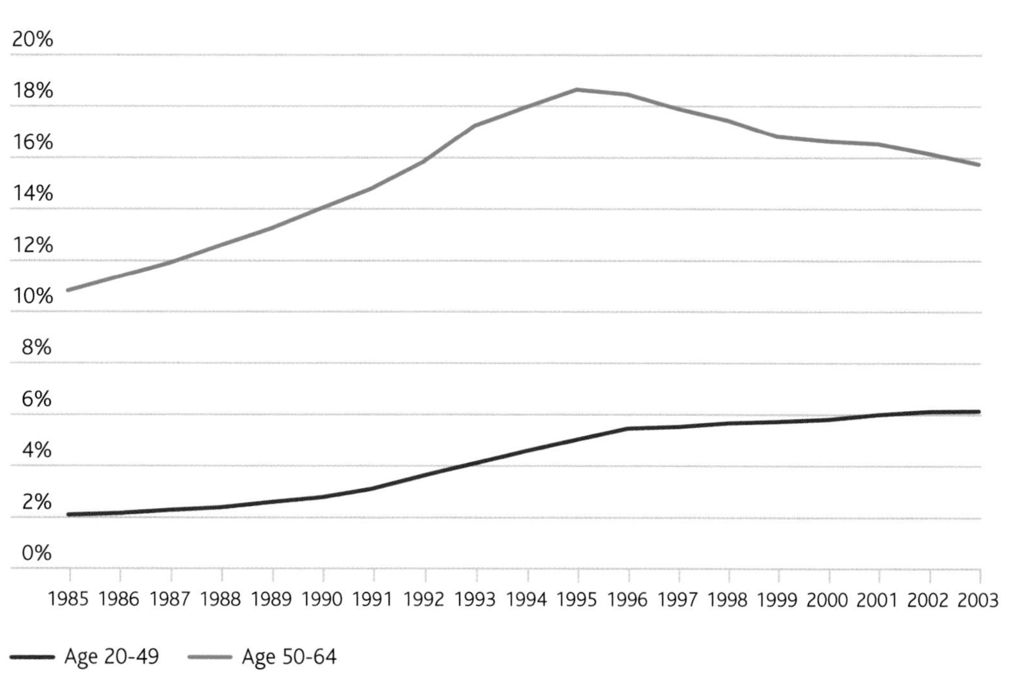

Source: Social Security statistics

Note: Invalidity Benefit or equivalent (Incapacity Benefit at the long term and short term higher rate), Severe Disablement allowance and incapacity "Credits Only" claimants.

- To illustrate the possible potential, we have therefore defined a stretching but feasible scenario which we have termed the "Higher Participation" scenario [See panel opposite]. Under this scenario, the overall employment rate for men aged 50-64 would rise from 72.0% to 79.3%, and for women from 54.8% to 71.6%. This employment rate also takes into account the equalisation of SPA for women. The average age of retirement would rise from 63.8 for men today to 64.2 and for women from 61.6 to 62.7.

Figure 2.15 Percentage of Women in receipt of Incapacity Related Benefits, by Age

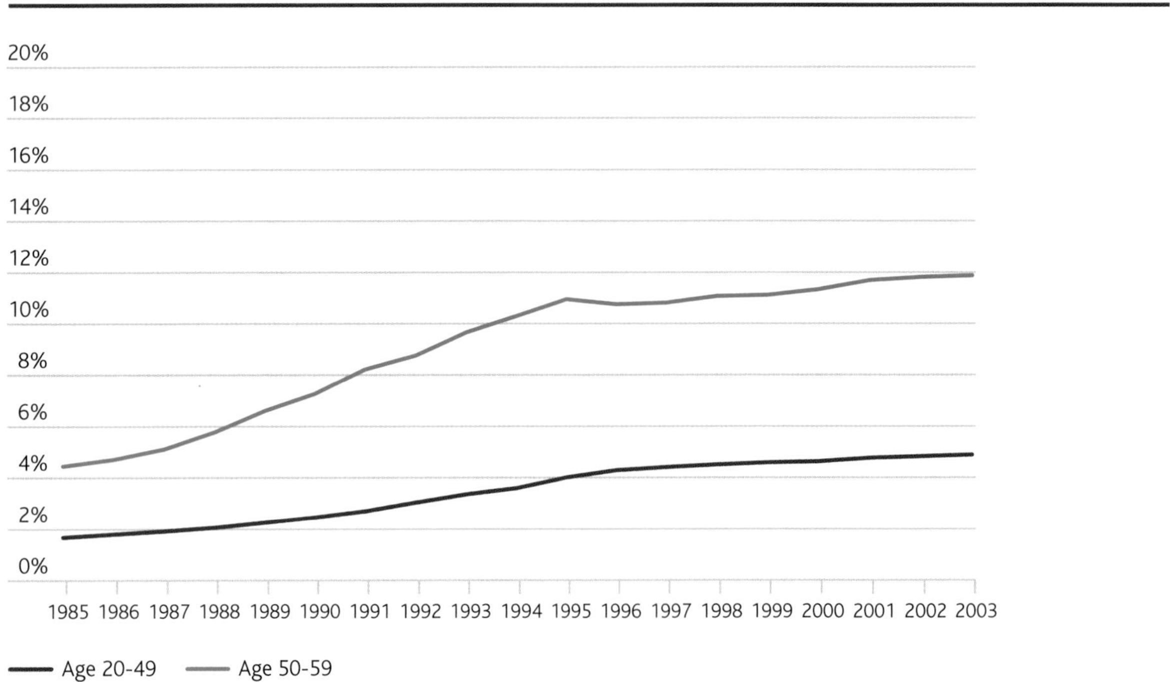

Source: Social Security statistics

Note: Invalidity Benefit or equivalent (Incapacity Benefit at the long-term and short-term higher rate), Severe Disablement allowance and incapacity "Credits Only" claimants.

The Higher Participation scenario

Employment rates among older workers have been increasing steadily over the last decade and there are good reasons to believe that further rises are possible.

To gauge the potential impact of further rises in employment rates on the dependency ratio we have constructed a "stretching but feasible" scenario of how employment rates might develop.

The scenario we have chosen assumes that employment rates increase for both men and women. The drivers behind these increases are, however, different for the two sexes.

Higher Participation Scenario for Men

Although employment rates for men have increased steadily across all regions over the last decade, there are still significant differences in employment rates across the country. Figure 2.16 illustrates the position for 50-64 year old men in early 2004.

Although some of the regional differences will be explained by differences in the skill and age composition of the male population, much of the difference will reflect incomplete adjustments to the economic restructuring of the last 10 to 20 years.

Our Higher Particpation scenario for men is that male employment rates across all regions gradually converge over 25 years to the current level observed in the South East of England.

Higher Participation Scenario for Women

Although there are regional differences in the employment rates of women, we have used a different approach to produce a Higher Participation scenario. In recent years there have been significant increases in female employment rates, particularly among lone parents and among married women with children. Part of this increase is due to ongoing improvements in the quantity and quality of childcare provision available.

We have looked at the employment situation for women in Sweden as an example of what can be achieved through a strong focus on measures to make it easier for women to combine work and family life, including better childcare. Figure 2.17 shows how employment rates in the UK and Sweden currently compare.

Our Higher Participation scenario for women assumes that over the next 25 years, the employment rates of women in the UK aged over 25 gradually converge on the rates currently prevailing in Sweden.

The current pension age for women in Sweden is currently 65. We assume that the employment rate of women aged 60-64 in the UK will move to the rate currently observed in Sweden after the equalisation of the SPA in the UK has been completed in 2020.

Figure 2.16 Employment Rates for Men aged 50-SPA, by Region

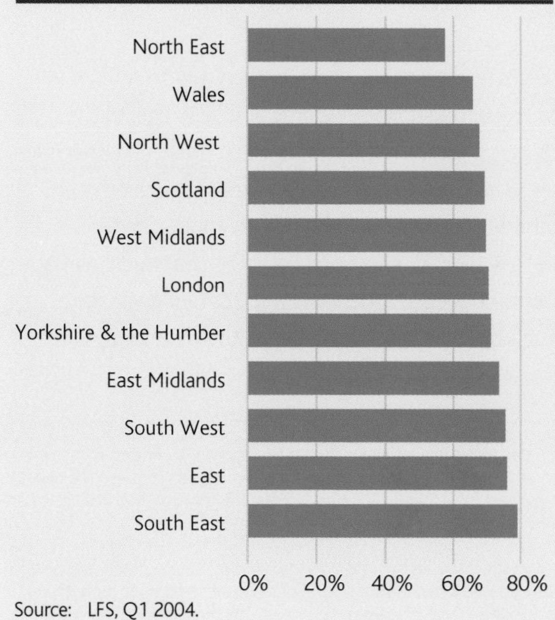

Source: LFS, Q1 2004.

Figure 2.17 UK and Sweden's Employment Rates for Women, by age

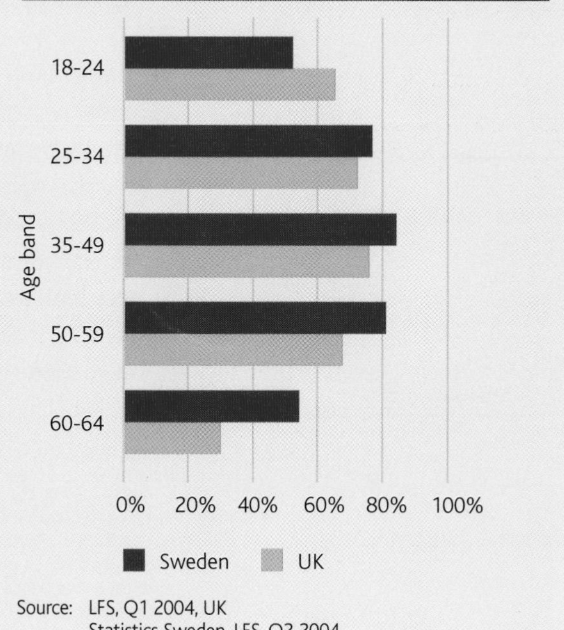

Source: LFS, Q1 2004, UK
Statistics Sweden, LFS, Q2 2004.

3. Working beyond the current SPA

Achieving this Higher Participation scenario would however have only a moderate impact on the increase in the dependency ratio.

- The Higher Participation scenario would reduce the ratio of above SPA non-workers to workers aged 20+ in employment from 58% to 54% in 2050. But this would still leave a significant increase from today's rate of 38% [Figure 2.18].

- And there are limits to achieving more than the Higher Participation scenario. A minority of people will always have the resources and will choose to retire early and a minority will be sick and disabled. Furthermore, caring responsibilities will mean that a further significant minority of people are working outside the formal economy.

This implies that for an increase in the average retirement age to make a major contribution to offsetting the dependency ratio rise, there will also have to be a significant number of people working beyond the current SPA. The number doing so is now slowly increasing but remains limited, with for instance only 17% of men aged 67 in employment [Figure 2.19].

Policies which make it easier for those who wish to work beyond the SPA are therefore desirable and should be pursued. These clearly include:

- Age discrimination legislation: this is now being introduced, and will make it illegal for companies to make people redundant solely on grounds of age. The Commission has already communicated to government its clear recommendation that in the enactment of this legislation there should either be no "default" age beyond which these workers' rights do not apply, or that if one is allowed, it should be different from and significantly higher than the current SPA, for instance 70.

- The flexibility to defer receipt of the state pension and to receive a higher pension (or the lump sum equivalent) at a later age: this is already in place, but at present individuals have to make an either/or choice on deferrals.[6] The Commission suggests that the government should consider whether a partial deferral option could also be introduced, making it easier for people to combine continued, perhaps part-time, work with the receipt of at least a portion of their state pension. It also suggests that the availability of the deferral option is more widely publicised.[7]

[6]Note: At present, for each year of deferral of claiming state pension, the pension is increased by 7.5% up to a maximum of five years. Proposals in the Pensions Bill will increase the reward for deferral to 10.4% per year and introduce the option to have a lump sum in the place of an increased weekly pension. For more details see Appendix F.

[7]Note: It should be noted that if deferral leaves the present value of state pension payments to each pensioner unchanged, it does not decrease the level of resource transfer to pensioners, i.e. in the framework of Figure 1.12's analysis, it does not decrease the numerator of the ratio (resource transfer as a percentage of GDP), but does increase the denominator by increasing the size of the work force.

Figure 2.18 Old Age Non-Workers to Worker Ratio: Current employment and Higher Participation Scenario

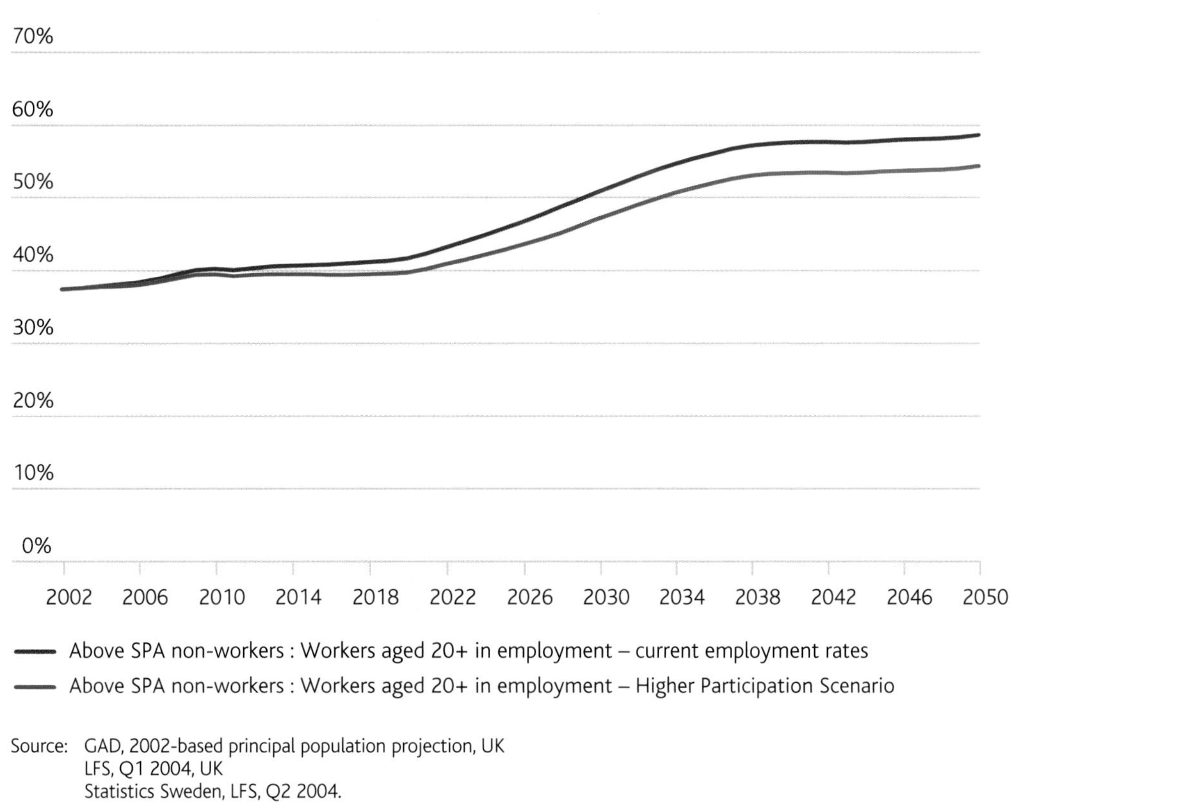

Source: GAD, 2002-based principal population projection, UK
LFS, Q1 2004, UK
Statistics Sweden, LFS, Q2 2004.

Figure 2.19 Employment rates for men and women aged 65-75

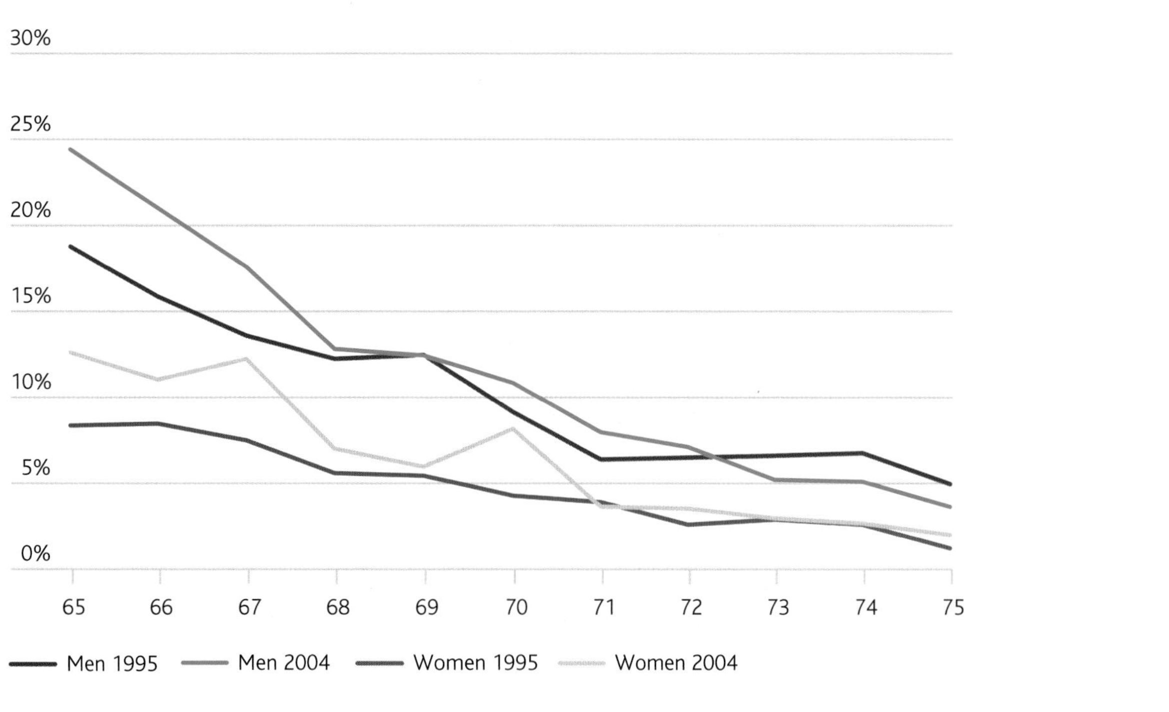

Source: LFS, Spring 1995, UK
LFS, Spring 2004, UK.

Beyond these policies, however, there may be other measures required to ensure that longer working lives can be both attractive to workers and highly productive. Retraining may have an important role. During the consultation period the Commission would be interested in ideas relating to these issues. It believes, moreover, that the debate may need to encompass attitudes to work/life balance at younger ages and work practices affecting that balance. Changes in working patterns which make it easier for people to combine work and family life during middle age, but which entail longer working lives and a gradual rather than sudden transition from full-time work to retirement, may be better both socially and economically than the pattern to which we have increasingly moved over the last 50 years, with a increasing percentage of life spent in total retirement, but with some indications that working life prior to retirement has become more pressured and stressful.

4. How high might average retirement ages rise?

While it is important to remove barriers to later working, and while average retirement ages will almost certainly rise, it seems unlikely that the increase which most people will wish to choose will be sufficient alone to offset the rise in the dependency ratio.

- To offset the rise in the dependency ratio solely by increasing the average age of retirement, it would need to rise from 63.8 for men today and 61.6 for women, to reach 69.8 for men and 67.4 for women. This would imply achieving the Higher Participation scenario for increased employment for 50-64 year olds, with an employment rate in the 60-64 age group of 65% for men and 54% for women, **and** in addition achieving for both men and women those same employment rates for 65-74 year olds [Figure 2.20].

- Such an increase in average retirement age would be more-than-proportional to the increase in adult life expectancy projected in GAD's principal projection for the next 50 years. Male life expectancy at 18 is forecast to rise from 64.8 today to 66.2 in 2050, an increase of 2.2%. An increase in the average retirement age from 63.8 to 69.8 would increase the years of adult life spent working by 13.1%. This more-than-proportional rise in retirement age would therefore increase the percentage of life spent working and decrease the percentage spent in retirement, the latter ratio falling from 30.5% in 2004 to 25.6% in 2050. This would reverse the trend illustrated in Figure 2.8.

  And while we have already stressed that life expectancy may well rise faster than official forecast, if it does so too will the required increase in retirement age, leaving the consequences for the proportion of life spent working unchanged.

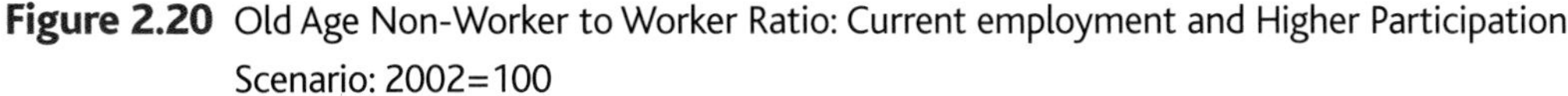

Figure 2.20 Old Age Non-Worker to Worker Ratio: Current employment and Higher Participation Scenario: 2002=100

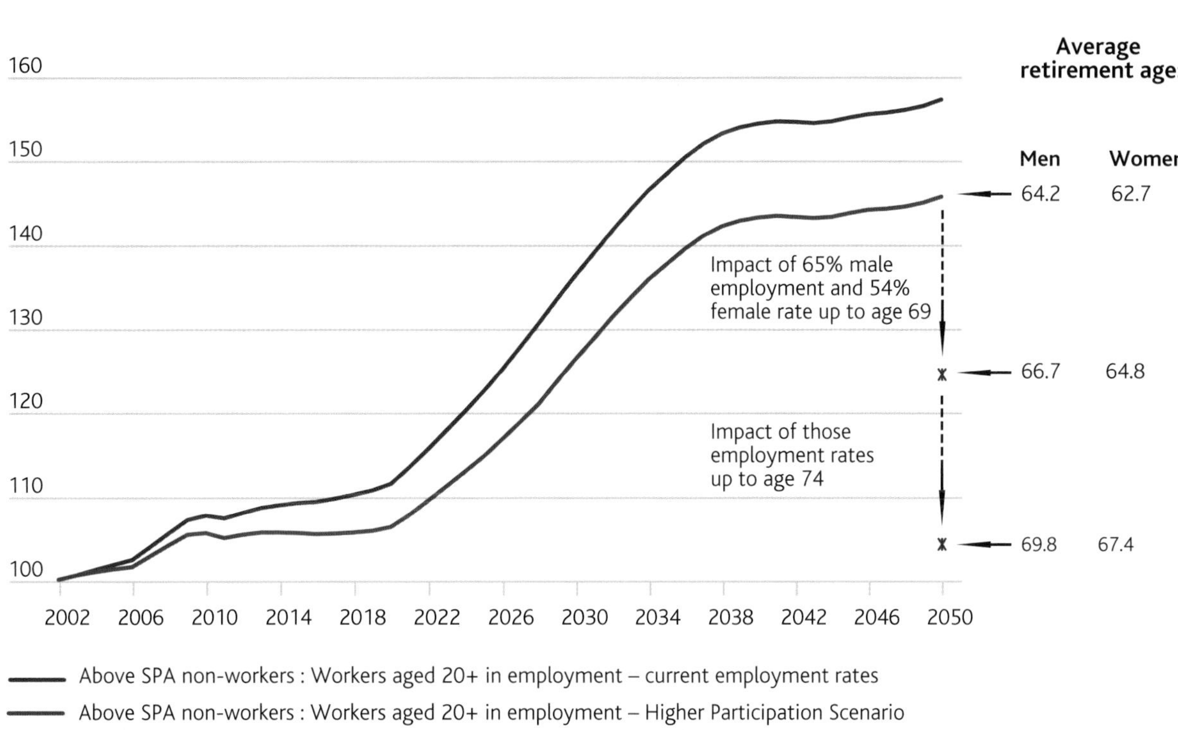

Source: GAD, 2002-based principal population projection,
UK LFS, Q1 2004, UK
Statistics Sweden, LFS, Q2 2004.

Note: The increase in average retirement age needed in 2050 to reduce the dependency ratio to the 2004 level is particularly high because of the specific shape of the UK's population distribution illustrated in Figure 1.5, with a particularly high number of people aged in their 60s and early 70s relative to the number of late 70 year olds and older.

- The reason that such a more-than-proportional increase is required is explained by the decomposition of movements in the dependency ratio presented in Chapter 1. If the only demographic change we faced over the next 30 or 50 years was the future increase in life expectancy from now on, then a proportional increase in the average retirement age would be a precisely sufficient response, with no need in aggregate for higher taxes/National Insurance (NI) contributions nor for higher savings. But as Chapter 1 explained, the impact of the baby boom has been to reduce the dependency ratio below its long-term trend for the last 30 years, and to concentrate the rise of the ratio into the next 30 years. Because of the baby boom, we will face over the next 30 years, the dependency ratio consequences of the increase in longevity which **has** already occurred between 1970 and 2000, as well as that which is still to come.

There is no science by which to determine what rise in average retirement ages should be preferred by society overall, nor what would be chosen on average in a system entirely driven by individual decisions. As a result, it is impossible to specify what level of tax increase or savings increase (Options 2 and 3 in the framework presented in Chapter 1) is required to close the resources gap illustrated in Figure 1.12. But two illustrative scenarios can be used as benchmarks to guide debate [Figure 2.21]:

- First a scenario in which average male retirement ages increase proportionately with life expectancy increases from now on. This would (on GAD's principal projections) require a rise in the average age of retirement from 63.8 to 66, which would entail achieving the Higher Participation scenario for 50-64 year olds, and in addition achieving a 65% employment rate among 65-68 year old men.

- Second a scenario in which average retirement ages rise more than proportionately, catching up by 2050 to the level they would have reached if they had increased in line with life expectancy since 1980. In this scenario we should **already** have increased male retirement ages by five years since 1980 (instead of the actual fall of 0.8 years), with a further 1.5 years to come. The scale of this required adjustment illustrates the impact of our lack of response to ageing over the last two decades.

The first scenario would reduce the percentage of GDP which needs to be transferred to pensioners (assuming no decline in relative pensioner income) from 15.1% to 13.1%. [See Figure 1.11 for the general framework for estimating required resource transfers.] The increase in resource transfer required above today's 9.9% would therefore be reduced to 3.2%. But achieving this 3.2% increase would still imply either the present day equivalent of a £36 billion increase in taxes/NI contributions, or an increase in pensions savings of somewhere between 50-100%.

The second scenario would fully offset the dependency ratio increase and leave no need at the aggregate level for additional taxes/NI contributions or additional pensions savings. (It would still however leave many individuals facing inadequate pensions or the need to accept higher savings or even higher average retirement ages, given the great inequalities in pension right accrual which Chapters 3 and 4 will describe.)

The Commission does not propose here any preference between these scenarios. And as stressed in Chapter 1, this choice will partly and should partly be left to individuals who will to a degree make their own trade-offs between savings levels, retirement ages and incomes in retirement.

Our current judgment, however, is that it is unlikely that society or individuals in aggregate will wish to choose an increase in retirement ages which is greatly more than proportional to future increases in life expectancy. If this is right, then in addition to higher retirement ages we will need either to accept increases in the aggregate level of taxes/NI contributions or achieve increases in aggregate pension savings.

5. Inequalities in life expectancy and health

On average life expectancy is increasing and on average ageing appears to be healthy. As argued above, this means that on average increased retirement ages are possible as well as required.

Figure 2.21 Increase in Average Male Retirement Age Required to Maintain Ratio of Retired Life to Working Life

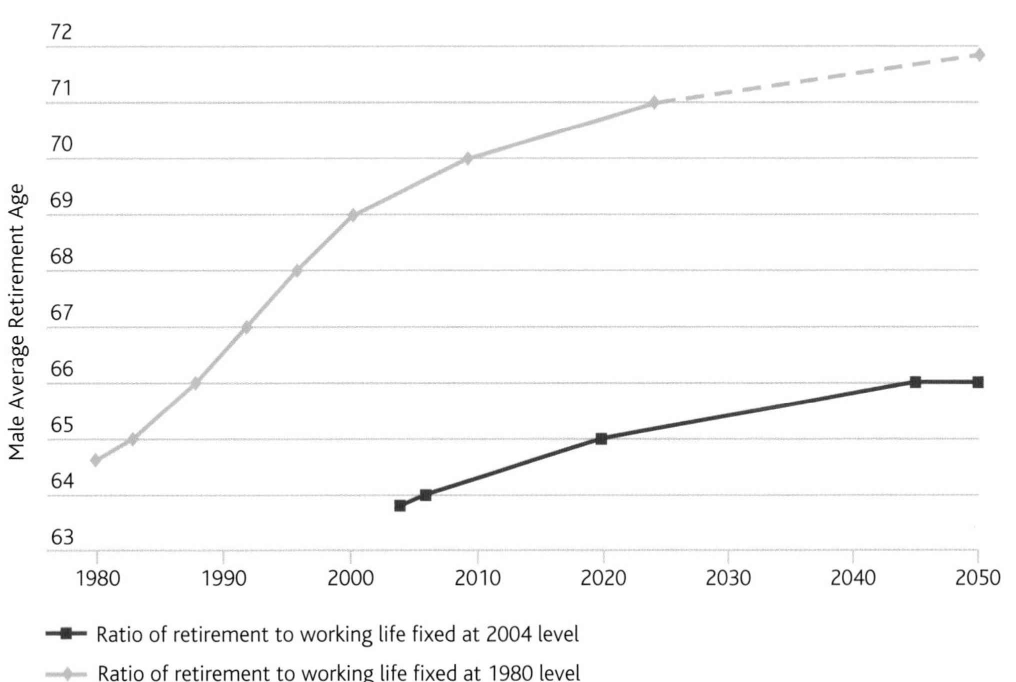

Source: Pensions Commission analysis

But averages do not tell the whole story: there are major inequalities in life expectancy and in health.

- Life expectancy varies significantly by socio-economic class. Among men, social class I life expectancy at 65 is about four years higher than social class V [Figure 2.22]. Among women, the gap appears to have widened significantly over the last 20 years [Figure 2.23].[8]

- Lower life expectancy tends to be associated with poorer health. Not only do lower socio-economic groups live for fewer years post-retirement, but a smaller percentage of these years appears to be free of sickness or disability [Figure 2.24]. And, as seen already in Figures 2.10 and 2.11, lower wealth groups are far more likely to leave the workforce early for health reasons.

Figure 2.22 Trends in Male Life Expectancy at 65, by Social Class

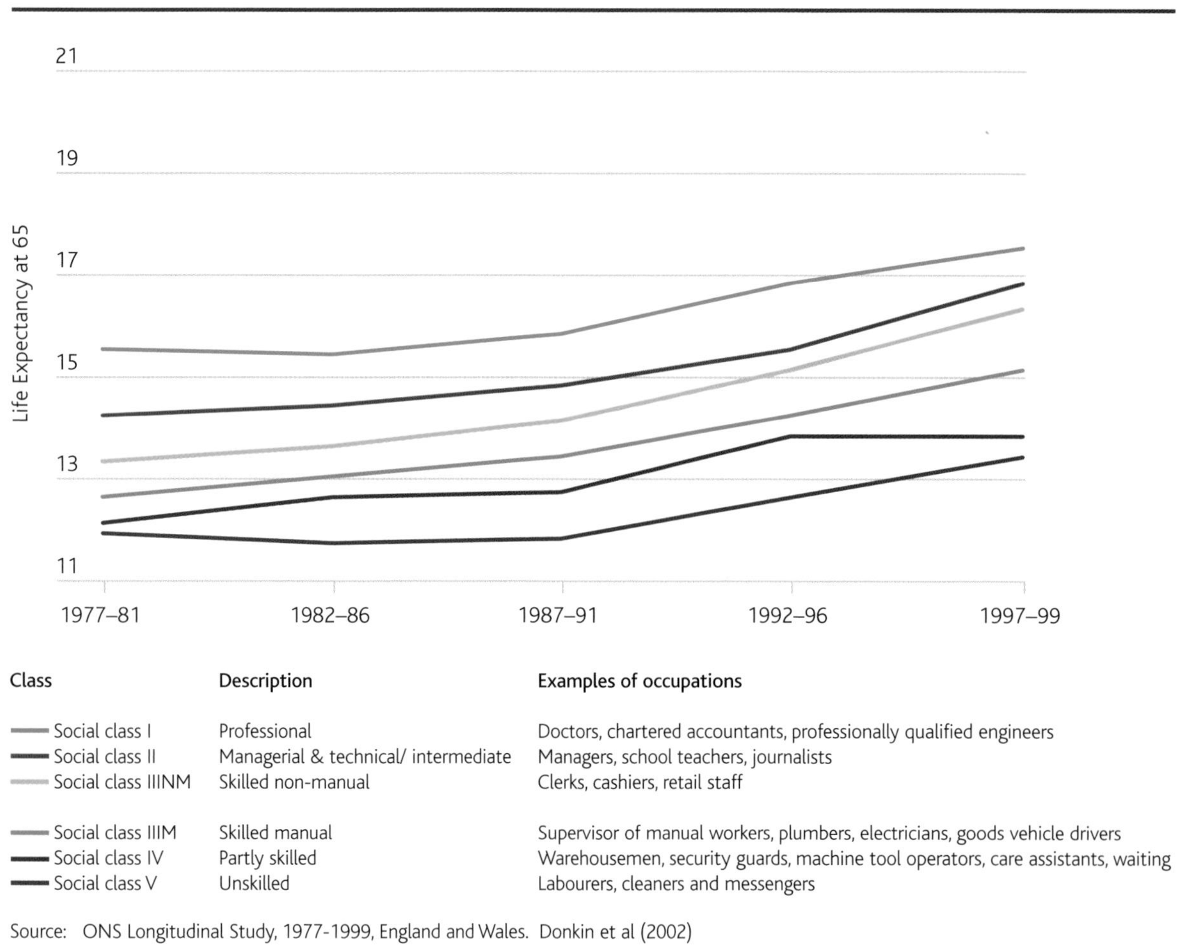

Class	Description	Examples of occupations
Social class I	Professional	Doctors, chartered accountants, professionally qualified engineers
Social class II	Managerial & technical/ intermediate	Managers, school teachers, journalists
Social class IIINM	Skilled non-manual	Clerks, cashiers, retail staff
Social class IIIM	Skilled manual	Supervisor of manual workers, plumbers, electricians, goods vehicle drivers
Social class IV	Partly skilled	Warehousemen, security guards, machine tool operators, care assistants, waiting
Social class V	Unskilled	Labourers, cleaners and messengers

Source: ONS Longitudinal Study, 1977-1999, England and Wales. Donkin et al (2002)

Note: Life expectancy is calculated on a period basis with social class assigned in 1971 maintained throughout.
Social classes I, II and IIINM are non-manual
Social classes IIIM, IV and V are manual.

[8]Note: It is also noteworthy that the gap is widening, for both men and women, when we look at life expectancy at 45 (ONS Longitudinal study analysis for the Pensions Commission, 2004). Lower socio-economic groups are not participating equally in the significant reductions in death rates between 45-65.

Figure 2.23 Trends in Female Life Expectancy at 65, by Social Class

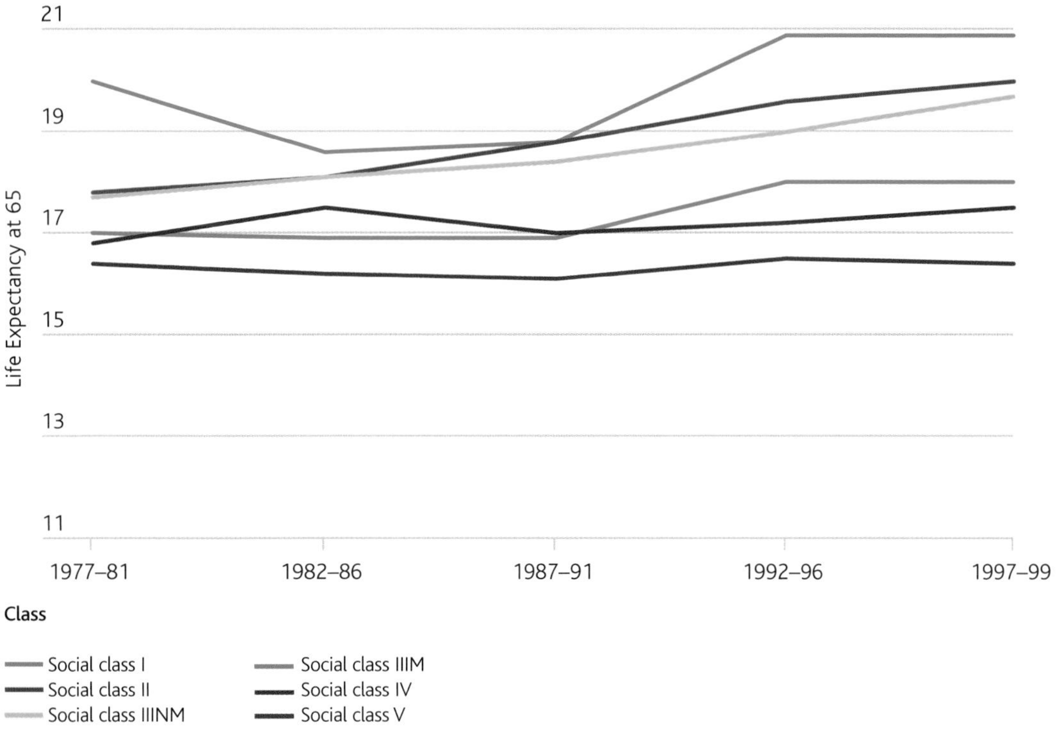

Life Expectancy at 65

21
19
17
15
13
11

1977–81 1982–86 1987–91 1992–96 1997–99

Class

Social class I
Social class II
Social class IIINM
Social class IIIM
Social class IV
Social class V

Source: See 2.22

Note: The falls in life expectancy of social class I between 1977-81 and 1982-86 are not statistically significant and are probably the result of small numbers of women in social class I at the age of 65 rather than any real short-term movement.

Figure 2.24 Expected Years of Life with and without Disability for Women at 65, by Socio-economic Category

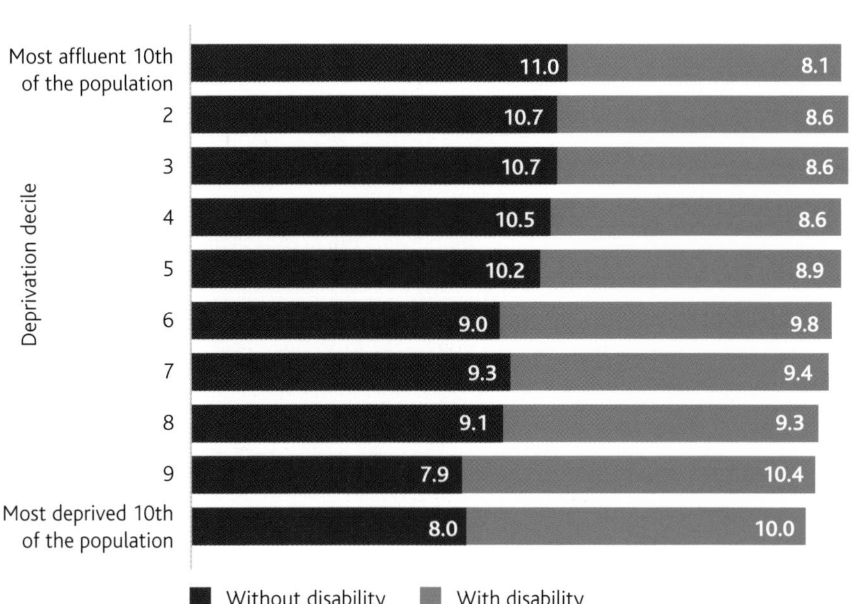

Source: HSE, 1996-1999, England. Bajekal (submitted for publication to the Journal of Epidemiology and Public Health).

Note: Life expectancy shown on a period basis. Deprivation deciles reflect four indicators of material deprivation.

This chart uses information on self-reported health similar to that discussed earlier in the chapter. While changes in people's expectations of health over time mean that these responses cannot necessarily be used to infer health trends over time, they are more likely to give robust information on a cross-sectional basis ie between social classes at any one time. It is possible that the expectations of higher social classes exceed those of the lower social classes, but this would imply that the social class gradient observed here is less than the true gradient.

- In part this reflects differences in key lifestyle predictors of future health. The proportion of people smoking has been falling in most social classes but most slowly in the lowest. Obesity is rising in all social classes, but from a higher level in the lowest social classes [Figures 2.25 and 2.26]. But work by Professor Michael Marmot looking at groups of civil servants whose working conditions are similar, and adjusting for any differences in lifestyle choices such as smoking, suggests a more general correlation of high income and high status with good health [Figure 2.27].

The implication of this is that there may be limits to the feasibility of across the board increases in retirement ages, particularly if increases are more-than-proportional to the increase in life expectancy. And that any increase in the SPA, even if offset by a more generous pension level, could raise issues of equity since it might tend disproportionately to affect socio-economic groups with the lowest life expectancy. Modelling of the financial incentive effects of an increase in the SPA suggests that it would be most likely to induce lower income workers to work longer and much less likely to induce higher income workers to work longer, since the state pension accounts for a larger share of total retirement income for these workers [Figure 2.28]. This effect might be partially offset by increased moves onto Incapacity Benefit.

A key issue therefore is how trends in life expectancy and health by social or economic class will develop in the future. An optimistic case could be made that the main occupational causes of health inequalities are now in the past, with the decline of mining and of other heavy industries and with improvements in workplace health and safety.[9] A pessimistic case would stress the increasing divergence of some lifestyle factors, especially the prevalence of smoking and obesity, between socio-economic groups and continuing differences in working conditions and factors such as stress.

Conclusion

This chapter has suggested that an increase in average age of retirement must be one element of our response to the demographic challenge. But it has also argued that retirement age increases alone are unlikely to be a sufficient response and may not be the response that most people will prefer, and that there may be barriers to across the board increases in retirement age.

If pensioner incomes are to be maintained relative to average net incomes, some increase in the percentage of GDP transferred to pensioners, either via the PAYG state system, or via an increase in private savings, is therefore required. The next chapter therefore considers the effectiveness of the UK pension system in delivering income to current pensioners, and how this is likely to change in future, given the trends in place.

[9]Note: The correlation between high life expectancy and better health in retirement across social classes is also in one sense encouraging. Like the Sweden/Russia comparison referred to earlier in this chapter, it supports the "healthy ageing" hypothesis that, in general, higher life expectancy is combined with better health, and it suggests that there is no inherent reason why "healthy ageing" could not apply to all social groups.

Figure 2.25 Trends in Smoking, by Sex and Social Class

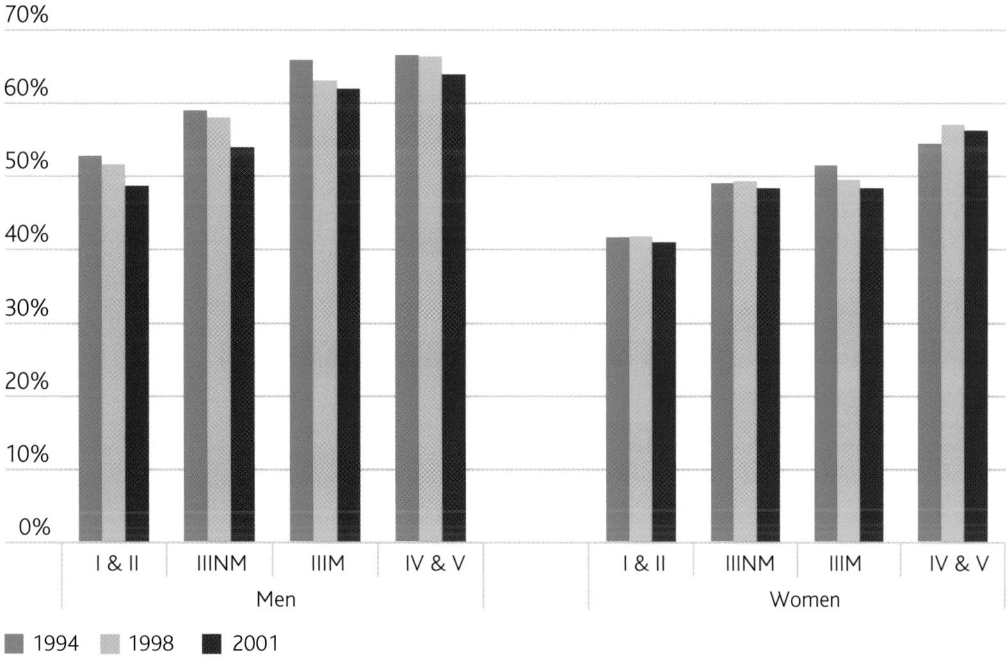

70%
60%
50%
40%
30%
20%
10%
0%
I & II
IIINM
IIIM
IV & V
Men
I & II
IIINM
IIIM
IV & V
Women
1994
1998
2001

Source: HSE 1994, 1998, 2001, England.

Note: Proportion of men and women 16 and over who have ever regularly smoked cigarettes by social class. Age standardisation for all years was based on 2001 Census figures.

Figure 2.26 Trends in Obesity, by Sex and Social Class

35%
30%
25%
20%
15%
10%
5%
0%
I & II
IIINM
IIIM
IV & V
Men
I & II
IIINM
IIIM
IV & V
Women
1994
1998
2001

Source: HSE 1994, 1998, 2001, England.

Notes: Proportion of men and women 16 and over classed as obese (with Body Mass Index>30) by social class. Age standardisation for all years was based on 2001 Census figures. Body Mass Index is calculated by dividing mass (in kg) by height squared (in m^2).

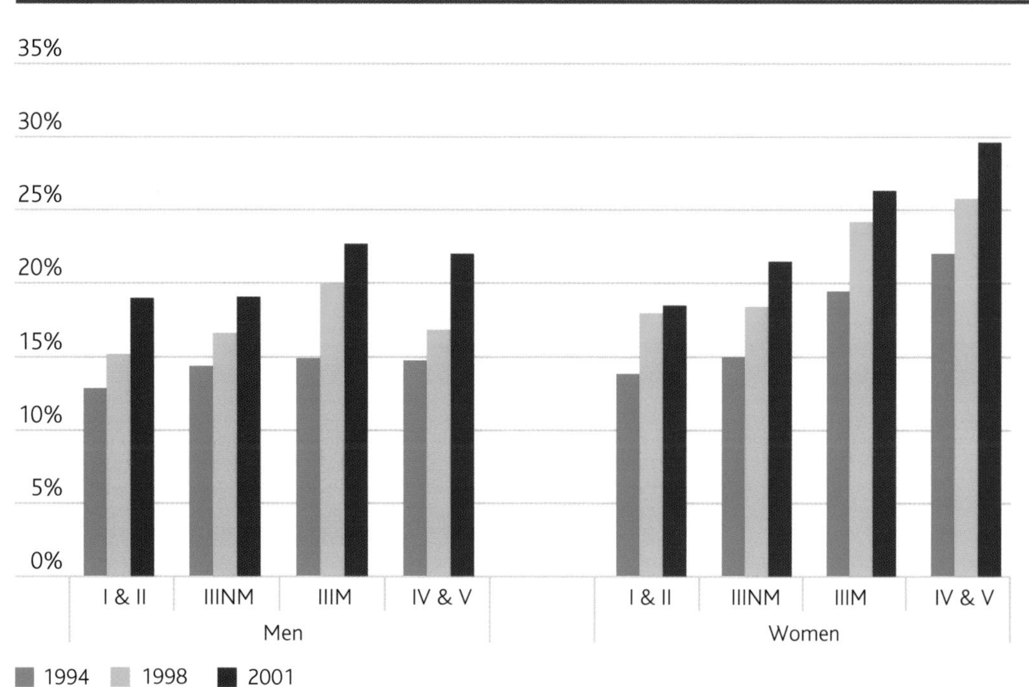

Figure 2.27 Percentage of Retired Civil Servants with Poorer Health Outcomes, by Employment Grade of Civil Servant

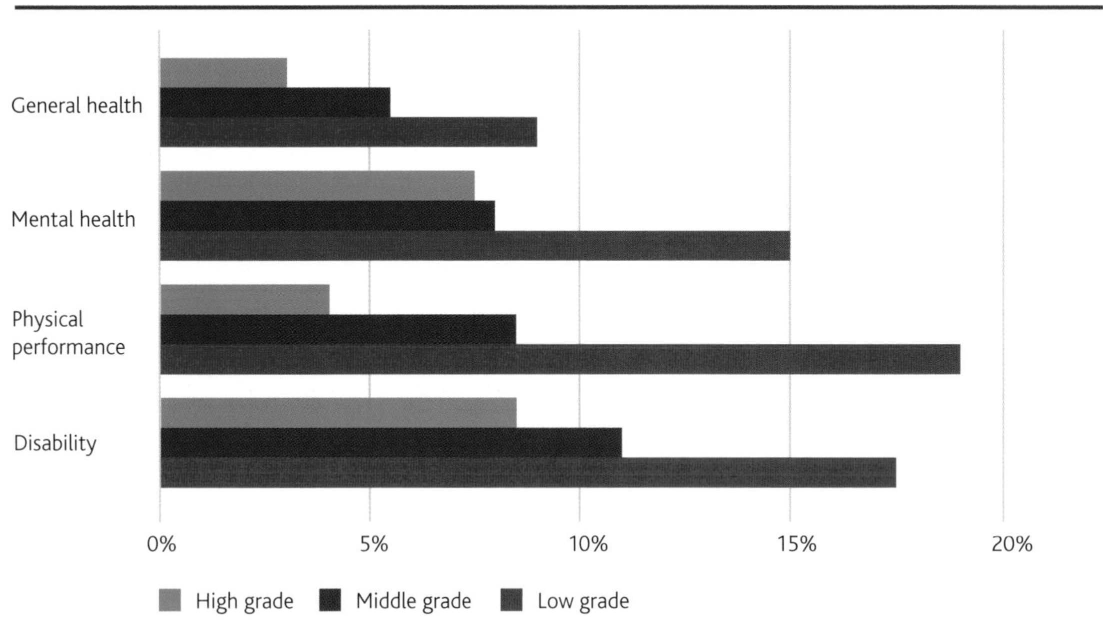

Source: Whitehall Study, 1997-1998. Breeze et al (2001).

Note: Percentage with poor health outcomes at resurvey by employment grade at baseline. Median age at resurvey was 77 (range 67-97). The morbidity data in this figure are not adjusted for risk factors.

Figure 2.28 Predicted Impact of Increasing SPA to 70 on the Full-Time Employment Rate of 65-69 year olds

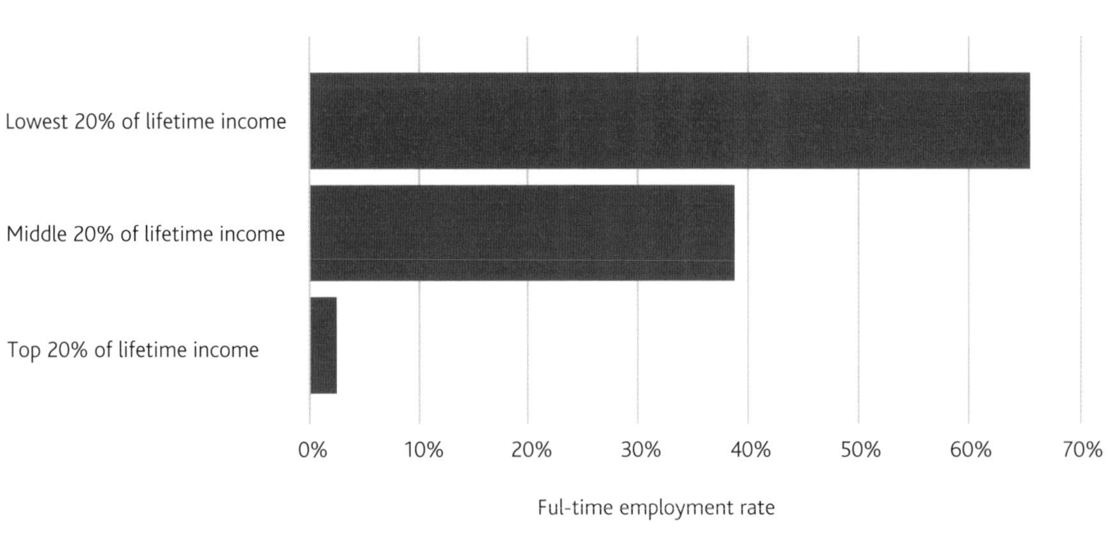

Source: Sefton and Van de Ven, 2004.

Defining the Average Retirement Age

Introduction

The use of the term "average age of retirement" needs to be clearly defined. It tries to capture the mean age at which someone who was at some time economically active (i.e. in work or seeking work) withdraws from the labour market (i.e. becomes economically inactive). It cannot therefore be calculated simply by observing the age at which the average employment rate falls below 50% since some people are economically inactive even in middle age (e.g. for family responsibility reasons) and because people sometimes return to work after periods of economic inactivity.

Methodology

A perfect measure of the mean age of retirement would use data that tracked the labour market behaviour of individuals over time, making due allowance for those people who return to the labour market after they first say they have "retired." In reality, such data is difficult to obtain and addressing the issue of subsequent returns to work is complicated.

As a result, most measures of the average retirement age use aggregate data and examine the age specific pattern of economic activity rates to draw inferences about the mean age of withdrawal from the labour force. Measures using the median age of retirement are not used because they cannot accurately capture the impact of changes in the distribution of retirement ages.

One measure of the mean retirement age would be the mean age of those people actually retiring in a given year. This would reflect not only the propensity of different age groups to retire but also the relative size of different age groups. One drawback of this approach is that changes in the relative size of different age groups might cause the mean retirement age to move up and down even in a situation where the likelihood that an individual of a given age should retire was stable.

An alternative measure would ignore the changing age composition of the population and simply estimate the mean age at which a typical individual would retire. This is the basis of the approach preferred by the Pensions Commission and it has the advantage of being unaffected by cohort sizes.

In recent years, the OECD and the EU have used different methodologies to produce estimates of the mean age of retirement for men and women in the UK. Although the Pensions Commission approach is slightly different from these two measures, we have found that all three methods tend to produce similar levels and trends.

In our approach, we examine age specific economic activity rates for men and women aged 50 and over in a given year and draw inferences about the likelihood that an economically active person of a given age will withdraw from the labour force. Having estimated the proportion of people retiring at a given age, it is a straightforward task to then calculate the mean age of retirement.

Implicit is the judgement that those people who are not in the labour force at the age of 50 do not rejoin it at a later date. Thus, we are trying to measure the mean age of retirement for those people who were in the labour force at the age of 50.

Results

Figure 2.29 shows the current pattern of age specific activity rates in 2004.

Figure 2.30 shows the distribution of retirement ages that is obtained from the manipulation of the data in Figure 2.29.

Figure 2.30 shows that, on average, men retire later than women. For women, the most frequent retirement ages are 59-61 while for men they are 64-66.[1]

Manipulating the information in Figure 2.30 produces an estimate of the mean age of retirement. Figure 2.31, shows the Pensions Commission estimates for recent years and also reports the long run series of estimates produced by the OECD. The estimated mean retirement ages in 2004 are 63.8 for men and 61.6, for women.

The figure shows that mean retirement ages have been increasing over the last 10 years, reversing the steady fall that had occurred since 1950.

[1] Note: Because we are manipulating aggregate data, we cannot pin down the precise age of retirement and, as a result, a retirement age of, say, 66 in the chart will actually cover retirements between 65 yrs + 1 day to 66 years + 364 days. Thus, many of the people classed as, say, 66 may have retired at 65.

Figure 2.29 Economic Activity Rates of Men and Women aged 50-75

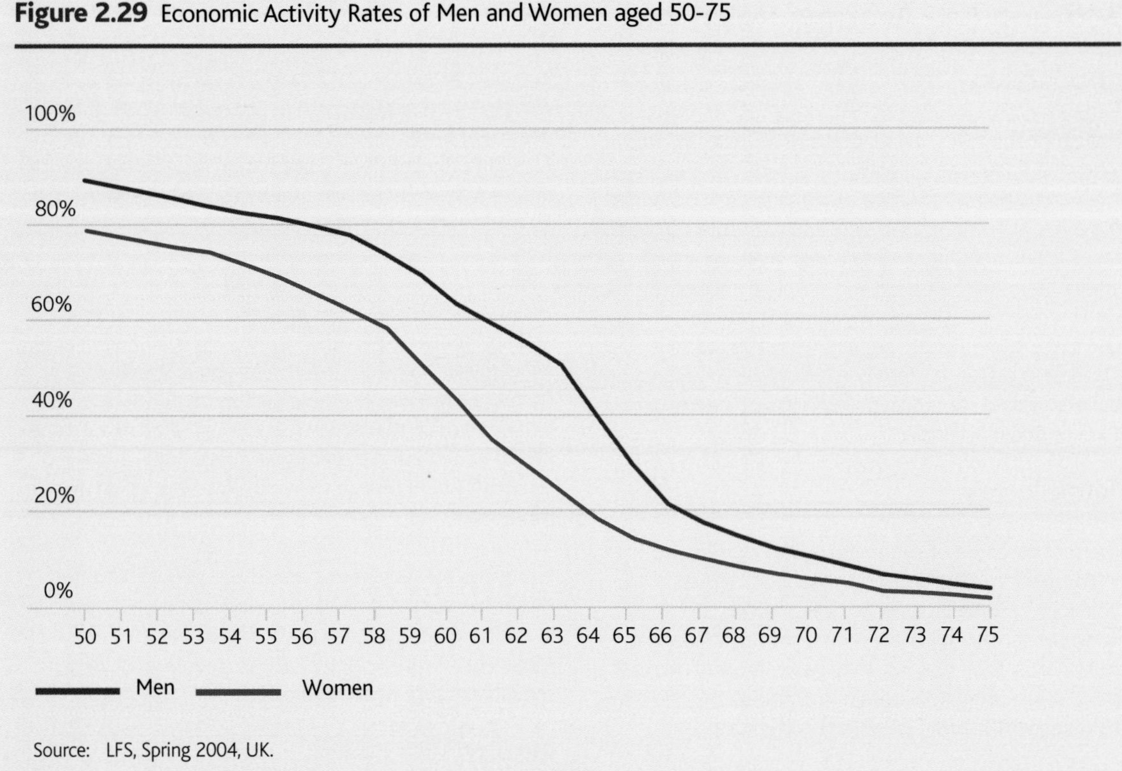

Source: LFS, Spring 2004, UK.

Figure 2.30 Estimated Distribution of Retirement Ages for 2004

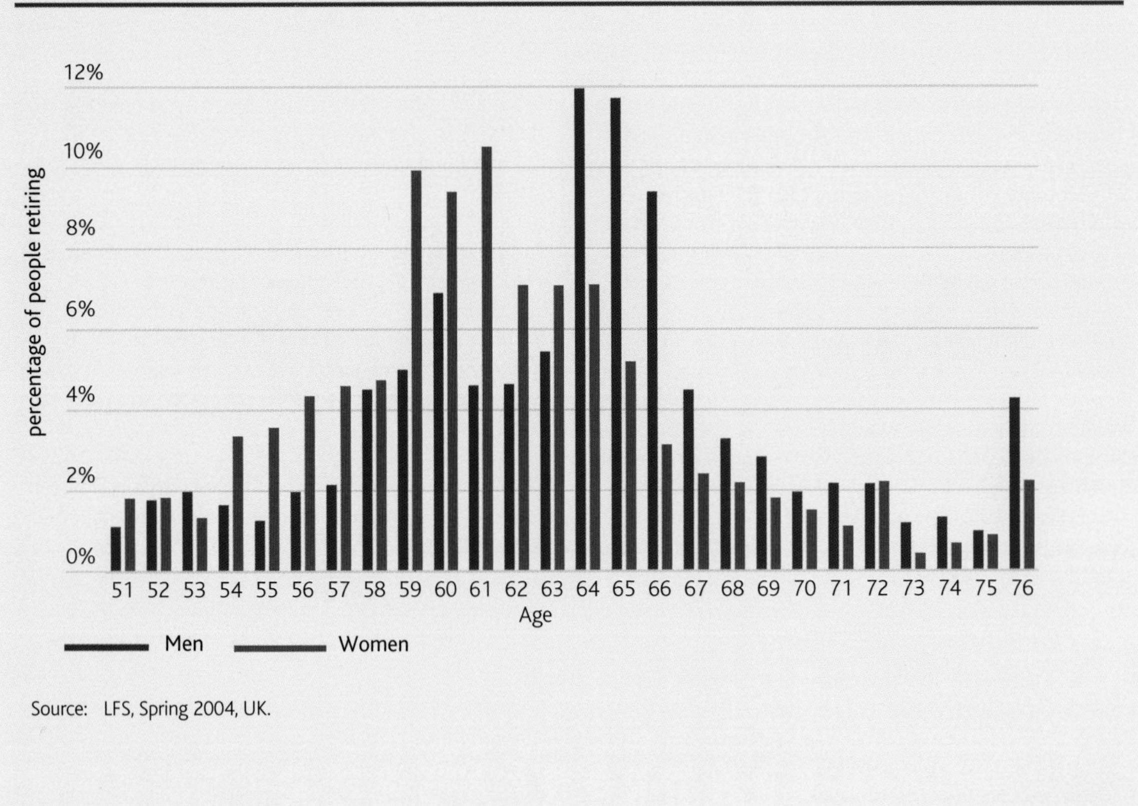

Source: LFS, Spring 2004, UK.

Figure 2.31 Trends in Mean Age of Retirement

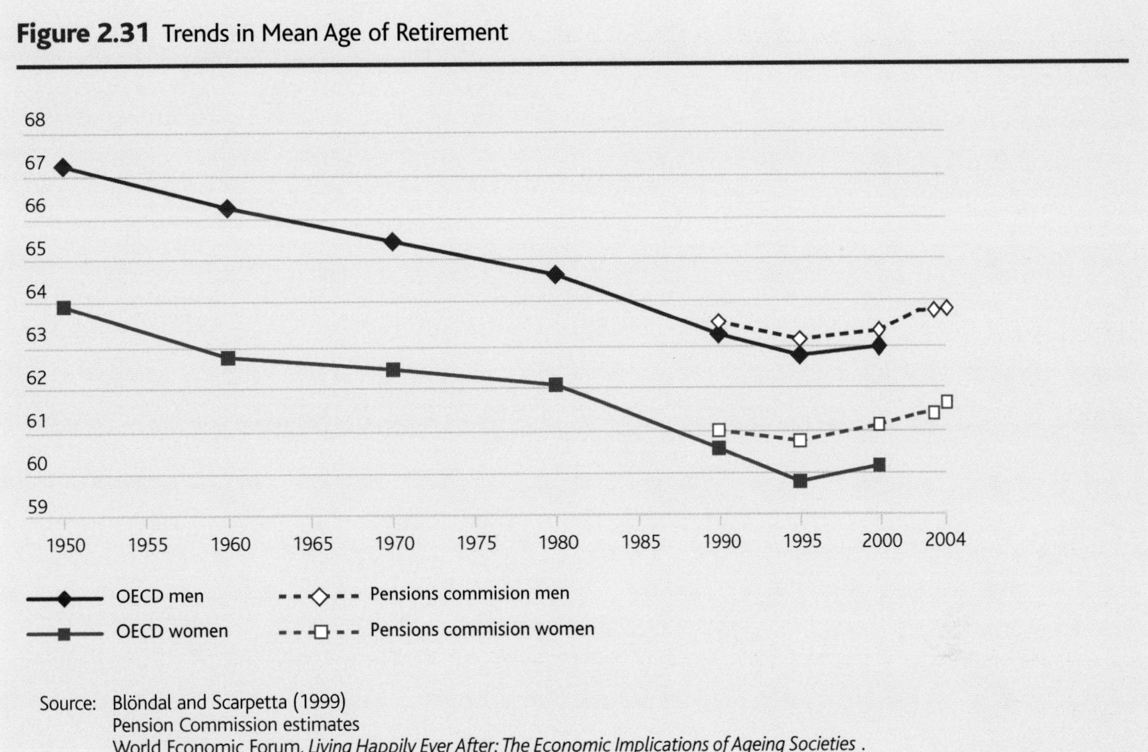

Source: Blöndal and Scarpetta (1999)
Pension Commission estimates
World Economic Forum, *Living Happily Ever After: The Economic Implications of Ageing Societies* .

The UK pension system: position and trends

3

The UK pension system appeared in the past to work well because one of the least generous state pension systems in the developed world was complemented by the most developed system of voluntary private funded pensions. This rosy picture always hid multiple inadequacies relating to specific groups of people, but on average the system worked, with the percentage of GDP transferred to pensioners comparable to other countries. But the state plans to provide decreasing support for many people in order to control expenditure in the face of an ageing population and the private system is not developing to offset the state's retreating role. Instead it is in significant decline.

The underlying trend in private sector employer pension provision has been downwards since the early 1980s, and the total level of funded pension saving is significantly less than official estimates have suggested. But irrational equity markets and delayed appreciation of life expectancy increases enabled many Defined Benefit (DB) schemes to avoid necessary adjustments until the late 1990s. As the fool's paradise has come to an end, schemes have been closed to new members, and a shift to less generous Defined Contribution (DC) schemes has followed. The underlying level of funded pension saving is falling, rather than rising to meet the demographic challenge, pension right accrual is becoming still more unequal, and risk is being shifted to individuals sometimes ill-equipped to deal with it.

This chapter covers seven points:

1 The inherited UK system: an ungenerous state system but extensive private provision.

2 The inherited UK system: the apparently rosy story always hid multiple inadequacies relating to specific groups of people.

3 Overall trends in second tier provision and key distinctions: PAYG versus funded: state versus non-state: public sector versus private.

4 The trends: Planned decline in state system generosity. Private system in underlying decline. Public employee pensions stable at increasing cost.

5 The consequences of decline: specific groups of people.

6 The consequences of decline: macro-estimates of pension saving.

7 A major shift in risk-bearing: from the state and employers to individuals.

1. The inherited system

The UK state pension system is among the least generous in the developed world. This can be measured by looking at the level of pension which different state systems deliver (as a percentage of average earnings) for individuals at different income levels during their working life.[1]

- The UK's state pension is clearly less generous than continental European systems, most of which provide the average earner with an income equal to at least 70% of working life earnings, and which provide a pension which increases with earnings up to a level of twice average earnings, and in some cases higher. The UK system, including fully paid-up State Earnings Related Pension Scheme or State Second Pension (SERPS/S2P), delivers to the average UK earner a gross replacement rate of just under 37% of earnings compared with 70% in the Netherlands, 76% in Sweden and 71% in France. At twice average earnings, the UK system delivers a replacement rate of 24%, compared with 70% in the Netherlands, 54% in France and 72% in Sweden [Figure 3.1].

- But it is also less generous than the US Social Security. At average earnings the US citizen receives a gross replacement rate of 45% of earnings versus 37% in the UK. At twice average earnings, the US gross replacement rate is 33% versus 24% in the UK. [Figure 3.2].

[1]Note: See Appendix F for a description of the UK state system. See Appendix D for international comparisons and for the assumptions made in Figures 3.1-3.3. Note that these Figures cover all mandatory pension provision. They therefore include the UK's SERPS/S2P and the mandatory savings of the Netherlands and Australian systems. They compare the position of a fully paid up member of each system. By fully paid-up we mean someone who has made the maximum number of years of contributions and therefore receives the maximum possible pension. In the case of SERPS/S2P the maximum number of years of contributions is 49.

Figure 3.1 Gross Mandatory System Pension Values: UK vs the 'Earnings-related' Systems

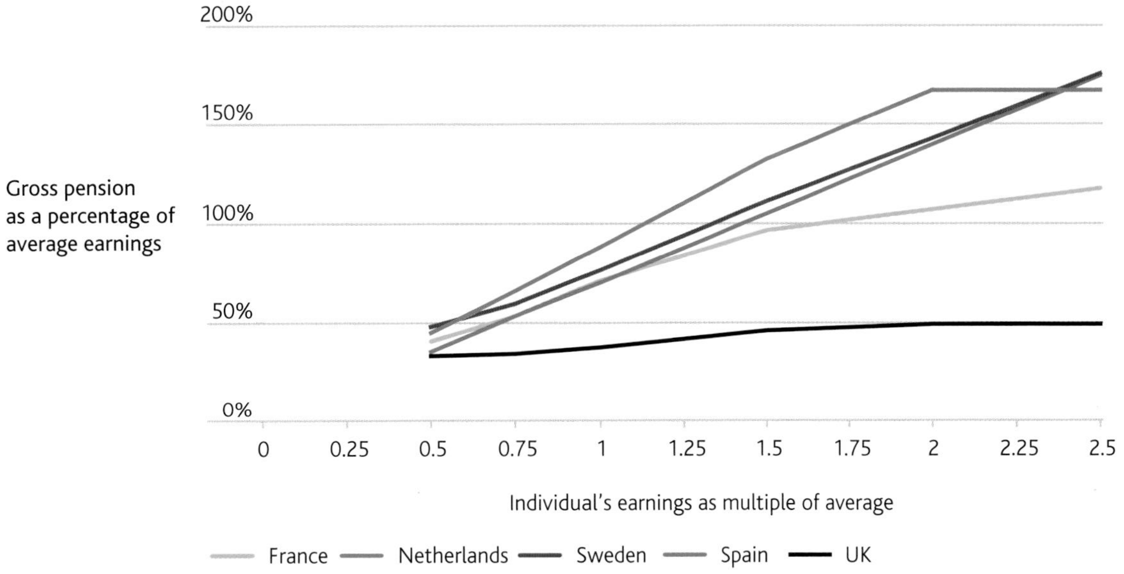

200%
150%
100%
50%
0%
Gross pension as a percentage of average earnings
0
0.25
0.5
0.75
1
1.25
1.5
1.75
2
2.25
2.5
Individual's earnings as multiple of average
France
Netherlands
Sweden
Spain
UK

Source: Monitoring Pension Policies, Annex: Country Chapters

Note: Netherland's figures reflect the impact of the quasi-mandatory private savings systems as well as the PAYG pension.

Figure 3.2 Gross Mandatory System Pension Values: UK vs the 'Intermediate' Systems

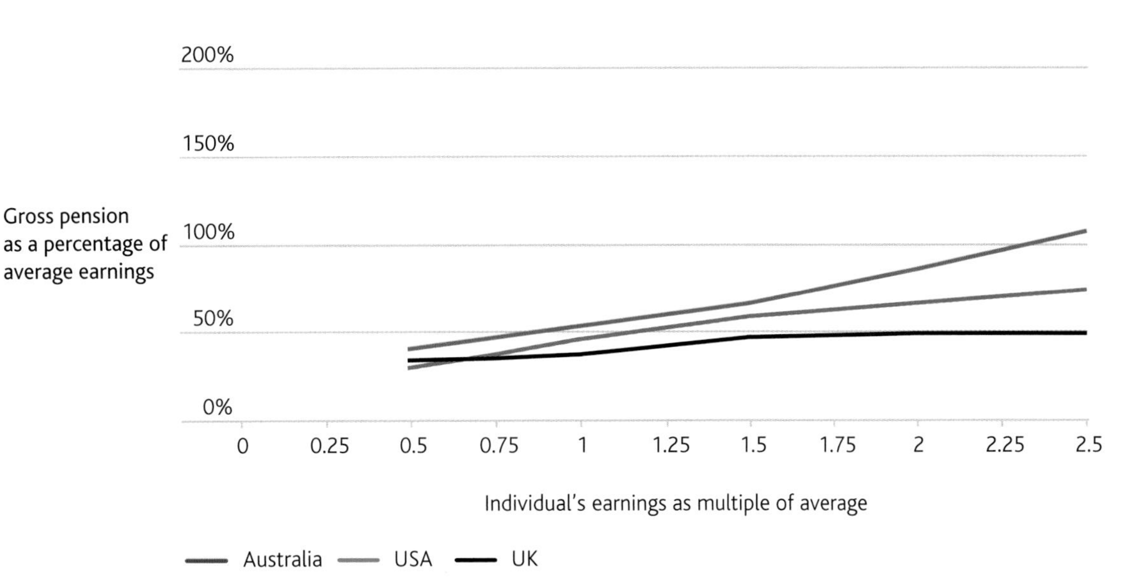

200%
150%
100%
50%
0%
Gross pension as a percentage of average earnings
0
0.25
0.5
0.75
1
1.25
1.5
1.75
2
2.25
2.5
Individual's earnings as multiple of average
Australia
USA
UK

Source: Monitoring Pension Policies, Annex: Country Chapters

Note: The Australian figures reflect the impact of the mandatory private savings system as well as the PAYG pension.

- Among the rich developed countries the UK is therefore in a specific group with Ireland, New Zealand and Canada, where the state pension is primarily designed to prevent poverty rather than to provide income replacement. In these systems replacement rates for those on half average earnings during working life are not far below continental levels but they are much lower for the average earner [Figure 3.3].

- It is worth noting that Australia was in this minimal provision group until the introduction of mandatory savings during the 1990s, and its PAYG pension alone would still put it in this category. But the impact of its compulsory savings scheme will, on reasonable rate of return assumptions, produce replacement rates significantly higher than the UK, but still short of continental levels. Like the US it is therefore now in the intermediate group [Figure 3.2].

The fact that the UK state system is relatively ungenerous has long been recognised. But this has been seen as beneficial from the point of view of fiscal sustainability, compared with the continental systems which face very large increases in taxes or social contributions as a percentage of GDP, if radical reforms are not enacted [Table 3.1]. And it has been seen as acceptable in terms of its implications for pensioner income because the UK has had one of the most extensive voluntary funded pension systems in the world, with a higher percentage of people in occupational schemes, mostly DB in nature, and large pension fund assets as a percentage of GDP [Figure 3.4].

Figure 3.3 Gross Mandatory System Pension Values: UK and Other 'Poverty Prevention' Systems

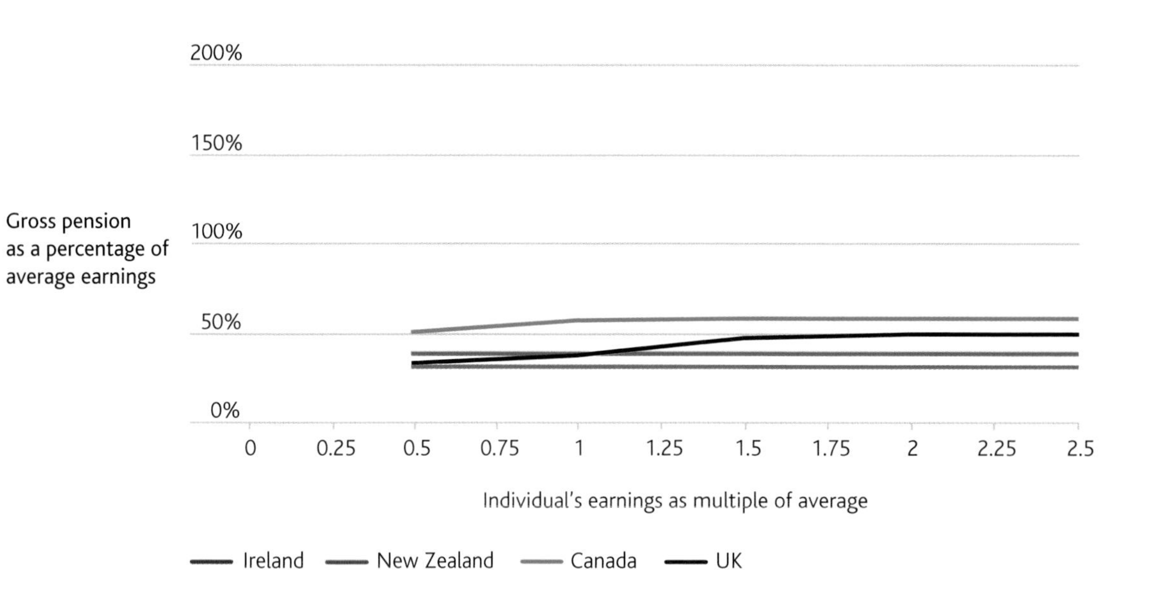

Source: Monitoring Pension Policies, Annex: Country Chapters

Table 3.1 Present and Forecast Public Pension Expenditures: Percentage of GDP[1]

	2000	2050	Percentage Point Change
Austria	14.5	17.0	2.5
Belgium	10.0	13.3	3.3
Denmark	10.5	13.3	2.8
European Union 15	10.4	13.3	2.9
Finland	11.3	15.9	4.6
France	12.1	15.8[2]	3.7
Germany[3]	11.8	16.9	5.1
Greece	12.6	24.8	12.2
Ireland[4]	4.6	9.0	4.4
Italy	13.8	14.1	0.3
Luxembourg	7.4	9.3	1.9
Netherlands	7.9	13.6	5.7
Portugal	9.8	13.2	3.4
Spain	9.4	17.3	7.9
Sweden	9.0	10.7	1.7
UK[5]	5.5	4.4	-1.1

Source: Economic Policy Committee (2001), "Budgetary challenges posed by ageing populations: the impact public spending on pensions, health and long-term care for the elderly and possible indicators of the long-term sustainability of public finances", Economic Policy Committee/ECFIN/655/01-EN final.

1. A number of countries introduced important reforms after 2000, or generated new national demographic projections. Latest national figures may therefore differ from here.
2. Figure is for 2040.
3. Updated German results based on the common EPC assumptions would show a 4.1% change.
4. For Ireland, the results are expressed as a percentage of GNP.
5. The UK figures differ from those used in other figures in this report (eg. in Chapters 1, 2 and 4) primarily because they are before both the introduction of Pension Credit, and latest demographic forecasts.

Figure 3.4 Pension Fund Assets as a Percentage of GDP

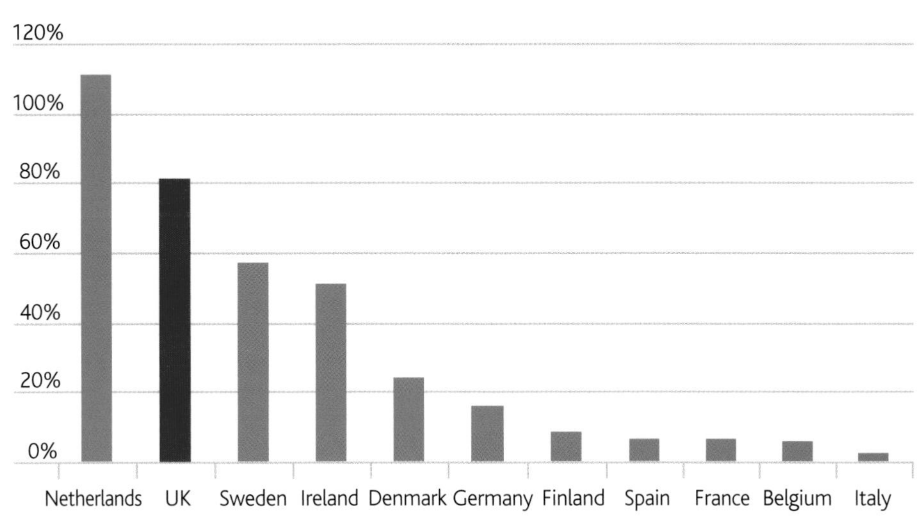

Source: CEPS, 2003

Note: The UK figures in this international comparison understate the UK pension assets, since they include only self-administered pension funds and exclude insurance company pension policies. Including the latter makes the total about 120% of GDP.

2. Apparently rosy story hid multiple inadequacies

This apparently rosy story was always exaggerated, because it failed to reflect the huge diversity of individual experience.

- In Britain in 2002-03, 11.3 million people in work were not making contributions to any private pension scheme and 8.8 million of them did not have a partner contributing. Unless they had accrued pension rights from previous arrangements they were therefore relying entirely on the state system [Figure 3.5].

- These non-contributors included about 1.7 million self-employed people. 53% of self-employed men and 67% of self-employed women were not contributing to any private pension scheme, and were thus relying on the Basic State Pension (BSP), since they were also not members of SERPS/S2P (which cover employees only).

- The non-contributors also include many employees of small firms. In 2003 only 29% of the employees of companies with 1-49 employees participated in an employer-sponsored scheme [Figure 3.6].

- Participation in private pensions has also varied hugely by sector. In 2003 85% of public sector employees were in occupational schemes. 59% of manufacturing employees participated in occupational or Group Personal Pension schemes (GPP), but only 41% of those working in the wholesale and retail sector. Some of these differences, e.g. the very low figures for hotels and restaurants, partly reflect the age profile of employment in the sector; but some do not [Figure 3.7].

- Participation also varies widely by earnings level. Seventy-two per cent of employees earning between £25,000-£39,999 were in an employer-sponsored scheme in 2003, but only 43% of those in the £9,500-£17,499 earnings band [Figure 3.8].

- Women, meanwhile, have in the past accrued on average significantly less occupational pension than men. Female pensioner incomes as a result are below those of men. [See Chapter 8 for details.] There have also been significant differences in pension provision by ethnic group. [See the panel on pages 66 and 67 for further details.]

Figure 3.5 Participation in Private Pension Schemes: 2002-03, millions

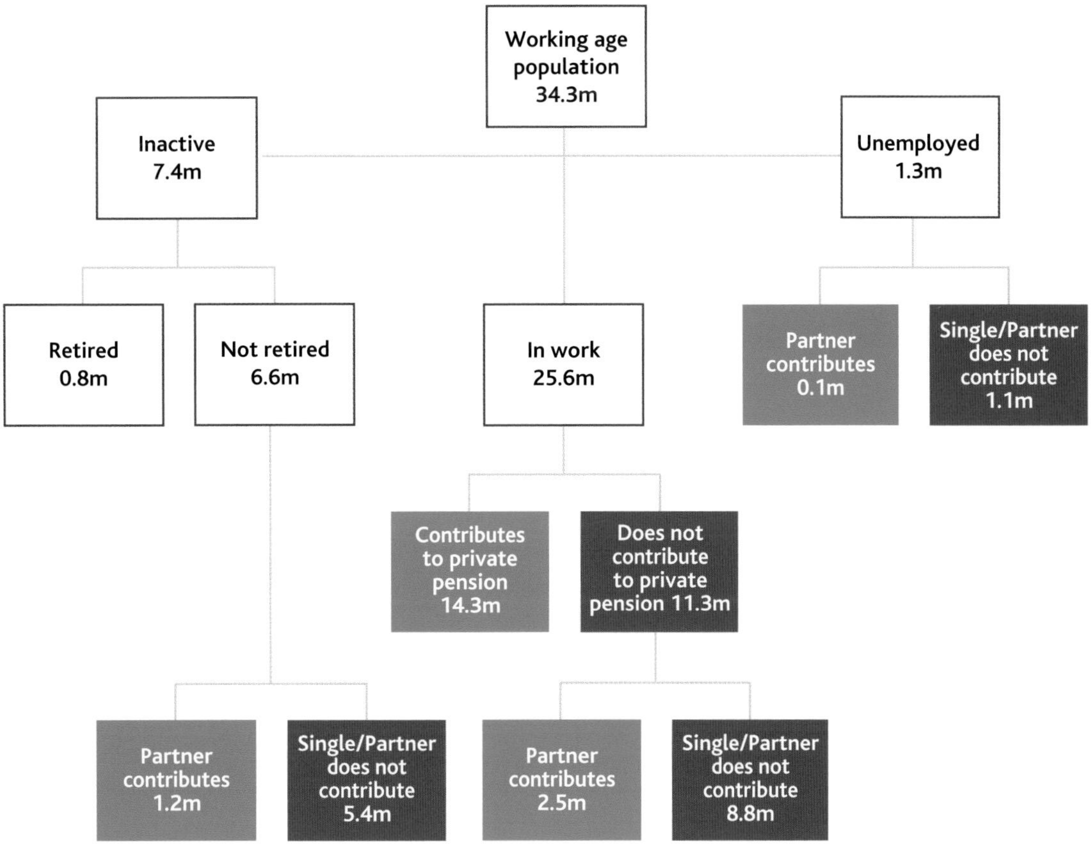

Source: FRS, 2002-03

Note: Those individuals with personal pensions that are only receiving contracted-out rebates have been counted among non-contributors since they will only accrue pension rights equivalent in value to the SERPS/S2P rights foregone (assuming that GAD calculations of appropriate rebates are fair).
As the numbers of inactive and unemployed individuals contributing to Stakeholder Pensions are small (fewer than 0.1m in FRS) they have been ignored for the purposes of this analysis.
Figures may not sum due to rounding.

Figure 3.6 Participation in Private Sector Employer-Sponsored Schemes, by Firm Size: 2003

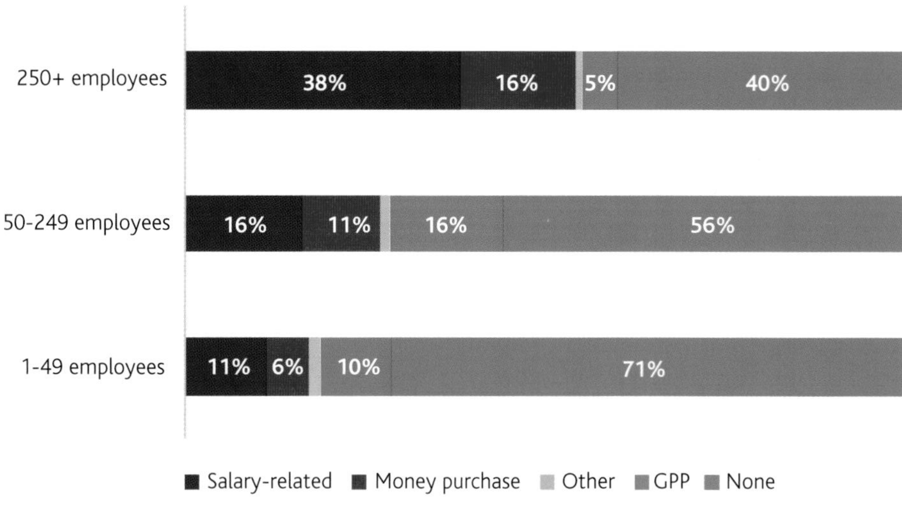

Source: Ungrossed NES, 2003

Note: Using ungrossed NES data may inflate the level of participation. For more information see Appendix A.

Figure 3.7 Participation in Employer-Sponsored Schemes, by Industry: 2003

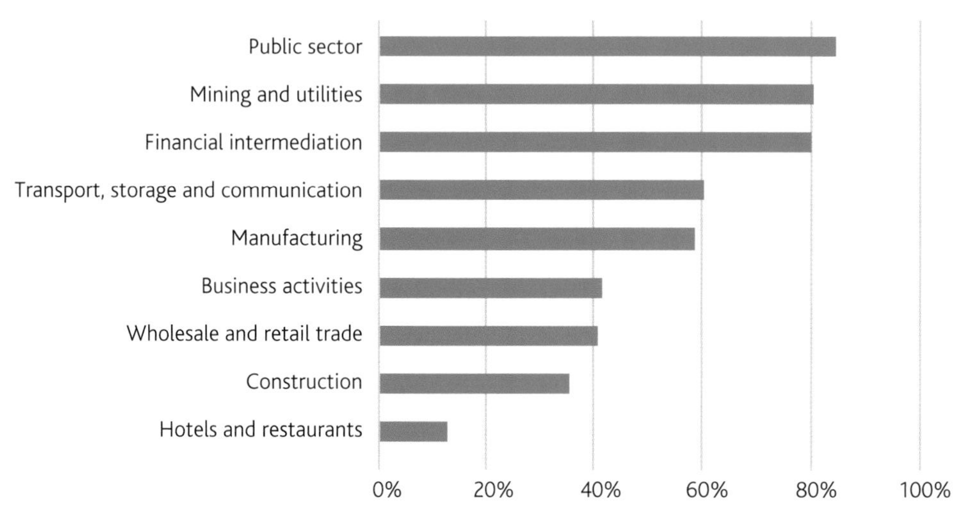

Source: Ungrossed NES, 2003

Note: Using ungrossed NES data may inflate the level of participation. For more information see Appendix A.

Figure 3.8 Participation in Private Sector Employer-Sponsored Schemes, by Earnings Band: 2003

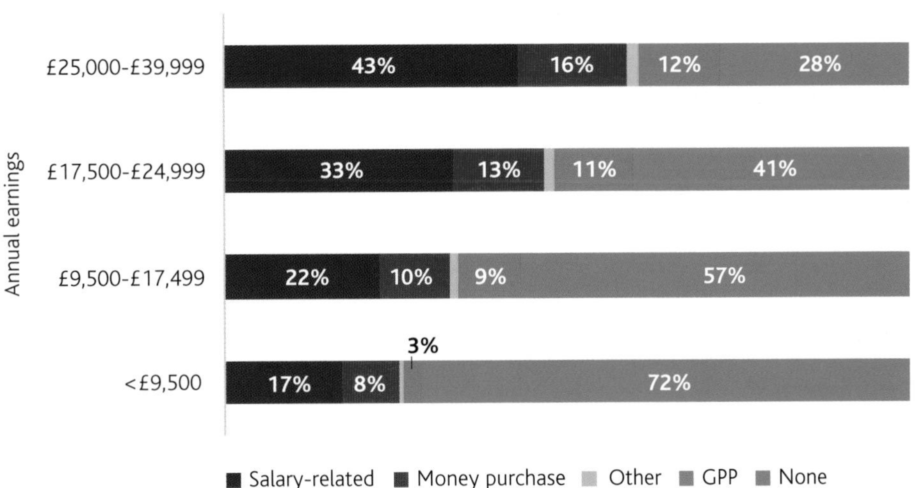

Source: Ungrossed NES, 2003

Note: Using ungrossed NES data may inflate the level of participation. For more information see Appendix A.

Ethnic Minorities: Pensioner Income and Private Pension Participation

Differences in current pensioner income among ethnic minorities results from the pattern of labour market participation interacting with the contributory nature of the state pension system. In 2001, 7.9% of the UK population came from a minority ethnic group. These groups have a younger age structure than Whites, reflecting past immigration and fertility patterns. In 2001 just 5.1% of non-White groups were aged 65 and over, compared with 16.9% for the White population [Figure 3.9].

Current Asian and Black pensioners have on average lower incomes than White pensioners. The level of state pension and benefit income is similar but occupational pension and investment income is substantially lower. Within the income from the state, however, the pension payments (i.e. BSP and SERPS/S2P) are considerably less for Asian pensioners, while means-tested benefits are higher [Figure 3.10].

These patterns of income reflect the labour market position of ethnic minority groups. There is a large variety of experience between different non-White ethnic groups [Figures 3.11, 3.12 and 3.13] but on average:

- Unemployment rates are higher for non-White ethnic groups, for both men and women, though more for Black Africans and Pakistanis and less for Indians.
- Economic inactivity rates also tend to be higher, though more for Bangladeshis and Pakistanis, and less for Black Caribbeans.
- Self-employment rates are significantly higher, particularly in the Pakistani and Chinese communities.

These patterns all reduce opportunities for membership of employer-provided pensions. These patterns are reinforced, for some ethnic groups, by sectoral patterns of employment, but not for others.

- Two-thirds of Bangladeshi and half of Chinese men in employment work in the distribution, hotel and restaurant sectors (which have lower average rates of pension participation), compared with just 17% of White British men.
- But half of Black Caribbean women work in the public administration, education and health sector, the highest proportion of any ethnic group, giving many the opportunity to participate in a public sector pension scheme.

The net effect of these different patterns is that non-White ethnic groups are significantly less likely to have private pension arrangements than Whites [Figure 3.14].

Figure 3.9 Population Distribution, by Ethnic Group and age

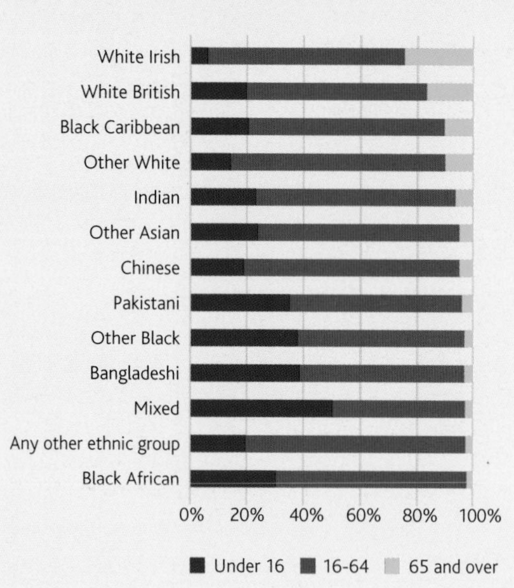

Source: Census 2001, ONS

Figure 3.10 Average Gross Pensioner Income, by Ethnic Group

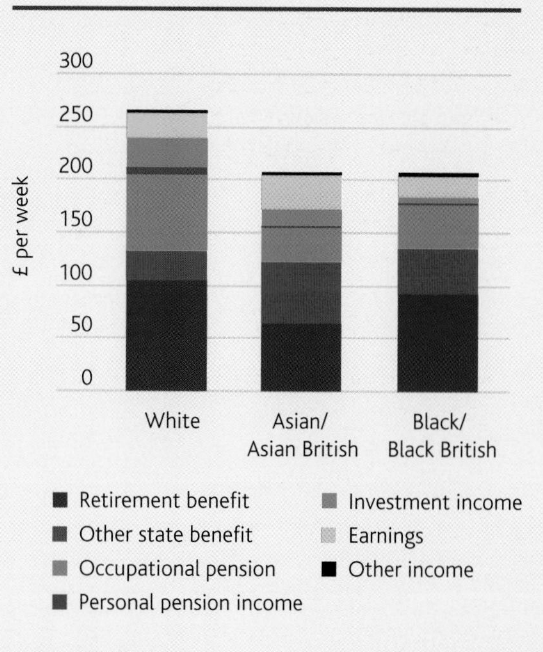

Source: FRS 2002-03

Figure 3.11 Unemployment Rates, by Ethnic Group and Sex: 2001/02

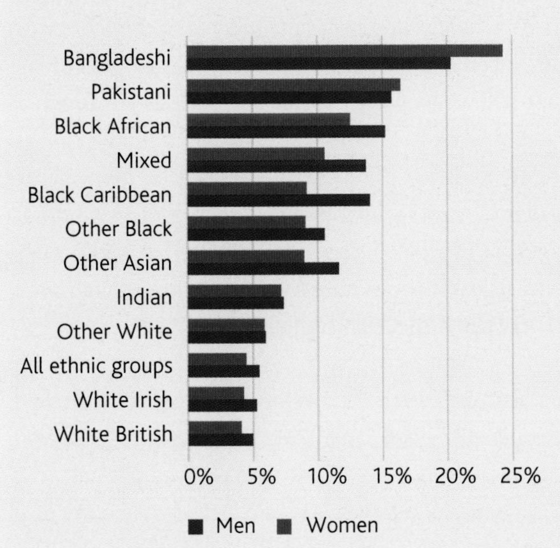

Source: Annual Local Area Labour Force Survey, 2001/02, GB, ONS

Figure 3.12 Economic Inactivity Rates, by Ethnic Group and Sex: 2001/02

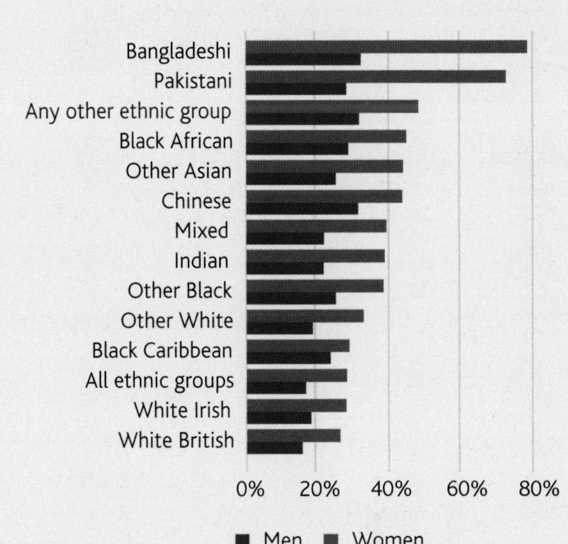

Source: Annual Local Area Labour Force Survey, 2001/02, GB, ONS

Figure 3.13 Self-employment as a Percentage of all in Employment, by Ethnic Group: 2001/02

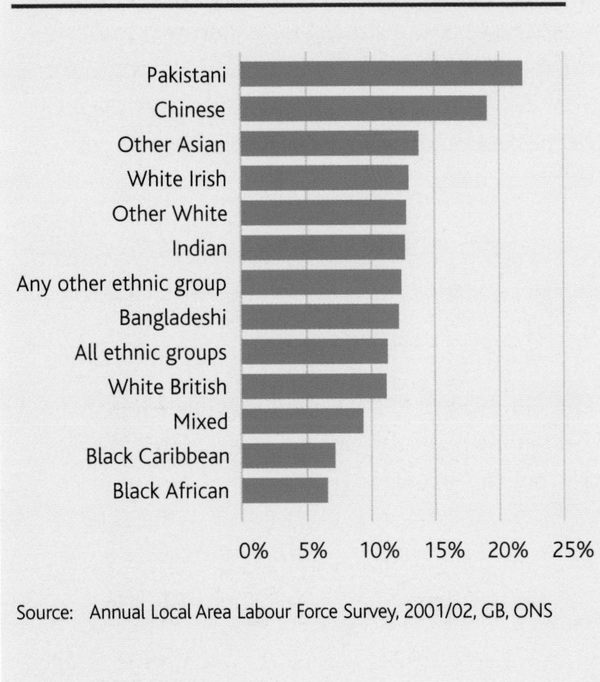

Source: Annual Local Area Labour Force Survey, 2001/02, GB, ONS

Figure 3.14 Private Pension Arrangements, by Ethnic Group: Age 20-59

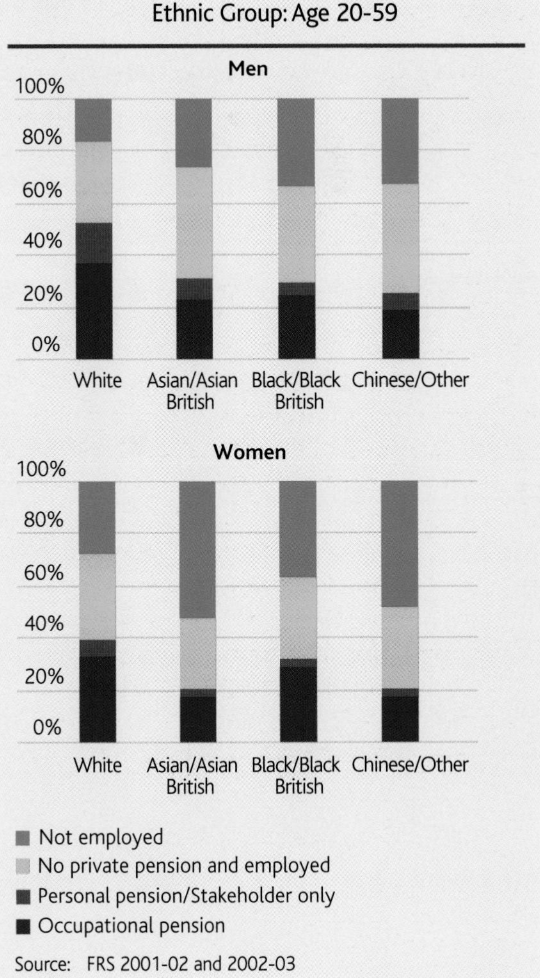

Source: FRS 2001-02 and 2002-03

These gaps for many people have co-existed with excellent provision for others.

- Private sector DB schemes have delivered to some top earners far higher levels of income replacement than typically found in any continental country, where state income replacement schemes typically level off at twice average salary, and where private sector DB schemes are rarer.

- Indeed while DB schemes deliver significant advantages for many people, and while their decline is resulting in both a decline in generosity and a shift in risk to individuals (discussed later in this chapter), it is important to note that DB final salary schemes have always entailed a significant redistribution from low earners to high earners.

- In addition, and in particular before improvements in leavers' rights were required by legislation in 1973 and 1986, DB schemes redistributed from early leavers to long-term employees. Those who enjoyed the full benefits of the DB schemes in their heyday were always a minority of the total number of members.

But despite these multiple gaps and inequalities, the public and private systems combined have produced a transfer of resources to pensioners comparable to that delivered by more generous state systems.

- In terms of the percentage of GDP flowing to pensioners in total, the UK appears to be not significantly out of line with other countries that have a similar demographic profile. (See Appendix D for the imperfections of the data which nevertheless tend to support this judgement.)

- The UK is below average in the EU15, but not dramatically so in terms of median pensioner incomes as percentage of the median household income [Figure 3.15]

- Pensioner poverty, as measured by the percentage of pensioners living on an income below 60% of median earnings, is higher than the EU15 average, but again not dramatically so [Figure 3.16].

Figure 3.15 Median Income of People Aged 65+ as a Percentage of Median Income of People aged less than 65: 2001

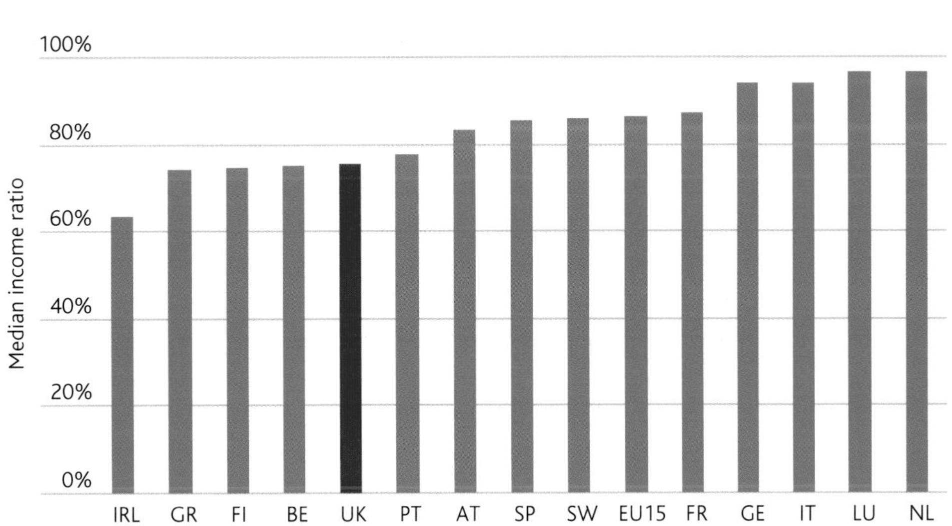

Source: Eurostat, ECHP-UDB, version July 2003

Note: The data for Sweden only includes people aged less than 85.

Figure 3.16 Percentage of People aged 65+ with Income Below 60% of Median Employment Income: 2001

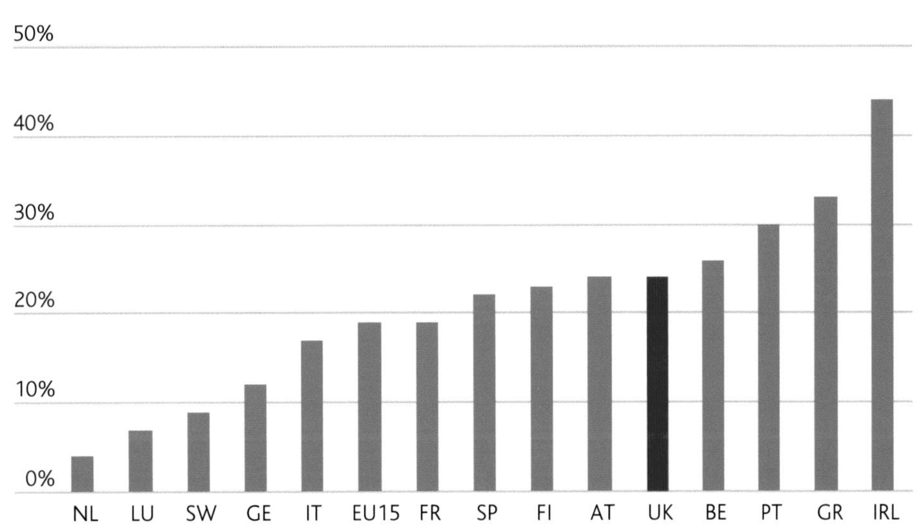

Source: Eurostat, ECHP-UDB, version July 2003

Note: The data for Sweden only includes people aged less than 85.

3. Overall trends and key distinctions

To understand the trends in state and private provision, it is important first to be clear about key definitions and conceptual distinctions, and about the context of previous and present government policy. Details of the UK state system are described in Appendix F and contracting-out is explained in detail in the panel on the following pages, but key points are:

- Since 1978, the UK has had for employees (but not for the self-employed) a compulsory "second tier" pension system. This requires employees either to be members of SERPS/S2P or to be "contracted-out" into an equivalent private system. When introduced this system produced a significant increase in the proportion of the people with second tier pension provision (i.e. provision in addition to the BSP). Since then this proportion has remained at around 60% [Figure 3.17]. The UK's position in the international comparisons in Figures 3.1-3.3 includes the impact of this second tier, showing the income replacement rate which would be achieved by a fully paid up SERPS/S2P member.

- The option of contracting-out into occupational schemes provided by employers existed from the beginning of SERPS, but it was expanded in 1987 to allow individuals to opt-out into Approved Personal Pensions. This produced an increase in the number of people covered by funded private pensions, and a fall in the numbers covered by SERPS. From the mid-1990s, however, as Figure 3.17 shows, the percentage of people in all contracted-out private arrangements has been in a decline, with an increase in membership of SERPS.

- The implications of these trends depend upon which question we are trying to answer.

  - From the point of view of the adequacy of pension provision for individuals, membership of SERPS could be as good a way to accrue pension rights as membership of a private funded scheme (though Figures 3.1-3.3 illustrate that compared with other countries' mandatory systems, SERPS provides a fairly limited benefit for people on average earnings).

  - If, however, it is the aim of public policy to encourage private funded savings rather than reliance on future taxes/National Insurance (NI) contributions to pay for PAYG benefits, then the shift back from private provision to SERPS is a step in the wrong direction. Both the previous Conservative Government and the present Government have been committed to an expanding role for private funded savings: the present Government has at times expressed this in terms of shifting the balance of pension income from 60% state: 40% private to 40% state: 60% private.

Figure 3.17 Percentage of the Population in a Second Tier Pension: Age 20-SPA

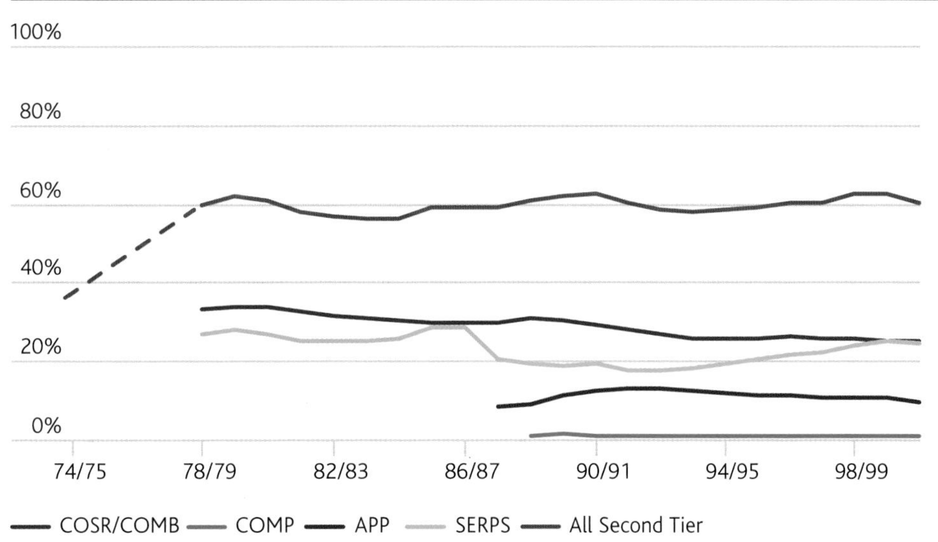

Source: GAD and LLMDB2, DWP

The UK "contracting-out" system

What is it?

The UK pension system includes (for employees but not the self-employed) a mandatory earnings-related tier, applying to a range of earnings between the Lower Earnings Limit (LEL) and the Upper Earnings Threshold (UET).[1] But it allows individuals an almost unique choice on how that earnings-related pension is secured.[2] One option is to join the State Second Pension (S2P) previously SERPS, which is run on a PAYG basis. The alternative is to 'contract-out' of S2P, with the relevant National Insurance (NI) contributions rebated to the individual and invested to build up a funded pension instead of S2P.

What people choose has implications for the timing of government receipts and expenditure. If people contract-out, present government revenue from NI contributions is reduced, but so too is the PAYG burden on future taxes/NI contributions. If people contract-in, government receives higher current revenue, but there is a higher future PAYG burden.

How does it work?

The operation of contracting-out is complex. Different arrangements are in place depending on whether someone contracts-out into an occupational salary related (i.e. DB) scheme, an occupational "money purchase" (i.e. DC) scheme or into an Approved Personal Pension. The rules and interactions between different parts of the system have changed many times. We explain below how the system works today.

Contracted-Out Salary-Related schemes (COSR)

An occupational DB pension scheme can contract-out of S2P if the scheme provides benefits that conform to the Reference Scheme Test, which define a minimum level of pension right accrual. If a scheme is contracted-out both employers and employees pay lower rates of NI contributions. In 2004-05 the total reduction is 5.1% (1.6% employee, 3.5% employer).

The Reference Scheme Test and the 5.1% rebate are not designed to ensure benefits fully equivalent to S2P, but rather to the now displaced SERPS, which was less generous for lower income levels. People who are contracted-out into COSR schemes and who earn below the UET therefore also accrue residual S2P rights equivalent to the difference between S2P and SERPS benefits. For example someone earning £10,000 per year will build up rights in their occupational scheme based on their earnings. In addition they will earn rights to S2P on the difference between what would have been accrued under SERPS and S2P. This is an addition of £37 per year for one year of earnings.

Contracted-Out Money Purchase schemes (COMP)

Occupational money purchase schemes can similarly contract-out and secure NI rebates. Contributions at least equivalent to this rebate ("the minimum payment") must be paid into a pension fund. The level of the rebate is calculated by GAD so that, on certain rate of return and cost of investing assumptions, the invested fund will produce benefits equal to the SERPS pension foregone. The present rebates have a flat-rate element (employee 1.6%, employer 1.0%) and an age related element, rising with age, to reflect the fact that later contributions earn fewer years of investment return.

Because the "minimum payments" are meant to secure a SERPS equivalent pension, this element of the fund ("the protected rights") has to be paid out in a fashion which mirrors the SERPS terms i.e. used to buy an index-linked annuity, based on a unisex rate, and, if the person is married, a joint life rather than single life annuity. The fact that the use of the "protected rights" has to mirror SERPS in structure, of course,

[1]Note: This panel refers to a number of different thresholds and limits in the NI system. The LEL (£4,108 per year or £79 per week in 2004/05) is the point at which individuals accrue entitlement to NI benefits, but employees and employers do not make contributions until earnings reach the Primary Earnings Threshold (£4,745 per year or £91 per week in 2004/05). The Lower Earnings Threshold (£11,600 per year or £211 per week in 2004/05) and the UET (£26,600 per year or £511 per week in 2004/05) affect the accrual of S2P. The Upper Earnings Limit (UEL) (£31,720 or £610 per week in 2004/05) is the point at which NI contributions for entitlement to benefits cease to be paid.

[2]Note: Only Japan has a somewhat similar system.

provides no certainty that the pension achieved will equal the SERPS benefits in terms of level: the pension achieved can be greater or less than the equivalent SERPS pension depending on the investment returns.

And, just as with COSR, since the aim is to mirror SERPS benefits rather than S2P benefits, people contracted-out into COMP who are earning less than the UET also accrue residual S2P equal to the difference between S2P and SERPS benefits.

Approved Personal Pensions (APP)

The option to contract-out through a personal pension was introduced in 1987. If someone is contracted-out in a personal pension plan, they initially pay the full rate of NI contributions, but at the end of each year the contracted-out rebate is paid directly to the pension fund by the government. These contracted-out rebates are age related, increasing with age, to reflect that for older people there are fewer years of investment return. Unlike for COSR and COMP the rebates for personal pensions are intended (on rate of return and cost of investing assumptions) to secure benefits equivalent to S2P (rather than to SERPS). To reflect the structure of S2P the rebates therefore have a banded structure, with different rates for the different bands of S2P accrual. This means that those who are contracted-out through a personal pension do not build up any element of entitlement to S2P.

The cost of rebates

Figure 3.18 sets out the level of total rebates paid over the last 24 years. These amount to almost £11 billion in 2002-03, therefore contracted out rebates are about one third of funded pension contributions.

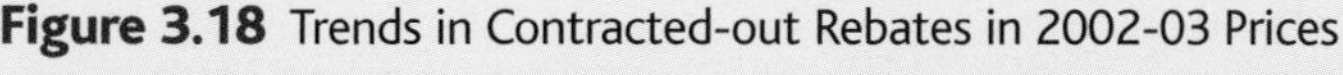

Figure 3.18 Trends in Contracted-out Rebates in 2002-03 Prices

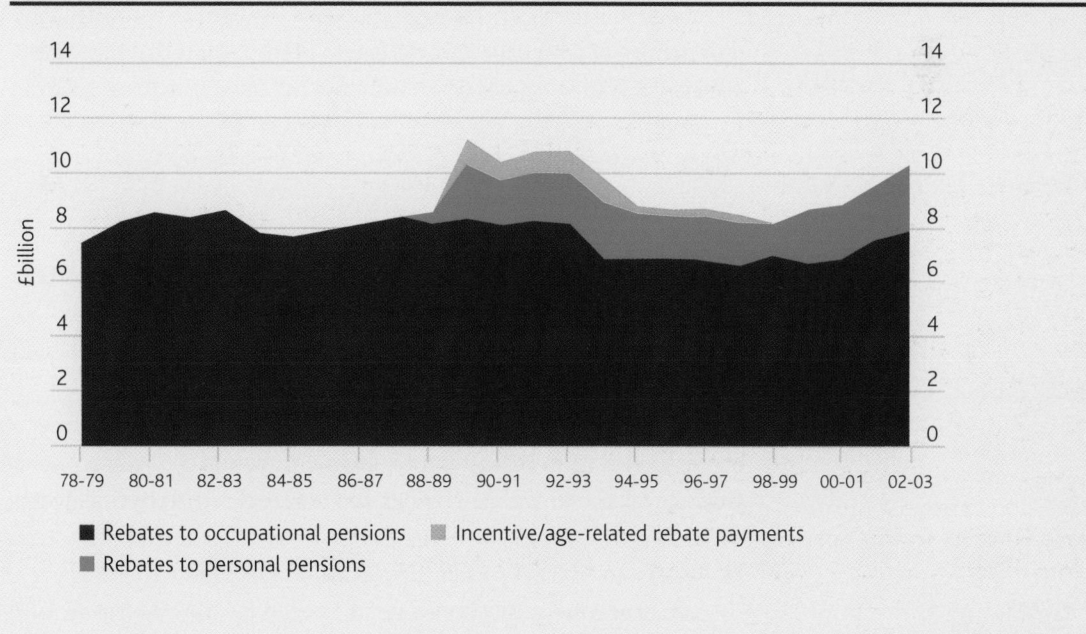

Source: GAD, GB

Note: The data above relates to GB.
Data on COMPs and incentive payments are available for the UK only. GB figures are derived using an assumed GB/NI split. It was necessary to estimate some of the payments to COMPs and some of the figures for the later years may be revised as more data becomes available.

- Finally, we need to be clear where public sector employee pensions fit in any figures presented. Public sector employee pensions are not included in "state pension expenditure," but if unfunded they will generate a claim on future tax revenues. There are about 4.7 million active members of public sector pension schemes. Of these 3.06 million are in unfunded (including 'notionally funded') government schemes while 1.5 million are in funded local government schemes. In addition 0.1 million are in what might be termed the "quasi-public sector" e.g. universities [Table 3.2]. As with the SERPS/S2P versus contracted-out distinction, which figures to look at depends upon the question asked.

  - If we are considering the adequacy of pension provision (state and employer combined) for the individual then public employee pensions should be considered as equivalent to private pensions. They are employment related benefits which are in addition to state pension scheme benefits.

  - If we are looking at the funded versus PAYG distinction, then the cost of the unfunded public schemes should be added to the state scheme cost, and only funded public sector pensions considered (along with private sector pensions) as non-state.

4. Trends: declining generosity in state and private systems: cost of public employment pensions increasing

The stated strategy of successive governments has been to encourage the development of private funded pensions, to offset the fact that they have been committed to policies which will make the state system less generous for average earners. But the private sector pension system is in significant decline. On current plans and trends only the public sector employee element of the overall system will deliver maintained (and indeed increasing) provision, but at increasing fiscal cost. We look in turn below at trends in the state system, the private funded system and in public sector employee pensions.

The state system: Present government plans will keep public expenditure on pensions roughly flat as a percentage of GDP. Faced with the demographic challenge, and if the state pension age does not rise further after equalisation at 65 in 2020, this must inevitably mean a declining per person provision relative to average earnings, and thus declining replacement rates.

- Relative to GDP per person and average earnings, state spending per pensioner is currently planned to fall by 26% by 2043/44 [Figure 3.19].

Table 3.2 Categories of Public Sector Schemes

	Explanation	Sectors covered	Number of active members (Million)	Annual cost* (£ Billion)
Unfunded	Paid for out of departmental spending	Civil service, armed forces, police and fire	1.04	£7.8
Notionally funded	Paid for by current departmental contributions to notionally purchase bonds from HM Treasury but unfunded at the level of the whole public sector	National Health Service, education	2.02	£8.2
Funded public sector	Pensions are paid by the pension funds to which contributions are made in cash	Local government	1.5	£4.4
Funded quasi-public sector		Universities	0.1	£0.7

* Annual costs are the actual pensions paid for the unfunded and notionally funded schemes and the actual contributions paid for the funded public sector and quasi-public sector.

Source: GAD, ODPM, University Superannuation Scheme Annual Report 2003

Figure 3.19 Projected State Spending Per Pensioner Indexed in Constant 2003/04 Price Terms

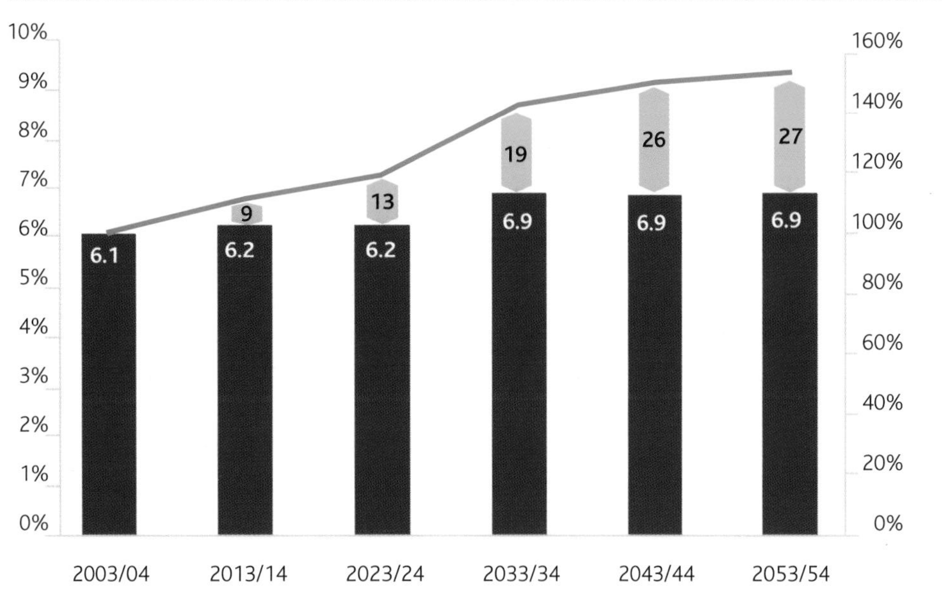

Source: Pensions Commission analysis of data from DWP and GAD

- The impact of this on the poorest pensioners will be offset by the increasingly flat rate and redistributive nature of state pension spending. The migration from SERPS to S2P will over time reduce the importance of the earnings-related element within the UK's state pension system. By 2050, under current plans, a maximum S2P pension will accrue at 108% of average earnings compared to 145% of average earnings in 2000 under SERPS. And between now and then the pension payable will rise in line with average earnings for someone on 27% of mean earnings or below, but will rise by less for anyone above this level [Figure 3.20]. Moreover while the BSP is projected to rise in line with prices, rather than average earnings, the effect of this on the lowest earners will be offset by the increasing role of means-tested income guarantee benefits, which on current indicative forecasts will rise in line with average earnings. As a result current indicative forecasts imply that an increasing percentage of UK state pension spending will be means-tested [Figure 3.21]. [See the panel in Chapter 6 on the possible evolution of Pension Credit.]

- But the unavoidable consequence of falling per person provision relative to average earnings, combined with greater redistribution, will be a significant reduction in the generosity of the state system at middle and higher income levels. The percentage of earnings replaced by non-means-tested state pensions will on current plans remain roughly constant for lowest income earners, but will fall significantly between now and 2050 for moderate and high earners [Figure 3.22]. The biggest impact of this change will be felt by middle income earners (say £15,000 to £30,000 per year) simply because at high and very high income levels state benefits are already such a small percentage of income in retirement that a further decline is of little importance. For people up to about average earnings who chose not to save the impact of this on income in retirement could be significantly offset by means-tested Pension Credit payments, but with the disadvantage, discussed in Chapter 6, of creating disincentives to private saving [Figure 3.23].

Figure 3.20 Composition of Income From the State Pension for a Single Man Retiring in 2000 and 2050 assuming no additional saving

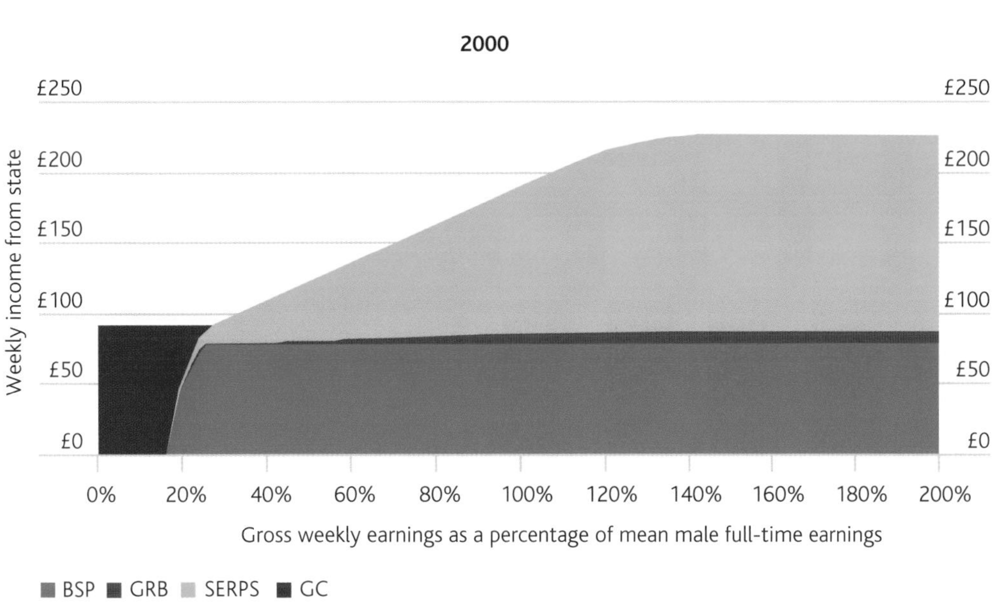

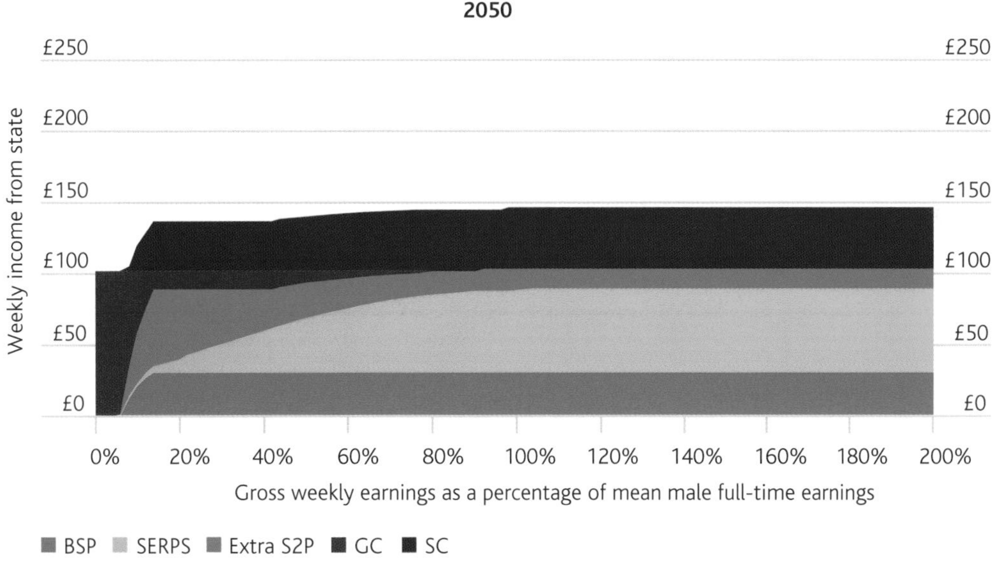

Source: DWP

Note: GRB = Graduated Retirement Benefit, GC= Guarantee Credit, SC = Savings Credit
Potential entitlement to Housing Benefit or Council Tax Benefit is ignored.
Amounts in 2003 Earnings Terms. This assumes a 44 year working life.

Figure 3.21 Breakdown of Forecast of State Spending per Pensioner if Current Indexation Plans Continued Indefinitely

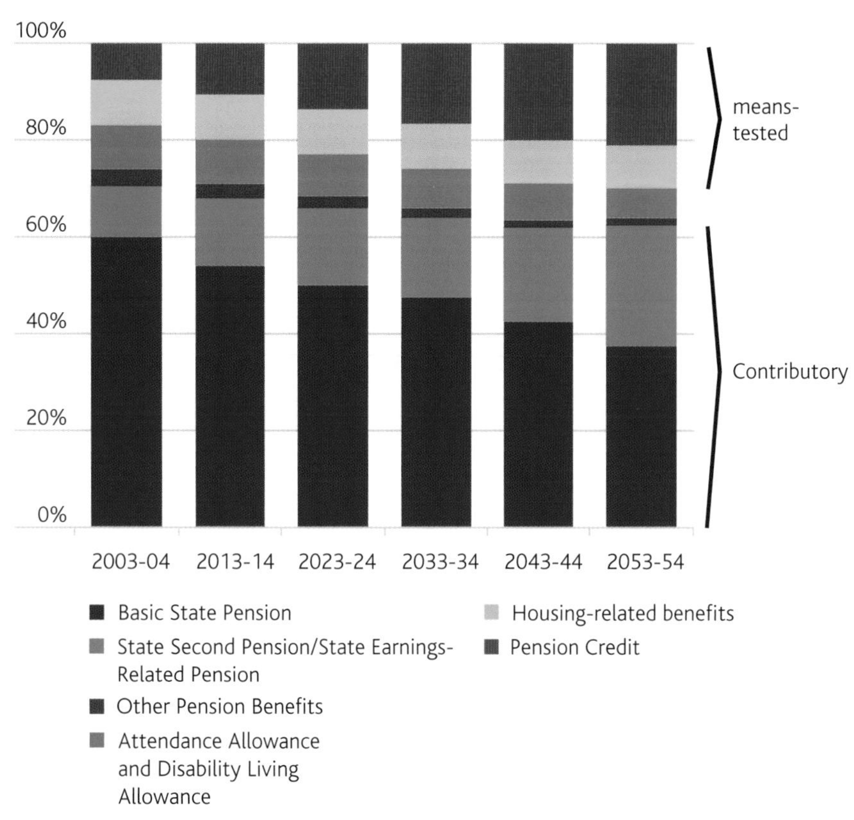

Source: Pensions Commission analysis of data from DWP and GAD

Figure 3.22 Gross Replacement Rate From the State for an Employee, by Earnings Level: Contributory Pensions Only

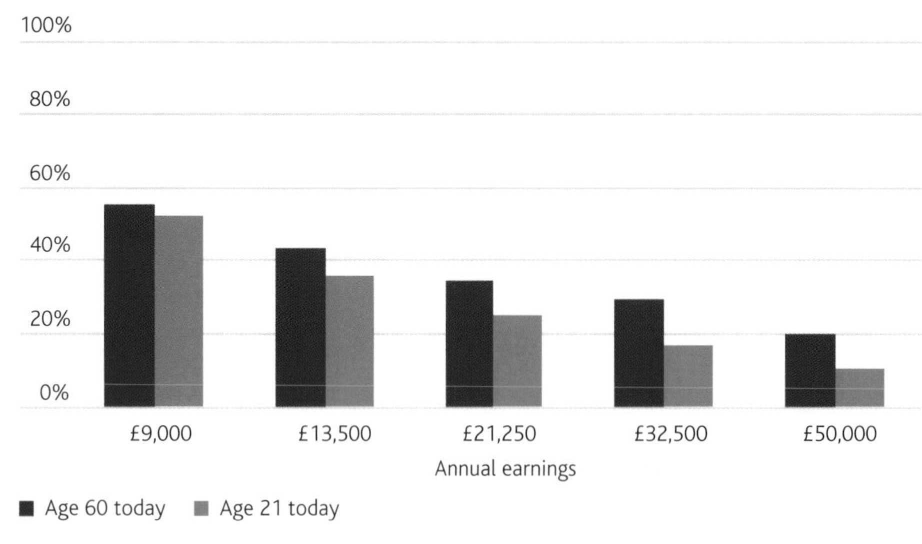

Source: DWP

Note: Assuming a 44 year working life for SERPS, S2P accrual and full BSP entitlement.

Figure 3.23 Gross Replacement Rate From the State Including Means-tested Benefits: For Employees by Age Today and Income Level, Assuming No Private Saving

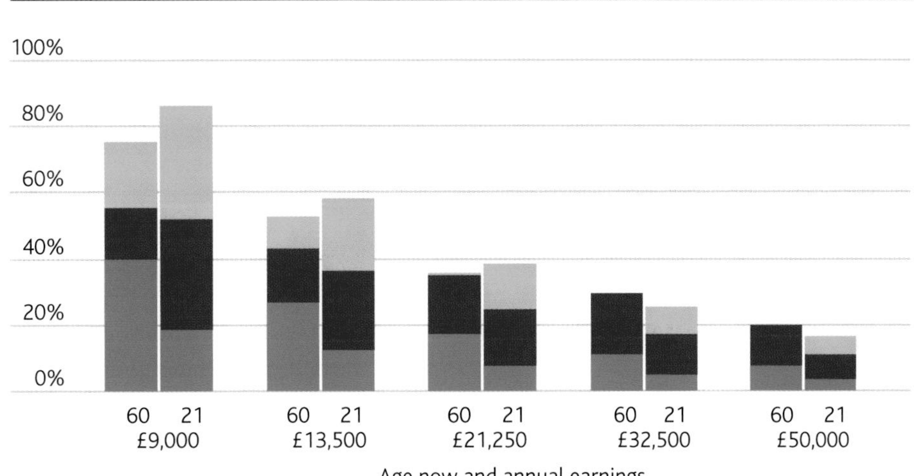

Source: DWP and Pensions Commission analysis

Note: Assuming 44 year working life for SERPS/S2P.

The private system: Rather than the private system expanding to fill the gaps left by state system plans, however, Britain's funded private pension system is in serious decline. The percentage of the workforce covered is not rising and the average level of pension provision is declining.

- Table 3.3 sets out the categories of private pension provision. The term "occupational" pension is used to refer to employer-sponsored pensions provided through the legal form of a trustee scheme. But employer-sponsored pensions can also be provided (and are increasingly provided) via a GPP scheme. In these the legal contract is between the individual and the insurance company provider, but with the employer facilitating the process, bulk negotiating the charges and usually making a contribution. The DB/DC distinction cuts across both the occupational/personal divide and the employer sponsored/individual divide.

- Private occupational pensions, and in particular DB final salary pensions, have been seen as the "jewel in the crown" of the UK pension system. But since the 1970s there has been an underlying downward trend. Despite the transfer to the private sector of the utilities (all of which previously provided DB schemes) active membership of private sector occupational schemes declined slightly from 1979-2000, while DB membership in particular fell significantly [Figures 3.24 and 3.25]. As a percentage of total private sector employment, occupational scheme membership, and in particular DB scheme membership, has been falling throughout the 1980s and 1990s [Figure 3.26]. The percentage of men contracted-out in DB schemes (combining both private and public sectors) has been in continuous decline, only partially offset by a rise in female DB participation [Figures 3.27 and 3.28].

Table 3.3 Types of Private Pension Provision

Occupational salary related	Occupational money purchase	Group personal pension	Individual personal pension
Occupational		Personal (contract based)	
Employer Sponsored			Not employer sponsored
DB	DC		

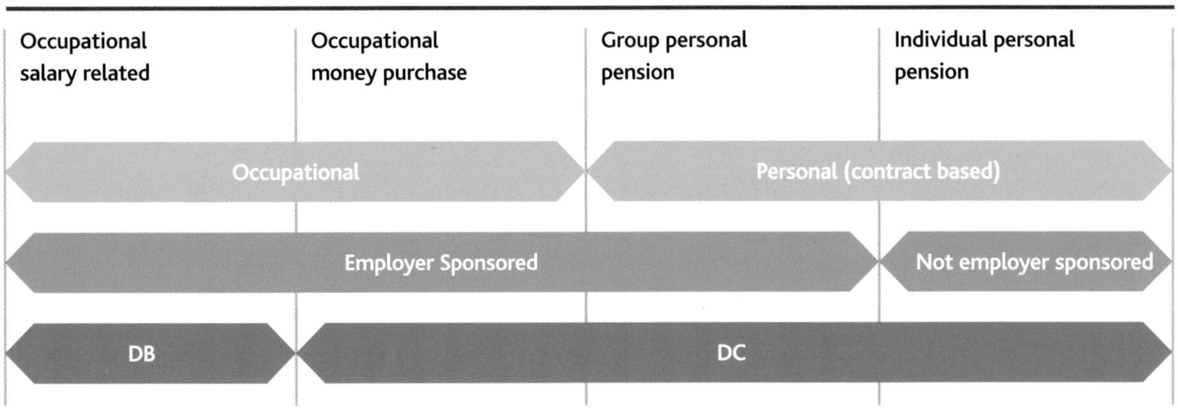

Occupational schemes can also be divided between self-administered and insurance managed. Most but not quite all DB schemes are self-administered.

Note: An occupational scheme is one with scheme trustees and governed by trust law. A personal pension (whether sponsored by an employer or not) has the legal form of a contract between an individual and a pension provider (usually an insurance company).
Individual personal pensions are most common among the self-employed and others who are not entitled to join occupational schemes such as those in partnerships. Stakeholder pensions are a subset of personal pensions and can be either GPP or individual personal pension in form.

Figure 3.24 Active Members of Occupational Pension Schemes, millions

15

10

Million

5

0

1953 1956 1963 1967 1971 1975 1979 1983 1987 1991 1995 2000

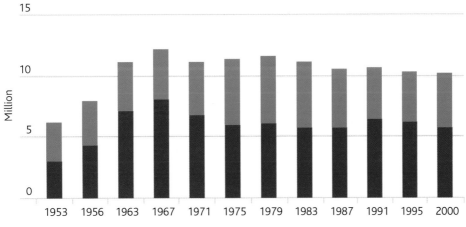

■ Private sector ■ Public sector

Source: Occupational pension schemes 2000, GAD

Note: Numbers for 2000 split between private and public sectors are not strictly comparable with numbers for earlier years. Members of schemes run by organisations such as the BBC are excluded from the public sector in 2000 but included in 1995. No adjustment has been made in 2000 for private sector employees who are members of schemes in the public sector (because their private sector employer participates in a public sector scheme such as a local authority scheme).

Figure 3.25 Active Members of Private Sector Occupational Pension Schemes, millions

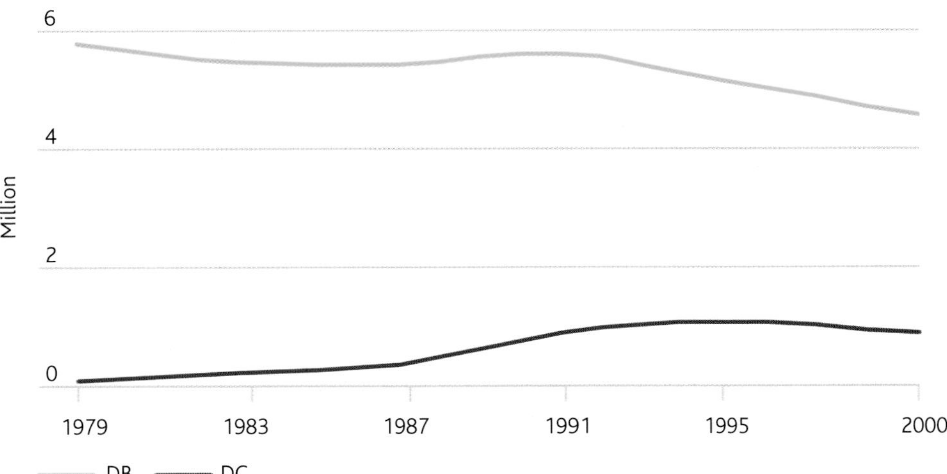

Source: Occupational pension schemes 2000, GAD

Figure 3.26 Estimated Percentage of Private Sector Employees Participating in Occupational Pension Schemes

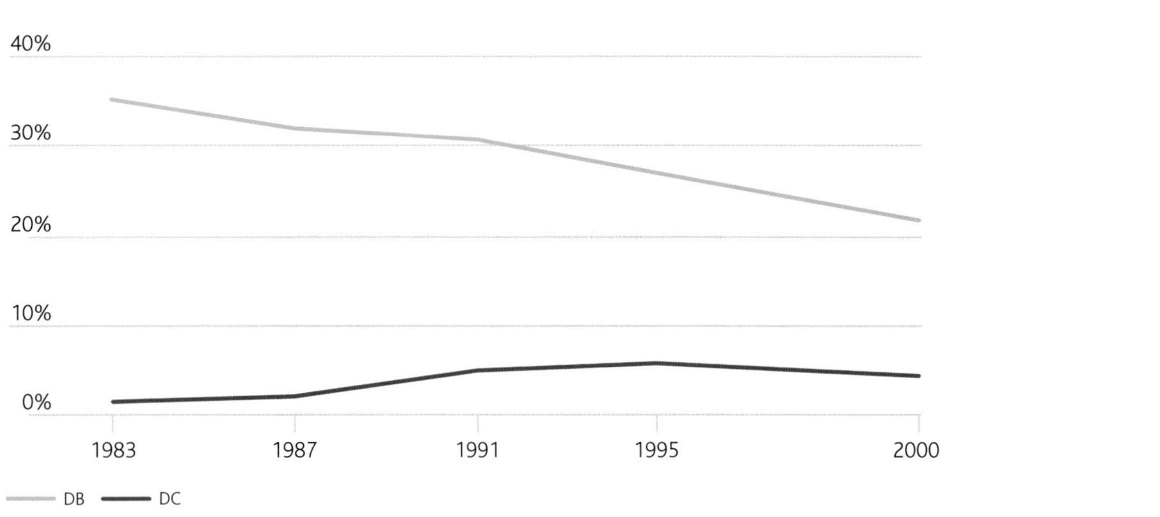

Source: Pensions Commission analysis based on occupational pension schemes 2000, GAD and ONS employment data.

Note: Definition of public and private sectors may vary between sources.

Figure 3.27 Percentage of Men in Contracted-out Salary Related Schemes, by Age

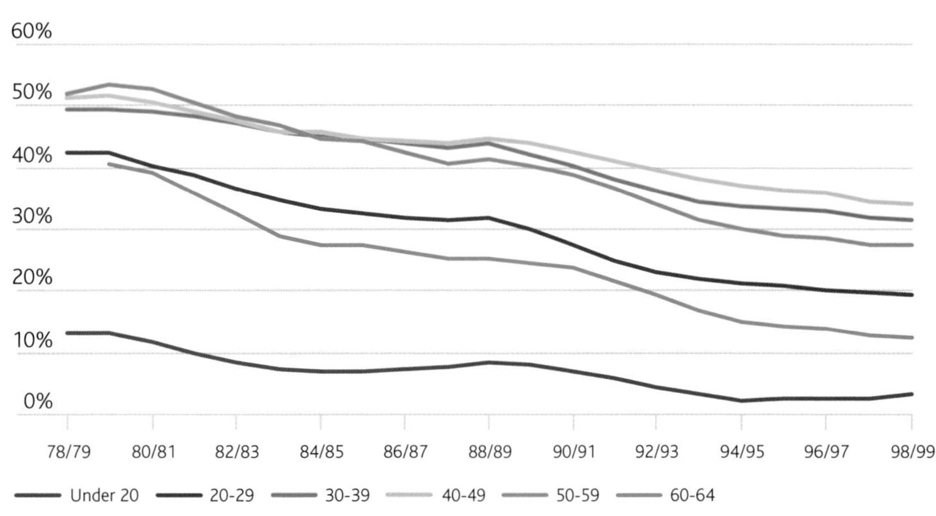

Source: LLMDB2, DWP

Figure 3.28 Members of Occupational Schemes, by Sector: Women, millions

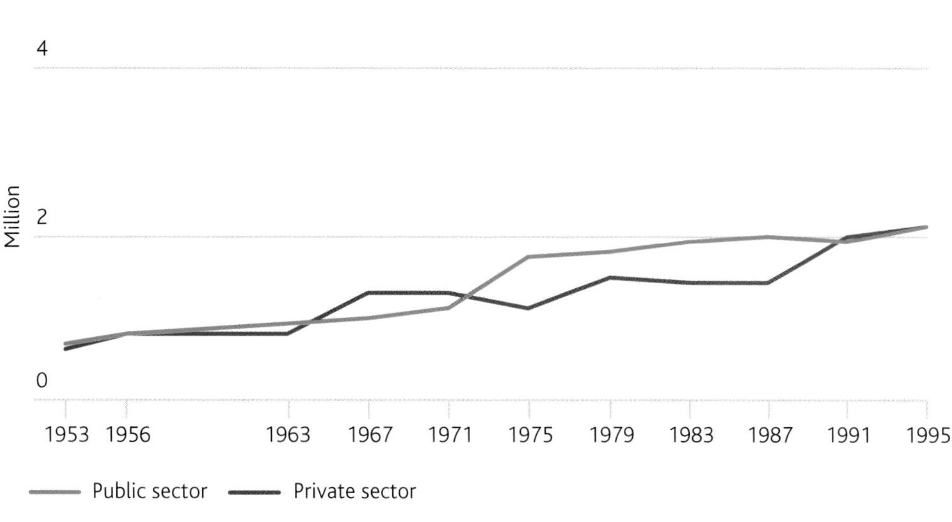

Source: Occupational Pension Scheme Surveys, GAD

Figure 3.29 Participation in Private Sector Salary-Related Schemes: Ongoing and New Employees

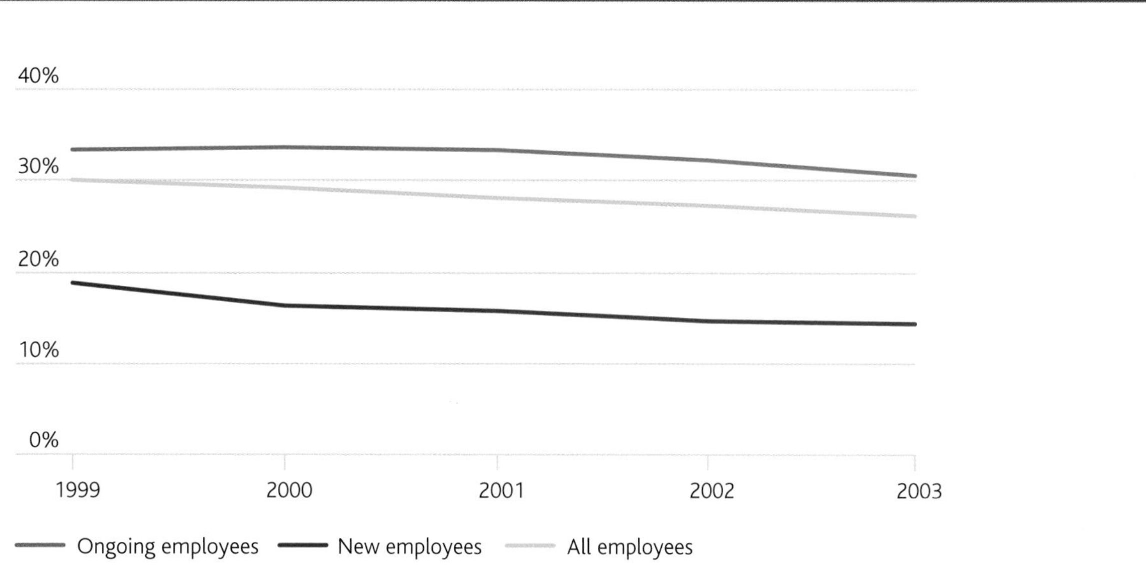

Source: Ungrossed NES, 2003

Note: Using ungrossed NES data may inflate the level of participation. For more information see Appendix A. In this analysis a 'new' employee is defined as one that has worked in the same job in the organisation for less than one year.

- This long-term trend has accelerated greatly in the last 10 years and, in particular, in the last four. There is no one data source which gives a definitive picture of the latest developments, but our best estimate is that active membership of open DB schemes in the private sector has fallen by 60% since 1995. In addition, a small but increasing percentage of schemes are now closed to accruals for existing members. [See the panel on the page opposite for our estimate of DB closures.]

- These closures will result in a steady further erosion of the percentage of employees in private sector DB schemes. Thus while the data from the New Earnings Survey (NES) suggests that about 26% of private sector employees are still members of salary related schemes, the figure for new employees shows that only 14% are in salary related schemes, down from 19% only five years ago [Figure 3.29].[2] Rolling these trends forward, and even if the rate of closure now slows considerably, DB scheme membership is likely to become a primarily public sector phenomenon. In 2000 there were about 4.6 million active members of private sector DB schemes, and a similar number in public sector schemes. Given current trends in scheme closure and reasonable assumptions on labour turnover, it is unlikely that more than 1.6-1.8 million private sector employees will be active members of DB schemes in 20 years time. This figure could be significantly lower.

- When DB schemes are closed they are usually replaced either by DC occupational or by GPP schemes. Different data sources suggest slightly different implications of this shift for the total membership of employer pension schemes DB and DC combined:

  - The 2002-03 data from the FRS [see Figure 3.5] when compared with the 1996-97 data [Figure 3.30] suggests that there are an increasing number of people with no private pension of any type [Figure 3.31].

  - The *Employers' Pension Provision Survey* (EPP) suggests a flat trend in large company membership and a slight decline in membership among small firms over the last seven years, but the movements could well be within the sampling error of the survey [Figure 3.32].

  - Data from the NES suggest that the percentage of private sector employees participating in any employer scheme is stable, with the decline in occupational DB scheme membership offset by the rise in occupational DC and GPP membership [Figure 3.33].

  No data source, however, suggests that private pension membership is growing to offset the state's retreating role. The best judgement from the data is that in terms of membership employer provision is either flat or very slightly in decline.

[2]Note: That NES survey data tends to suggest slightly higher participation in any pension scheme, and in salary related schemes, than do other sources. This reflects the NES's imperfect coverage of lower income part-time workers falling below the National Insurance LEL.

Estimates of the DB to DC Shift

Over the last 10 and, in particular, the last four years there has been a major wave of closures of DB (usually final salary) schemes in the private sector. On average these are replaced by significantly less generous DC schemes, with lower contribution rates. The closure wave will, therefore, over time reduce aggregate pension saving in the UK, and reduce the level of future pension income. To assess the adequacy of pension saving looking forward we therefore need to estimate how far the closure wave has progressed and at what level of DB provision it is likely to end. This requires judgement drawing on many imperfect data sources.

A DB scheme can be closed in three different senses:[1]

- Closed to new members but still open to further accruals for existing members. This is the predominant form of scheme closure.
- Closed to both new members and to new accruals of rights for existing members. This is rarer, but has become slightly more common over the last two years.
- Fully closed or wound up, with bulk annuities purchased to meet the liabilities. This is currently very rare.

The best data sources for the position at the beginning of the closure wave are the GAD survey figures for 1995 and 2000. These suggest that in 1995 there were 5.2 million active (i.e contributing) members of private sector DB schemes.[2] Of these 5 million were in open schemes, 0.2 million in closed. By 2000, GAD estimated that there were 4.6 million active members, of which 0.5 million were members of already closed schemes, 4.1 million of open schemes, implying a closure rate of 16% between1995 and 2000. If there had been no more scheme closures after 2000, our best estimate would have been that total membership of DB schemes would fall over the years (at a pace determined by job turnover and retirement rates) to bring the total number into line with the number for open schemes, and with the eventual figure slightly lower than 4 million because of DB scheme concentration in sectors of declining employment.

Since 2000, however, the closure wave has gathered pace, as illustrated by numerous surveys. None of these surveys provides the definitive picture of membership today. Most of them measure the proportion of schemes which have closed, but it is sometimes difficult to infer the implied start date for these closures. Most surveys also count numbers of schemes, with imperfect information by which to weight the result by number of members. And a closed scheme may never have been open to all employees. But all sources suggest a major wave of closures in the last four years.

- NAPF annual surveys have suggested that 10% of private sector final salary schemes closed to new entrants in 2001, 19% in 2002 and 26% in 2003. As a percentage of open DB schemes in 2000 the closure rate would have been significantly higher, implying a total closure rate across all three years of well over 50%, but double-counting may have occurred if respondents mistakenly included the same closure in more than one year's response.
- An ACA survey in 2003 found that 63% of final salary schemes were closed to new members and a further 9% to new accruals, but the results may be skewed towards smaller companies.
- A Pensions Commission study of FTSE350 company accounts conducted in summer 2003 and reflecting latest published data (usually end 2002) suggested that 60% of active members of DB schemes were in closed schemes.
- The *Employers' Pension Provision Survey 2003*, conducted in spring 2003, suggested that the percentage of employees, in organisations with 20 or more employees, who were members of open DB schemes had fallen 33% between 2000 and 2003.
- Since 2003 closures have continued, but the rate may be slowing. A 2004 CBI/Mercer survey suggests a 41% closure rate over the last two years, but an intended closure rate of 10% over the next year.

No definitive estimate can be derived from these different sources. The evidence suggests that active membership of open private sector DB schemes has so far fallen by 60% since 1995. And for the purposes of modelling we have assumed that active membership of private sector DB schemes will ultimately fall by 60% from the 2000 level. This would imply a long-term floor of perhaps 1.6-1.8 million active members. These estimates are however highly uncertain. Next year's GAD survey should provide better data for the Pensions Commission's 2005 report.

[1]Note: In addition to these three major closure routes, a scheme could of course become insolvent. In future however the PPF will be able to take over and administer the scheme rather than close it.

[2]Note: This figure is stated on a comparable basis to the 2000 figures i.e. treating BBC, London Regional Transport, and universities as in the private sector. In the original GAD 1995 figures these were counted in the public sector, reducing the private figure by around 0.1 million.

Figure 3.30 Participation in Private Pension Schemes: 1996-97, millions

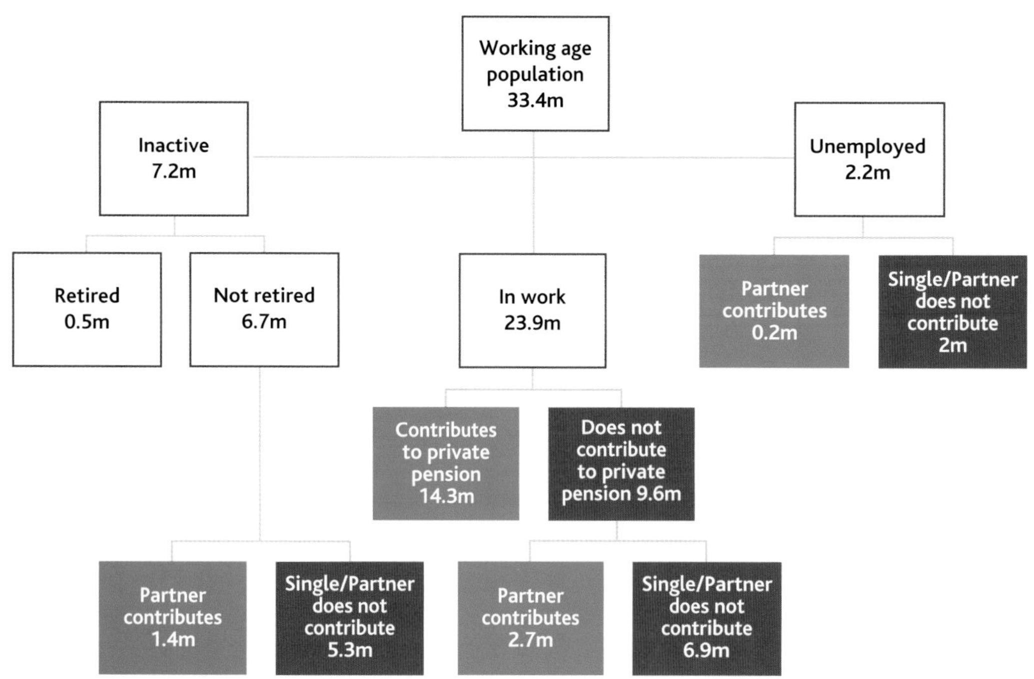

Source: FRS, 1996-97

Note: Figures may not sum due to rounding.

Figure 3.31 Change in Private Pension Participation: 1996-97 to 2002-03, millions

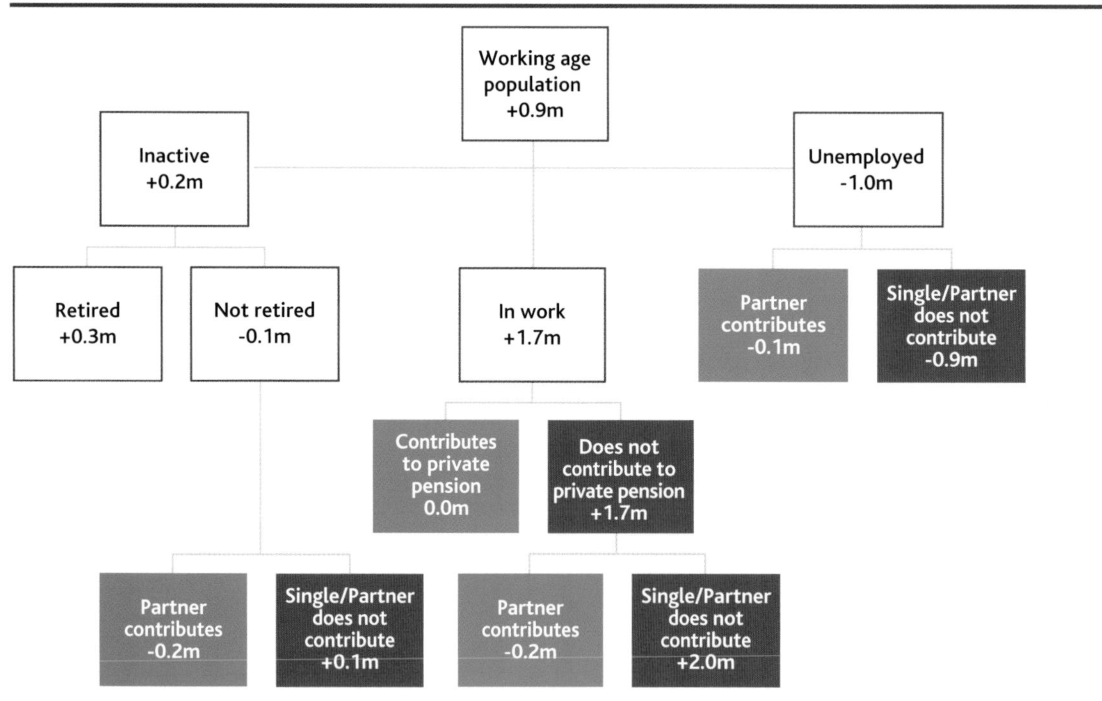

Source: FRS, 1996-97 and 2002-03

Note: Those individuals with personal pensions that are only receiving contracted-out rebates have been counted among non-contributors since they will only accrue pension rights equivalent in value to the SERPS/S2P rights foregone (assuming that GAD calculations of appropriate rebates are fair).
As the numbers of inactive and unemployed individuals contributing to Stakeholder Pensions in 2002-03 are small (fewer than 0.1m in FRS) they have been ignored for the purposes of this analysis.
Figures may not sum due to rounding.

Figure 3.32 Percentage of Employees who are Members of Any Private Sector Employer-Sponsored Pension Schemes, by Size of Organisation

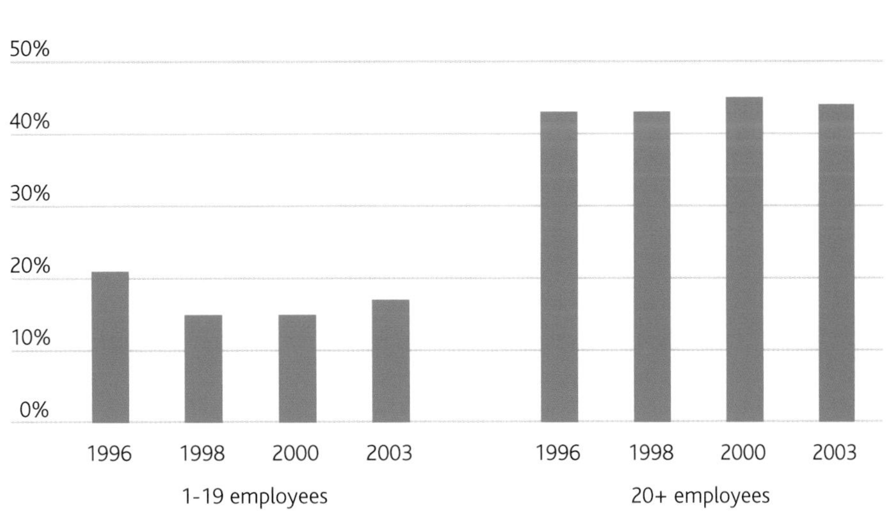

Source: Employers' Pension Provision Survey 2003, DWP

Note: Percentage of employees that are members of any type of scheme

Figure 3.33 Percentage of Employees Participating in Private Sector Employer-Sponsored Pension Schemes

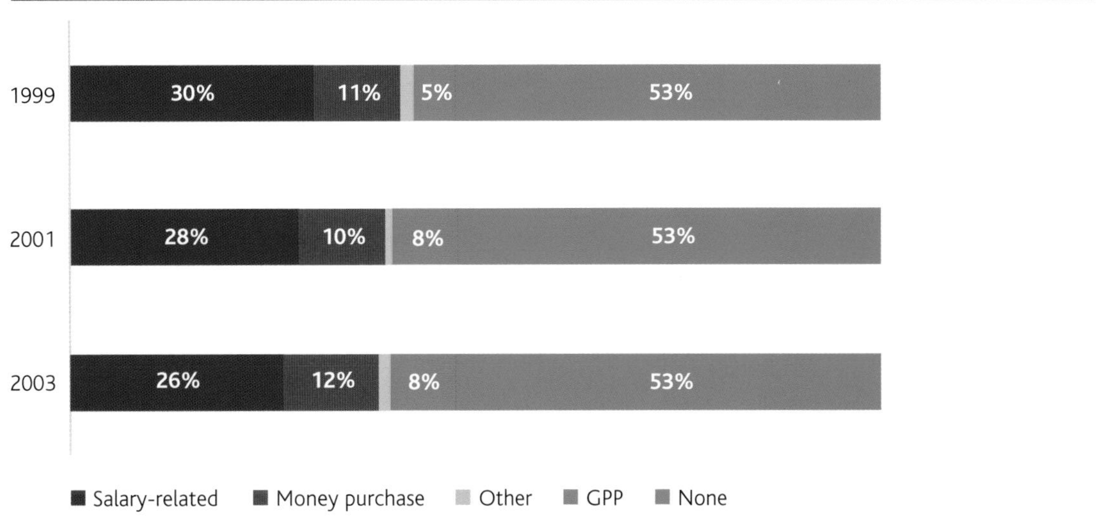

Source: Ungrossed NES.

Note: Using ungrossed NES data may inflate the level of participation. For more information see Appendix A.

- But while the trend in total scheme membership is uncertain, what is clear is that average employer contributions to occupational DC schemes and GPP schemes are much lower than for DB schemes.
  The comparison of DB and DC contributions is complex because DB contribution rates can be different from the value of pension rights being accrued and from the rates required to fund the pension promise over the long-term. Until recently many DB pension funds were taking contribution holidays (total or partial) and aggregate data on average contribution rates reflects this. But the overall pattern is clear:

  – Analysis of GAD's latest data, which is comprehensive but now four years out of date has to be supplemented by analysis of more recent but less comprehensive surveys. All the data sources however show far higher employer contributions to DB schemes than to DC and slightly higher employee contributions [Figure 3.34]. Total DB contributions are broadly in the 16-20% range (11-14% employer and 5-6% employee), while total DC contributions are around 7-11% (4-7% employer and 3-4% employee).

  – The National Association of Pension Funds (NAPF) survey responses also suggest, however, that long-term average contributions to DB schemes will be higher still (around 16-18% for employers with employee contributions in addition).

  – This is confirmed by the Pensions Commission's estimate which suggests that total employer and employee contributions need to be about 22-26% to fund a final salary scheme with an accrual rate of one 60th of salary per year and with a retirement age of 65 [Figure 3.35].

  Almost no generally available DC schemes (as against some "Executive Pension schemes") have contributions at this level. The average suggested by the different surveys is about 7-11%. There is moreover no evidence that the DC or GPP schemes which are replacing closed DB schemes are on average more generous than long-established DC schemes, and thus no necessary tendency for DC/GPP contributions rates to increase over time. And while DB schemes are more likely to be contracted out of SERPS/S2P, so that some of the higher contributions are paid for by rebates of National Insurance, adjusting for this can only explain about 3% out of an underlying difference in total contributions of 12% or more [Figure 3.36].[3] The total level of employer contributions to pensions schemes is thus falling significantly, while employee contributions to employer-sponsored schemes appear to be declining slightly.

[3]Note: also that while the fact that DC schemes are more likely to be contracted-in means that the fall in pension rights being accrued is falling slightly less than the difference between gross DB and DC contributions suggests, in terms of the level of funded pension savings occurring, it is the gross contribution comparison which matters.

Figure 3.34 Contribution rates to Employer-sponsored Pension Schemes

Occupational DB
EPP 2003
ACA 2004 last year
ACA 2004 current
NAPF 2003
GAD 2000
Occupational DC
EPP 2003
ACA 2004 last year
ACA 2004 current
NAPF 2003
GAD 2000
GPP
ACA 2004 last year
ACA 2004 current
0% 5% 10% 15% 20% 25%
Percentage of salary
■ Employer ■ Employee

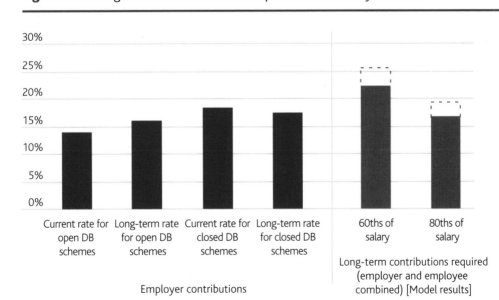

Source: Occupational pension schemes 2000 GAD. Annual Survey 2003 NAPF. Smaller Firms Pensions Survey 2004 ACA, Employers' Pension Provision Survey 2003, DWP

Note: GAD data for private sector schemes excluding schemes with zero contribution rates.
EPP data for employer's contributions only based on open schemes with 10 or more active members.
NAPF employer contributions for private sector main open schemes, excluding zero contributions, and non-contributory schemes. DC scheme could be money purchase, GPP or Stakeholder.

Figure 3.35 Long-term Contribution rates Required for Final Salary Schemes

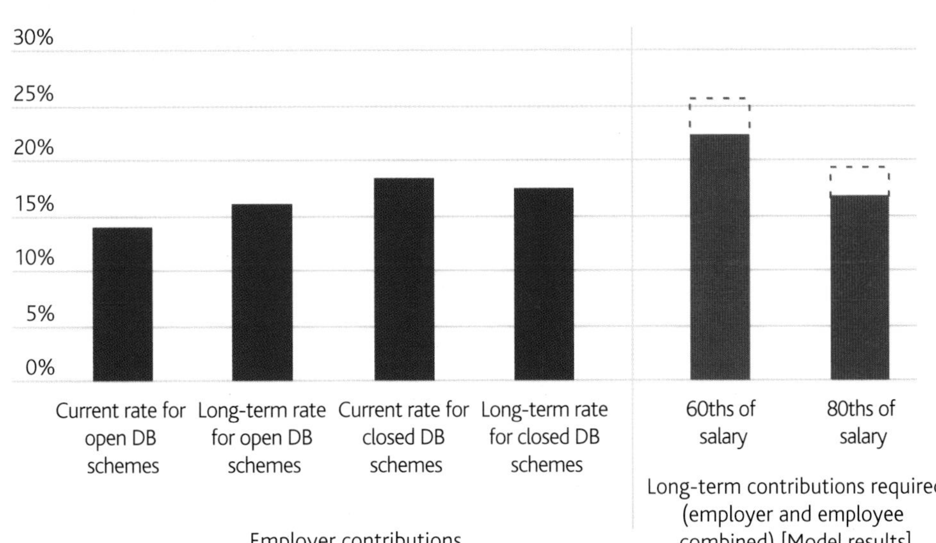

Source: Annual Survey 2003, NAPF and Pensions Commission analysis.

Note: Excluding schemes with zero employer contributions.
Model results show total contributions needed to receive 60ths or 80ths final salary pension at age 65.
Lower figures based on 40 years' accumulation, higher figures based on 30 years' accumulation.
Model assumes: earnings growth of 1.5% per year, constant proportion of gross salary paid into pension, portfolio starts in equities and gradually shifts to bonds in later years of accumulation
real rates of return of 4% on equities and 2% on bonds.
Fund is annuitised at 4.83%, the best rate available from the Annuity Bureau in August 2004 for joint life indexed annuity with man and woman both aged 65.

- This retreat of employer provision has not been offset by an increase in contributions to individual (i.e. non-company sponsored) personal pensions. Personal pension contributions have increased, even relative to average earnings, during the 1990s, but most of this increase is explained by the GPP contributions already discussed, which are largely replacing previous occupational scheme contributions [Figure 3.37]. The role of **individual** personal pensions for employees cannot be distinguished from the figures. But discussions with insurance companies and Independent Financial Advisers (IFAs) suggest that individual personal pensions for employees (i.e. as distinct from the self-employed) account for a small percentage of the total, and that new sales of personal pensions to employees are almost entirely concentrated among higher income groups. Very few individual personal pensions are now sold to employees on average earnings or below. The percentage of self-employed people with private pension provision meanwhile has fallen between 1996-97 and 2002-03 [Figure 3.38].

Figure 3.36 Average Contribution rates as a percentage of salary, by scheme type: Adjusted for contracting-out rebates

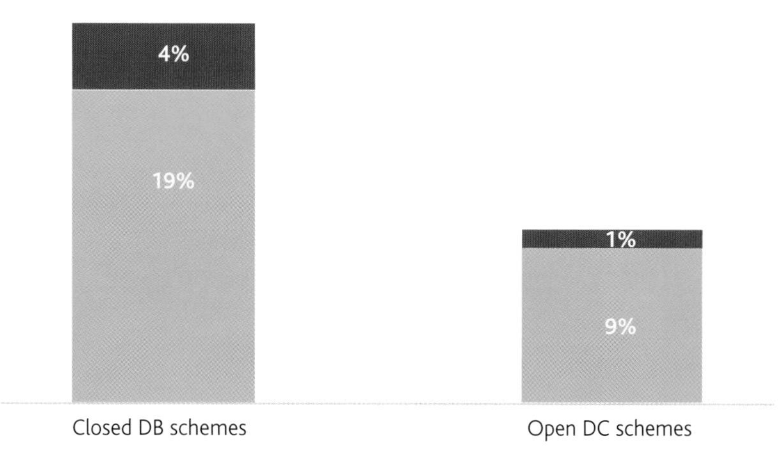

Source: Pensions Commission analysis based on Annual Survey 2003, NAPF.

Note: NAPF figures show that 80% of DB schemes are contracted-out, compared with 23% of DC schemes. The contracted out rebate is 5.1% of salary. Therefore contracted-out rebates account for 4.1% of salary across all DB schemes and 1.2% across all DC schemes.

Figure 3.37 Contributions to Personal Pensions in 2002 Earnings Terms

£billion in 2002 earnings terms

12
10
8
6
4
2
0

1991 1992 1993 1994 1995 1996 1997 1998 1999 2000 2001 2002

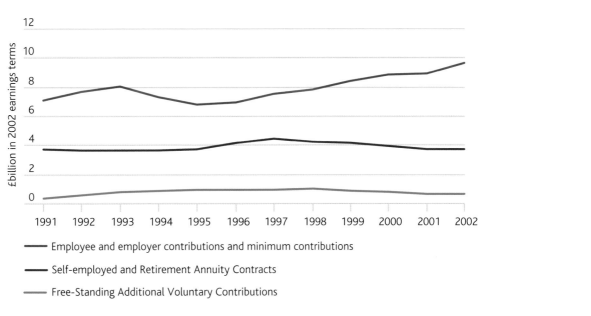

- Employee and employer contributions and minimum contributions
- Self-employed and Retirement Annuity Contracts
- Free-Standing Additional Voluntary Contributions

Source: Inland Revenue

Figure 3.38 Percentage of the Self-employed Contributing to Any Private Pension, by sex

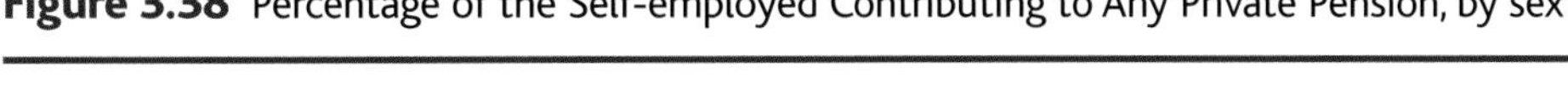

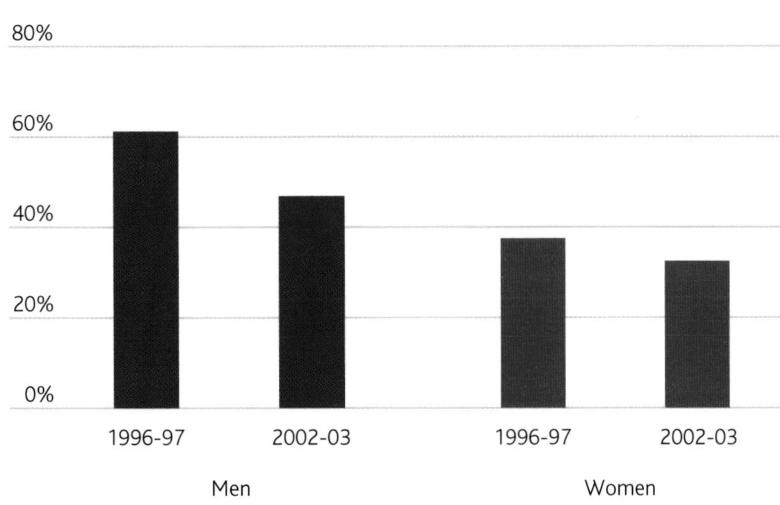

Source: FRS, 1996-97 and 2002-03

- Finally, one of the Government's policies to respond to gaps in private provision, Stakeholder Pensions, has had only limited effect. The vast majority of small company Stakeholder schemes are empty shells with no contributing members. Sixty-five percent of companies with 5-12 employees have nominated a Stakeholder supplier, but only 4% are making contributions [Figure 3.39]. And the "new premiums" which have gone into Stakeholder Pensions include a large element which previously were going into other types of pension scheme. There is little evidence of a net increase in ongoing pension contributions flowing into personal and GPPs as a result of the introduction of Stakeholder pensions.

Public sector pensions: This is currently the most stable part of the UK pension system. An increasing percentage of public sector employees have become members of public sector schemes over the past 10 years. These schemes are almost entirely DB final salary in nature and, unlike in much of the private sector, are still open to new members [Figure 3.40]. The cost of these pensions to the state, whether in explicit current contributions to the funded schemes or in the future PAYG tax burden, will however, grow with increasing life expectancy unless retirement ages are increased, or terms are changed in other ways. The Government has proposed that the normal pension age within most public sector pension schemes should rise from 60 to 65 years, but full details have yet to be finalised.

Overall, therefore, looking at current trends across all three elements of the system, the level of pension right accrual in the UK is likely to decline rather than rise in the face of the demographic challenge. The biggest element of this decline is the reduction in the generosity of employer pension contributions. The Annex at the end of this chapter explains why this reduction has occurred. The essence of the story is that:

- Over the last 20 years the value to employees, and the underlying long-term cost, of salary related pension provision has grown in a fashion neither planned nor anticipated when schemes were initially put in place. This has been the result of increased longevity, more generous treatment of early leavers and surviving spouses, and increasingly full indexation.

Figure 3.39 Percentage of Employers Providing Access and Making Contributions to Stakeholder Pensions: 2003

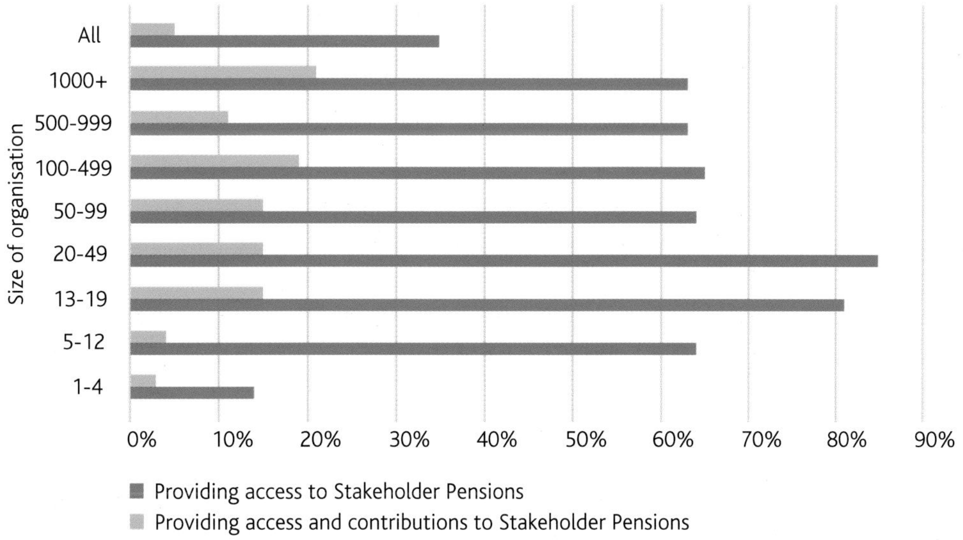

Size of organisation

All
1000+
500-999
100-499
50-99
20-49
13-19
5-12
1-4

0% 10% 20% 30% 40% 50% 60% 70% 80% 90%

Providing access to Stakeholder Pensions
Providing access and contributions to Stakeholder Pensions

Source: Employers' Pension Provision Survey 2003, DWP

Figure 3.40 Percentage of Employees Participating in Public and Private Sector Occupational Pension Schemes

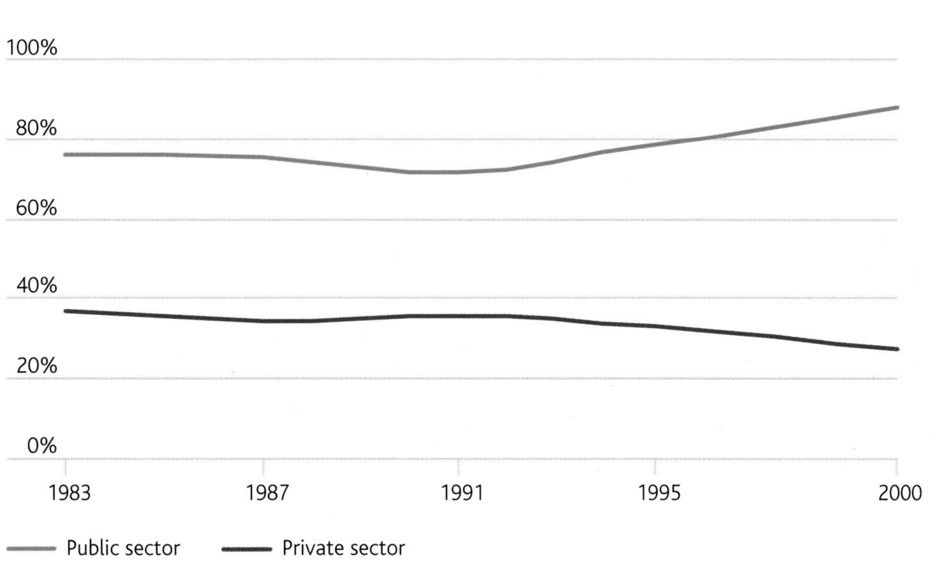

Source: Pensions Commission analysis based on occupational pension schemes 2000, GAD and ONS employment data.

Note: Definition of public and private sectors may vary between sources.

- To avoid this extra cost some employers have been slowly moving away from DB schemes since the late 1970s and many growing companies, especially in service sectors, have never put such schemes in place. But for many existing schemes the scale of the extra cost was hidden by two factors: (i) delays in realising how significant the increase in life expectancy was; and (ii) the long equity bull market which made increasingly generous pension promises look painlessly affordable. As a result, while the underlying cost of salary related pension schemes was relentlessly rising, employer pension contributions fell dramatically as the bull market developed [Figure 3.41 and Figure 3.42]. And for 20 years companies failed to make the adjustments (either increased contribution rates or less generous pension terms) which rising life expectancy would eventually require.

- In the last four years we have seen the end of this fool's paradise. Increased life expectancy estimates, more realistic equity return expectations, lower real bond returns, and tighter accounting standards, have all forced companies to face the true cost of pension liabilities. Contribution rates have therefore had to increase, both to match the pension rights being accrued, and through "special contributions" to cover past pension right accruals. But many companies have also responded by closing DB schemes to new entrants, dramatically reducing the generosity of pension provision to new employees while in most cases preserving terms for existing members.

Some reversal of the unplanned and unanticipated increase in the generosity of DB pension promises was inevitable at some time. But the scale of the reversal, its sudden acceleration, and its uneven treatment of new versus existing employees, when combined with a state system planning to become less generous, has major adverse consequences for the adequacy of the UK pension system, both in terms of specific groups of people, and in terms of the total level of pension saving in the economy as a whole.

Figure 3.41 Occupational Pension Contributions as a Percentage of GDP

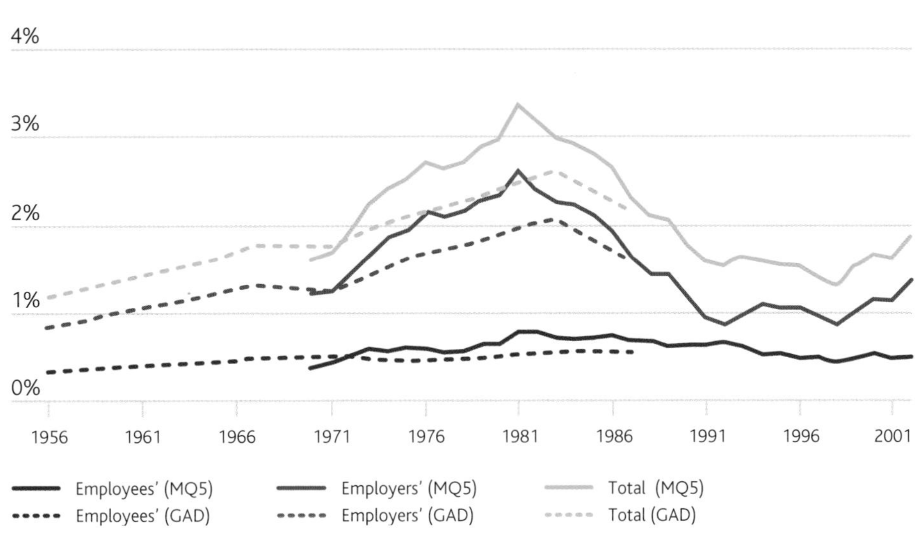

Source: ONS and GAD

Note: ONS MQ5 figures are both public and private funded schemes, GAD figures are private sector only.

Figure 3.42 Employer Contribution Rate to Self-Administered Occupational Pension Funds as a Percentage of Wages

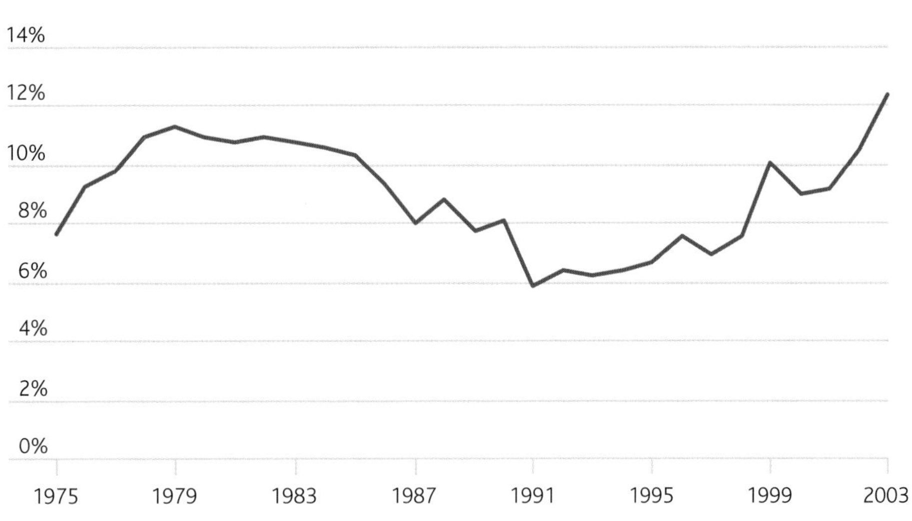

Source: Annual Survey, NAPF.

Note: Average level of employer contributions for schemes which are contributory.

5. The consequences of decline: specific groups of people

Figure 3.31 suggested that the percentage of people making no private pension provision may be growing. Certainly a large number of people are accumulating smaller pensions than in the past.

This decline in pension right accumulation is found in all income and age groups. One feature of what is occurring indeed is a somewhat random spread of severe undersaving. DB schemes are usually being closed only to new members, introducing a major inequality between different groups of workers within the same company. And not only do DC schemes (occupational and GPP) have lower average contribution rates than DB, but the dispersion is greater, with a wide spread of contribution rates by company [Figure 3.43].

But the decline is clearly biased towards the private sector not the public sector, and is slightly biased towards:

- **Middle and higher earnings groups rather than lower earnings groups:** While participation in salary-related schemes is falling in every earnings quintile, it is falling most significantly in middle bands and above [Figure 3.44].

- **Men rather than women:** A slightly increasing percentage of men are not participating in any employer sponsored pension scheme, while for women the trend is marginally in the other direction [Figure 3.45]. Similarly, male participation in private sector salary-related schemes is falling rapidly, while female participation is more stable [Figure 3.46]. These trends reflect the fact that an increasing percentage of women working part-time are covered by pension schemes, and that women are more likely to be employed in the public sector, where no shift from DB to DC is occurring.

- **Larger and medium-size firms rather than small:** While non-participation in any pension scheme is much higher in smaller firms (70% in firms with 1-49 employees versus 40% in firms with 250+ employees) the decline in the coverage of salary-related pensions is concentrated in large and medium size firms, simply because the coverage in small firms has always been very low [Figure 3.47].

An interesting feature of the trends is that while the "savings gaps" of the past were concentrated in particular labour market groups (women, the lower paid, the self-employed, employees of small firms), they are probably spreading most rapidly among middle income earners and above, often male, in mid and large as well as small firms.[4] It is noticeable indeed that a deterioration in private pension savings is occurring in the same group most affected by the planned reduction in the generosity of state pension provision i.e. middle income earners.

[4]Note: The use of the term "savings gap" will be considered in Chapter 4.

Figure 3.43 Employer Contributions to Open Money Purchase Schemes: Percentage of firms contributing at different rates

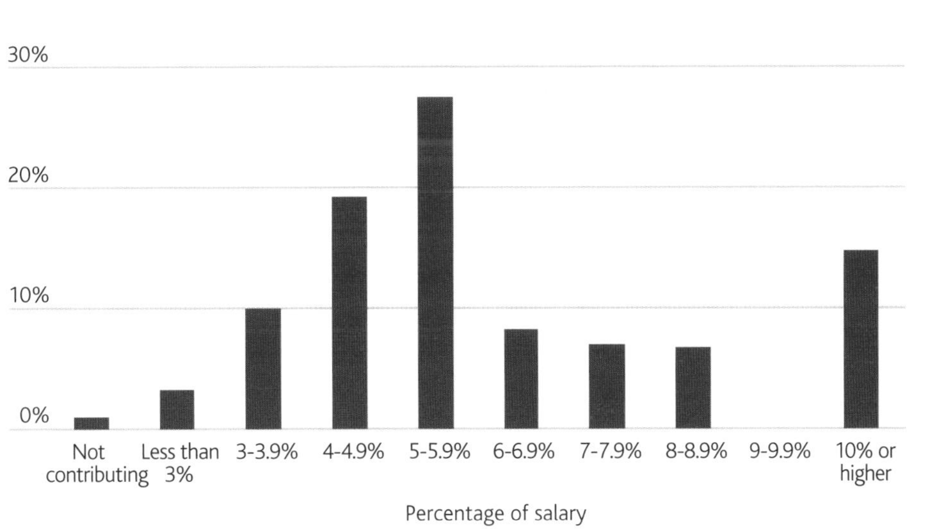

Source: Employers' Pension Provision Survey 2003, DWP

Note: Base is all open schemes with at least 10 members.
While within DB schemes there is a spread of accrual rates and retirement ages, GAD 2000 reports that 63% of active members of private sector Defined Benefit schemes are in a scheme with an accrual rate of 1/60ths of salary.

Figure 3.44 Percentage of Employees Participating in Private Sector Salary-related Pension Schemes, by Earnings Quintile

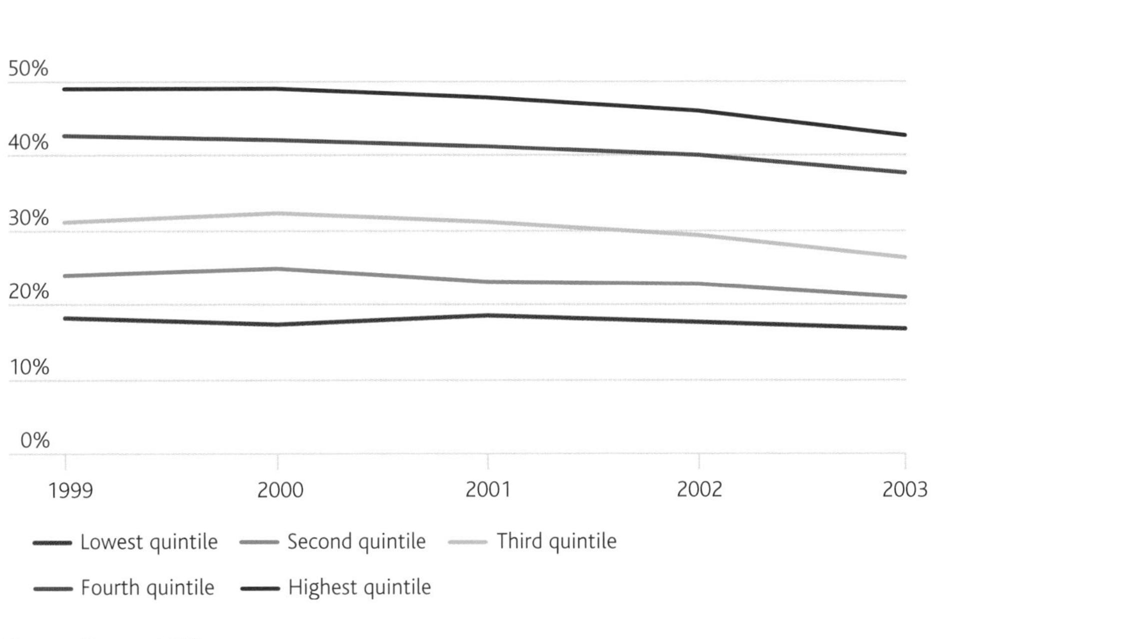

Source: Ungrossed NES

Note: Using ungrossed NES data may inflate the level of participation. For more information see Appendix A.
The earnings quintiles were calculated using annual pay for ongoing employees.

Figure 3.45 Percentage of Employees that are Members of Current Employer's Pension Scheme, by Sex and Full-time/Part-time Status

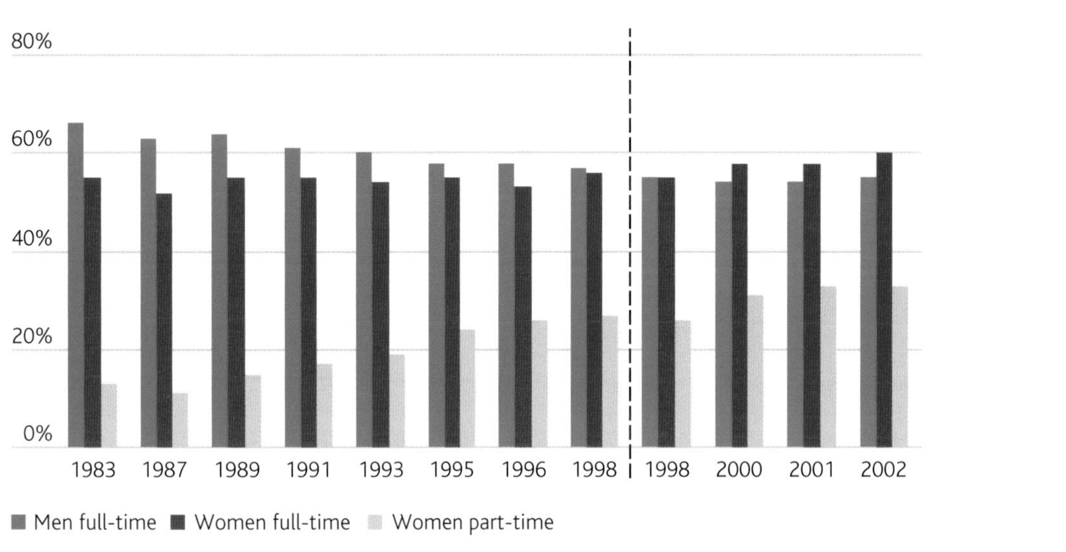

Source: Living in Britain, GHS 2002

Note: Trend data show unweighted and weighted figures for 1998 to give an indication of the effect of the weighting introduced in 1998.

Figure 3.46 Percentage of Employees Participating in Salary-Related Pension Schemes, by Sex and Sector

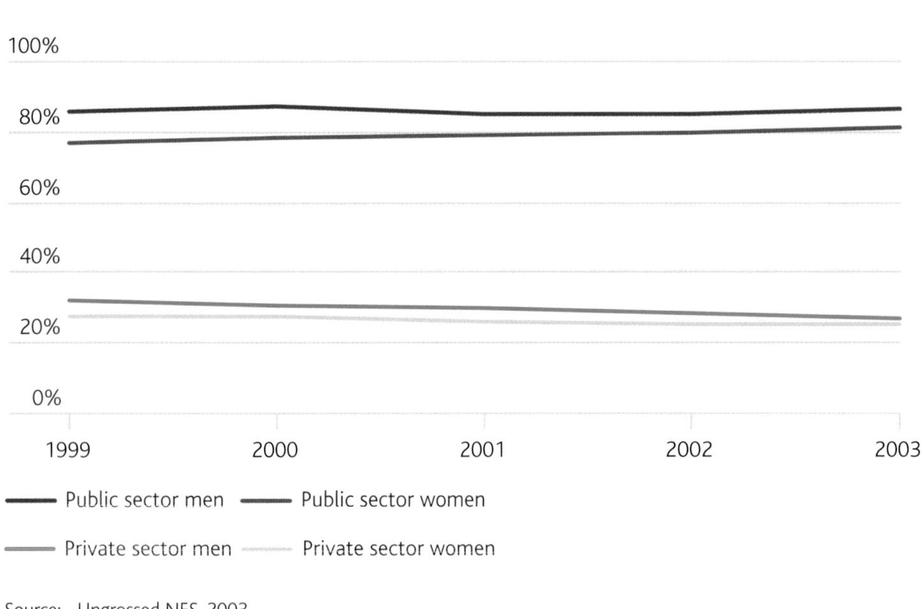

Source: Ungrossed NES, 2003

Note: Using ungrossed NES data may inflate the level of participation. For more information see Appendix A.

Figure 3.47 Percentage of Employees Participating in Private Sector Salary-Related Employer-Sponsored Pension Schemes, by Size of Firm

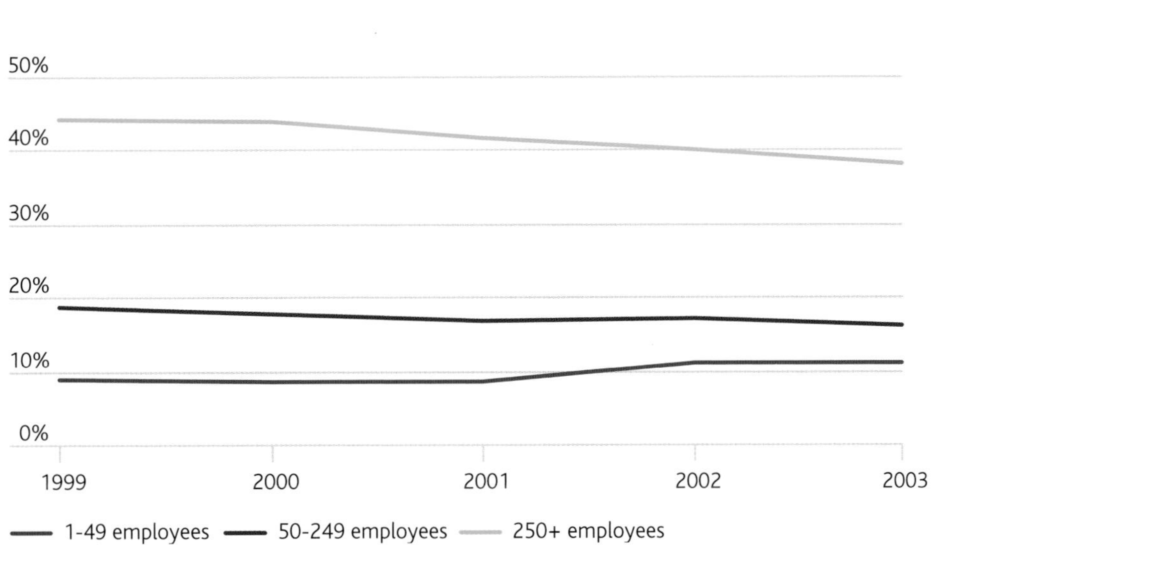

Source: Ungrossed NES, 2003

Note: Using ungrossed NES data may inflate the level of participation. For more information see Appendix A.

6. The consequences of decline: macro estimates of pension saving

Assessment of the level of total private pension saving in the UK is hampered by significant errors and uncertainties in National Statistics. Raw data provided by insurance companies on pension contributions includes a large element of double-counting, and ONS procedures have in the past only succeeded in removing a proportion of this. In addition there are several significant methodological errors and inconsistencies in the way that ONS have been manipulating the data, introducing errors to estimates of benefits as well as contributions. These problems, and the derivation of the Pensions Commission's best estimates of contributions and benefits, are discussed in Appendix A. The Pensions Commission has worked in close collaboration with ONS staff in the analysis of the problems and in the development of new estimates. The new estimates presented in this Report are broadly in line with those in the ONS document *Private Pension Estimates and the National Accounts*, issued in July 2004 [Tables 3.4 and 3.5].

The effect of these errors is that the figures included in past Blue Books (National Income and Accounts) for contributions to both insurance company managed occupational schemes and to personal pension schemes (whether GPP or individual) are hugely overstated. The correct figure for personal pensions can be derived from Inland Revenue data on the level of tax relief paid, which indicate a contribution level of about £14 billion per year rather than the £20 billion figure implicit within Blue Book figures. Contributions to insurance company managed occupational schemes are more difficult to discern, but the Pensions Commission believes that they are probably about £6-8 billion per year, versus the Blue Book figure of £21 billion. For these insurance company occupational schemes, there is no independent Inland Revenue source of data: rather Inland Revenue estimates for tax relief on insurance company occupational schemes are derived from the ONS figures. The error in the occupational scheme figure therefore means that estimates of tax relief granted are also wrong. We estimate that the correct figure for total tax relief is about £3 billion lower than the official estimate of £13.9 billion for 2003/04.

Table 3.4 Sources for ONS, Inland Revenue and Pensions Commission Figures for Total Pension Contributions

	ONS – Blue Book	Inland Revenue	Pensions Commission
Self-administered occupational	MQ5 data	MQ5 data	MQ5 data
Insurance company managed occupational	MQ5 data	MQ5 data	ABI survey data
Personal pensions	MQ5 data	Based on Inland Revenue administrative data for tax relief	Based on Inland Revenue administration data for tax relief

Table 3.5 ONS, Inland Revenue and Pensions Commission Figures for Total Pension Contributions: 2002

£ billion	ONS – Blue Book	Inland Revenue	Pensions Commission
Self-administered occupational	19.5	19.5	19.5
Insurance company managed occupational	21.2	21.2	6.1
Personal pensions	20.2	14.0	14.0
Total	60.9	54.7	39.6

Note: The ONS figures are as in the Blue Book. The revised estimates published by ONS in July 2004 in *"Private pension contributions and the National Accounts"* are in line with the Pensions Commission figures presented here, but are not reflected in the latest (2004) Blue Book.

Our new estimates suggest not only that the previously quoted figures for pension contributions are too high, but also that the trend of the last 10 years is not as suggested by official figures. Figure 3.48 sets out the total level of private pension contributions (combining self-administered pension schemes, insurance company managed occupational schemes, and personal pensions) according to the original ONS figures, Inland Revenue figures, and the Pensions Commission's best estimates. Figure 3.49 shows these figures as a percentage of GDP. The ONS figures suggest significant growth in the percentage of GDP invested in pension funds. Inland Revenue figures suggest some growth. We believe that the level has been roughly flat at about 3.8% of GDP.

Looking at these figures by category, however, suggests that the underlying trend is still less favourable than this flat total might imply [Figure 3.50].

Thus:

- The largest and most dynamic category of contributions is self-administered pension funds, which include the vast majority of the DB schemes. But these contributions have been swollen recently by the ending of contribution holidays, and by "special contributions" to plug pension fund deficits. Many of the contributions being made to DB schemes are essentially securing already accrued pension rights, rather than creating new accruals for the future. As the closure of DB schemes to new members and their replacement with lower contribution DC schemes works through, contributions to the self-administered schemes are likely to decline as a percentage of GDP. If we assume that contribution rates to DC schemes are on average 50% of the underlying DB level, pension savings as a percentage of GDP could, in the absence of other changes, shift down to 2.9% of GDP [Figure 3.51].

Figure 3.48 Total Pension Contributions to Funded Pensions in Nominal Prices: £ billion

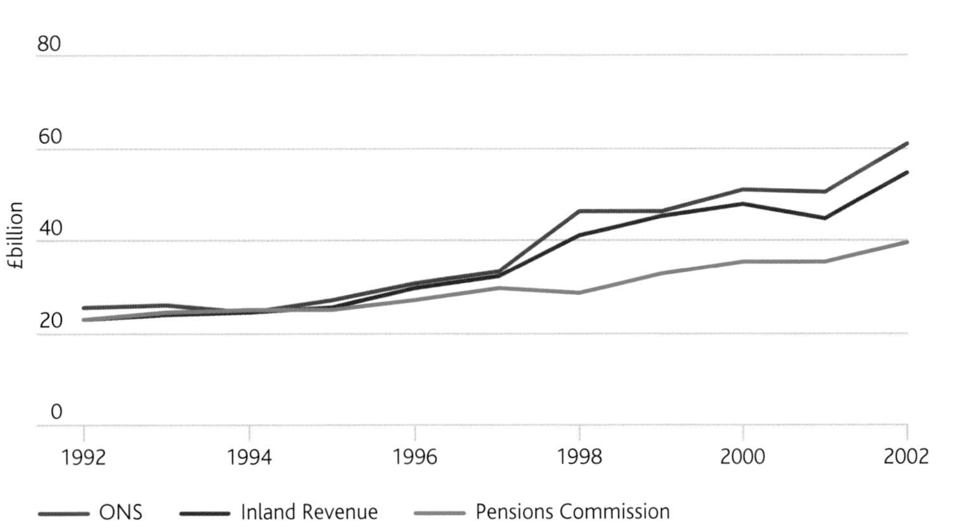

Source: ONS, Inland Revenue and Pensions Commission estimates

Figure 3.49 Pension Contributions as a Percentage of GDP

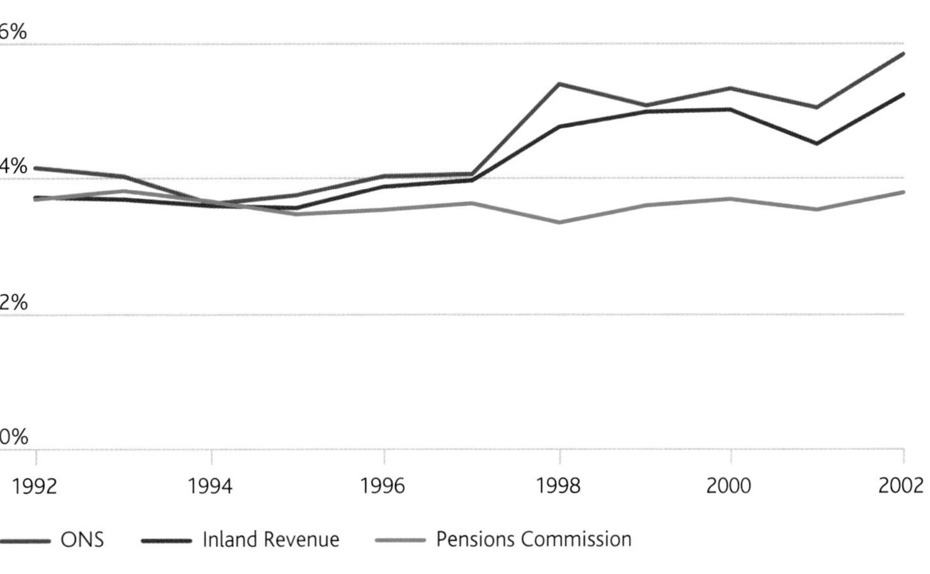

Source: ONS, Inland Revenue and Pensions Commission estimates.

- It should be noted moreover that about £10 billion of the £39 billion contributions are not really voluntary contributions, but contracted-out rebates, which would otherwise have to be paid into the SERPS/S2P scheme. Voluntary funded saving amounts to about £29 billion, of which about £4.4 billion pounds relates to the funded element of local government pension schemes. Voluntary private sector funded pension savings even today may be as low as 2.4% of GDP and if trends do not change this percentage is more likely to decline than grow given the effect of DB scheme closures. The consequences of this for future pensions as a percentage of GDP are set out in Chapter 4, where we model the implications of different levels of pension saving, and different rates of return, for the pensioner income which funded schemes will deliver. But it is clear that the total level of private pension saving is lower than has in the past been believed, and that at least over the last 10 years it has not been growing to meet the demographic challenge.

7. A major shift in risk bearing

The declining level of pension right accumulation is being accompanied by a major shift in risk from the state, employers, and insurance companies to individuals. One aspect of this, a shift in long-term longevity risk to individuals, could have advantages. But the shift of investment risk to individuals of modest income is of significant concern. This section sets out some key issues relating to risk-sharing on which the Commission would like to hear views during the consultation period.

Pension provision and pension savings entail either the provider or the individual absorbing four different categories of risk: longevity risk, of which there are three subtypes, investment return risk, default/political risk and earnings progression risk. Different forms of pension provision allocate these risks differently. In state PAYG schemes and in private DB schemes with price indexed benefits the provider bears almost all of these risks and the individual none. In DC schemes invested directly in equities or bonds only longevity risk post retirement is absorbed by the providers of annuities; all other risks are borne by the individual. [See the panel on the next page for explanation of the different types of risk and how they are shared in different pension systems.]

Figure 3.50 Components of Funded Pension Contributions as a Percentage of GDP

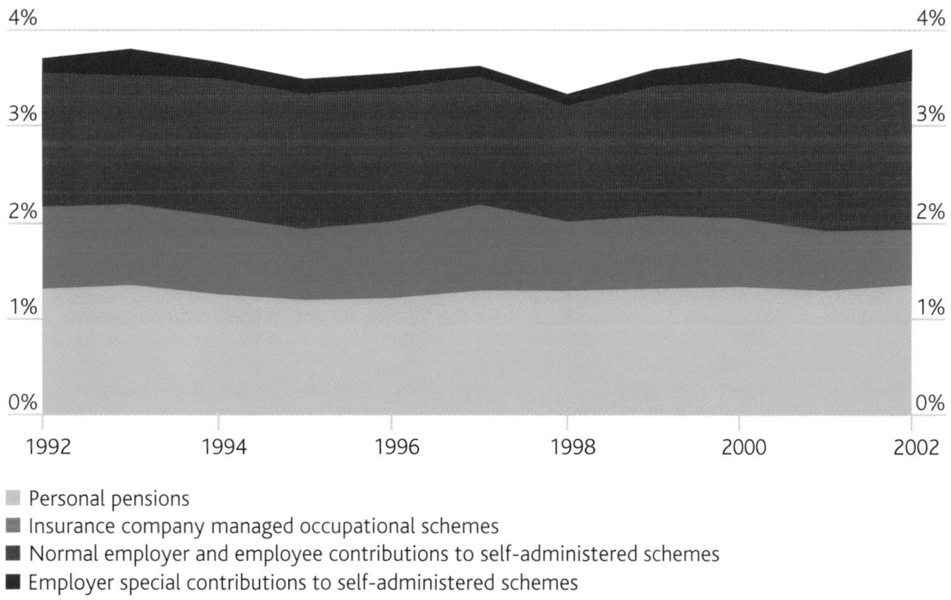

4%
3%
2%
1%
0%
1992
1994
1996
1998
2000
2002
Personal pensions
Insurance company managed occupational schemes
Normal employer and employee contributions to self-administered schemes
Employer special contributions to self-administered schemes

Source: Pensions Commission estimates as defined in Table 3.4.

Figure 3.51 Change in Pension Savings as a Percentage of GDP with the Maturing of the DB-DC Shift

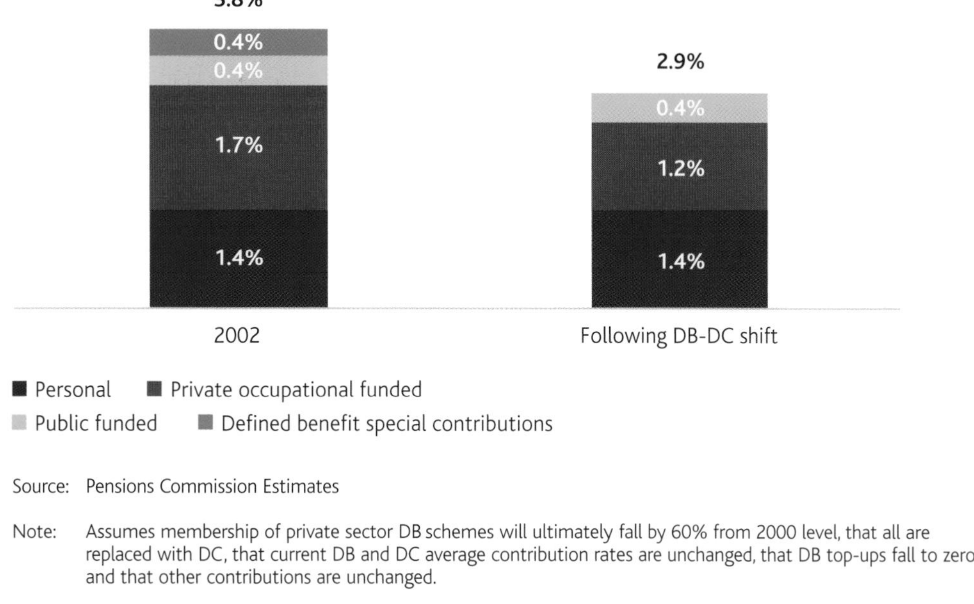

3.8%
0.4%
0.4%
1.7%
1.4%
2.9%
0.4%
1.2%
1.4%
2002
Following DB-DC shift
Personal
Private occupational funded
Public funded
Defined benefit special contributions

Source: Pensions Commission Estimates

Note: Assumes membership of private sector DB schemes will ultimately fall by 60% from 2000 level, that all are replaced with DC, that current DB and DC average contribution rates are unchanged, that DB top-ups fall to zero and that other contributions are unchanged.

Pensions and risks

There are four components of risk inherent in any system of pension provision, one of which (longevity risk) needs to be considered in terms of three sub-categories.

Investment return risk

- In funded pensions, the return on the assets in which the fund invests will vary with market returns and prices. In a DB scheme with pre-committed price indexation this risk is borne by the scheme provider. In a DC scheme the risk in the pre-retirement phase is borne by individuals, except to the extent that financial products (such as with-profits funds) absorb some of the risk. Post-retirement the risk for a DC pension is absorbed by the annuity provider (though only in real terms if an index-linked annuity is bought).

- In PAYG schemes there is an implicit return, i.e. a relationship between the benefits paid out relative to the contributions paid in. The sustainability of this return is linked to the overall growth of the economy. Who bears the risk of poorer economic returns (government or individual) depends on the precise nature of the promise made (e.g. price uprating versus earnings uprating) and whether the promise is actually delivered.

Longevity risk: three sub-categories must be distinguished

- **Specific longevity risk, post-retirement:** i.e. the fact that an individual at point of retirement does not know how long he or she will live, even if we could know with certainty the average life expectancy of the individual's age cohort at that date. This risk is almost never borne by individuals but by either a DB scheme provider, an annuity provider or by the government. Indeed one of the key defining characteristics of a "pension" is that this risk is not borne by the individual.

- **Average cohort longevity risk post-retirement:** e.g. uncertainty in 2004 as to how long on average the entire age cohort of those currently aged 65 will live. As for specific longevity, this is typically absorbed by scheme providers, annuity providers or the government. But concerns have been raised about the capacity of the insurance industry to absorb this risk at acceptable prices, for example by the ABI in their report on the future of the pension annuity market (2003).

- **Long-term average longevity risks pre-retirement:** e.g. the fact that we are very uncertain about what the life expectancy at 65 will be of someone who is 30 years old today. This risk is borne by DB scheme providers and by the government if they commit in advance to retirement ages which will apply far into the future. In DC schemes individuals bear this risk, (via changing annuity rates) and will need as they approach retirement to make a trade-off between later retirement and lower income in retirement if their future life expectancy turns out to be higher than they anticipated.

Default / Political Risk

- In DB schemes there is a danger that the scheme/ sponsoring company could become insolvent and unable to meet pension promises in full. This risk has in the past been borne by individuals (though with a very unequal order of payout between retired members and employees), but in future will be partially absorbed by the Pension Protection Fund.

- In DC schemes the danger of default is less applicable up to the date of retirement since no provider has promised a certain pension. After retirement the individual bears the risk that the annuity provider (i.e. insurance company) could default, but this should be very small[1].

- The equivalent risk for government PAYG schemes is that a future government can change the pension promise unilaterally. This risk is borne by individuals.

- There is also a political risk to the private pension sector that the government can change the tax rules and regulatory regime for private pensions.

[1]Note: The risk of insurance company default on annuities is also at least partially covered by the Financial Services Compensation Scheme.

Earnings progression

- Many people appear to think about pension "adequacy" in terms of replacement rates, i.e. they want a higher pension the higher their income during life, and perhaps specifically the higher their income at the point of retirement.
- But at the beginning of their working life they do not know what their future income will be: there is therefore a risk that individual pensions accumulated may fail to meet individual aspirations, even in a world of no investment risk and no longevity risk. In a DB final salary scheme this risk is taken off the individual and absorbed by the provider. In a DC scheme it resides entirely with the individual (though higher income will tend to make higher savings easier). If state pensions are flat-rate this risk resides entirely with the individual: if they are strongly earnings related they are absorbed by the government.

Table 3.6 Summary of current risk bearing: who bears which categories of risk?

Risk Category	Classic DB	Classic DC	UK State Pension
Investment pre-retirement	Employer	Individual[1,2]	State[4]
Investment post-retirement	Employer	Annuity provider	State[4]
Specific longevity post-retirement	Employer	Annuity provider	State
Average cohort longevity post-retirement	Employer	Annuity provider	State[4]
Long-term average cohort longevity pre-retirement	Employer[3]	Individual	State/Individual[5]
Default/political	Individual (in future partly covered by PPF)	Individual[6]	Individual
Earnings progression	Employer	Individual	Largely individual

[1]Note: May be partially absorbed through with-profits funds.

[2]Note: When investment return is very poor however this risk is partially absorbed by the state if there is a means-tested element in the state pension system, e.g. a DC investor who does badly will in the UK receive more Pension Credit.

[3]Note: Employer absorbs this risk if (as in most DB schemes) the age of retirement is contractually committed far in advance.

[4]Note: May be partially passed on to individuals by changing the value of pensions in payment.

[5]Note: Depends upon whether the state is committed to a State Pension Age set far in advance and whether it delivers on this promise.

[6]Note: Partly recovered by Financial Services Compensation Scheme.

The issue of who should ideally bear **longevity risk** raises complex issues:

- State PAYG and private DB schemes which provide price indexed pensions absorb almost all the longevity risk. They absorb longevity risk post-retirement by giving people a pension at, say, 65 and promising to maintain it even if the average life expectancy of all the people then retiring turns out higher than expected.[5] But they also absorb long-term average longevity risk (**longevity risk pre-retirement**) by promising people (implicitly in the case of the state, and contractually in a private DB scheme) a specific pension at a specific age many years in advance of the individual reaching retirement.

- DC pension schemes shift this latter long-term longevity risk to the individual. Given huge uncertainty about the long-term trend in life expectancy, this has some advantages. It gives individuals the freedom to choose their own preferred trade-off between higher savings, later retirement, and lower retirement income, and it thereby provides incentives for freely chosen later retirement. As we saw in Chapter 2, people with DC pensions who face this long-term longevity risk retire later than those with DB pensions.

- Once people reach retirement age, however, there is considerable merit (for both individuals and for society) in individuals being assured of pensions which will last throughout their retirement irrespective of their own specific longevity, and irrespective of unexpected changes in the average longevity of their specific age cohort from then on. It is these two risks (**specific longevity post-retirement** and **average longevity post-retirement**) which the annuity market absorbs. But the shift from DB to DC will greatly increase demands for annuities, while rising life expectancy is increasing the number of years which annuities on average have to cover. This raises issues about the capacity of the insurance industry to meet that demand at attractive prices, given the current limited supply of appropriate underlying instruments (such as long-dated gilts and index-linked gilts), and given the industry's capital capacity to absorb risk. For this reason some commentators have questioned whether the state should actually take post-retirement longevity risk back to itself, by issuing annuity-equivalent forms of debt.[6]

The Commission will consider these issues further over the next year.

[5]Note: In DB schemes which are not fully price-indexed, as was predominantly the case when DB schemes were initially put in place, both the average cohort and the specific longevity risk post-retirement is partly borne by individuals, since the longer they live the more the real value of their pension may degrade.

[6]Note: For more information see David Willets, *The Pension Crisis,* Politeia July 2004; and David Blake and William Burrows, *Survivor Bonds: Helping to Hedge Mortality Risk*, The Journal of Risk and Insurance, 2001

The appropriate allocation of **investment return risk** is equally complex. But it is clear that the shift of this risk to individuals, which is a key consequence of the DB to DC shift, exposes them to major uncertainty about the value of their future pension, given the volatility of rates of return over periods relevant to pension savings.

- Equity returns have historically been hugely volatile even over 20 year periods [Figure 3.52]. Only over 50 year periods do they appear to be more predictable. But this finding has to be treated with caution. There are insufficient independent 50 year periods in the history of stock market capitalism to draw any clear conclusions about past patterns, let alone about whether they will be repeated in the future.

- Real returns on fixed rate non-indexed bonds have also been extremely volatile [Figure 3.53]. This has been mainly driven by unanticipated increases and decreases in inflation, and it may be that improvements in macroeconomic management will make inflation considerably less volatile in future. But this cannot be assumed, and only investment in inflation-indexed bonds can eliminate the inflation risk. However real rates of return on index-linked bonds have also varied significantly over the last 15 years [Figure 3.54].[7]

In the UK pension system as it had evolved by the early 1990s investment return risks were for many pension savers absorbed by the providers. This enabled many pension scheme members to benefit from the long-term superiority of equity rates of return while taking none of the volatility risk. But a very major shift in risk bearing is now occurring for three reasons:

1. The state is becoming less generous. This tends to shift risk from the state to the private sector. Essentially a state PAYG promise can be considered as providing a guaranteed rate of return on contributions roughly in line with the rate of growth of GDP. The smaller the role of the state PAYG scheme, the smaller the percentage of peoples' pension that comes in this guaranteed return form.[8] Means-tested benefits such as Pension Credit, however, off-set this risk shift at lower income levels, with the state partially absorbing the consequences of poor investment return.

2. The decline of DB shifts investment return risk from employers to the individual. The desire of many companies to cease running a risky fund management business alongside their core business may be rational from a business perspective, but it has large consequences for the risks borne by individuals.

[7]Note: See Appendix C for detailed discussion of reasonable expectations of rates of return, and their variability, for equities, bonds and for other asset categories.

[8]Note: The guarantee of return only holds if the state actually delivers the implicit promise of future PAYG benefits. These promises can however be changed by future governments.

Figure 3.52 Distribution of Real Returns on UK Equities over 20 Year Periods: 1899-2003

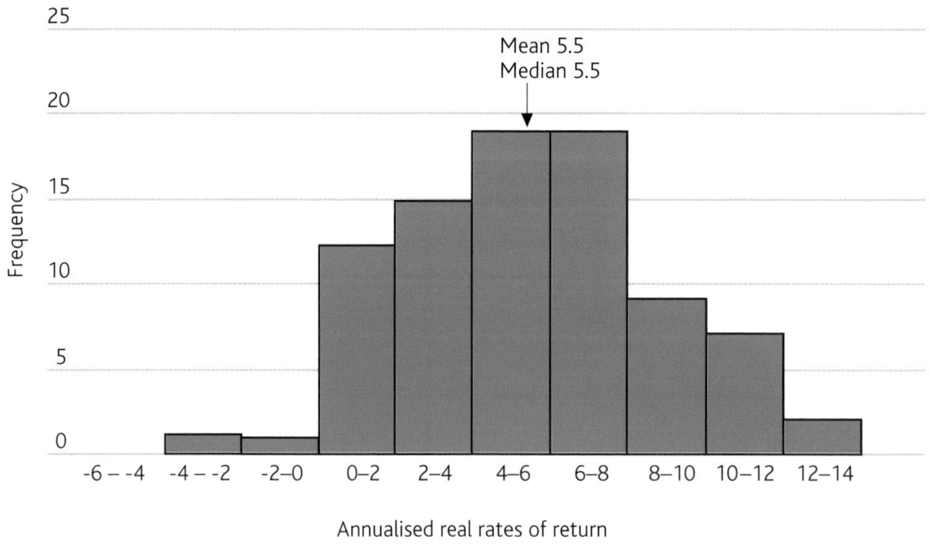

Mean 5.5
Median 5.5
Frequency
-6 – -4 -4 – -2 -2–0 0–2 2–4 4–6 6–8 8–10 10–12 12–14
Annualised real rates of return

Source: Barclays Equity Gilt Study, 2004

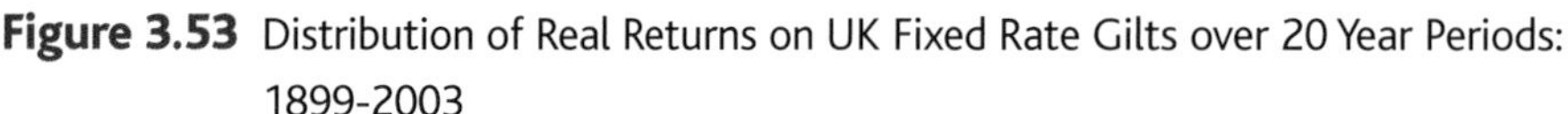

Figure 3.53 Distribution of Real Returns on UK Fixed Rate Gilts over 20 Year Periods: 1899-2003

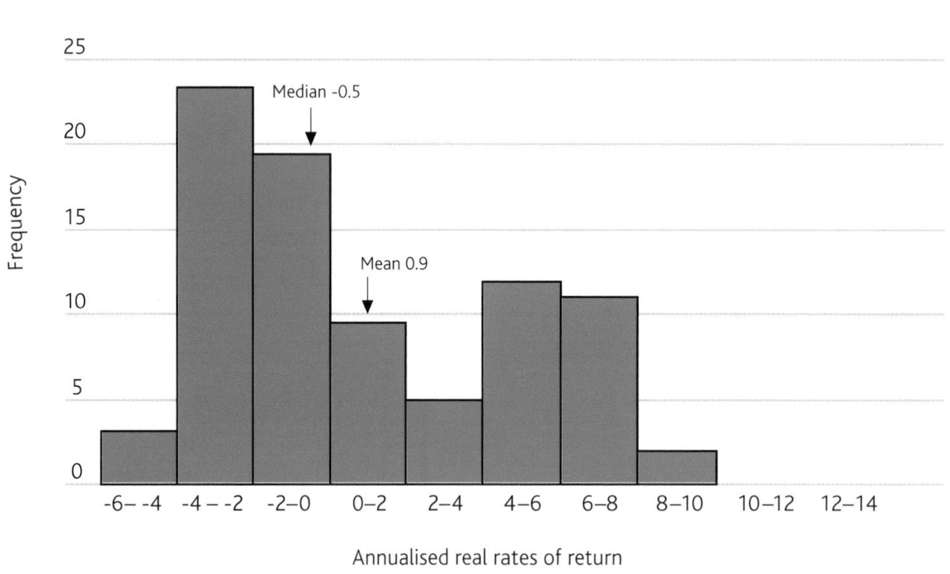

Source: Barclays Equity Gilt Study

Note: These are the real inflation adjusted returns on normal fixed rate bonds. Real returns on index-linked gilts are shown in Figures 3.54.

Figure 3.54 Real Yields to maturity on 20 Year UK Government Index-linked Bonds

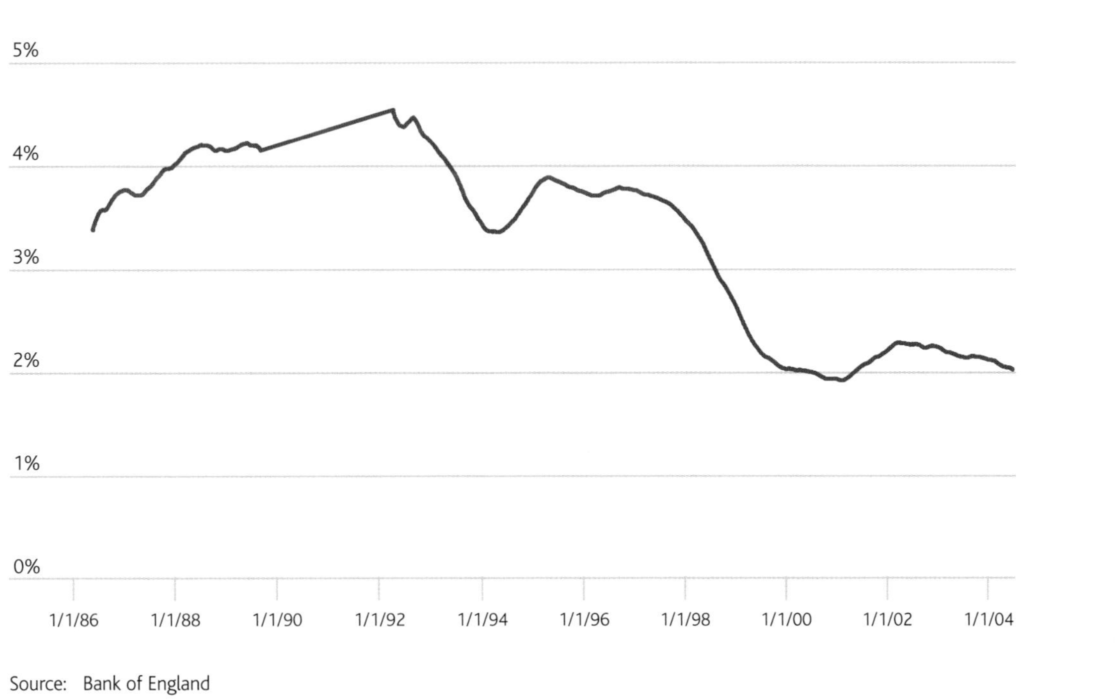

Source: Bank of England

Figure 3.55 Investment Choice for New Personal Pension Contracts by Value of Premiums: £ billion

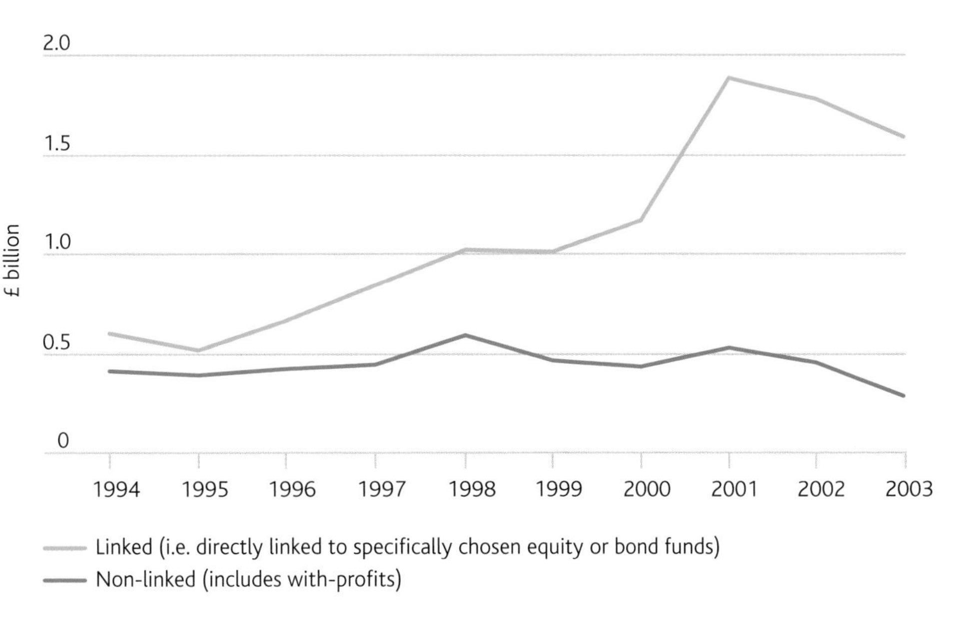

Source: ABI

3. Finally the with-profits product, which has been a return smoothing and risk absorption product available to pension savers in occupational DC and personal pensions, is in wholesale retreat. Volumes sold are falling, and investment via insurance companies is switching rapidly to a unit-linked form [Figures 3.55 and 3.56]. Remaining with-profits funds are shifting investment strategies from equities to bonds [Figure 3.57]. Traditional with-profit funds were rightly criticised in the Sandler Report for both poor transparency (i.e. the extent of return-smoothing guarantees was vague and poorly understood by customers) and for high charges. And from a financial stability point of view the Financial Services Authority (FSA) is right to argue that implicit guarantees should be supported by adequate capital (as required by CP 195). But the net effect of the decline of with-profits products is to remove from many people of modest savings levels the option of investing in equities in a risk-mitigated fashion.

As a result of this shift in risk bearing, individuals' income in retirement will be increasingly influenced by the investment decisions they make. Individual pension savers are therefore increasingly faced with a choice between (i) accepting equity return risks which they are often ill-equipped to evaluate and which will introduce a random variation into the distribution of pensioner incomes; or (ii) moving to lower risk, bond-rich investment strategies which on average imply lower expected rates of return, which in turn implies that higher contributions will be required to deliver a given level of pension income.

The appropriate allocation of both longevity and investment return risk between the state, employers and individuals is therefore a complex issue on which the Commission intends to focus attention over the next year. It is worth noting at this stage, however, that innovative combinations of risk sharing are possible, avoiding the "all with the individual" or "all with the provider" choice which has tended to dominate in the past. Hybrid schemes, part DC and part DB, can ensure that people at least have a base load of guaranteed retirement income, but at lower risk to the corporate provider than an entirely DB scheme. Company DB schemes can be designed which deliver guaranteed investment returns, but which shift the long-term longevity risk to individuals (e.g. American "cash balance" schemes).[9] State PAYG schemes can similarly be redesigned to shift long-term longevity risk to the individual, while keeping both investment return risk and the longevity post-retirement risk with the state (the "notional defined contribution" tier within the Swedish state pension takes this form).[10]

The Commission would like to hear views on the appropriate balance of risk sharing between government, employers, the financial services industry and individuals during the consultation period.

[9]Note: In an American "cash balance" scheme, individuals (and their employees) make contributions to a fund on which the rate of return is guaranteed by the provider. The value of the pension pot at the time of retirement is therefore not subject to investment return risk. But the value of the annuity which the accumulated fund will buy is determined by real interest rates and by average cohort life expectancy at the point of retirement.

[10]Note: The Swedish "notional defined contribution" scheme works in a similar way as the American cash balance scheme, though the funds are not in fact invested in market funds but are liabilities of the state pension system.

Figure 3.56 Investment Type for all Regular Personal Pensions Premiums Whether Old or New Contract

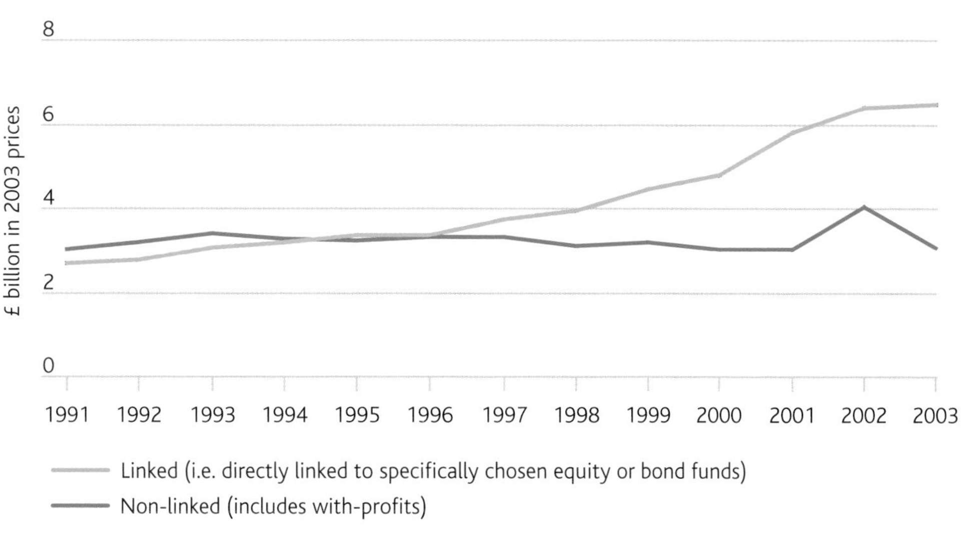

Source: ABI

Figure 3.57 Investment Holdings of Non-linked Insurance Company Funds

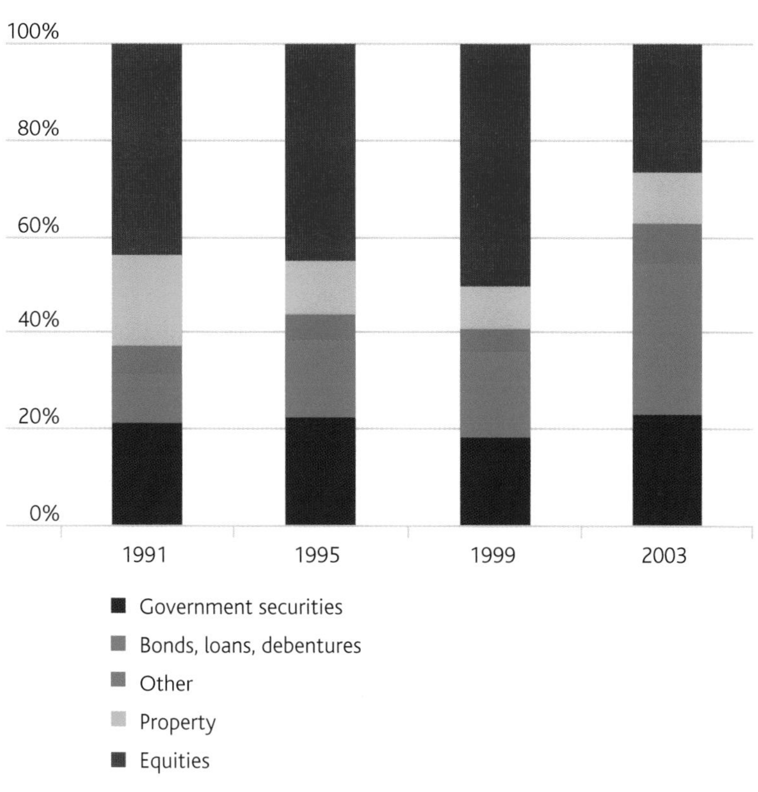

Source: ABI

Chapter 3 Annex : The Rise and Decline of the Defined Benefit Final Salary Pension: A Brief History

Over the last 10 years there has been a major shift of private sector pensions provision from Defined Benefit (DB) to Defined Contribution (DC). We estimate that the number of active members of open DB schemes in the private sector has fallen by 60% since 1995, by 50% since 2000, and could fall by a further 10-20% in the future. This means that the final salary promises have been replaced with much less generous DC provision.

But it is important to place this dramatic short-term movement in its long-term context. Underlying trends in private occupational provision have been heading down for 20 years. And only the impact of irrational equity market exuberance prevented more dramatic decline. The interaction of demographic and economic trends, combined with regulation, meant that by the mid-1990s many companies were making pension promises that they would never have to put in place on a voluntary basis given more realistic expectations of future rates of return. For 20 years irrational exuberance allowed firms to avoid the adjustments (either increased contributions or less generous promises) that would eventually be required.[1]

Those adjustments are now being made but at a pace and in a fashion which is creating major gaps, risks and inequalities in Britain's pension provision.

This Annex first sets out the long-term trends of occupational pension provision, and then our interpretation of why those trends have occurred.

The long-term trends

Figures 3A.1 and 3A.2 show trends in membership of occupational schemes, in the private and public sectors, for men and women, from 1953-1995. From the early 1950s to the late 1960s, membership soared, particularly in the private sector. But since the 1970s total occupational scheme membership has fallen. While the raw figures suggest that this has occurred in both the public and private sectors, once the impact of privatization is allowed for it is clear that the decline has been concentrated entirely in the private sector. There were 1.6 million people in nationalised industry occupational pension schemes in 1975. If we define the private sector to include the nationalised (and subsequently privatised) companies even in 1975, private sector occupational scheme membership has fallen steadily, while in the public sector it has increased [Figure 3A.3].

[1]Note: Irrational equity market exuberance refers to the1980s and 1990s when equity returns were above their long-term historical averages and some people also expected that future returns would continue to be above the historical averages.

Figure 3A.1 Members of Occupational Schemes, by Sector: Men, millions

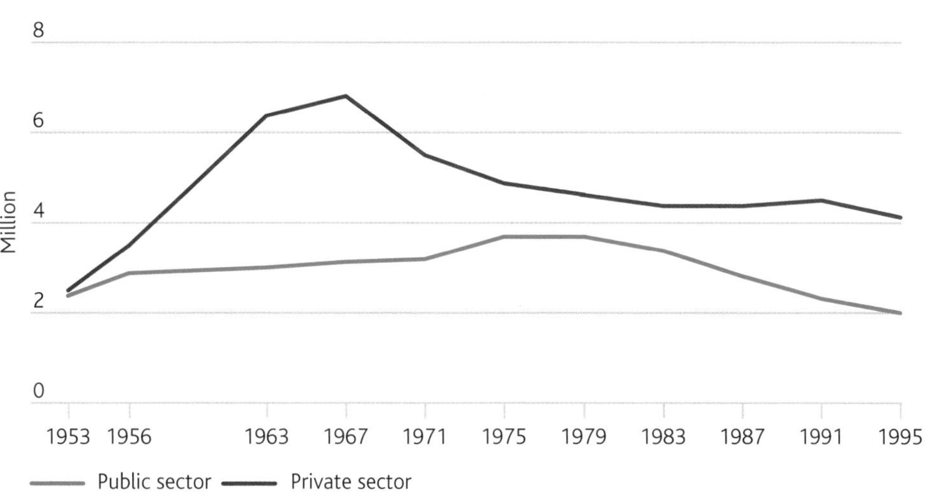

Source: Occupational pension scheme surveys, GAD

Note: These figures are affected by the changing composition of the sectors. The apparent fall in public sector scheme membership in the 1980s and 1990s is explained by privatisation.

Figure 3A.2 Members of Occupational Schemes, by Sector: Women, millions

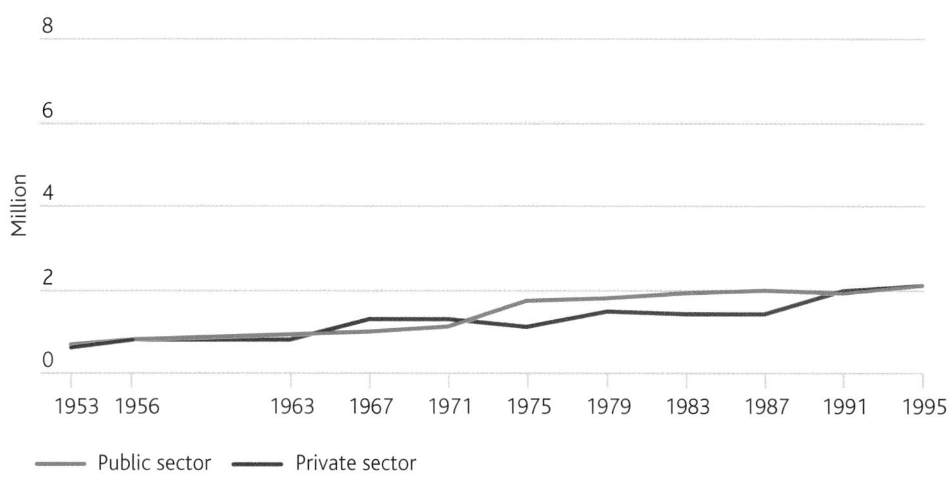

Source: Occupational pension scheme surveys, GAD

The fall has been entirely concentrated among men. In 1975, 58% of men in private sector employment were in occupational schemes, but only 17% of women. By 1995, the proportion of men in occupational schemes had fallen to 34% and for women had risen to 27%.

Most of these occupational schemes were DB in nature, but in the private sector in 1963 only 23% of active members were in a final salary scheme. Membership of average salary related schemes, and schemes giving a flat sum per year of service, was more prevalent. By 1979, however, membership of final salary schemes (always the dominant form in the public sector) dominated the private sector too [Figure 3A.4]. Steadily over the 1980s and 1990s however, there was a private sector shift from DB to DC [Figure 3A.5]. It is this slow change which has become a flood in the last eight years. In 1995 there were 5.2 million private sector active members in DB schemes. Pensions Commission estimates suggest that the number of active members in open private sector DB schemes (and eventually therefore in all private sector DB schemes) is unlikely to stabilise above 1.6-1.8 million [see the panel "Estimates of the DB-DC shift" in the main body of Chapter 3].

This rise and then fall in pension scheme membership is reflected, but in a greatly exaggerated form, in the history of contributions to funded occupational pension schemes. Different sources give slightly different figures, but the overall pattern is clear. Contributions soared up till about 1980, then fell abruptly as a percentage of GDP throughout the 1980s with a slight rise in the late 1990s. And it is the variation in employer pension contributions which explains almost all of the change: employee contributions, after the steady growth of the 1950s and 1960s, have been more stable [Figures 3A.6 and 3A.7].

Finally the impact of the rise in membership during the 1950s and 1960s, together with other factors considered below, can be seen in rising occupational pension income as a percentage GDP from 1980 onwards, as workers of the 1950s and 1960s began to enter retirement [Figure 3A.8].

Figure 3A.3 Percentage of Employees Participating in Occupational Pension Schemes: Public and Private Sector Adjusted for Nationalised Industries

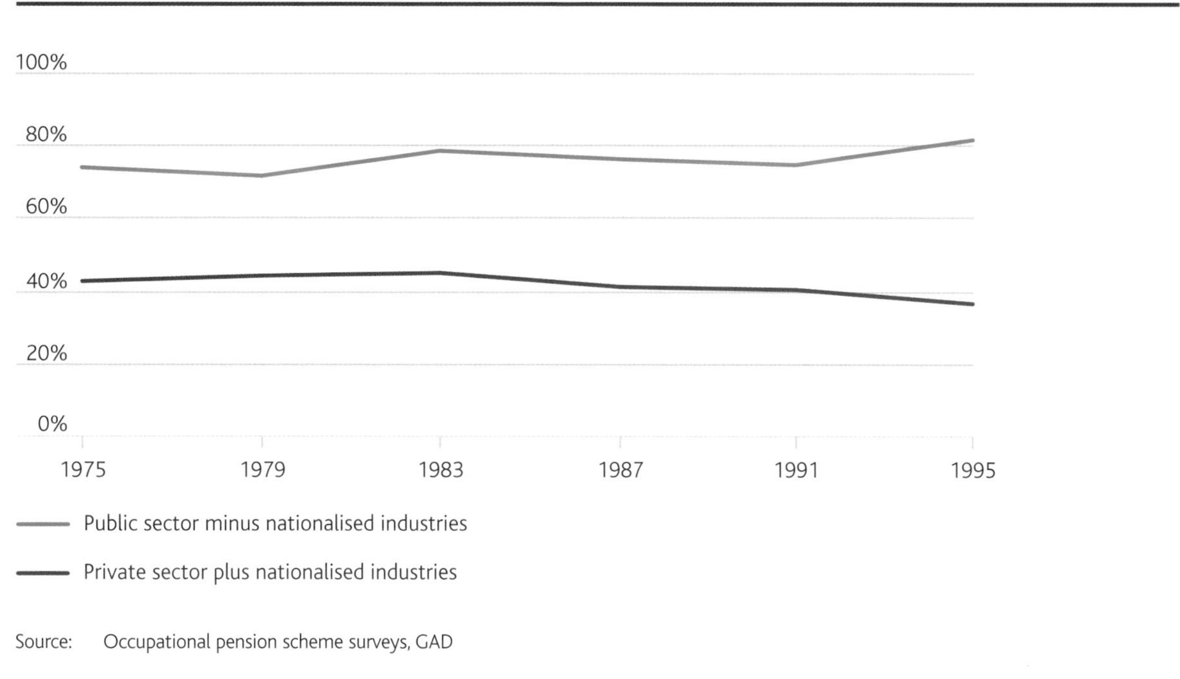

Source: Occupational pension scheme surveys, GAD

Figure 3A.4 Distribution of Type of Private Sector Schemes, by membership

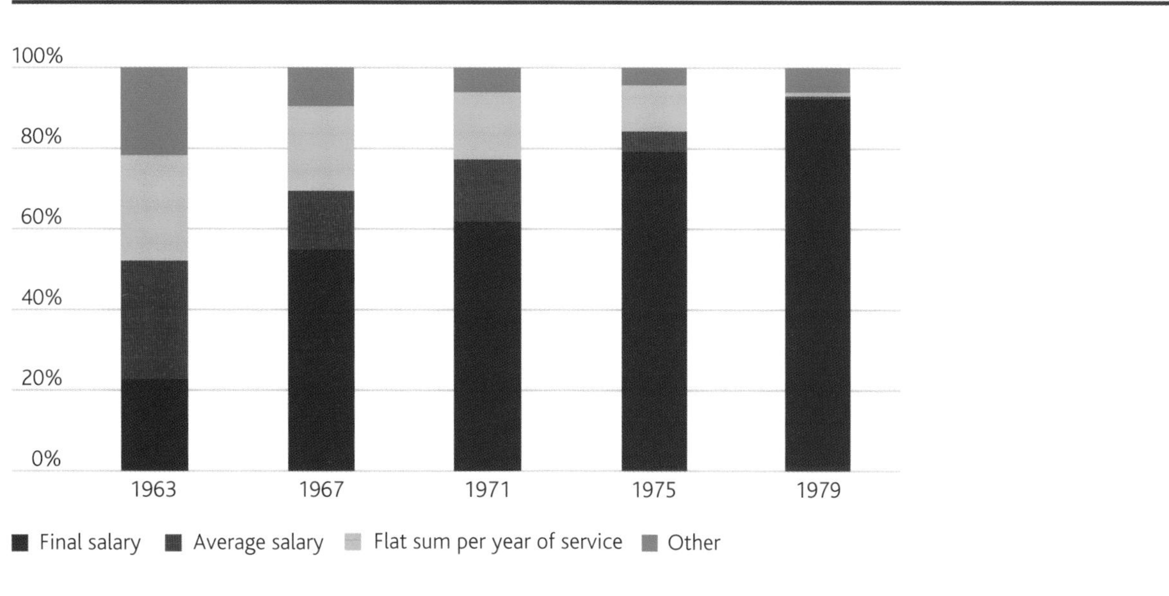

Source: Occupational pension scheme surveys, GAD

Figure 3A.5 Estimated Percentage of Private Sector Employees Participating in Occupational Pension Schemes

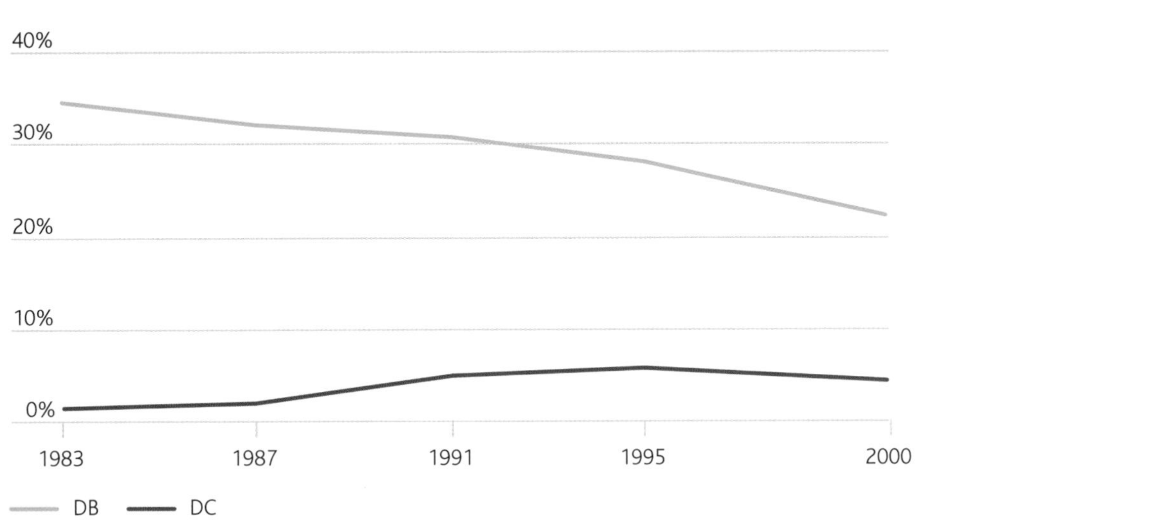

Source: Pensions Commission analysis based on occupational pension schemes 2000, GAD and ONS employment data.

Note: Definition of public and private sectors may vary between sources.

Figure 3A.6 Occupational Pension Contributions as a Percentage of GDP

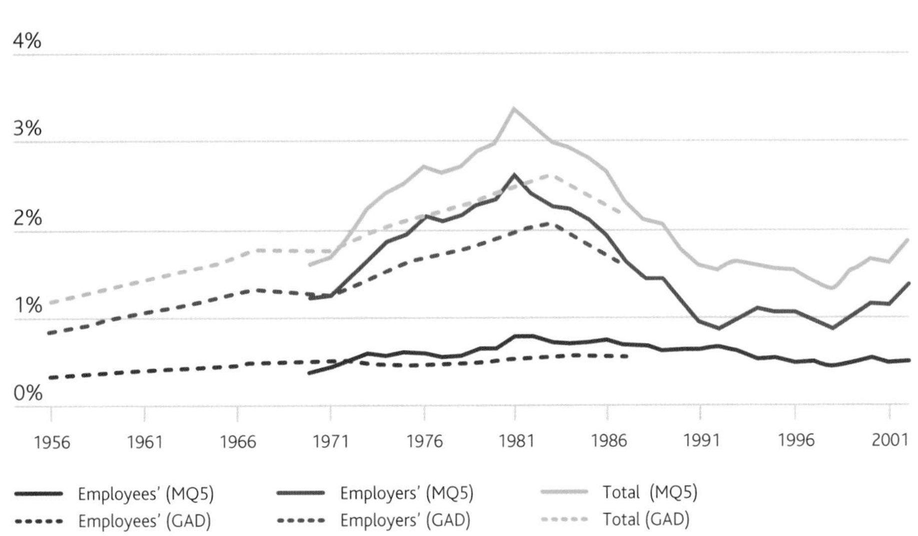

Source: ONS and GAD occupational pension scheme surveys

Note: ONS MQ5 figures are both public and private funded schemes, GAD figures are private sector only.

Figure 3A.7 Employer Contribution Rate to Self-Administered Occupational Pension Schemes as a Percentage of Wages

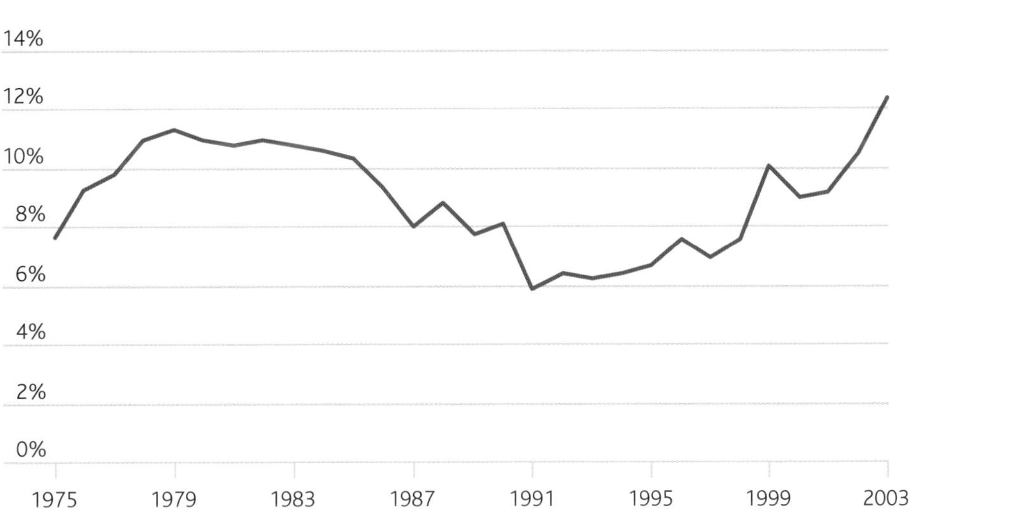

Source: Annual Survey, NAPF

Note: Average level of employer contributions for schemes which are contributory.

Figure 3A.8 Pensioner Income From Occupational Pensions as a Percentage of GDP

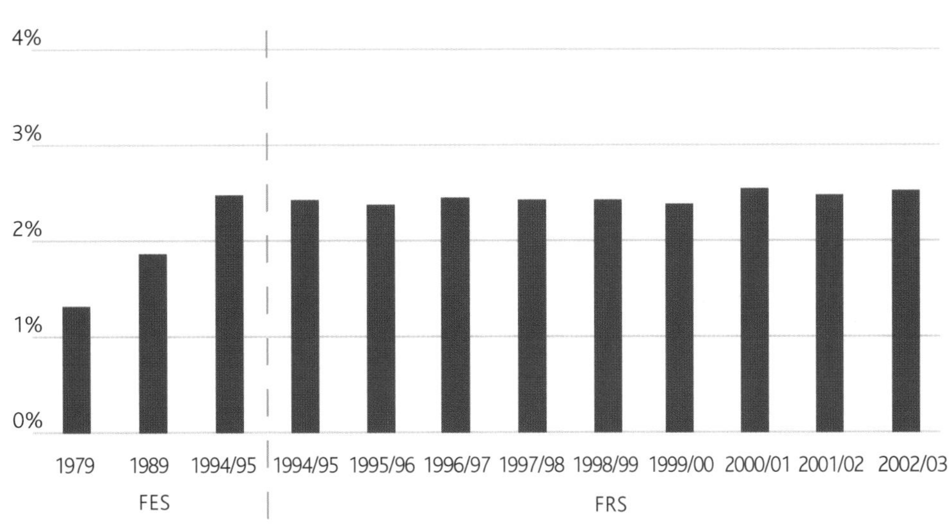

Source: The Pensioners' Income Series 2002/03

Explaining the trends: the affordable rise

To a degree the initial rise of the employer provided pension in the 1950s and 1960s simply reflected a society of growing prosperity and longevity, in which pensions were offered as part of the overall compensation package needed to attract workers, and were seen as increasingly important negotiating objectives by trade unions.

But the scale of the development also reflected specific factors which made pension provision appear easily affordable and highly desirable to company management: and the dominance of the final salary form reflected an interaction of regulatory requirements and specific economic circumstances.

- Major income tax benefits, in an era of higher marginal tax rates than today, made pension schemes a tax-efficient way of paying people, in particular senior managers.

- Firms also gained corporation tax efficiencies (at a time when marginal rates were over 50%) since pension fund contributions enabled them to smooth profits over the economic cycle.

- Income policies in the 1960s and 1970s also made pension schemes attractive. Pension right accrual could be a means of increasing the total compensation package at a time when the cash element was constrained.

- The fact that when schemes were put in place they tended to be salary related, reflected not only the assumed preference of workers and managers, but also regulatory requirements. Only salary related schemes could be contracted out from the Graduated Retirement Pension introduced in 1961, or from SERPS when first introduced in 1978. It was only in 1987 that DC forms of pension provision could be contracted-out.

- The shift from average salary to final salary schemes, meanwhile, appears to have been the product of rising inflation. Final salary schemes were always favoured by management as a means of providing high non-cash compensation to executives. Initially they tended to be opposed by trade unions, due to their regressive distributive effect, but as inflation gathered pace in the 1960s and 1970s, they were accepted as a means of ensuring price indexation at least up to the point of retirement.

- The final salary schemes which developed, however, appeared easily affordable, since the generous promise to some workers was effectively cross-subsidised by the poor treatment of others. Not only were final salary schemes significantly redistributive from average to high earners, they also redistributed from leavers to stayers. Before 1975, there was no requirement to preserve pensions for those who left prior to pension age; as a result, the total cost of generous pension promises to those who stayed, was easily afforded.

- Finally it should be noted that when initially introduced, final salary pensions did not have to be offered to women as well as men, often did not provide assured spouse benefits, and were not price indexed (except at the discretion of the trustees) during retirement.

One implication of this story is that it is wrong to see the heyday of the DB final salary scheme as an unalloyed "Golden Age". Many women were outside the system. Many scheme members who changed jobs, or whose relative income did not progress during working life, participated only to a minimal extent in the generosity of the system. More people were covered by some form of pension provision than ever before: but the easy affordability of the promises made depended on the highly unequal distribution of both the promises, and of delivery against them. And the survival of the system throughout the 1970s depended on one crucial feature of the initial design: the absence of requirements for price indexation of contributions up to retirement and of pensions in payment during retirement.

Explaining the trends: survival in the 1970s

From the start UK pension funds tended to invest heavily in equities. In 1974 world stock markets crashed, and the UK stock market lost 50% of value between October 1973 and September 1974, not regaining its real 1973 level again until 1980. In real terms this was a far bigger stock market adjustment than in 2000-03. But unlike in the latter case it was not accompanied by a major closure of DB pension schemes. This reflects two facts. First that the schemes were far less mature. This meant that the ratio of contributing workers to pensioners receiving payment was much higher, thus allowing the adjustment to the emergence of deficits to be managed over a longer time period. Secondly, and crucially, pensions in payment were adjusted to prices only at the discretion of the trustees, with indexation neither required by regulation nor a pre-commitment in most schemes. The impact of high inflation was therefore able to fall on pensioner incomes, rather than on the viability of the fund.

Explaining the trends: the growth of unplanned and unanticipated costs

By the late 1960s private industry had voluntarily put in place extensive pension provision, but this provision appeared easily affordable and proved so during the 1970s, precisely because of its complex cross-subsidies, its poor treatment of some workers, and its ability to shift inflation risk to pensioners. Over the next 30 years, the inequalities were removed and the generosity of the pension promise improved by regulatory intervention.

The key changes were:

- Equal access to pension schemes for women and men, and as a knock-on consequence for part-time workers under provisions of the Social Security Pension Act of 1975 and the European Community Directive on Equal Treatment of 1976, although the full effect of these rules was not felt until successful legal challenges in the early 1990s.

- Better treatment of early leavers under the Social Security Acts of 1973 and 1985. This reduced the cross-subsidy from early leavers to stayers, by giving the right to a refund of contribution for those who left within five and then two years, and a preserved pension for those who had stayed for longer.

- The Social Security Act of 1985 also introduced the requirement for schemes to index the preserved pension of early leavers. This initially applied to pension accrued after 1985. But under the Social Security Act 1990, anyone who left after 1 January 1991 had their entire deferred pension revalued.

- Required provision of widow's benefits from 1978 in order to contract-out of SERPS. From 1988 a requirement to provide widower pensions applied.

- Under the rules for contracting-out of SERPS, the Guaranteed Minimum Pension (GMP), has had to be revalued at the point of retirement in line with average earnings growth. Before 1988 the State took the responsibility of post-retirement uprating of the GMP. In 1988, however, schemes became responsible for indexing any GMP accrued since 1988 by up to 3%. Since 1997, in order to contract-out of SERPS defined benefit schemes have been obliged to provide indexing of up to 5% for all pension accrued since 1997, under the provisions of the Pensions Act 1995.

Each of these measures made the occupational pension system fairer or more transparent, but each added considerably to the cost of any given pension promise. That cost was further increased by:

- The fall in inflation during the 1980s and 1990s: while compulsory indexation was introduced in 1987 and increased in 1997, it was limited to the lower of the RPI or 3% (and of the RPI or 5% after 1997). When inflation was above 3 or 5% therefore, some of the cost of inflation was still borne by existing pensioners. When inflation fell below 5% none of the inflation risk was borne by pensioners. This, along with the general maturing of the system, explains the increase during the 1980s in occupational scheme pension payments as a percentage of GDP. Pensions during retirement were no longer being eroded by inflation. But the impact was higher underlying cost.

- The increase in life-expectancy in retirement. In the 1950s, when many of the major corporate pensions plans were put in place, with predominantly male members, male life expectancy at 65 was 12 years. Today it is 19. Most of this rise has occurred since 1980.

The combined impact of all these changes is that the total long-term cost (i.e. the required combination of employer and employees contributions) of a final salary pension, calculated on 60ths of salary, and with a retirement age of 65, has increased from something like 10-14% when many schemes were initially introduced, to about 22-26% today.

Explaining the trends: irrational exuberance delays necessary adjustments.

Given this huge increase in underlying cost, what is surprising is not the slow drift away from DB pension provision between the 1970s and late 1990s, but that the movement was so slow, and that within the DB pension schemes which have stayed open, there was little change in scheme design until the 1990s. Faced with disappearing cross-subsidies and increasing costs we might logically have expected to see either:

- Reduction in the generosity of the headline terms (e.g. a shift from say 60ths of salary to 80ths): There was no sign of such a trend.

- An increase in average retirement ages to balance increased longevity: In fact the the percentage of scheme members with a normal retirement age of 65 fell until the early 1990s, while retirement at 60 became more common. Only since the mid-1990s have the trends reversed [Figure 3A.9].

Figure 3A.9 Normal Retirement Ages in Private Sector Schemes

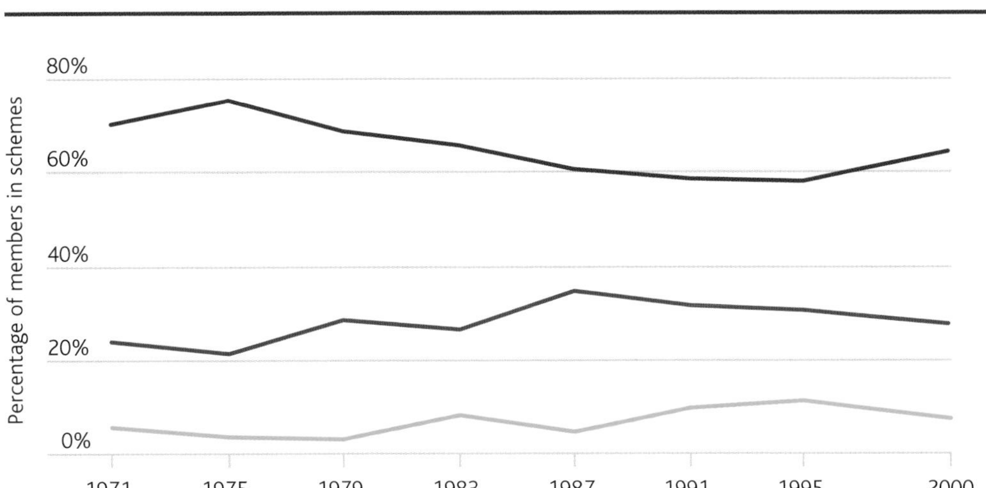

Source: Occupational pension scheme surveys, GAD

- Increases in contributions to meet the more generous promise: In fact, as Figure 3A.6 shows, the trend was down throughout the 1980s.

One partial explanation of this discrepancy between long-term actuarial requirements and observed behaviour is that the increase in longevity occurring was consistently underestimated. In 1981, GAD estimated that life expectancy for a 65 year old man would be 14.8 years: today this life expectancy is estimated to be 19 years.

But the bigger explanation is the impact of the long equity bull market of the 1980s and 1990s, which in retrospect appears as a period of irrational and unsustainable exuberance. From 1974-2000 the average annual real return on UK equities was 13%. The very long-term historic average is 5.5%. With UK DB pension schemes heavily invested in equities, this made increasingly expensive pension promises appear not only affordable without increased contributions, but even with decreased contributions. Contribution rates had increased during the 1970s to help repair the damage to scheme finances caused by the equities slump of 1974, but as the equity market recovery gathered pace they fell rapidly.

Indeed not only did they fall but they were required to fall by deliberate government policy. HM Treasury had by the early 1980s become concerned that companies were using large pension fund contributions as a means of managing down corporate tax liability in years of high profit. The Finance Act of 1986 therefore required pension funds to identify whether (on certain actuarial assumptions), they had a surplus of 5% or more, and to take action to remove the surplus within five years, or else lose some part of their tax-exempt status. The deep dip in contributions seen in the period 1988-91 in Figure 3A.6 almost certainly reflects the impact of this policy.[2]

Even with much lower contributions, however, the impact of high equity market returns was so positive that large surpluses were in many cases still left. These were therefore also used to pay for large early retirement packages in the corporate downsizings of the 1990-92 recession, as an apparently costless alternative to cash redundancy payments. (The latter were charged to the profit and loss account; early retirement packages were not.)

Finally pension funds surpluses appeared to be so resilient that HM Treasury believed that it could increase tax on pension fund investment return (through the dividend tax changes of 1997) without endangering the continuity of the system. Tax relief on pension fund investment income fell from £7.1 billion in 1996-97 to £3.3 billion in 2002-02 (on Inland Revenue figures).

In retrospect the actions both of government (in 1986 and in 1997) and of employers were predicated on assumptions about the sustainability of long term returns which were over optimistic.

[2]Note: The current Pensions Bill proposes reviewing the treatment for schemes to eliminate fund surpluses.

Conclusions and implications

The exceptional equity returns of the 1980s and 1990s thus enabled many private sector DB schemes to ignore the rapid rise in the underlying cost of their pension promises. Irrational exuberance allowed them to put off for 20 years the necessary adjustments, either increased contributions, less generous pensions, or increased retirement ages, which would eventually be required. Now that the fool's paradise of irrational exuberance has come to an end, the adjustment has been made abruptly, with the closure of schemes to new members.

Some reduction in the generosity of the DB pension promises as they had developed by the mid-1990s was inevitable. As this brief history has explained, that generosity was not a result of a consciously planned employer approach to competition in the labour market, and would never have resulted from voluntary employer action well informed by foresight as to the eventual cost, or operating within rational expectations of equity market returns. It resulted from the unplanned interaction of scheme design, government regulation, unanticipated changes in inflation and longevity, and irrational exuberance which made improved promises appear costless.

But the suddenness of the delayed adjustment, its extremely unequal impact as between existing and new members, and the major shift of risk occurring as many people move from DB to DC provision, have severely exacerbated the gaps that have always existed in Britain's pension system.

Looking forward: pension adequacy if trends unchanged

4

Given present trends many people will face "inadequate" pensions in retirement, unless they have large non-pension assets or are intending to retire much later than current retirees.

Current government plans and private savings levels imply that total pension income flowing to normal age retirees will rise from today's 9.1% of GDP to a mid-point estimate of 10.8% by 2050, and that there will be no significant shift in the balance of provision from state to private sources. This level of transfer in turn implies either poorer pensioners relative to average earnings or significantly higher average retirement ages.

The burden of adjustment will, however, be very unequally distributed. We estimate that at least 75% of all Defined Contribution (DC) scheme members have contribution rates below the level likely to be required to provide adequate pensions. Our estimates suggest that around 9 million people may be under-saving, some by a small amount, some severely. But the significant minority of people in still open private sector Defined Benefit (DB) schemes will enjoy more than adequate pensions and most public sector employees will be well provided for, as will some higher paid employees in Senior Executive schemes. The present level of pension right accrual is both deficient in total and increasingly unequal.

The implications of this for pensioner income will be more serious in 20-25 years time than in the next 10. And over that long time span many adjustments, for instance to savings rates and retirement ages, may naturally occur. A muddle-through option does therefore exist. But it is highly likely that the muddle-through option will produce outcomes both less socially equitable and less economically efficient than we could achieve with a consciously planned response to the problems we face.

As Chapter 3 describes, the level of pension saving in the UK is not rising to meet the demographic challenge, and may indeed be on an underlying downward trend. But whether this implies a "savings gap," and the size of that gap, depends on what level of pension income is required/desired, and on whether present pensioner income relative to average net incomes is equal to, more than or less than the required/desired amount. This chapter therefore assesses present pension savings against measures of adequate retirement income. It concludes that the distribution of pension right accrual is becoming increasingly unequal, with significant minorities well provided for, but many others heading for what they will consider inadequate pensions.

The chapter has eight sections:

1 The philosophical issue of "adequacy": what responsibility should government take for ensuring adequate income in retirement?

2 The empirical issue: what income replacement rates are "adequate"? Are current UK pensioner incomes a sensible benchmark?

3 The macroeconomics of saving: what do present aggregate pension savings imply for future aggregate pensions? Why the balance of pension provision will not shift from state to private.

4 Required savings levels: what contribution rates are required to meet benchmarks of adequate pension? Explanation of group modelling assumptions.

5 Future pension adequacy: deficient for many people. Group modelling results.

6 Future pension adequacy: increasingly unequal.

7 The impact over time: why the problems will be bigger in 20 to 25 years time rather than over the next 10 to 15 years.

8 The do-nothing option: how the problems would resolve themselves, but why that is not the best way forward.

1. The philosophical issue: should government ensure "adequate" pensions?

The definition of an "adequate" pension system is debatable in both a philosophical and an empirical sense.

Philosophically we have to decide what the responsibility of government in pension provision should be. One possibility would be to argue that the state's role is only to provide a minimal poverty prevention safety net and that if individuals fail to make "adequate" provision on top of this, that is their problem and not the rest of society's. By this standard, the UK system could be defined as adequate if we believed that the minimum level of income which means-tested benefits aim to ensure (currently the Guarantee Credit of £105.45 per week) provides an acceptable minimum standard of living. (And if we could be confident that means-tested benefits were taken up by all who were eligible for them.)

An alternative point of view is that government should try to ensure that people make provision which they would consider adequate for their retirement, for three reasons:

1. A purely free market for private provision may be severely inefficient given the inherent imbalance of knowledge between customers and providers, the short-sightedness which many consumers display, and the large, one-off, and in some cases irreversible nature of the decisions that consumers must make;

2. Large numbers of dissatisfied future pensioners will be a large future social problem, even if in an ideal world they should have made provision for themselves and if equipped with foresight would have done so;

3. Many of those who make inadequate private provision are likely to wind up reliant on the state in any case.

Fully resolving one's approach to these issues would involve a wide-ranging political and philosophical debate. For the purposes of this Report, the Commission has decided to take a pragmatic mid-point position and to assume that there is a social interest in ensuring that people of modest or average means (e.g. those up to the 75th percentile of earnings – at present about £29,000) have made provision which they would consider adequate, but that above some level of income (say above the 90th percentile – currently about £40,000) a purely individualist approach is appropriate.

During the consultation period the Commission would like to hear reactions to this proposed approach, and alternative points of view, and would encourage those submitting specific policy proposals to make clear the philosophy of approach which underlies them.

2. The empirical issue: what pension level is "adequate"?

Chapter 3 illustrated that total pension saving in the UK is not rising to meet the demographic challenge and may indeed be on an underlying downward trend. But we cannot take this as evidence that higher pension savings are essential since it is possible that current levels of retirement income are on average higher than necessary or desired, or retirement ages unnecessarily low, and that pension income should therefore be allowed to fall as a percentage of GDP. Benchmarks of adequate or desirable levels of pension therefore need to be developed, drawing on evidence from international comparisons, time trends, analysis of expenditure patterns, actual replacement rates observed today and people's stated expectations and preferences.

International comparisons and time trends of pensioner income suggest that for some pensioners the 1990s was a golden age, but that pensions in general are not unnecessarily high.

- International comparisons, cited already in Chapter 3 [see Figures 3.15 and 3.16] suggest that the UK's pensioners are on average slightly (but only slightly) poorer relative to median incomes than pensioners in other rich developed countries. This evidence would caution against the assumption that pensions on average are currently too high. And as Figure 1.17 illustrated, when people are asked to choose between the four options for solving the pension challenge, only a small minority believe that lower retirement income is the appropriate response.

- It is also true, however, that the percentage of GDP transferred to pensioners increased significantly between the 1970s and 1990s, with total pension income rising proportionately more than the number of pensioners [Figure 4.1]. As a result, average pensioner incomes have increased faster than average earnings, both for singles and couples, and for both recently retired and over 75 year olds [Figure 4.2]. This rise reflects two factors.

  - The maturing of the occupational pension schemes built up during the 1950s and 1960s and, among the older pensioner groups, the decline of the influence of inflation, which resulted in a significant erosion in the real value of private pensions during the high inflation of the 1970s.

Figure 4.1 Pensioner Income as a Percentage of GDP

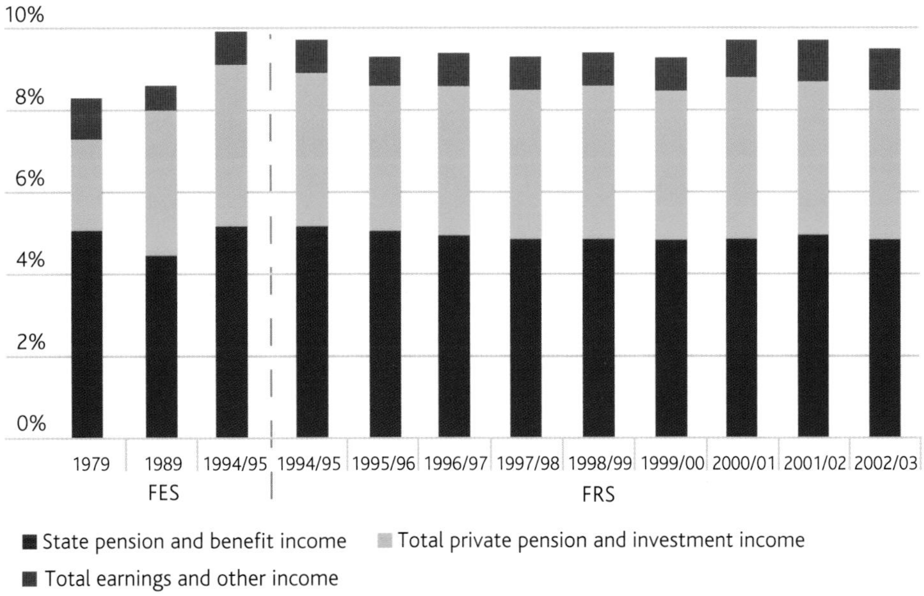

10%
8%
6%
4%
2%
0%

1979 | 1989 | 1994/95 | 1994/95 | 1995/96 | 1996/97 | 1997/98 | 1998/99 | 1999/00 | 2000/01 | 2001/02 | 2002/03

FES | FRS

■ State pension and benefit income ■ Total private pension and investment income
■ Total earnings and other income

Source: Pensioners' Incomes Series 2002/03

Figure 4.2 Change in Mean Income of Pensioners Relative to Average Earnings

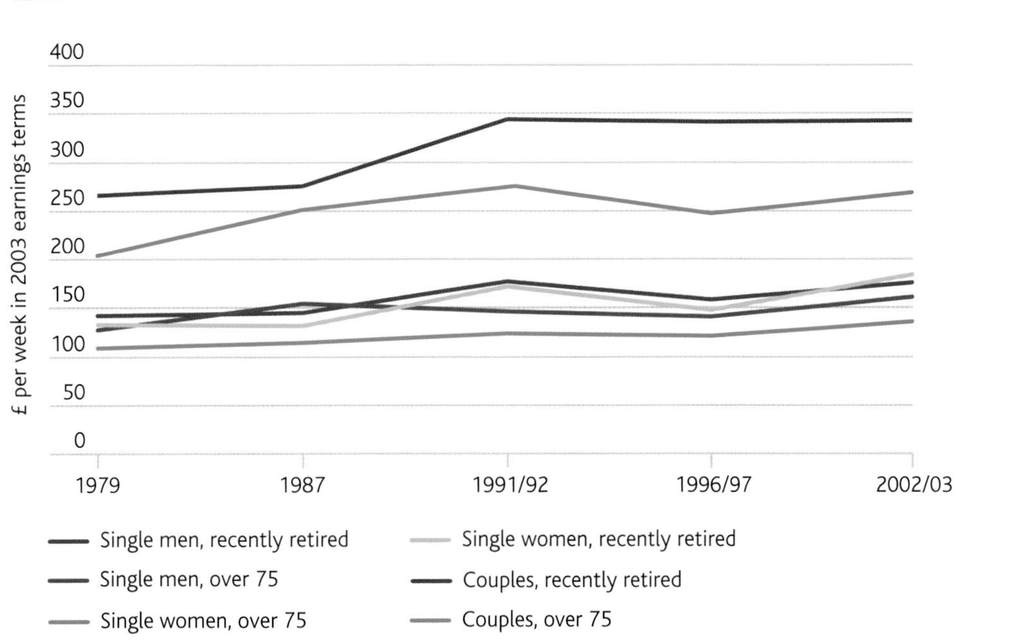

Source: Pensioners' Incomes Series 2002/03

Notes: Incomes net of taxes, pension contributions and housing costs
Incomes are in 2003 earnings terms

- The maturing of the SERPS system and the generous level of SERPS benefits accrued by SERPS members in the 1980s, which meant that the average earner with maximum state pension rights retiring in the late 1990s enjoyed an income replacement rate from the state higher than ever before (as well as higher than planned looking forward) [Figure 4.3].

For some pensioners therefore the 1990s was indeed a "golden age" of retirement, with a combination of the generous level of SERPS and the unanticipated generosity of the DB schemes [described in Chapter 3] enabling some pensioners to retire with a combination of a retirement income, retirement age, and life expectancy more favourable than in any previous generation.

- But this rise in pensioner incomes relative to average earnings was unequally distributed, with the top quartile of pensioners achieving the largest percentage increases, while lowest quartile pensioners received much smaller or zero increases [Figure 4.4]. This reflects the fact that Basic State Pension (BSP) benefits (i.e. excluding SERPS) on which lower income earners are more reliant, have actually fallen slightly relative to average earnings, even when allowance is made for the increasing generosity of income related benefits as supplements to the BSP. [Figure 4.5]. Overall, therefore the evidence on trends in pensioner income over time might suggest that there is a case for accepting lower pensions relative to lifetime average annual earnings than those enjoyed by the most favoured retirees of the 1990s, but that we cannot assume that pensions in general are unnecessarily high.

Figure 4.3 State Pension at Point of Retirement Assuming Full Contribution Record for a Person who has been on Average Full-time Earnings Throughout Their Working Life: Percentage of Average Earnings

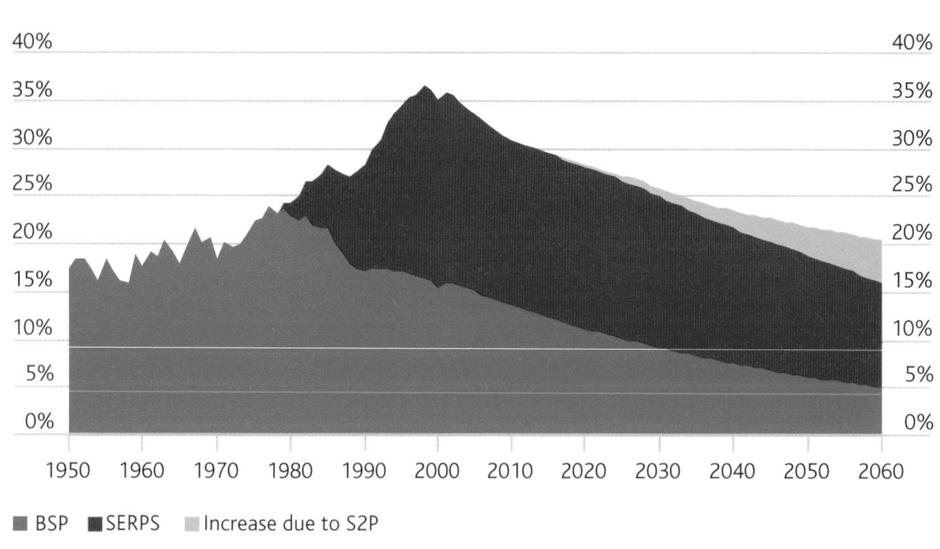

Source: Government Actuary's Quinquennial Review of the National Insurance Fund as at April 2000, GAD

Figure 4.4 Percentage Change in Pensioner Incomes Relative to Average Earnings, 1979-2002/03

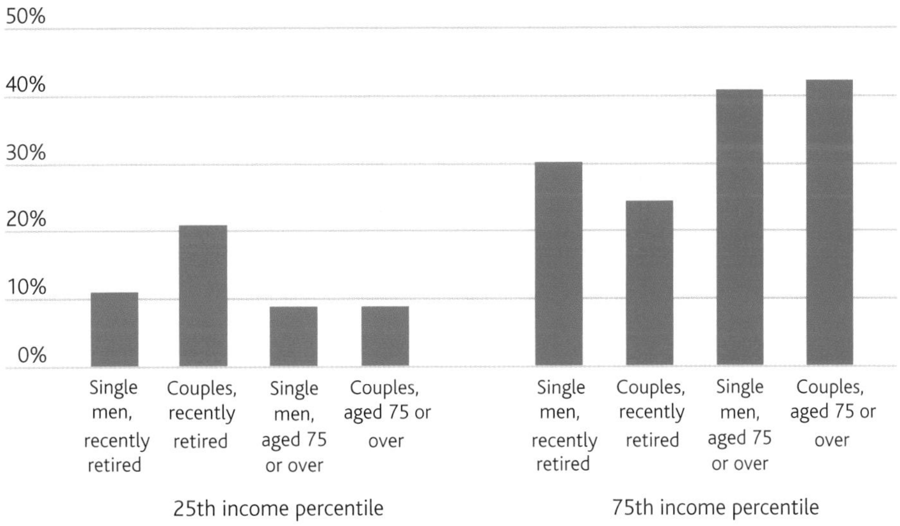

50%
40%
30%
20%
10%
0%

Single men, recently retired | Couples, recently retired | Single men, aged 75 or over | Couples, aged 75 or over
25th income percentile

Single men, recently retired | Couples, recently retired | Single men, aged 75 or over | Couples, aged 75 or over
75th income percentile

Source: Pensioners' Incomes Series, DWP

Figure 4.5 Full BSP and Income Support as a Percentage of Male Earnings

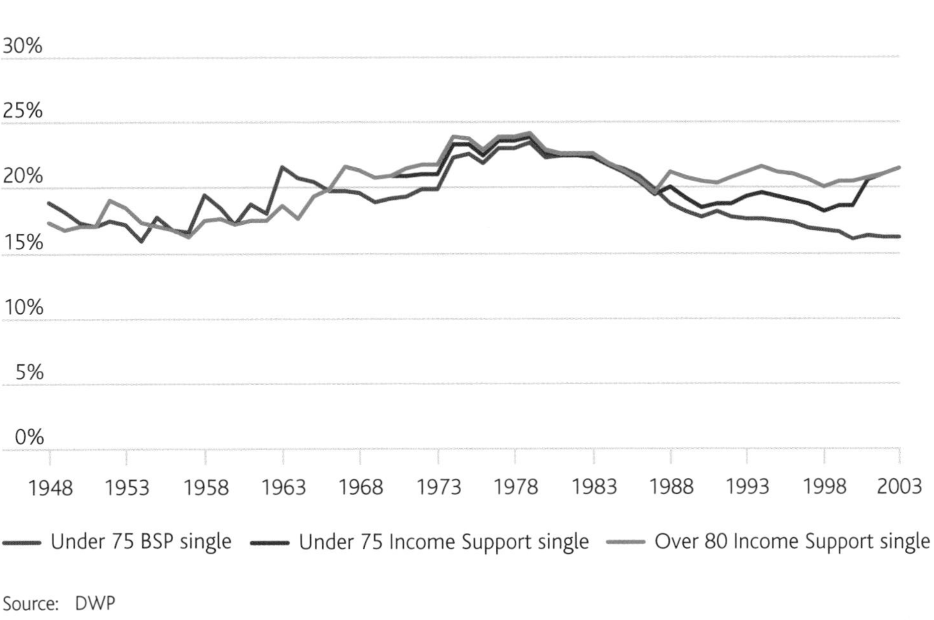

Source: DWP

Note: The Income Support line includes Supplementary Benefit which was the predecessor benefit and the Minimum Income Guarantee and Guarantee Credit as sucessor benefits.

Analysis of consumption patterns throughout life provides another way of thinking about pension adequacy. Pensions, whether PAYG or funded, enable people to smooth consumption across their life, sacrificing consumption during working life to allow consumption in retirement. Reasonable assumptions about how people make that trade-off, combined with analysis of actual expenditure patterns pre and post-retirement suggest four conclusions.

1. High consumption replacement rates (i.e. consumption maintained during retirement at close to working life levels) can be delivered with significantly lower rates of gross income replacement. There are two reason for this:

   (i) Retirees pay less tax and National Insurances: For someone on average earnings a net post-tax replacement rate of 80% could be achieved with a gross pre-tax replacement rate of about 67% [Figure 4.6];

   (ii) Retirees save less: A large element of financial savings (and in particular pension saving) is accumulated during working life and spent during retirement. Housing assets tend to be bought during working life and maintained (but not added to) during retirement.

   Combining these two effects, someone on average earnings who saved 10% of gross income during working life might well be able to maintain consumption at 100% of their working life level with a gross replacement rate of 77%.

2. While desired consumption replacement rates are high, they can be slightly below 100% and still allow standards of living to be maintained. This is because some categories of expenditure (e.g. commuting expenses) fall away in retirement, although others (for instance for care) may increase, particularly later in retirement. [See the panel on the following page.]

3. The required gross replacement rate is higher for lower income people than those with higher income for two reasons:

   (i) The savings effect is greater, because high income people are more likely to have been saving for bequest motives as well as to smooth consumption across the life-cycle; and

   (ii) Lower income people may need a high consumption replacement rate to be assured of what society considers a minimum acceptable standard of living. There is, therefore, a generally accepted role for government to intervene to ensure higher replacement rates at low income than would result from individually chosen consumption-smoothing.

4. The issue of the evolution of income replacement **during retirement** is complex but important and will become more so as longevity increases. Most people will desire their standard of living to be maintained during retirement and the most obvious benchmark is therefore that pensions should maintain the same real value, i.e. rise with prices. If, however, the prices of goods and services which pensioners tend to consume (e.g. holidays and household services rather than computers) rise faster than prices on average, this benchmark may be insufficient to maintain their perceived standard of living. Conversely, some categories of expenditure may naturally decline as pensioners grow older, suggesting that even real income maintenance might not be absolutely essential. There is no clear theoretical resolution of these issues and empirical evidence tells us little, since it is impossible to infer how far changing patterns of actual expenditure by age are simply the result of available resources rather than a reflection of changing need. But what is clear is that the correct definition of adequacy during retirement becomes more important as life expectancy post-retirement grows.

Figure 4.6 Gross Replacement Rates Required for 80% Replacement Rate Net of Income Tax and National Insurance Contributions

Source: Pensions Comission analysis

Expenditure patterns of those aged 65-74 compared to those aged 50-64

The Expenditure and Food Survey carried out by the Office of National Statistics provides detailed breakdown of expenditure by households. It makes possible analysis of how expenditure varies across age groups and household types.

On a cross-sectional basis the income and expenditure of households headed by someone aged 65-74 is about 60%, slightly lower than we have seen from other surveys. This is probably because these figures are on a household basis and because the pre-retirement age group used for comparison covers a wider age band.

Table 4.1 shows that expenditure declines over all categories, although the rate of decline varies, as the age of the household increases. One reason for this is the decline in household size over the age groups, which means that consumption **per person** does not decline as much. The average size of a household headed by someone aged 50-64 is 2.2 but 1.7 for households headed by someone aged 65-74. Therefore although household expenditure declines by 40%, expenditure per person only declines by 22%.

Expenditure declines by £180 per week between the 50-64 year olds and the 65-74 year olds when using this cross-sectional source. Table 4.2 presents the contribution that each expenditure category makes to this reduction. The most significant groups are transport, recreation and culture, restaurants and food, and other expenditure items.

Table 4.1 Household Expenditure and Income According to the Age of Household Reference Person (£ per week)

	50-64	65-74	75 and over
Food & non-alcoholic drinks	47.80	38.90	29.40
Alcoholic drinks, tobacco & narcotics	13.40	8.50	5.10
Clothing & footwear	24.00	11.60	7.80
Housing, fuel & power	35.30	29.30	25.90
Household goods & services	36.90	22.00	14.90
Health	6.30	5.90	3.50
Transport	72.40	35.10	15.60
Communication	10.60	6.90	5.10
Recreation & culture	65.60	42.10	23.00
Education	6.40	[1.00]	..
Restaurants & hotels	38.50	20.10	11.50
Miscellaneous goods & services	34.70	22.20	16.90
Other expenditure items	59.30	27.40	17.80
Total expenditure	**451.40**	**270.90**	**177.20**
Total income	493	303	234
Percentage of income spent	92%	90%	76%
Average household size	2.2	1.7	1.4
Average expenditure per person	202.50	157.30	122.60

Source: Expenditure and Food Survey 2003

- The reduction in transport costs may be largely due to the removal of travel to work costs and to the significant public transport concessions which older people enjoy and the greater ability to travel off-peak.

- The "other expenditure" items include mortgage repayments. These decline for the older age group as most people plan their finances to pay off their mortgages prior to retirement. Spending while on holiday also declines significantly.

- The reduction in spending on recreation and culture may not necessarily mean that consumption has fallen. One of the significant contributions to the reduction is less spending on purchasing electrical equipment, and although spending on recreational and cultural services also declines, this could reflect concessions in prices for older people. Spending on the purchase of package holidays declines very little.

- The reduction in spending on hotels and restaurants could reflect a decline in consumption relative to those of working age driven by budget constraints, and among later age groups, mobility constraints.

Spending falls by a further £94 per week for those aged 75 and over compared to younger pensioners, although income only declines by £69 per week. The major contributions to the reduction in expenditure are food and non-alcoholic drinks, transport, recreation and culture and other expenditure items

- The reduction in expenditure on food may suggest a decline in living standards compared to younger pensioners. But it does also reflect smaller households.

- Transport expenditures decline in all sub-categories. This could reflect the lower mobility of older people as their health declines.

- Recreation and cultural spending also declines, this may also reflect less active lifestyles as people age. One contribution to the reduction is free television licences for any household with someone aged over 75.

- "Other expenditure" also declines because housing costs continue to decline. Spending while on holiday declines even further.

Table 4.2 Contributions to the Total Reduction in Household Expenditure for Different Age Groups

Category	Contribution to total reduction in spending for households aged 65-74 compared to 50-64 year olds	Contribution to total reduction in spending for households aged 75 and over compared to 65-74 year olds
Food & non-alcoholic drinks	4.9%	10.1%
Alcoholic drinks, tobacco & narcotics	2.7%	3.7%
Clothing & footwear	6.9%	4.0%
Housing, fuel & power	3.3%	3.6%
Household goods & services	8.3%	7.5%
Health	0.2%	2.6%
Transport	20.7%	20.7%
Communication	2.1%	1.9%
Recreation & culture	13.1%	20.3%
Education	3.0%	1.1%
Restaurants & hotels	10.2%	9.2%
Miscellaneous goods & services	7.0%	5.6%
Other expenditure items	17.7%	10.3%

Source: Expenditure and Food Survey 2003

These four theoretical assertions are reflected in the **actually observed pattern of replacement rates at retirement** (i.e. income just after retirement as a percentage of income just before), though less so when we consider real income trends during retirement.

- A striking feature of the data is that replacement rates vary very significantly even at the same income levels [Figure 4.7]. But on average most studies find replacement rates of about 70-80% for men and find that replacement rates vary in line with income in the way that the theoretical models predict [Table 4.3 and Figure 4.8].

- The empirical data suggests however that the decline of relative real income during retirement may be more severe than theory suggests is optimal. Older pensioners have significantly lower income than recent retirees [Figure 4.9]. This is bound to be true to a degree if new retiree pensions rise in line with average earnings, while pensions in retirement rise at best with prices. But it is exacerbated by the fact that DB price indexation has only recently become widespread, and by the fact that the vast majority of annuities bought out of maturing DC pension funds are non-indexed and single rather that joint life annuities. It also reflects the fact that older pensioners will have accrued nil or small SERPS rights. The problem of inadequate pensioner income late in retirement may therefore decline in the short-term, as cohorts with SERPS entitlements move through, but over the long-term is likely to grow significantly as life expectancy grows and as the importance of DC schemes increases.

Finally, **survey evidence of people's preferences** suggests that desired, as well as actual, replacement rates are higher at low income levels [Table 4.4]. It also however suggests that expectations vary greatly, and that the median replacement rates desired are considerably higher than those currently experienced by all income groups [Figure 4.10].

Figure 4.7 Replacement Rates Two Years After Retirement Compared to Two Years Before Retirement

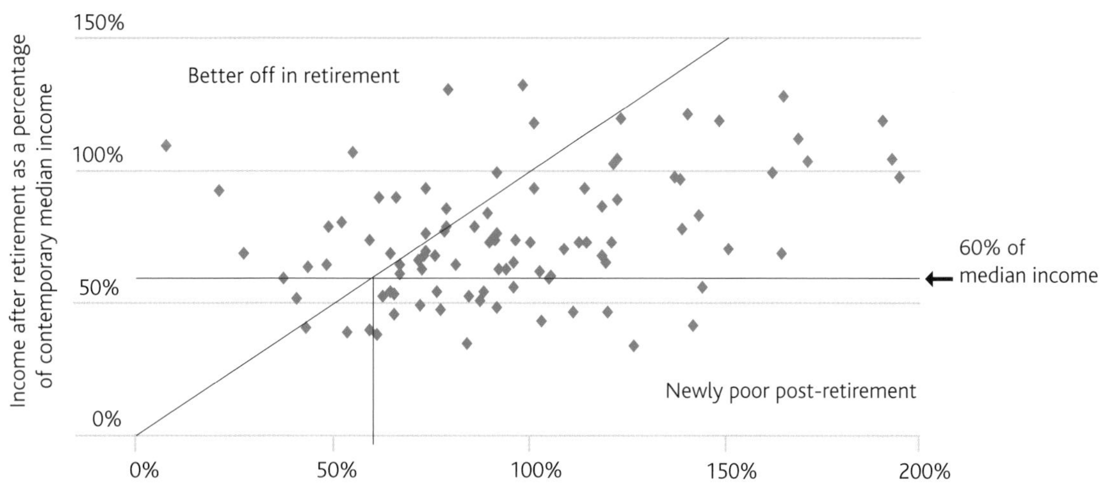

Source: Case analysis of BHPS data (based on Bardasi, Jenkins and Rigg (2002))

Note: Compares average of net incomes two and three years before retirement with net incomes two and three years after retirement.

Table 4.3 Summary of replacement rate survey evidence

Source and year	Measure of income used	Basis of comparison	Replacement rate
Family resources survey 1999/2000	Income net of taxes	Recently retired households to households not yet retired	Singles – 70% Couple – 74%
Retirement survey 1988 – 1994	Net weekly income in real terms	Longitudinal analysis of individuals	Mean for men – 79% Mean for women – 97% For men who reached SPA between 2 waves, replacement rates ranged from 74% for bottom quartile to 56% for the top quartile
British Household Panel Survey 1991-97	Equivalised net income	Longitudinal analysis of households	Median for men 5 years before to 5 years after retirement – 78% Median for women 5 years before to 5 years after retirement – 91%

Source: DWP
Blundell & Tanner 1999
Bardasi, Jenkins & Rigg, 2002

Figure 4.8 Net Replacement Rates Observed for People Retiring Between 1988 and 1994

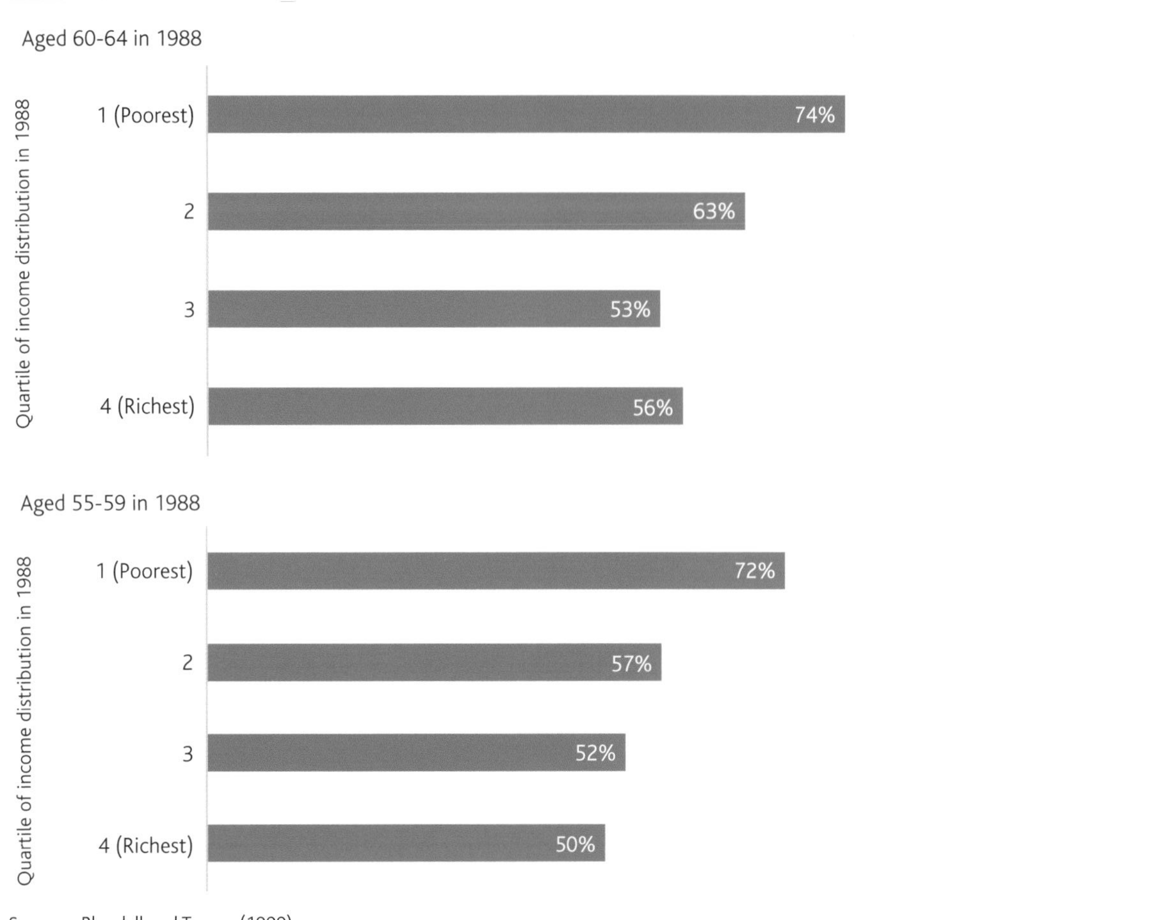

Source: Blundell and Tanner (1999)

Note: Income is defined as usual net weekly income, so includes income from benefits after tax
The Retirement Survey was a longditudinal survey carried out over two waves. Wave one in 1998 and wave two in 1994.

Figure 4.9 Average Gross Income of Single Pensioners, by Age: 2002/03

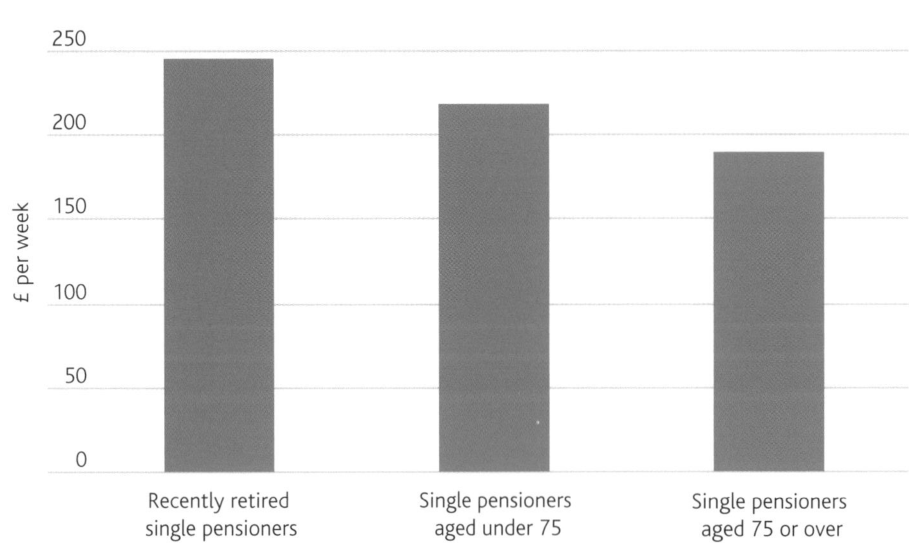

Source: Pensioners' Incomes Series

Table 4.4 Relationship between current income and desired income in retirement for people aged 45-54

What income is considered enough to live on in retirement?	Currently weekly income (column percentages)							
	<£100	£100-£157	£158-£199	£200-£259	£260-£359	£360-£499	£500+	All
Less than current income	0	10	13	40	59	81	67	45
About the same as current income	7	21	40	31	34	15	33	27
More than current income	93	69	47	29	6	4	0	29
Median	£150-£199	£150-£199	£150-£199	£200-£249	£200-£249	£250-£349	£350-£499	£200-£249

Source: Additional analysis of Pensions 2002

Note: People who did not give details of either current income or desired future income have been excluded from these results.

Figure 4.10 Estimated Median Desired Replacement Rates for People Aged 45-54

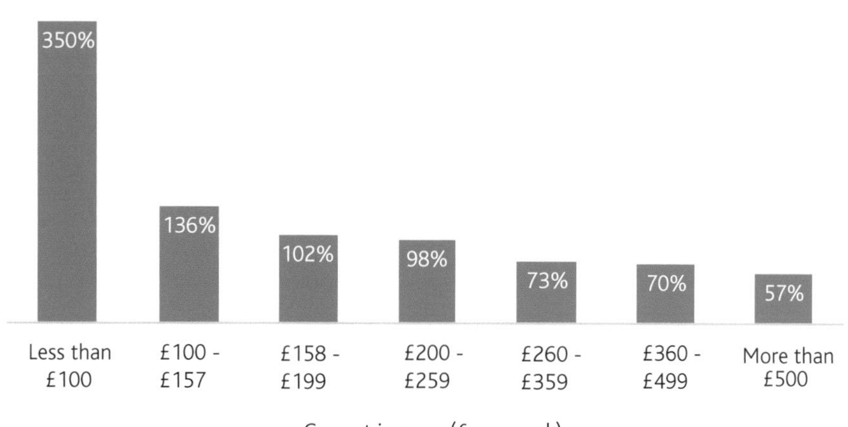

Source Pensions Commission analysis of Pensions 2002

Note: People who did not give details of either current income or desired future income have been excluded from these results

Considering this evidence together there can be no clear definition of pension adequacy. And it is important to remember that the generosity and affordability of pension provision is dependent on two factors: the level of the pension but also the age from which it is taken. But a reasonable judgement to guide assessment of adequacy might be as follows:

- It is possible that the income replacement levels enjoyed by some higher income retirees in the 1990s were unnecessarily high. And highly likely that the combination of retirement age, life expectancy and annual pension enjoyed by some long-service retirees in final salary plans was more favourable than for any previous generation and both unintentionally and unnecessarily generous.

- But there is no evidence that average income replacement rates have been significantly higher than most people desire and consider adequate.

- It is therefore reasonable to use current actual replacement rates as a benchmark when assessing the adequacy of pension right accrual. In our analysis below we use benchmark replacement targets of 80% of gross earnings for lowest earners, declining to 67% for median earners and to 50% for top earners [Figure 4.11]. We illustrate the level of pension contribution needed to deliver those pension incomes given a variety of different retirement ages.

We would be interested to hear views on the definition of "adequacy" during the consultation period.

Figure 4.11 Benchmark Replacement Rates Assumed for Pensions Commission Modelling: Percentage of Gross earnings

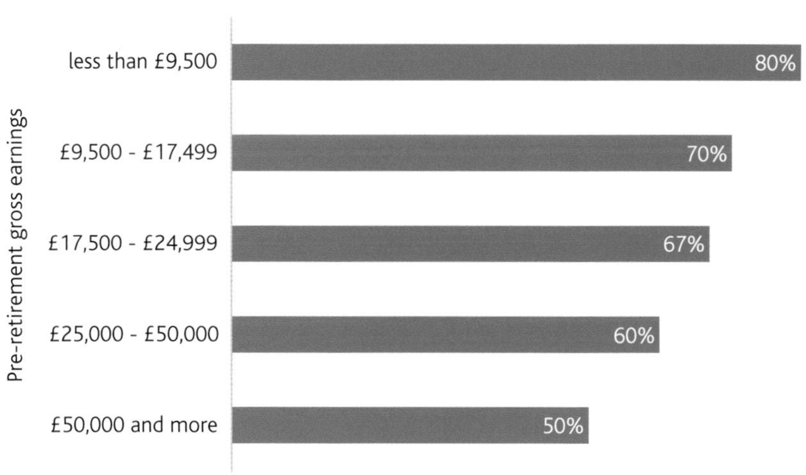

Source Pensions Commission analysis

3. Present pension saving and future pension incomes: the macro relationship

Chapter 1 identified [Figure 1.12 repeated as Figure 4.12] that the percentage of GDP transferred to pensioners via pensions would have to rise from 9.1% to 16.1% of GDP between now and 2050 to keep pensioner incomes in line with average net incomes with unchanged retirement ages, and to 13.9% even after considering the possible impact of equalisation of the male and female SPA. It suggested that part of this increase will not and should not occur, and instead average retirement ages would need to rise still further. But it also identified that a significant increase in the percentage of GDP transferred would probably still be required. Current state plans and private savings patterns, however, will only deliver a small increase and contrary to the government's stated aspiration, the balance of provision will not shift from state to private savings.

As Figure 4.12 shows government expenditure on pensioners of normal retirement age is currently planned to increase from 6.1% to 6.9% of GDP.[1] This is the increase that will be driven by demographic change even given current plans to increase the BSP only in line with prices. In addition, public unfunded pension currently cost 1.5% of GDP (of which 0.8% flows to normal age retirees as pension income) and are likely to cost at least this in future. If retirement ages do not rise (apart from the equalisation of male and female average retirement ages), private funded savings flowing to normal age retirees would need to rise from 2.2% to 6.2% of GDP to fill the gap.

The current level of private pension saving however is unlikely to produce any significant increase in future funded pensions as a percentage of GDP. The panel on pages 148 and 149 describes the Pensions Commission's model of future pension incomes, and our detailed assumptions and outputs [See also Appendix B for further details]. Key points are:

- As Chapter 3 described, the underlying level of private pension saving is now in decline. Actual contributions over the last 10 years have been roughly constant at about 3.5-3.8%, but half of this relates to private DB schemes, over 60% of which (weighted by number of active members) are closed to new members. If scheme participation and contribution patterns do not change, private pension contributions will fall from 3.8% to about 2.9% of GDP over the next 15 years [see Figure 3.51].

- The relationship between pension savings today and future pension income depends on a complex set of factors described in the panel. But reasonable assumptions on rates of return and growth rates, suggest that the current underlying level of saving may produce funded pensions as a percentage of GDP of 3.4-4.2% compared to the current level of total funded pension income of 3.8%.[2] The implications of this for the resource transfer to pensioners over 65 depends on how much of this income flows not to over 65 years olds but to early retirees [Figure 4.12].

[1]Note: See the panel at the end of Chapter 1 for state spending as a percentage of GDP according to different definitions.

[2]Note: It is possible however that this percentage will rise above this level over the next 15 years before falling, given the significant number of people still benefiting from membership of DB schemes closed to new members.

Figure 4.12 The Implications of Current Plans and Savings Behaviour for the percentage of GDP transferred to pensioners

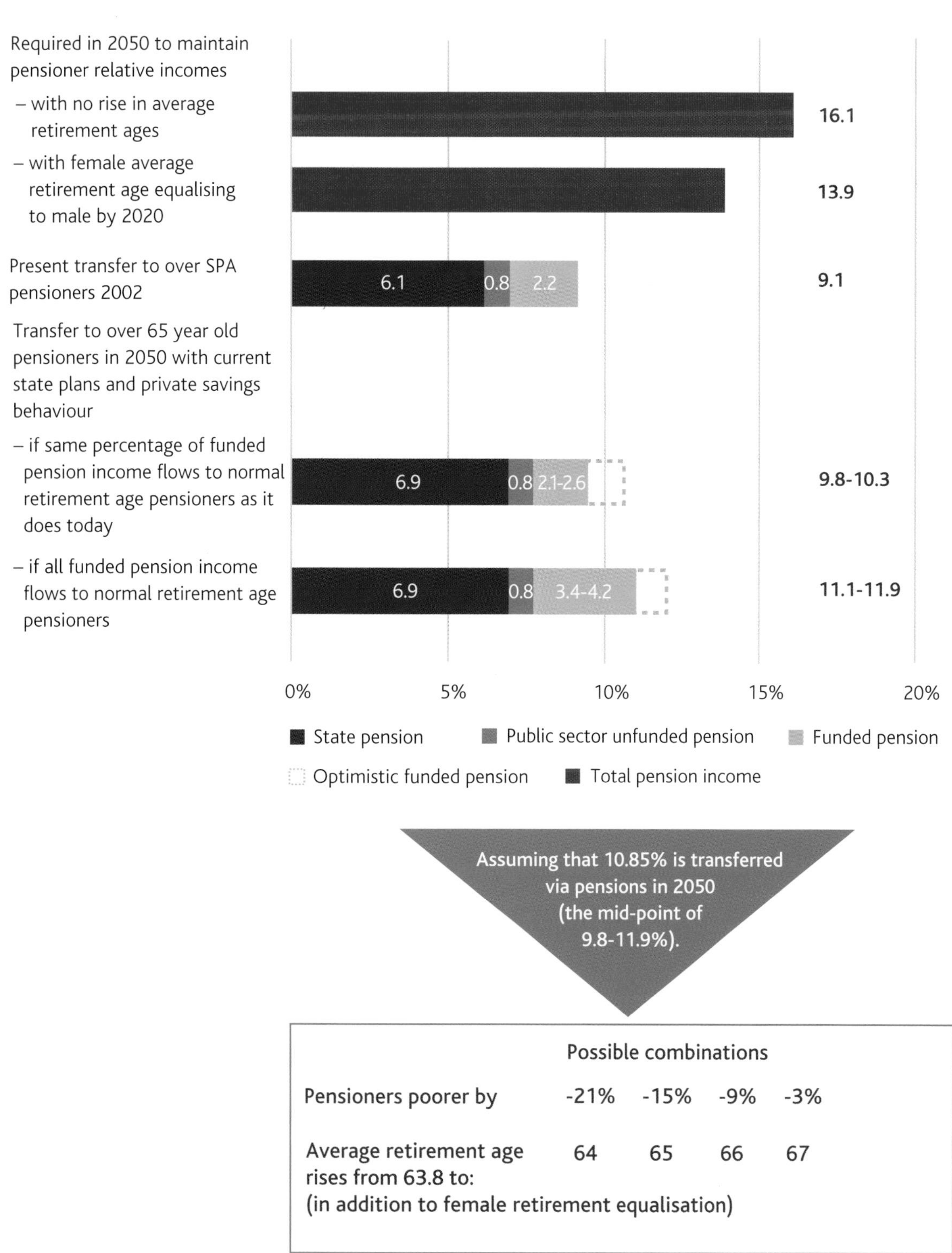

Source: Pensions Commission analysis

[1]Note: This implies a total transfer including investment income of 12.05%

- If the proportion of funded pension income flowing to early retirees continues at the current 40%, funded pension income reaching over 65 year olds in 2050 will be only 2.1%-2.6%, similar to the current 2.2%, and the total resource transfer via pensions would be 9.8%-10.3% versus 9.1% today.

- If all future funded pension income flowed to over 65 year olds, the total resource transfer via pensions would be 11.1%-11.9%.

- This proportion of GDP transferred to pensioners implies either significant reductions in average pensioner incomes relative to average net incomes, or a rise in retirement ages significantly more than proportional to the rise in life expectancy [as Figure 4.12 illustrates].

- Contrary to the Government's stated aspirations, moreover, around 60% of this income is likely to come from public expenditure on state pensions and benefits, and around 70% (i.e including also public sector employee pensions) will be a charge on PAYG public expenditure rather than funded. In the Green Paper on Pension Reform of 1998, the Government projected that government expenditure on pensions would remain constant as a percentage of GDP, and set a target that the balance of pensioner income should shift from 60% public: 40% private to 40% public: 60% private. This aspiration is extremely unlikely to be met, both because latest public expenditure plans, reflecting the new demographic projections, assume an increase in public pension expenditure as a percentage of GDP, and because private funded pensions are unlikely to grow if current pension savings behaviour continues. The future of British pension provision will therefore on current plans be far more state dominated than is often suggested. This is even more the case if we note that a quarter of all private funded pension contributions are accounted for by National Insurance contracted-out rebates, i.e. are products of the UK's existing compulsory earnings related pension system.[3]

- Obviously our modelling results are sensitive to the assumptions made on contribution rates as a percentage of GDP, and on rates of return. Table 4.5 illustrates how future private pension income could vary with different assumptions. We believe that the base case we have presented reflects reasonable assumptions. But we would like to hear views during the consultation period on whether these assumptions appear over optimistic or over pessimistic.

[3]Note: National Insurance rebates for contracted-out schemes amount to £11 billion per annum out of £37 billion of pension contributions. But this proportion may grow over time as the total contribution level comes down with the DB-DC shift.

Table 4.5 Funded Pension Income as a Percentage of GDP: Sensitivities

	Real Rate of Return on Investments			
Contribution Rate as a % of GDP	**2%**	**3%**	**4%**	**5%**
2.0%	1.9%	2.3%	2.9%	3.6%
2.9%	2.8%	3.4%	4.2%	5.2%
4.0%	3.8%	4.7%	5.8%	7.1%

Presented as our base case

Note: The real rate of return is after all costs, implicit and explicit. See Chapter 6 and Appendix C for assumptions.

Modelling total future income from funded pensions

The level of future pension income produced by the funded pension system will depend on the size of present and future contributions, the rate of return earned, and future trends in demography. Appendix B sets out the details of the model the Pensions Commission has built to forecast future pensioner income, and some of the key points of the theory of funded pensions which need to be understood in interpreting the model.

Theory and Model Structure

- In a funded pension system existing workers accumulate assets through both cash contributions and reinvested investment income. They then liquidate these assets by selling them on to the next generation of workers, with an annuity income representing both a continuing element of investment income, and a gradual sale of the underlying assets.
- Part of workers' cash contributions are effectively used to purchase existing assets off the existing pensioners, but part is used to fund new capital investment. Even though each individual worker accumulates and then entirely liquidates their own specific pension assets, a society with a stable demography but growing per capita income will have a total capital stock growing in line with GDP, and an element of each year's cash contributions is therefore directed not to buying existing assets (and thus funding pensioner consumption) but to new capital investment.
- The level of future funded pension income as a percentage of GDP in an economy in equilibrium is therefore given by the equation set out below:

$$\text{Funded Pension Income as \% of GDP} = \text{Cash Contributions as \% of GDP} + \text{Investment Income on Pension Funds as \% GDP} - \text{Net Capital Investment as \% GDP}$$

Which in turn implies

$$\text{Funded Pensions as \% of GDP} = \text{Cash Contributions as \% of GDP} + \left(r_w \times \text{Capital Stock owned by workers}\right) + \left(r_p \times \text{Capital Stock owned by pensioners}\right) - \left(g \times \text{Capital stock}\right)$$

Where: r_w is the rate of return earned by workers during the accumulation phase of pension saving

r_p is the rate of return implicit within an annuity during the decumulation phase

g is the rate of growth of the economy

Note: In this model we have ignored non-pension saving and the investment financed by it.
But conclusions would not be affected by the addition of explicitly modelled non-pension savings.

The future level of pension income is therefore dependent on the rate of cash contributions, the rate of return being earned, but also future demography. This latter factor enters the equation because if the present generation is followed by a smaller generation, a lower growth rate of capital stock is required, and thus the fourth term of the equation becomes a smaller negative. Thus, for any given combination of cash contributions and rates of return, a birth rate below two will tend to increase pension income as percentage of GDP (compared to a birth rate of two in the base case), since more of the workers' cash contributions are financing pensioner consumption and less are financing capital investment.

Assumptions for modelling

Our base case assumptions for the variables are:

- Cash contributions as percentage of GDP 2.9% once the DB-DC shift has worked through [Figure 3.51].
- An average real rate of return, after all relevant costs, of between 3-4% during the accumulation phase. (See Appendix C for the basis of these assumptions: the 3% case assumes a real equity return of 6%, corporate bonds 2.7%, and government bonds 2.0%, and deducts relevant implicit and explicit costs.)
- An average real rate of return of 1.3% during the decumulation phase (this is the rate of return currently implicit in annuity pricing).
- GDP per capita growth of 2% per annum, with total growth in GDP, in the capital stock, and thus in the percentage of savings devoted to capital expenditure, driven also by the UK's forecast demographic development.

Model outputs

With these assumptions the model suggests that funded pension income as a percentage of GDP will be about 3.4-4.2% in 2050 (i.e. once the DB-DC shift is fully worked through). This is similar to the level currently being produced by the funded pensions system, which we believe to be about 3.8%. But this similar overall result is the product of three offsetting trends.

- Future cash contributions as a percentage of GDP below that of the last 10 years and well below the levels of the late 1970s and early 1980s illustrated in Chapter 3.
- A considerably lower average rate of return than has been achieved in the 1980s and 1990s, when equity and bond returns were far above long-term historical averages.
- But, offsetting these negatives, demographic trends which, by decreasing the ratio of workers to pensioners, increase the proportion of cash contributions devoted to pensioner consumption rather than to capital investment.

The contribution which funded pensions might make to meeting the demographic challenge is illustrated in Figure 4.12, which shows that funded pensions flowing to people above state pension age might rise from 2.2% to 3.4-4.2%.

But it is important to understand that almost all of this increase derives not from a projected increase in the total income flow from the funded pension system, but from the fact that we assume that all of this will flow to normal age retirees, and none to early retirees.

At present, as the panel in Chapter 1 (Pensions and Pensioner Incomes as a percentage of GDP) sets out, early retirees receive about 40% of all funded pension income. This percentage was swollen by the generous early retirement packages offered by DB schemes in the 1990s and is bound to decline. But an assumption that it will decline to zero is extreme. The income gap to be filled (by higher taxes, higher savings, or higher retirement ages) may therefore be higher than the lowest bar on Figure 4.12 suggests.

4. Required savings rates for different categories of individual: Explanation of the group modelling assumptions

The rate of pension contribution which an individual needs to make to secure an "adequate" pension depends upon a very wide range of factors including:

- The individual's desired income replacement rate, and their planned retirement age.

- What level of income replacement he or she can expect to receive from the state system. As Figure 4.13 shows this varies by income and also by current age reflecting the planned decrease in the generosity of the state system. It also varies between employees (who are members of SERPS/S2P) and the self-employed (who are not). Finally it varies between low income renters (who receive housing benefits) and low income owner-occupiers (who do not).

- The number of years over which an individual saves, and the rate of return on investment.

- Future life expectancy after retirement and thus future annuity rates (either explicit within a DC scheme or implicit within a DB scheme).

Figure 4.13 Gross Replacement Rates from the State System Assuming that No Private Saving Takes Place: If Current Indexation Approaches were Continued over the Long-Term

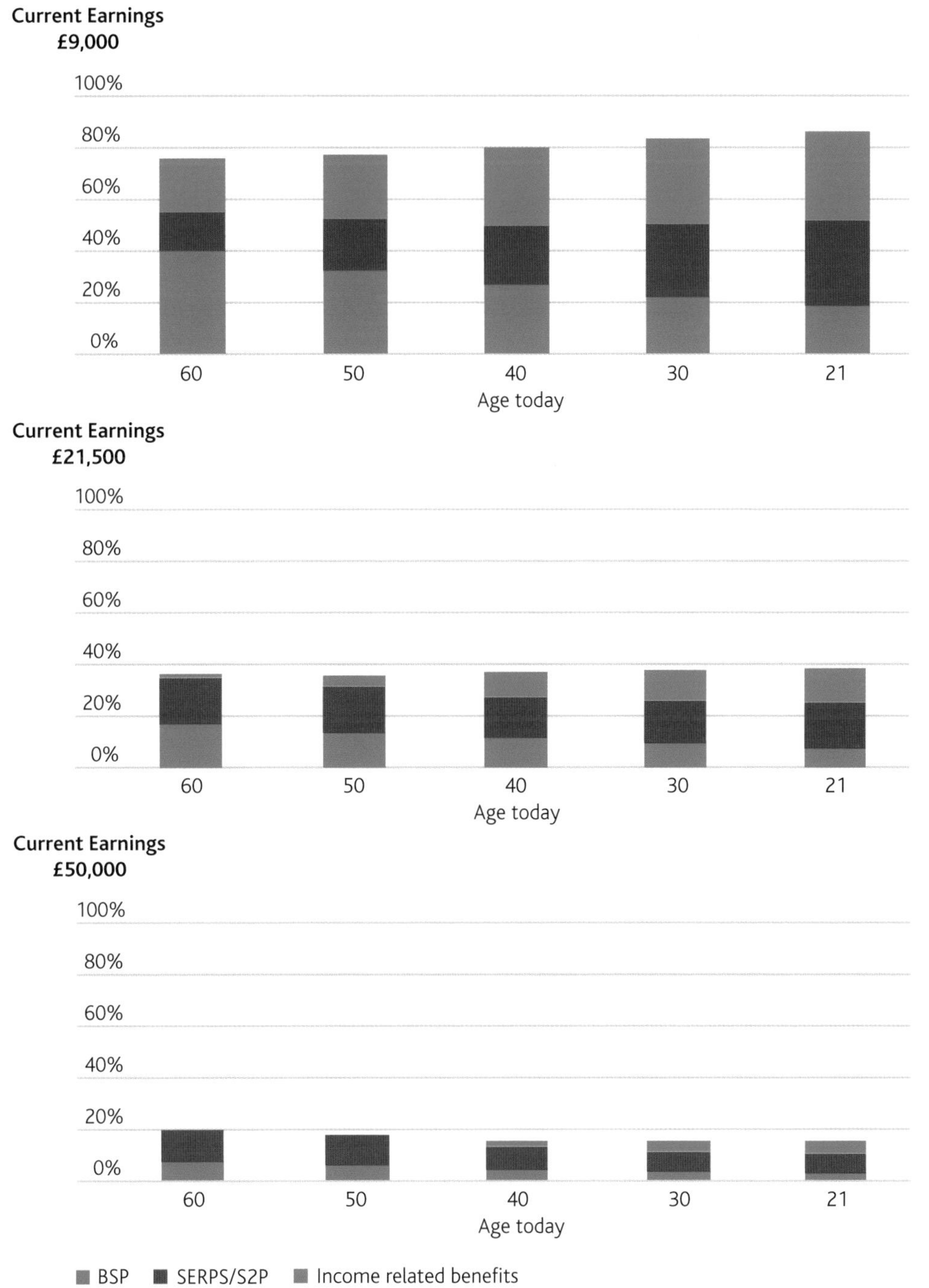

Source: Pensions Commission analysis based on DWP data

Note: These replacement rates assume the continuation over the long-term of current indexation approaches: BSP indexed to prices. Guarantee Credit indexed to average earnings.

Tables 4.6-4.8 illustrate the savings rates which would be required to achieve different levels of replacement from private saving alone (i.e. assuming no state pension). They show how this varies on different assumptions for one particular category of person: a 40 year old male owner-occupier employee on about median earnings.

- Table 4.6 illustrates how required savings rates as a percentage of earnings would vary with the target income replacement level and the number of years of saving, given a planned retirement age of 65, and assuming rates of return of 3.3% real during the accumulation period and 1.3% during the annuity.

- Table 4.7 illustrates savings rates required as target replacement rates and retirement ages vary, assuming 30 years of savings and other assumptions as in Table 4.1.

- Table 4.8 provides the matrix of required contribution rates given different combinations of target replacement rate and rates of return during the accumulation period.

The wide range of possible results carries one obvious implication: some of the trade-offs included, e.g. between savings rates and retirement age, cannot be determined by policy makers and government and should to a significant degree reflect personal choice, which needs to be as well-informed as possible. There are moreover severe data availability barriers to modelling at the level of detail required to capture all these different variables.

Table 4.6 Required contribution rates to achieve target replacement rates: depending on the number of years of saving

Total gross replacement rate from private saving	Start saving at 40	at 35	at 30	at 25
20%	9%	7%	6%	4%
30%	14%	11%	8%	7%
40%	19%	14%	11%	9%
50%	23%	18%	14%	11%

Source: Pensions Commission analysis

Note: Assuming a man aged 40 earning £21,500 per year, rate of return 3.3% and retiring at 65.
Gross replacement rate from contributory state pensions is 28%, assuming a 44 year working life.

Table 4.7 Required contribution rates to achieve target replacement rates: depending on the age of retirement

Total gross replacement rate from private saving	Retire at 55	at 60	at 65	at 70
20%	9%	8%	7%	6%
30%	14%	12%	11%	9%
40%	19%	17%	14%	12%
50%	24%	21%	18%	15%

Source: Pensions Commission analysis

Note: Assuming a man aged 40 earning £21,500 per year, saving for 30 years, with a 3.3% rate of return. Gross replacement rate from contributory state pensions is 28%, assuming a 44 year working life.

Table 4.8 Required contribution rates to achieve target replacement rates: depending on the rate of return on saving

Total gross replacement rate from private saving	Rate of return 2.5%	3%	3.5%	4%
20%	8%	7%	7%	6%
30%	12%	11%	10%	9%
40%	16%	15%	14%	13%
50%	20%	19%	17%	16%

Source: Pensions Commission analysis

Note: Assuming a man earning £21,500 per year, saving for 30 years from age 35 and retiring at 65. Gross replacement rate from contributory state pensions is 28%, assuming a 44 year working life.

But to develop an initial indication of current pension saving adequacy for different groups of people we have used the following **assumptions and simplifications.**

- Benchmark income replacement rates which fall from 80% for someone on £9,000 per year to 50% for someone on £50,000. We assume 67% for someone on median earnings as shown in Figure 4.11. We also consider an alternative scenario with lower replacement rates in Appendix G.

- The average retirement age is 65, compared with current retirement ages of 63.8 for men and 61.6 for women. While this is a feasible rise for those currently, say, 30, it may not be possible to achieve this rise for older age groups, and our figures may therefore understate the savings gaps for these groups. Future development of our model will allow more realistic modelling of possible retirement ages over time.

- A real rate of return after all costs of 3.8% for occupational schemes and 3.3% for personal pensions during the accumulation period, and of 1.3% during the annuity phase. These different assumptions for occupational and personal pensions reflect the different average administrative costs of these schemes, which are considered in Chapter 6. [See also Appendix C for details]. We also consider an alternative scenario with higher rates of return in Appendix G.

- People start saving aged 35 and keep saving for 30 years. We also consider an alternative scenario in which saving starts at 25 years old and last for 40 years. It is important to note that both these variants assume that when we observe, say, a 55 year old man saving at 8% of earnings we can assume that he has been saving at that level since he was either 35 or 25 years old. This is a hugely simplifying assumption, necessitated by severe data deficiencies which we outline below, and will almost certainly lead us to underestimate the number of under-savers.

Combining these assumptions with Figure 4.13's description of what the state will deliver, allows us to define the level of private saving required at different ages and different incomes. These levels assume that people are contracted-in to SERPS/S2P. For someone who is contracted-out required savings rates would be on average about 5% higher.

- Table 4.9 illustrates how these savings rates vary for a man who starts saving at age 35. The required savings rate of a man aged 35-44 with income of £9,000 is zero because employees on that income will receive the target 80% replacement rate from state pensions and benefits. The required rate declines slightly at high income levels because of the lower target replacement assumed. It is higher for those currently aged 35-44 than for older groups because the state pension system is becoming less generous over time and because life expectancy is increasing, reducing the assumed annuity rate.

- Table 4.10 illustrates the lower savings rates required if savings starts at 25 years old. They are significantly lower, but many people do not start saving this early.

- Table 4.11 illustrates how required rates vary by gender and employment status, for two combinations of age and income. Women require slightly higher savings rates than men because of greater life expectancy and lower annuity rates. Self-employed people require higher rates because they are not members of SERPS/S2P.

It is obvious that many people fall well short of these average savings rates. Not only are many people not saving for a pension at all; but most members of DC schemes will also fall short of these levels given the distribution of total employer plus employee contributions typically being made. People with earnings above £17,500 per annum who start saving at 35 usually need to be saving 10% or more of gross earnings (either via their own or via employer contributions) **in addition to National Insurance SERPS/S2P contributions or rebates.** But the Pensions Commission estimates that around 90% of all DC scheme active members have combined contribution rates (on a contracted-in basis) below this level, many significantly so [Figure 4.14].

Looking at personal pensions, Inland Revenue data also suggest that for many individuals contribution rates are below this level [Figure 4.15].

The next section of this Chapter explores how many such under-savers there may be.

Table 4.9 Required Contribution Rates to an Occupational Pension for a Male Employee Starting Saving at 35 and Retiring at 65: Assuming Contracting-In to SERPS/S2P

		Age today			
Replacement rate	**Income**	**25-34**	**35-44**	**45-54**	**55-64**
80%	£9,000	n/a	0%	1%	6%
70%	£13,500	n/a	11%	9%	8%
67%	£21,250	n/a	13%	11%	10%
60%	£32,500	n/a	13%	11%	9%
50%	£50,000	n/a	12%	10%	9%

Source: Pensions Commission analysis

Note: [1]Assuming 3.8% rate of return. For personal pensions a 3.3% rate of return is assumed and this increases the level of required contribution rates by about 1%.
[2]For anyone contracted-out, the required contribution rates would be about 5% higher.

Table 4.10 Required Contribution Rates to an Occupational Pension for a Male Employee Starting Saving at 25 and Retiring at 65: Assuming Contracting-In to SERPS/S2P

		Age today			
Replacement rate	**Income**	**25-34**	**35-44**	**45-54**	**55-64**
80%	£9,000	0%	0%	1%	4%
70%	£13,500	6%	6%	6%	5%
67%	£21,250	8%	8%	7%	6%
60%	£32,500	8%	8%	6%	6%
50%	£50,000	8%	7%	6%	5%

Source: Pensions Commission analysis

Note: [1]Assuming 3.8% rate of return. For personal pensions a 3.3% rate of return is assumed and this increases the level of required contribution rates by about 1%.
[2]For anyone contracted-out, the required contribution rates would be about 5% higher.

Table 4.11 Required Contribution Rates, by Sex and Employment Type

	35 – 44 year olds earning £13,500 per year	**45 – 54 year olds earning £21,250 per year**
	Target replacement rate 70%	**Target replacement rate 67%**
Male employee	11%	11%
Female employee	12%	13%
Male self-employed	18%	18%
Female self-employed	20%	21%

Source: Pensions Commission analysis

Note: Assuming 3.8% rate of return for occupational pensions for employees and a 3.3% rate of return for personal pensions, starting saving at 35 and retiring at 65.

Figure 4.14 Estimated Distribution of Combined Employee and Employer Contribution Rates in Occupational DC Schemes Adjusted for Contracting-Out

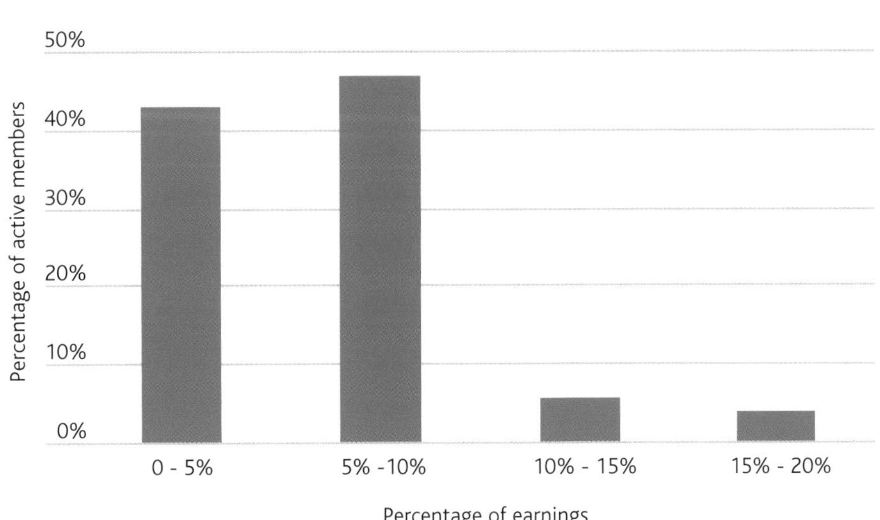

Source: Pensions Commission estimates based on data from occupational pension schemes 2000, GAD

Note: Results are based only on those schemes that responded to the question.

Figure 4.15 Distribution of Employer and Individual Contribution rates to Personal and Stakeholder Pensions

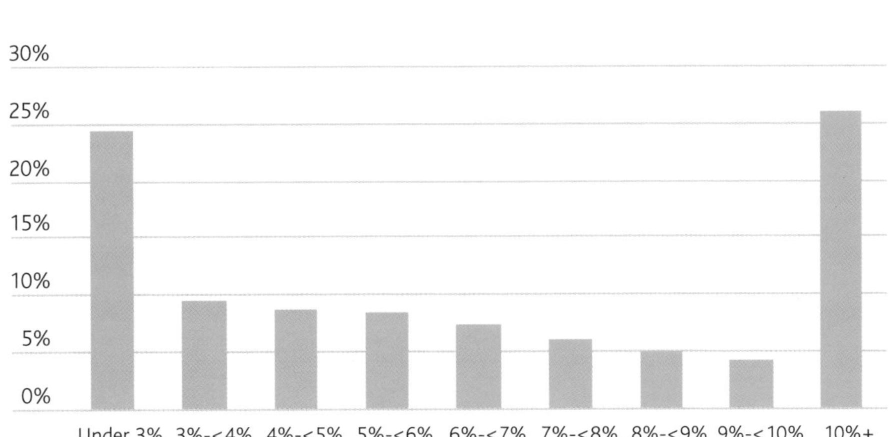

Source: Inland Revenue estimates based on Third Party Information 2001-02 and Survey of Personal Incomes 2000-01.

Note: Percentage of workers (employed/self-employed) with earnings during the year and contributions to personal, Group Personal or Stakeholder Pensions.
The Inland Revenue have matched a sample of the Third Party Information (TPI) cases to the Survey of Personal Incomes (SPI) by NI number in order to obtain corresponding earnings. The SPI and TPI data that are matched refer to different years due to different timings of availability.
Where both the employer and the individual contribute to an arrangement, their separate contributions are summed.
If an individual has two arrangements the contributions from both are summed.
This excludes any contracted-out NI rebates.

5. Future pension adequacy: deficient for many: Group model results

To identify accurately whether individuals are on target to meet the benchmarks of income replacement, we would need to know both their rate of current pension saving and their accumulated stocks of past pension savings. In fact, as Appendix A explains, the data available does not allow this: it is highly imperfect in respect to rates of new pension saving, and almost entirely non-existent on accumulated pension stocks.

We have therefore had to make a number of simplifying assumptions. Most of these will tend to result in an underestimate of the number of people making inadequate provision.

Our key simplifying assumptions are:

- People save continuously throughout life, starting at 35 (or 25). In fact many people, particularly women, and part-time workers, have interrupted savings patterns.

- All people accrue full BSP rights, and all employees at the relevant income levels accrue 44 years of SERPS/S2P rights. In fact many people, and again particularly women and part-timers, do not.

- We have modelled on an individual basis, ignoring the fact that some people may be able to rely on a spouse's pension. This partly reflects the unavailability of data, but also the principle, proposed in Chapter 8, that we must increasingly focus on an individual rights approach to assessing pension adequacy, given the increasing number of women and men who are entering retirement not part of an on-going marriage.

- We assume that all current members of private sector DB schemes and public sector pension schemes will be adequately provided for whatever the current contribution rates. This reflects the fact that almost all DB pension promises have an underlying value to the employee of more than 20% of salary, (and of close to 20% even on a contracted-in basis) and that future contribution rates will have to rise to fund these obligations. But while this is true for those who stay in their current employment, many current members of DB schemes will leave their employer before retirement and in the majority of cases move to a less generous DC scheme. Our estimates therefore represent a snapshot of under-savers today. The situation will get worse as the DB-DC shift works through.

- The distribution of DC contributions is the same for all age, sex and income groups. In fact we know that the upper tail of the distribution is heavily influenced by executive pension schemes. We may therefore tend to underestimate the number of DC scheme under-savers of average and lower earnings. One factor that might offset this slightly is that we have used the GAD 2000 source for the distribution of occupational DC contributions, and it is possible that DC contributions have increased slightly since then.[4]

- For low income house renters we assume that the higher percentage of income replaced by the government (as a result of housing benefit) fully offsets the higher replacement rate needed to cover rent expenditure, (ie we have assumed no difference in required savings between homeowners and renters). This is an over-generous assumption used for reasons of modelling simplicity. In fact housing benefit does not always fully offset the costs of renting. We may therefore underestimate the number of under-savers among low income renters.

Our estimates should therefore be treated as indicating the **minimum number of people under-saving in pensions**. [The issue of whether some of them will be adequately provided for because of housing and other non-pension assets is considered in Chapter 5]. The true figure for pensions under-savers is probably already substantially higher and will grow over time with the DB-DC shift. Over the next year the Pensions Commission aims to develop a more realistic model of under-saving, building on the Pensim 2 model being developed within DWP, and drawing on data on the stock of accumulated pension saving being developed (though only for the 50-65 year old group) from the ELSA survey.

Our initial base case results suggest that there are **around 9.6 million people who are either not saving for pensions or are under-saving**, and illustrates some important features of how the problem varies by age and income group. However it is important to note that some of these people are under-saving by relatively small amounts. Running an alternative scenario with target replacement rates which are 5 percentage points lower reduces the number of people who are not saving or under-saving to 8.5 million. This illustrates the sensitivity of results to the adequacy benchmarks selected.

[4]Note The assumption of the same distribution for all ages is also simplistic given that many DC schemes have contributions increasing with age. But this is offset by the fact that we are assuming that the savings rates required and actually observed are flat with age, whereas a sophisticated life-cycle consumption model would suggest that they should be lower for younger age groups and higher for older.

Our findings for the base case assumption that people start saving at 35 are summarised in Figure 4.16. The alternative scenario, with saving starting at 25, is summarised in Figure 4.17. Some key features to note are:

- There is a significant group of people in income bands below £9,500 who do not need to save because the state system itself will on current plans deliver an adequate replacement rate. Note however, that this assumes full BSP and 44 years of SERPS/S2P accrued. For those not achieving that accrual there will still be a savings gap not shown in our current estimates.

- In Figure 4.16, where we assume that savings should start at 35, people below 35 are assumed to be in the "don't need to save" category. But if we assume, as per Figure 4.17, that saving should and does start at 25, large numbers of 26-35 year olds show up as under-savers. Conversely in this scenario the percentage of those aged over 35 years who are under-saving goes down, since the required rate of savings would be reduced if savings did indeed start at age 25.

The total number of under-savers suggested by Figure 4.16 (i.e. with savings starting at age 35) is 9.6 million [Table 4.12], of which 5.2 million are not saving at all and 4.4 million are saving, but not enough. Sixty per cent of all in work aged over 35 are under-saving in our base case [Table 4.13]. With the alternative 40 years of saving assumption, the percentage under-saving falls to 54% of all 26-59/64 year olds, while the estimated number of under-savers rises to 12.1 million, reflecting the fact that it is assumed that 25-34 year olds should now be saving.

These under-savers moreover are not concentrated solely among the groups which were always ill-provided for in the UK system: women, the self-employed and part-timers. Sixty-six per cent (0.6 million) of employed men aged 36-45 and earning from £17,500-£24,999 appear to be not saving enough to achieve the income replacement benchmark [Figure 4.18].

Figure 4.16 Base Case Results: Savings Start at Age 35

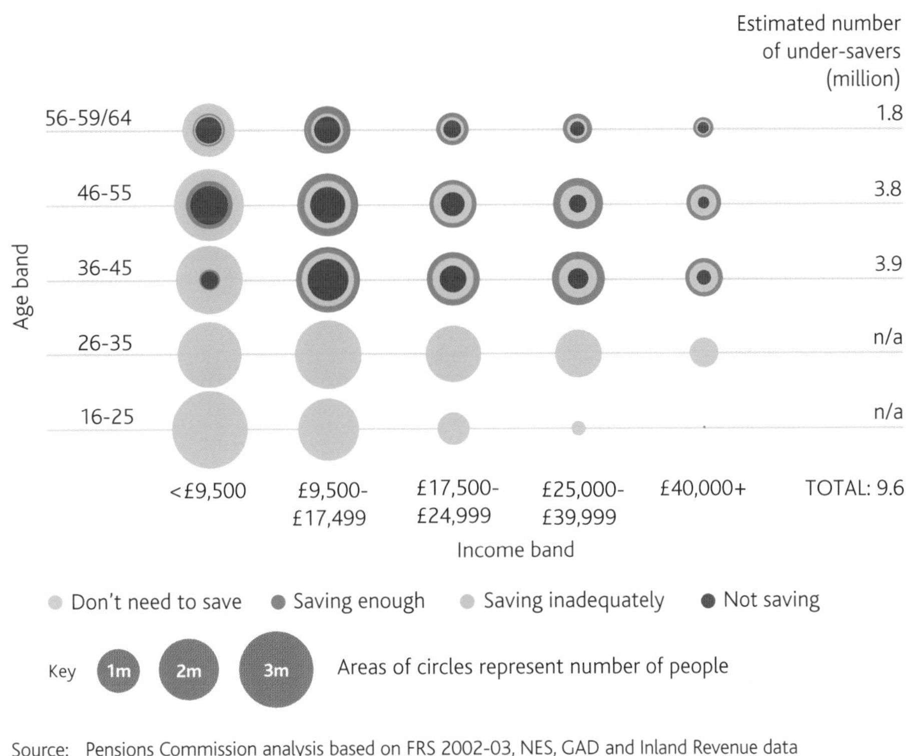

Source: Pensions Commission analysis based on FRS 2002-03, NES, GAD and Inland Revenue data

Note: See Appendix G for further details.
Under-savers includes those saving inadequately and those not saving.

Figure 4.17 Alternative Scenario 1 Results: Saving Starts at Age 25

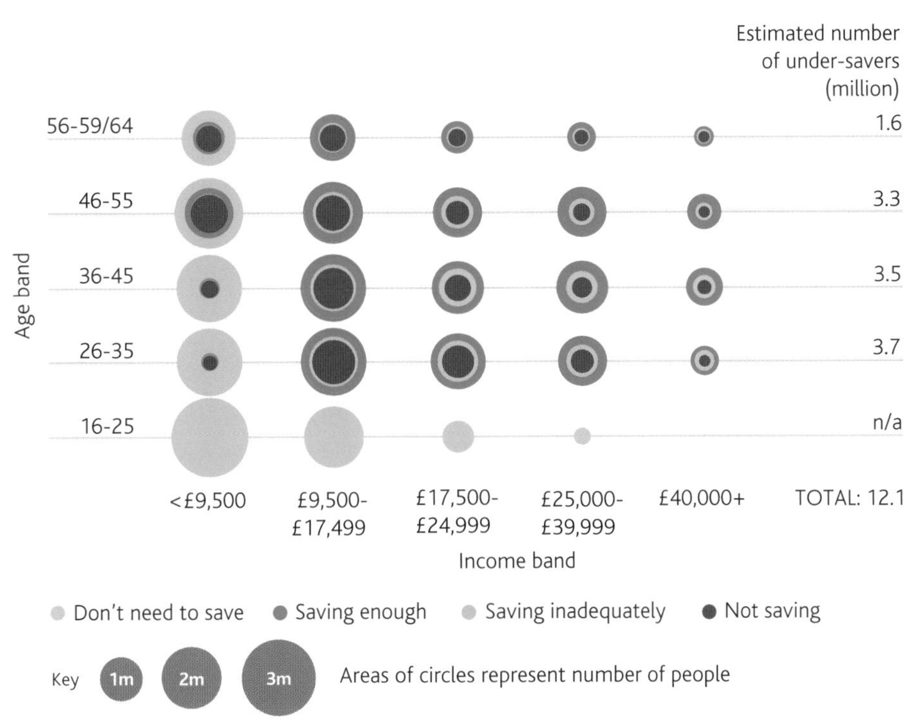

Source: Pensions Commission analysis based on FRS 2002-03, NES, GAD and Inland Revenue data

Note: See Appendix G for further details.
Under-savers includes those saving inadequately and those not saving.

Table 4.12 Numbers of Under Savers and Non-savers (millions), Assuming Savings Start at 35

Age band	26 - 35	36 - 45	46 - 55	56 - 59/64	All over 35
Income band					
< £9,500	n/a	0.2	0.8	0.5	1.5
£9,500-£17,499	n/a	1.4	1.2	0.6	3.3
£17,500-£24,999	n/a	0.9	0.8	0.3	2.1
£25,000-£39,999	n/a	0.9	0.7	0.3	1.8
£40,000+	n/a	0.5	0.4	0.2	1.0
Total	n/a	3.9	3.8	1.8	9.6

Source: Pensions Commission analysis based on FRS 2002-03, GAD, NES and Inland Revenue data

Note: Totals may not add due to rounding.

Table 4.13 Numbers of Under-Savers and Non-savers: Assuming Savings Start at 35: as a percentage of those in work

Age band	26 - 35	36 - 45	46 - 55	56 - 59/64	All over 35
Income band					
< £9,500	n/a	16%	66%	77%	49%
£9,500-£17,499	n/a	73%	67%	69%	70%
£17,500-£24,999	n/a	63%	64%	64%	64%
£25,000-£39,999	n/a	57%	51%	56%	54%
£40,000+	n/a	62%	53%	59%	58%
Total	n/a	57%	61%	67%	60%

Source: Pensions Commission analysis based on FRS 2002-03, GAD, NES and Inland Revenue data

Note: Percentage of working age population over 35 years old in work.

Figure 4.18 Percentage of Non-savers and Under-Savers Among Men aged 36-45 Earning from £17,500 to £24,999: Base Case

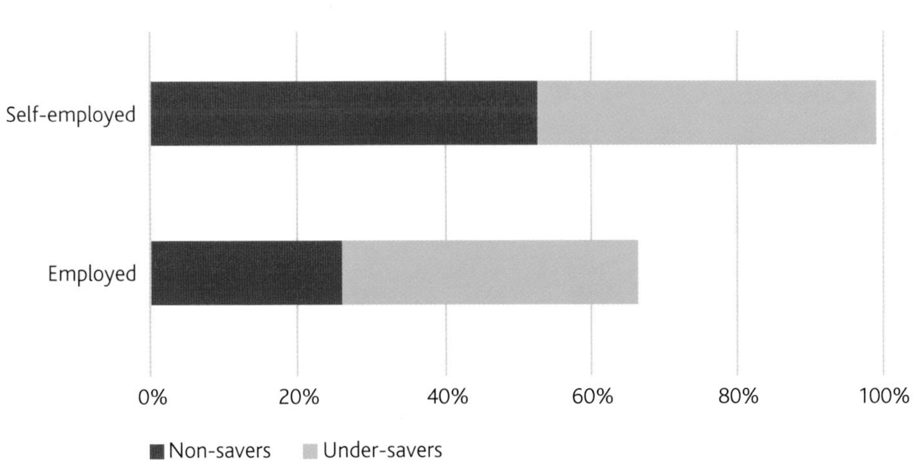

Source: Pensions Commission analysis based on FRS 2002-03, NES, GAD and Inland Revenue data

Note: As self-employed earnings can vary dramatically between years, so can their pension contributions.

This page has been left intentionally blank.

6. Future pension adequacy: increasingly unequal

Around 9 million people may therefore be heading towards inadequate retirement income, and this number is likely to increase as the DB to DC shift has an increasing effect. These people will tend to be concentrated among the groups identified in Chapter 3, where pension provision has always been deficient (women, the self-employed, employees of small firms, part-timers) but members of these groups will also be joined by an increasing number of full-time, middle earners, men and women, who are members of a pension scheme, but with inadequate contribution rates.

But conversely there are still many people on target for pensions equal to or above benchmark adequacy. A striking feature of present pension right accrual and of the outlook for pension income is the increasing inequality between different groups of people.

- **People continuing to accrue rights under DB pension schemes will be very well provided** for unless major changes are made affecting not only new members, but existing ones. Final salary pension schemes based on 60ths of salary and retirement ages of 65 have an implicit underlying contribution rate of 22-26%, far above the levels necessary to achieve our benchmark replacement rates, and over double those seen in the average DC and GPP schemes. These DB pension scheme members will include:

  - Future members of private sector DB schemes which stay open to new members. We anticipate, however, that this is unlikely to amount to more than about 1.6-1.8 million employees, and possibly far fewer, with private sector DB provision limited primarily to a small number of large companies. [See the panel "Estimating the DB to DC shift" in Chapter 3.]

  - Members of private sector DB schemes closed to new members, but still open to new accruals for existing members: There are probably about 2 million employees in this category today. For the next 40 years the workforce will include at least some employees in this category; and over a still longer period of time some will be receiving pensions. But within 20 years the vast majority will have retired or (through job changes) ceased to accrue DB rights, making this group only marginally relevant to the pattern of pension incomes for cohorts retiring from, say, 2025 onwards.

- About five million members of public sector schemes: These fall into 3 categories: the unfunded (e.g. central civil service and the armed forces); notionally funded (teachers, NHS); and the funded but guaranteed (local government). [See Table 3.2 in Chapter 3]. In addition, there are 0.1 million members in institutions (e.g. universities), which can be considered as "half way" between the public and private sectors. Given the decline of private DB schemes, these public sector schemes now represent a large and growing percentage of all pension right accrual in the UK. While the public sector accounts for 18% of all employment and a similar (17%) percentage of all earnings, it accounts for about 36% of all the already accrued occupational and personal pension rights [Figure 4.19]. And if nothing changes either in the design of public sector schemes or in the level of private pension savings, public sector schemes will over time account for a still higher proportion of all new pension right accrual, as the impact of the private sector DB scheme closure works through.

- In addition to these DB scheme members, **employees in DC schemes which do enjoy high levels of employer contributions will also be well provided for**. These people are predominantly higher income, and often in schemes only open to senior executives. Thus while there is a tail of DC schemes with employer contributions over 10%, this is predominantly explained by senior executive schemes [Figure 4.20]. And over half the regular premiums being paid into DC occupational schemes managed by life companies relates to the small minority of employees in executive pension plans [Figure 4.21].

- Finally, it should be noted again that **the lowest earners**, while obviously facing the lowest absolute level of income, **will not under present plans suffer any decline in relative position,** as long as the Guarantee Credit continues to rise with average earnings, and people claim their entitlement (which at present a significant number do not).

The conclusions from the analysis of both the macro level of future pension income and its adequacy for different groups of individuals can therefore be summarised as follows. Overall pensioner income will not rise in line with increased needs, and average pensioner incomes will fall relative to average net incomes unless average retirement ages rise by more than increased life expectancy. But with the lowest earners protected, and with some high earners, some private DB scheme members and the public sector continuing to enjoy a historically unique level of pension generosity, the impact of this decline will be concentrated on middle income earners working in the private sector.

Figure 4.19 Pensions Assets and Accrued Rights: Public and Private Sector Estimated Percentage Shares at end 2002

Source: Pensions Commission analysis based on employment data from ONS and earnings data from ungrossed NES

Notes: Total pension funds (self administered and insurance companies) £1080bn (Source: ONS Blue Book and Pensions Commission estimates). Of which self-administered are £620 billion but value of liabilities is £700 billion (with £80 billion deficit). Out of which £700 billion, 17% (£119 billion) related to public sector schemes.

Unfunded public sector liabilities estimated at £475 billion: GAD estimate for end of March 2003 £425 billion adjusted to allow for FRS 17 equivilent discount rate.

Therefore total private equals £1041billion (£1080billion plus £80 billion deficits minus £119 billion funded public sector). Total public sector £594 billion (£475 billion unfunded plus £119 billion funded).

Figure 4.20 Average Rates of Employer Contributions to Occupational DC Schemes for New Employees

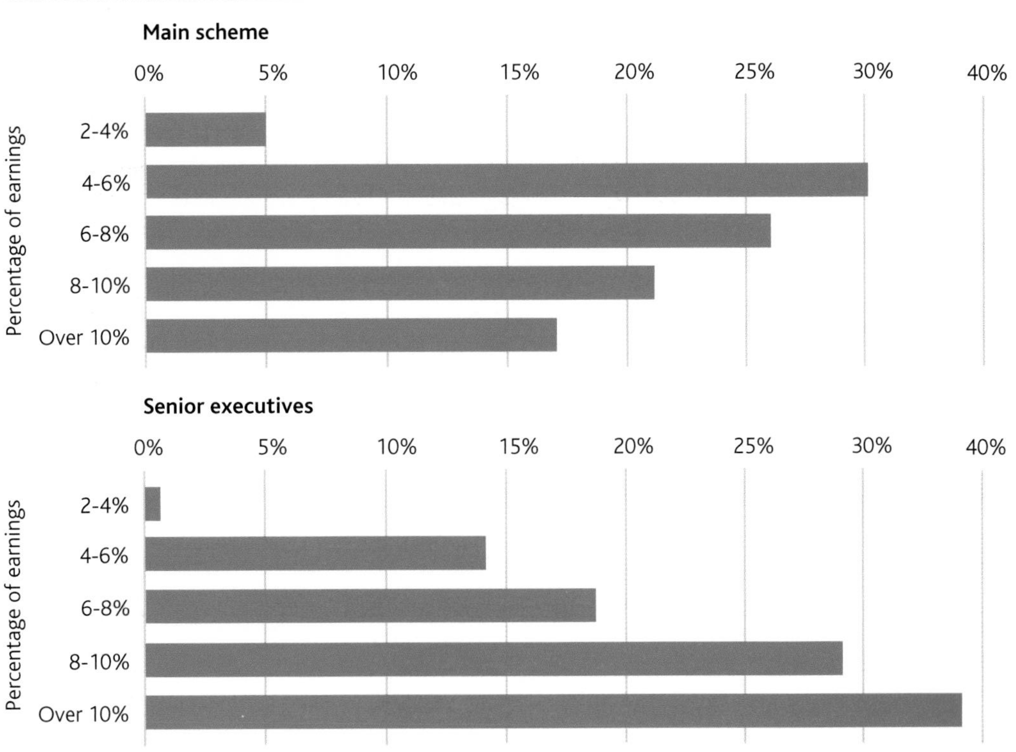

Source: Towers Perrin, Survey of Defined Contribution pension arrangements, June 2004

Note: The figures here for employer contributions to main schemes are higher than the employer element within the total contribution figures from GAD 2000 shown in Figure 4.14. This is primarily explained by the fact that we have adjusted down the GAD figures by 2.5% to reflect the contracted-in assumption in our estimates of required contribution rates. The remaining small difference may reflect sampling differences or suggest that DC contribution rates are beginning to rise. Also these results are scheme based whereas the GAD results are member based.

7. Effects over time: the biggest problems will occur in 25 years' time rather than in 10

Our analysis above has focussed on the outlook for pension provision once existing trends are fully worked through, i.e. pension adequacy given present saving levels, but given also planned changes to the state system, and the gradual working through of the DB closure effect. Within 25 years these trends will produce a severe problem of pension adequacy. But for the next 10-15 years the impact on actual pensioner income will be muted because:

- There will be many people retiring with good pensions from DB plans which have now closed to new members, but in which they have significant accumulated rights. And while there have been unfortunate cases of pension schemes closing with funds inadequate to meet these rights, looking forward the impact on total pensioner incomes is likely to be a small effect relative to the total, particularly with the creation of the Pension Protection Fund (PPF).

- There will also be a cohort of people retiring with significant SERPS rights, providing an earnings-related element to their state pension provision which will not be enjoyed by later cohorts, who will retire after the evolution towards a flat rate system has occurred. Thus although SERPS/S2P rights for a fully paid up member are forecast to become less generous over time as shown in Figure 4.3, total expenditure on SERPS/S2P pensions in payment is on a strong upward path as more people reach retirement age with significant rights [Figure 4.22].

Even in the near future there remain significant problems. The long-standing gaps in the UK pension system outlined in Chapter 3 mean that many individuals are reaching retirement with minimal private pension savings, and require means-tested benefits to achieve adequate income. Many individuals in DC schemes have suffered significant asset price falls in the last 3 years, and face lower annuity rates. Increasing numbers are likely to reach retirement age with inadequate resources even over the next 10-15 years.

But at the macro and "on average" level the major challenge we face is more concerned with getting the pension system right for those people retiring from, say, 2025 onwards, than fixing problems likely to be reflected in pensioner incomes over the next 10 years.

Figure 4.21 Contributions to Insured Occupational Pension Schemes, by Type: 2002 Prices

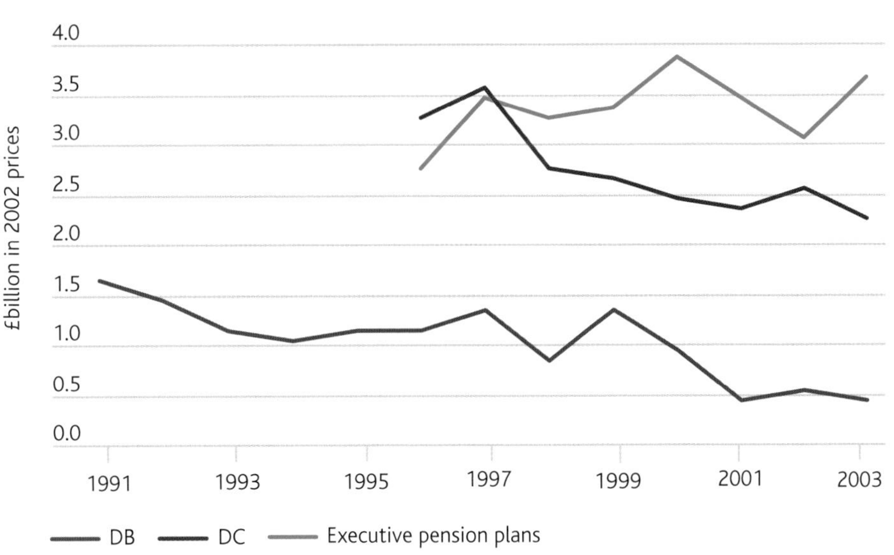

Source: ABI Long Term Insurance Statistics

Figure 4.22 Forecast SERPS/S2P Expenditure as a Percentage of GDP

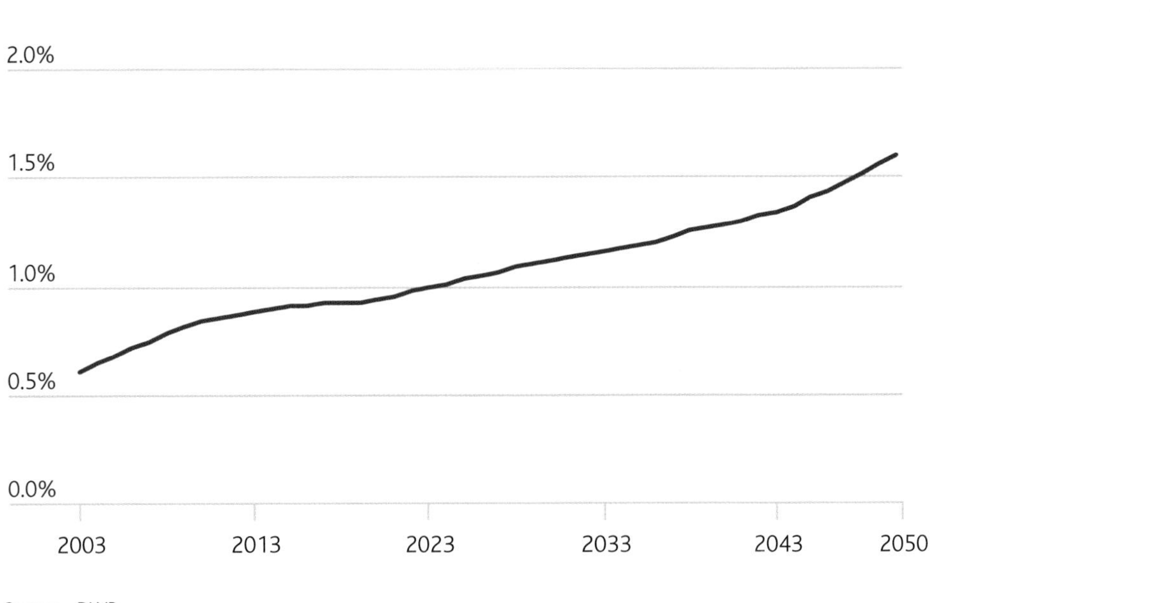

Source: DWP

8. The do-nothing option: possible, but not the best way forward

If policy and behaviour do not change many British people will face retirement incomes which they will consider inadequate. But it is worth noting that there is a do-nothing option. If we do nothing, many people, in particular of middle income levels, will reach their planned retirement age with inadequate pension funds, and will then have to accept lower than planned pension income, or keep working longer than they had intended. Others will retire on attractive pensions, and feel no need to delay retirement. In some fashion, the numbers will balance out.

But this is not the best way forward for society. People who fail to foresee later retirement are unlikely to make the career and training decisions which will maximise their job opportunities and income in later working life. Excessively generous pensions for some people will allow them to take earlier retirement than others, reducing total economic resources available. The increasing inequality of pension provision will create major social stress; and those who lose out are likely to lobby and vote for *ad hoc* rather than intelligently planned changes to the state system, and will be a powerful political force given the increasing proportion of elderly people in the population. Such unplanned changes are likely to produce results both less socially equitable and economically less efficient than could be achieved with a more forward-looking and planned approach.

The do-nothing option is not an attractive one. We need to achieve a better way forward than muddle-through will provide.

Non-pension savings and housing

5

In addition to occupational and personal pension funds worth £1,300 billion and unfunded public sector pension rights worth about £500 billion, the personal sector owns about £1,150 billion of non-pension financial assets, some of which could also provide resources for retirement income. But the ownership of these assets is very unequally distributed, and for the majority of people they can only provide a modest contribution to their standard of living in retirement.

Housing assets are more significant, both because they are much bigger (£2,250 billion net of mortgage debt) and their ownership is more equally distributed. While the liquidation of housing assets during retirement will likely remain limited in scope, the inheritance of housing assets by people who already own a house may play an increasing role in retirement provision for many people. But house ownership does not provide a sufficient solution to the problem of pension provision given (i) uncertainty over future house prices; (ii) other potential claims on housing wealth such as long-term care; and (iii) the fact that housing wealth is not significantly higher among those with least pension rights.

Business assets, meanwhile, are important stores of wealth and potential sources of retirement provision, but for only a small minority of people. The fact that pension saving among the self-employed is not increasing therefore remains concerning.

This chapter covers eight topics:

1 Overview of personal sector wealth: how large are non-pension assets?

2 Non-pension financial assets: unequal distribution means that for the average person these will provide only modest retirement income.

3 Housing assets: almost twice as big as pension assets and more evenly distributed.

4 The macroeconomics of houses as pensions: no reason why not, but there are specific risks.

5 Using houses to fund retirement: trading down, equity release, buy-to-let, inheritance.

6 Other claims on housing assets: need for integrated life-cycle analysis.

7 Why housing is not a sufficient solution: house ownership not correlated with pension gaps.

8 Private business assets: important, but for a small minority.

1. Personal sector wealth: the overall picture

While pension fund saving plays a major role in the UK's economy and in provision for retirement, it accounts for less than 30% of net personal sector wealth held in financial and physical assets, and for about a fifth if the value of the state pension and of unfunded public sector pensions is taken into account. Table 5.1 sets out an estimate of total UK personal sector wealth with figures rounded to the nearest £50 billion to reflect the uncertainty of precise estimates. The total of £6,400 billion can be broken down into four main blocks:

- Non-pension financial wealth amounts to around £1,150 billion, with £1,300 billion of financial assets offset by £150 billion of consumer debt. In addition, the value of unquoted equity (i.e. private businesses) is estimated at about £100 billion.

- Housing wealth is now about £3,000 billion at the gross level, and £2,250 billion net of mortgage debt.

- Pension assets held by self-administered pension funds and life companies amount to about £1,300 billion. In addition, the unfunded accrued rights of public sector employees are worth about £500 billion, bringing total non-state pension assets or rights to £1,800 billion.

- The value of already accrued state pension rights (Basic State Pension (BSP) plus SERPS/S2P) is estimated at about £1,100 billion.

Table 5.1 Total personal sector balance sheet end 2003: Estimated figures to the nearest £50 billion

	Assets	Liabilities		
Cash and deposits[1]	650	150	Short-term consumer debt	Non-pension financial wealth 1,150
Securities (equities and bonds including via mutual funds)	350			
Insurance company policies (excluding pensions)	300			
Unquoted equity	100			
Residential housing	3,000	750	Mortgage debt	Net housing wealth 2,250
Pension funds and policies[2]	1,300			Non-state pension rights 1,800
Unfunded public sector pension rights[3]	500			
Accrued state pension rights	1,100			State pension rights 1,100
TOTAL	7,300	900		Net personal sector wealth 6,400
Of which				
– market assets and liabilities	5,700	900		Net market assets 4,800
– PAYG claims on future tax resources	1,600			

Source: ONS Blue book, ONS Financial Statistics, ONS MQ5, GAD, Pensions Commission estimates

[1]Note: The 'Cash and Deposits' figure is as per M4 for individuals in ONS Financial Statistics. This figure is below the figures recorded in the Blue Book Household sector balance sheet, since the household sector includes non-incorporated businesses and charities. Small judgemental adjustments to exclude these latter two groups have been made to derive personal sector estimates for other asset categories e.g. for Securities, for which the total household sector figure is £400 billion.

[2]Note: The personal sector claim against pension funds can be higher than the value of assets, to the extent of pension fund deficits (and was by about £70 billion at end 2003). Personal sector funded scheme rights might therefore alternatively be expressed as £1,400 billion, but only if there is no risk of pension fund insolvency.

[3]Note: See Table 3.2 for an explanation of the types of public sector pension schemes. £475 billion is the Pensions Commission's broad estimate of the value of unfunded liabilities at March 2003. The GAD estimate for March 2003 is £425 billion, but this will increase significantly once it is recalculated using the latest life expectancy estimates, and using an equivalent discount rate to that used in the private sector.

Of the total of £6,400 billion, £1,600 billion represents a Pay As You Go (PAYG) claim on future tax resources (for the state pensions and public sector unfunded pensions), while £4,800 billion represents the balance between £5,700 billion of marketable assets, either directly held by individuals or via pension funds and life companies, offset by £900 billion of debt.

The scale of this market-based wealth relative to GDP, and the relative importance of different categories, has changed significantly over the last 20 years and in particular over the past five.

- Over the 20 years to 1999, wealth held via pension funds and life companies grew to overtake net housing wealth. But since 1999 there has been a major reversal of this trend, with housing wealth now worth over 40% more than all pension fund and life policy wealth. Meanwhile, net financial assets held outside pension funds and life companies also grew during the 1990s with equity price rises, but are now roughly at the same level (75% of GDP) as they were in 1990 [Figure 5.1].

- Within these categories, however, an important trend towards increased gearing (borrowing against assets) is evident. Gross housing value as a percentage of GDP has fluctuated, but has grown over the whole period and is now higher than at any previous peak. However, this has been partly offset by a steady rise in mortgage debt as a percentage of GDP [Figure 5.2]. Similarly, the breakdown of net non-pension financial assets reveals three separate underlying elements: the value of securities (held either directly or via mutual funds/unit trusts) has fluctuated in line with equity price movements, but with no clear trend as a percentage of GDP; holdings of cash deposits and savings accounts show a gradual increase; while consumer debt increased gradually until the late 1990s and then rapidly in the last five years [Figure 5.3].

The significant fluctuations in the value of several of the wealth categories and the increasing level of gearing raise complex issues about the sustainability of some of these stores of wealth, in particular housing. But in principle all of these forms of wealth provide their owners with resources which could be used to support consumption in retirement. The defining characteristic of pension wealth is that it is held in a legal vehicle which requires the owner to use most of it for retirement purposes, leaving nothing to bequeath.[1] Other categories of wealth can either be run-down in retirement or bequeathed. But even if bequeathed, such assets might become relevant to retirement income adequacy in the next generation.

Given the scale of this non-pension wealth, we therefore need to consider whether it makes a significant difference to the "pension adequacy" story told in Chapters 3 and 4. This chapter considers first non-pension financial assets, then housing assets, and finally and briefly, private business assets.

[1] Note: The exception to this requirement in the UK pension systems is the "lump sum on retirement". This can be either used to fund consumption in retirement or held onto and bequeathed, and once paid is therefore a part of non-pension financial wealth. It is however locked-up until the point of retirement.

Figure 5.1 Pension Funds, Net Housing and Net Financial Assets as a Percentage of GDP

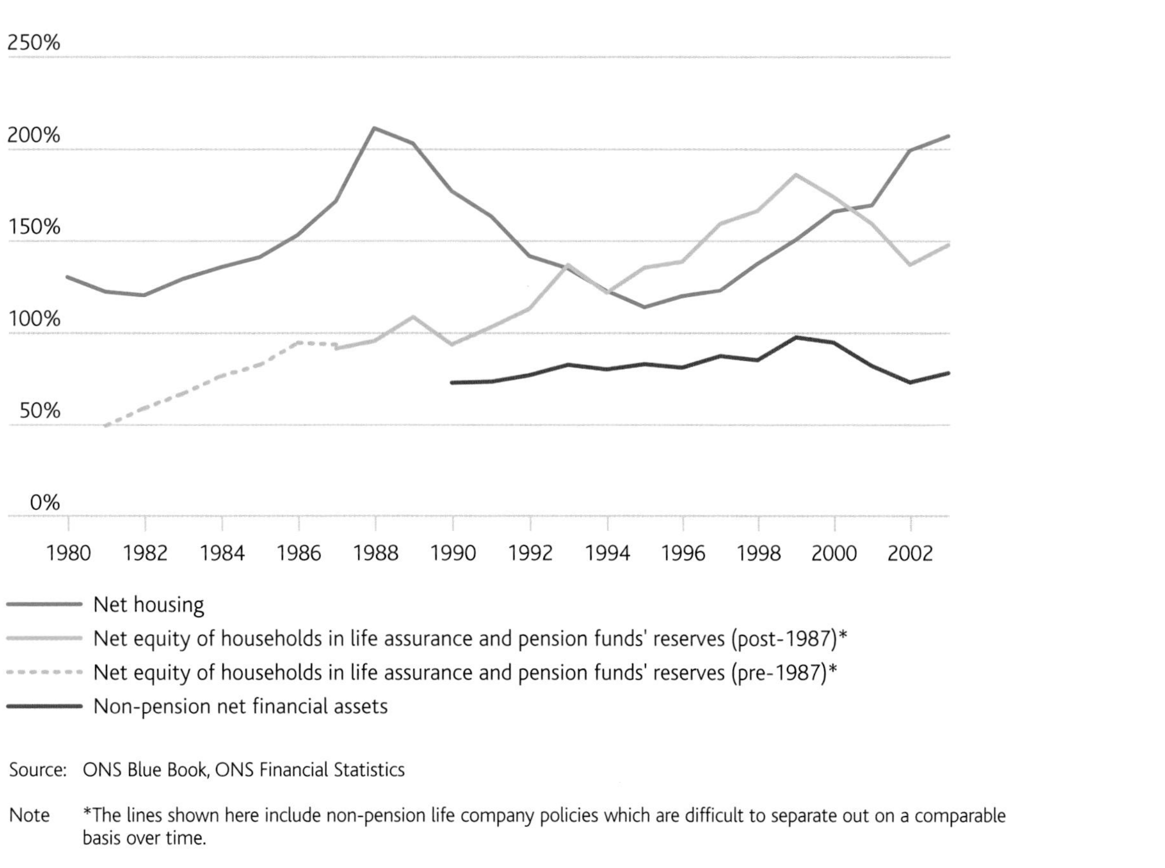

Source: ONS Blue Book, ONS Financial Statistics

Note *The lines shown here include non-pension life company policies which are difficult to separate out on a comparable basis over time.

Figure 5.2 Gross Housing Assets and Mortgage Debt as a Percentage of GDP

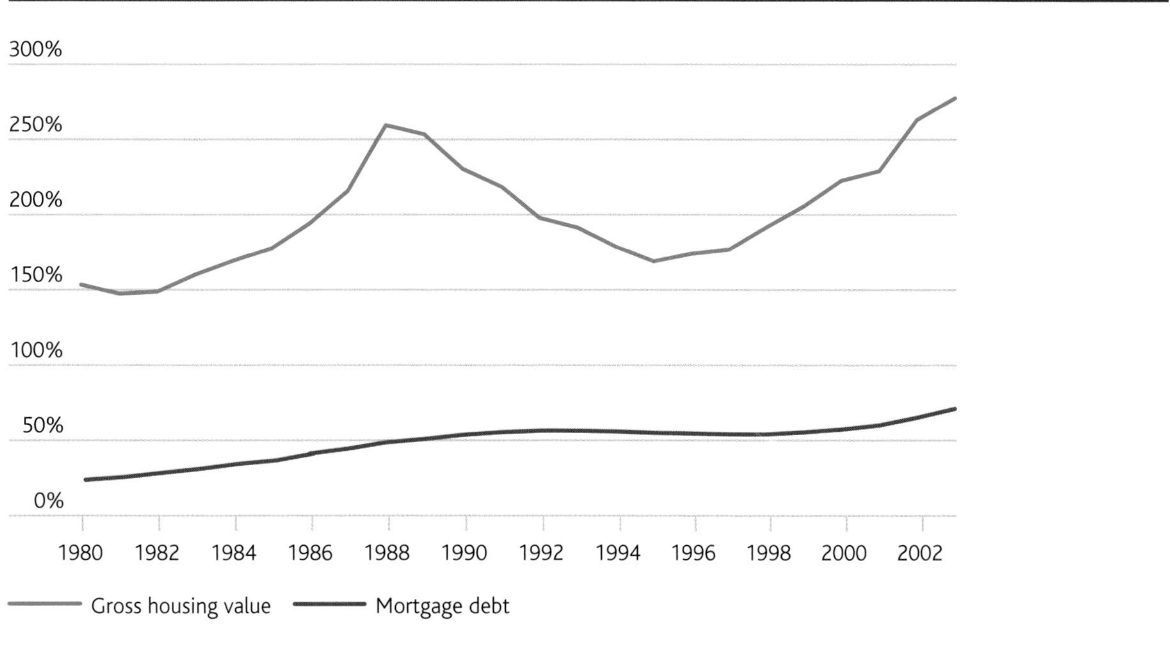

Source: ONS Blue Book

2. Non-pension financial assets

Non-pension financial assets amount today to £1,300 billion, and to £1,150 billion net of non-mortgage consumer debt [Table 5.2]. This figure overstates the extent to which financial wealth could supplement pension and housing wealth for two reasons. First, something like £50 billion derives from lump sum pension payments and this amount does not therefore add to the resources for retirement already considered in Chapter 4's analysis. Second, of the £300 billion in life company policies a significant proportion is accounted for by mortgage endowments, which are accumulated in order to repay mortgages and which (particularly given recent falls in payouts) are unlikely to provide any significant financial resources once the mortgage is repaid.[2]

However, even after these deductions (and assuming £100 billion for the mortgage endowments) £1,000 billion of net financial wealth is a large figure relative to £1,300 billion held via pension funds and life company pension policies. For some people it could make a significant difference to pension adequacy.

But for most people it will not. While financial assets are large in total, the distribution of their ownership is highly unequal and those who have deficient pensions are not more likely to have significantly more non-pension wealth. As Appendix A explains, data on the distribution of financial wealth holdings is imperfect since many people are unable or unwilling to calculate or reveal their total wealth. The surveys which provide comprehensive coverage of all age groups, such as the British Household Panel Survey (BHPS) or the MORI Financial Services Survey, produce estimates of individual wealth which do not reconcile to aggregate totals, while the new English Longitudinal Study of Ageing (ELSA), which achieves a better reconciliation to the aggregate figures, only covers people over the age of 50. Improvements in the quality of data gathering, for example through the implementation of the ONS' planned Wealth and Assets Survey, are therefore a priority to support evidence-based policy.

[2]Note: The inverse of excluding mortgage endowment policies from estimates of non-pension financial assets is that the underlying level of mortgage debt outstanding is effectively lower by the same amount.

Figure 5.3 Non-Pension Financial Assets and Non-Mortgage Debt as a Percentage of GDP

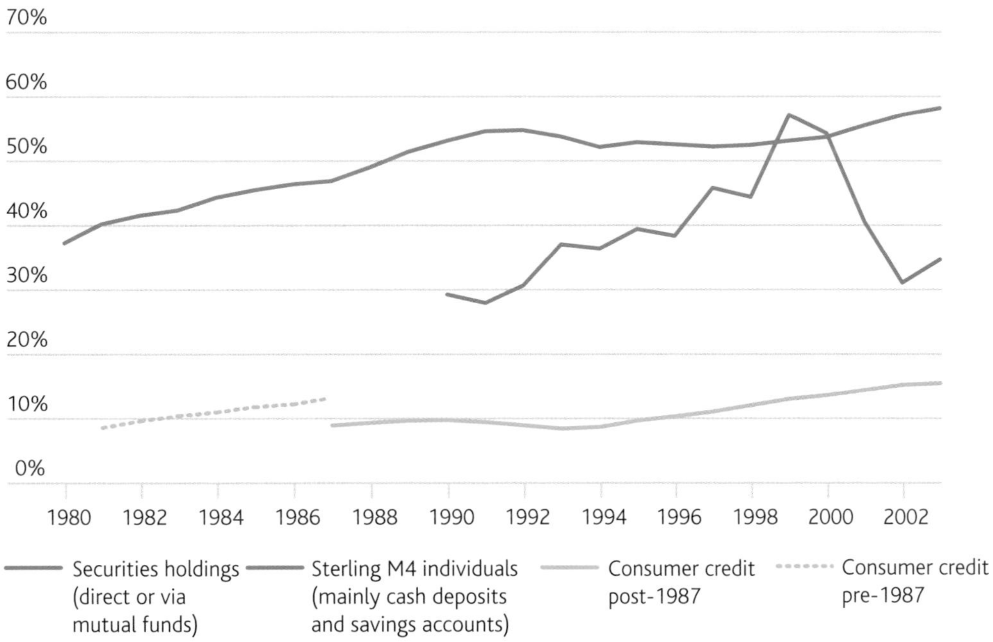

Source: ONS Blue Book, ONS Financial Statistics

Note: Data on consumer credit for individuals (excluding sole proprietor businesses and non-profit making bodies) are only available back to 1987. Data for previous years are not on a comparable basis; data were available for the personal sector, which additionally covered partnerships and sole proprietorships. In addition, the personal sector series of UK bank lending included lending by offshore banks.

Table 5.2 Personal sector non-pension financial assets: 2003

	Assets (£ billion)	Liabilities (£ billion)	
Cash and deposits	650	150	Non-mortgage consumer debt
Securities held directly[1]			
– Equities	up to 200		
– Bonds	up to 40		
Securities held via mutual funds/ unit trusts	up to 135		
Insurance company policies (non-pension)	300		
ESTIMATED TOTAL	1,300	150	

Source: ONS Blue Book, ONS Financial Statistics

[1]Note: Securities holdings are denoted as "Up to x", since a portion is held by charities and unincorporated businesses.

Nevertheless, key features of the distribution of the ownership of non-pension financial wealth by age and income can still be discerned from the existing data and are confirmed by each of the different sources:

- Non-pension financial wealth holding reveals a fairly strong life-cycle pattern, with very limited asset holding among people under 40, significant accumulations by people in their 50s, and then a significant liquidation of assets during retirement years. This pattern is found whether we look at the mean for each age group or at the median, which is always considerably lower due to the concentration of wealth holding at the top of the wealth distribution [Figures 5.4 and 5.5]. This concentration also explains why the median figure falls proportionately more during retirement than the mean. The median person (the person in the middle of the wealth distribution), and indeed people at the 75th percentile of wealth, probably liquidate the majority of their net financial wealth during retirement while at the top end of the wealth distribution the majority of net financial wealth is bequeathed [Figure 5.6].

- Financial wealth is also very unequally distributed even within the same age band. Looking at the ELSA survey for the 55-59 year age group (the group which has the highest mean wealth level and which is approaching retirement age) we find that average holdings of financial wealth are much more unequally distributed than housing wealth [Figure 5.7]. People in the £25,000 plus income bracket have over seven times as much financial wealth as those in the under £9,500 band, compared with two and a half times as much housing wealth. And even for people within the same age and income band, a high level of inequality is found. Among 55-59 year olds with income of £17,500-£24,999, the ratio of holdings of financial wealth between those at the 75th and at the 25th percentile is 10:1, while for housing wealth it is slightly less than 3:1 [Figure 5.8]. In total the ELSA figures suggest that 50-59 year olds own at least £165 billion of non-pension financial assets, but since the top quarter owns 84% of this, the relevance of large non-pension financial assets to the issue of pension adequacy is greatly diminished.[3]

[3]Note: Since surveys of wealth holding tend to undersample the very wealthy, these figures will probably be an underestimate of aggregate holdings of this group.

Figure 5.4 Net Non-Pension Financial Wealth Holding, by Age: MORI MFS Estimates

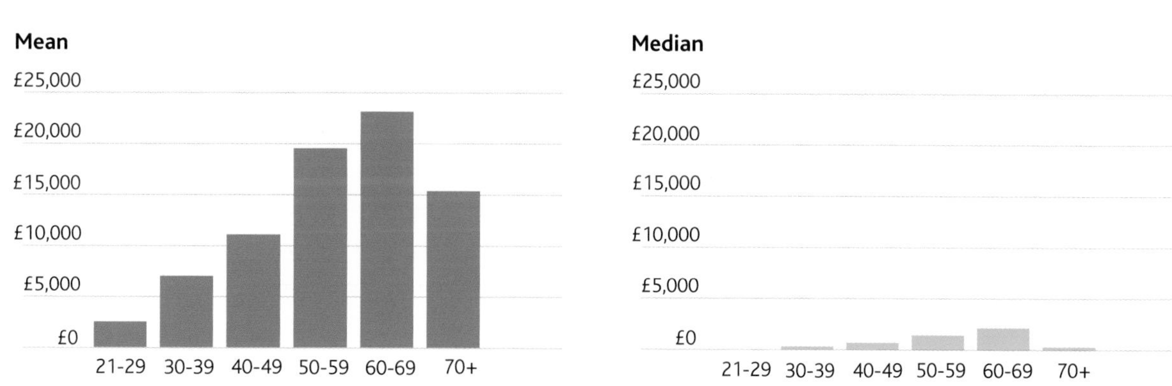

Source: MFS, 2003, GB

Note: Only personal loan and credit card debt are offset against savings and investments, as values for other types of debt were not available for 2003. These figures probably understate the level of assets in all age groups, but the finding of increasing holdings with age is believed to be robust as it is confirmed by other data.

Figure 5.5 Net Non-Pension Financial Wealth Holding, by Age for Those Aged 50 and over: ELSA Estimates

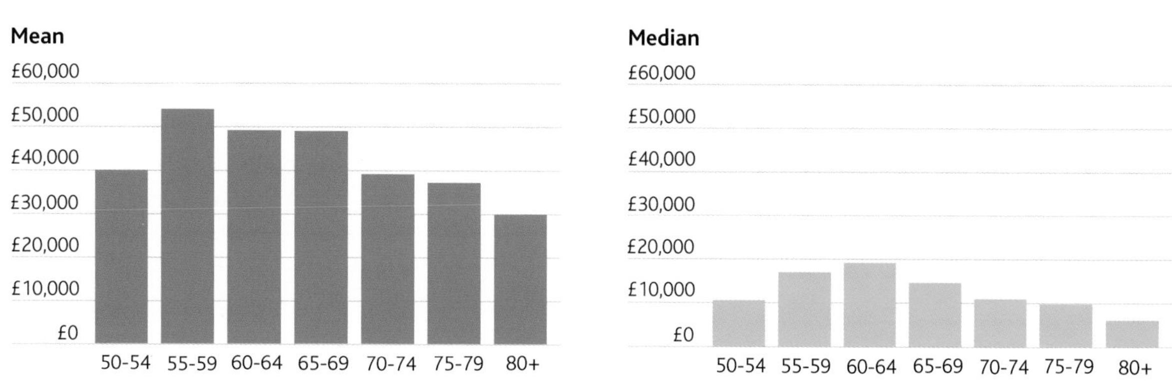

Source: ELSA, 2002, England

Note: Net financial wealth of families in the above age groups; not adjusted for family size.

The non-pension financial wealth suggested by the ELSA survey is considerably higher than that suggested by MFS or the BHPS, and reconciles better to the aggregate totals.

Figure 5.6 Net Financial Assets During Retirement, by Age for Those Aged 60 and over

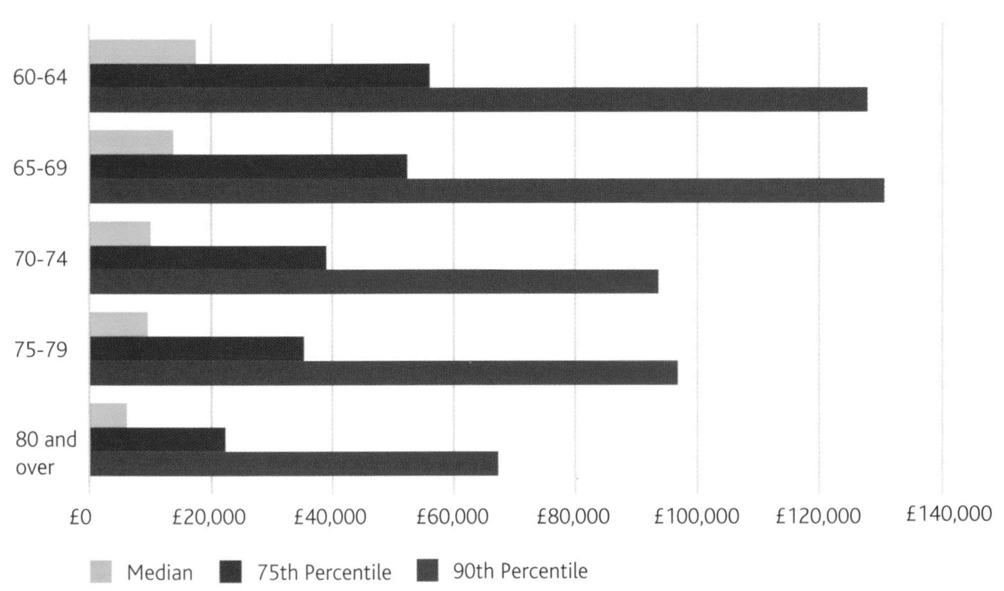

Source: Banks J, Emmerson C and Oldfield Z (2004)

Note: Percentiles of net non-pension financial wealth of population 60 years and older not in paid work.
Net financial wealth of families in the above age groups; not adjusted for family size.
The extent to which people run down their wealth with age is not fully established by this data as ELSA is not yet longitudinal.
The actual life-cycle effect could be more or less extreme than we observe.

Figure 5.7 Mean Net Financial Wealth and Mean Net Housing Wealth among those approaching Retirement, by Income

Source: Banks J, Emmerson C and Oldfield Z (2004)

Note: Data is shown for non-retired 55-59 year olds.
The non-retired include all those in work and all not in work who do not describe themselves as retired, even though some of these may never work again. Income is on an equivalised family basis and is net of income tax. Equivalisation refers to adjustments made to wealth or income to take account of the size of the family with a claim on that resource. ELSA uses the OECD equivalence scale which gives a weight of 0.5 to another adult, 0.3 to a child aged 0-13 years and 0.5 to a dependent child aged 14-18 years. Wealth is calculated on a family basis and is not equivalised.

Figure 5.8 Percentiles of Net Financial Wealth and Net Housing Wealth Among Those Approaching Retirement with Income £17,500-£24,999

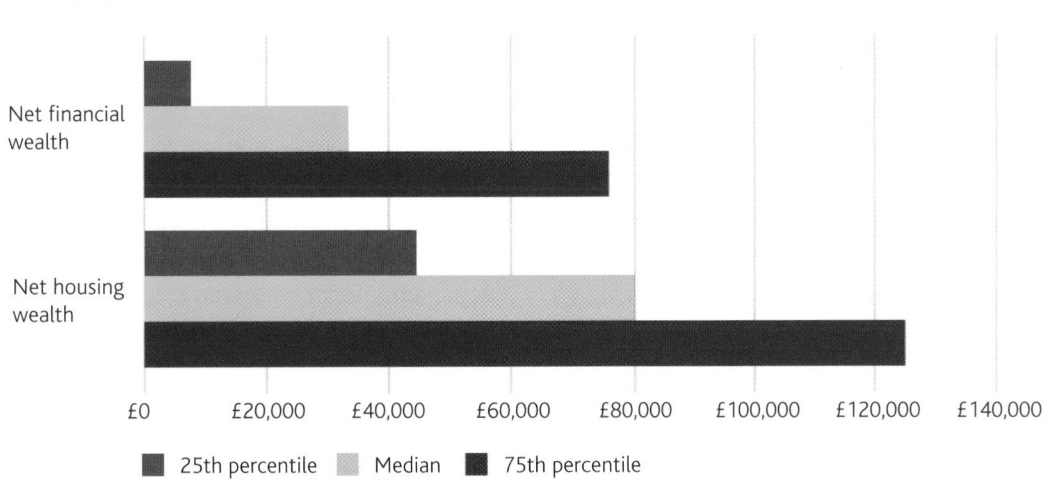

Source: Banks J, Emmerson C and Oldfield Z (2004)

Note: Data is shown for non-retired 55-59 year olds with income £17,500-£24,999.
The non-retired include all those in work and all not in work who do not describe themselves as retired, even though some of these may never work again.
Income is on an equivalised family basis and is net of income tax. Wealth is calculated on a family basis and is not equivalised.

The impact of this unequal distribution is that when we look at the financial wealth of the median person we find holdings which, while not trivial, will only make a moderate difference to pension adequacy in retirement:

- A useful benchmark is to note that the implicit value of a fully accrued Basic State Pension (BSP) at retirement is about £80,000 for men and about £88,000 for women even after State Pension Age equalisation.[4] Table 5.3 sets out median net financial assets held by non-retired 55-59 year-olds and these assets as a percentage of the BSP value. For income bands up to £17,500, the value is relatively trivial, only 3.6% for those with an income below £9,500, and 15% for those with an income between £9,500-£17,499. Only for incomes above £25,000 does the median 55-59 year old person have financial assets approaching the value of the BSP.

- And if we consider a non-retired 55-59 year old individual on median full-time earnings of around £21,000, who, according to our adequacy benchmark outlined in Chapter 4, might wish for a retirement income of almost £14,000 per year, and who might receive a full BSP of £4,139 per year, the median net financial wealth of around £33,000 will produce only about 12% of the retirement income required to achieve the adequacy benchmark [Figure 5.9].

[4] Note: These calculations are based on single-life indexed annuity rates of 5.2% and 4.7% for 65 year old men and women respectively. A fully accrued BSP is currently £4,139.20 per year.

Table 5.3 Median Net Financial Wealth among those approaching Retirement and as a Percentage of the Implicit capital value of a Fully Accrued BSP

Income Band	Median net financial wealth	As a percentage of implicit capital value of the BSP for 65 year old man
Under £9,500	£2,901	3.6%
£9,500 to £17,499	£11,950	14.9%
£17,500 to £24,999	£33,420	41.8%
£25,000 and over	£57,800	72.3%

Source: Median net financial wealth from Banks J, Emerson C and Oldfield Z (2004).
Annuity rates from Annuity Bureau, Current Rates, 2 August 2004.

Note: Data is shown for non-retired 55-59 year olds.
An implicit BSP capital value of £80,000 was calculated for a 65 year old man with a single life index-linked annuity.

Figure 5.9 Adequacy of Retirement Income Based only on BSP and Median Net Financial Wealth Among Those Approaching Retirement

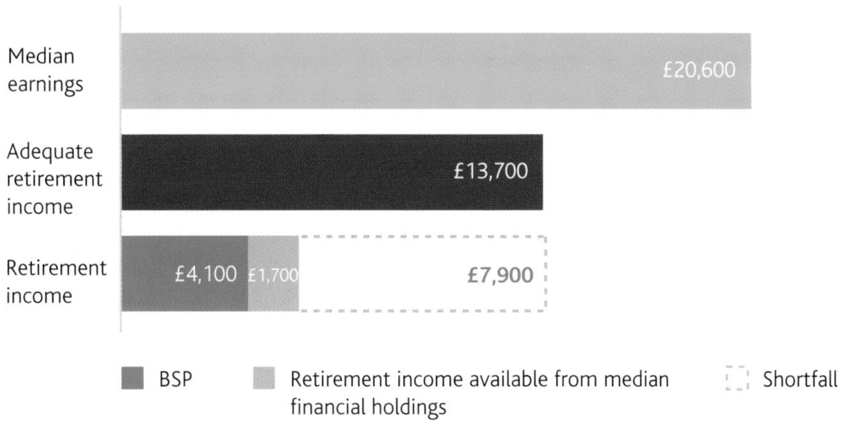

Source: NES, 2003, GB and Pensions Commission Analysis

Note: Data is shown for non-retired 55-59 year olds.
The non-retired include all those in work and all not in work who do not describe themselves as retired, even though some of these may never work again.
Median earnings is median full-time gross annual earnings for the population of male and female employees whose pay for the survey period was not affected by absence. Adequate retirement income is derived as two thirds of median gross earnings, as an example benchmark. The retirement income available from median non-pension financial holdings is derived using an annuity rate of 5% and median net financial wealth of £33,420.
The figure compares the income of an individual with the possible annuity income from the financial wealth of a couple, so that the contribution to the shortfall is an overestimate.

For the median person, therefore, net financial savings amount to a useful, non-trivial additional resource for retirement but, even if run down to zero during retirement, cannot make more than a modest contribution to income replacement. For the 50% of the population with wealth holdings below the median, the contribution to income replacement of non-pension financial assets will be still less. Such assets therefore make only a marginal difference to the assessment of pension adequacy set out in Chapter 4, unless it is the case that the people with inadequate pensions tend to be those with largest financial assets. The ELSA data suggest that this may be true to an extent, with non-pension financial assets likely to produce a larger percentage uplift to retirement income for those expecting very low private pensions, than for those expecting higher ones [Table 5.4]. But overall the pattern is that people without private pensions do not in general have significantly higher levels of financial savings than those who do [Figure 5.10].

Overall, therefore, while non-pension financial assets are large in total and non-trivial even for the average person, their liquidation during retirement can only modestly enhance the standard of living of the average pensioner. Conversely, however, the fact that, as Figure 5.6 demonstrated, they are (for the median person) largely liquidated in retirement means that inheritance of non-pension financial assets is for most people relatively trivial. If assets other than pensions are to be a major factor in retirement resources, it is to housing assets that we will have to look.

Table 5.4 Net Financial Wealth among those approaching Retirement, by Expected Private Pension Income

Expected private pension income band	Median expected pension (£)	Median net financial wealth (£)	Annuitised income from median net financial wealth (£)	Annuitised income as percentage of median expected pension
£0	0	2,350	118	n/a
£1-£2,500	1,200	12,637	632	53%
£2,501-£6,000	4,000	18,800	940	24%
£6,001-£12,500	8,750	22,510	1,126	13%
£12,501 and over	20,833	35,750	1,788	9%

Source: Median net financial wealth and median expected pension from Banks J, Emmerson C and Oldfield Z (2004). Annuity rates from Annuity Bureau, Current Rates, 2 August 2004.

Note: Data is shown for non-retired 55-59 year olds.
The non-retired include all those in work and all not in work who do not describe themselves as retired, even though some of these may never work again.
A single life indexed annuity for a 65 year old man was assumed, yielding a rate of 5%.
Median net financial wealth is on a family basis while expected pension income is on a family basis but adjusted for family size.

Figure 5.10 Net Financial Wealth among those approaching Retirement, by House Ownership and Pension Scheme Membership

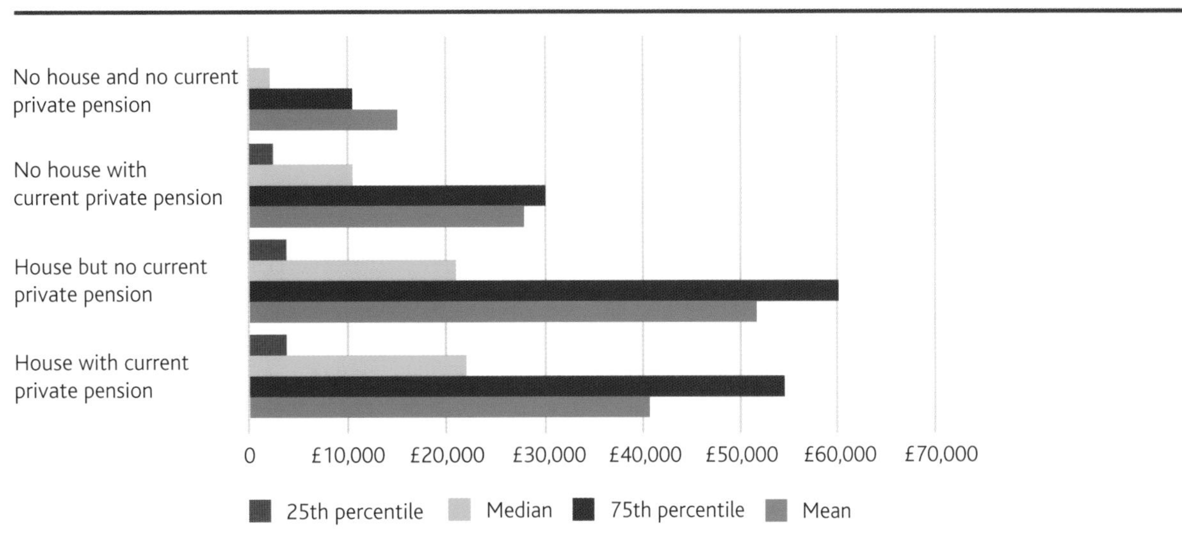

Source: Banks J, Emmerson C, Oldfield Z (2004)

Note: Data is shown for non-retired 55-59 year olds with net equivalised family income in £9500-£24,999. The non-retired include all those in work and all not in work who do not describe themselves as retired, even though some of these may never work again.

3. Housing assets

A significant proportion of people say that they see equity in their home as an alternative or additional retirement asset [Figure 5.11]. Press reports and anecdote suggest that this attitude is growing, both among the majority of people who own and occupy one home and among the small but rapidly growing minority involved in buy-to-let activities[5].

These attitudes reflect the reality that housing is potentially a far more important source of retirement income than non-pension financial assets for two reasons. First, it is in aggregate much larger, £2,250 billion of net housing equity compared to £1,150 billion of non-pension financial assets. Second, housing equity is much more evenly distributed. While inevitably, higher income people own more valuable houses, and while there are still 26% of people over 40 who do not own their own house[6], among non-retired 55-59 year olds who do, the net value of housing equity rises slightly **less** than proportionately with income, i.e. middle income people have slightly larger housing assets, relative to their income, than high income people [Table 5.5]. Housing equity at middle income levels is as a result significant in relation to the pension adequacy calculations of Chapter 4. People with income of about £21,000 have on average about £96,000 of net housing equity by the time they are 55-59 years old. **If** this were all available to fund retirement, it could give an inflation indexed pension of around £4,800[7], making a significant contribution towards the benchmark replacement income of £14,000, when combined with approximately £4,100 of BSP.

Moreover, the potential importance of housing assets is likely to increase further as the large increase in owner-occupation that occurred during the 1970s and 1980s (partially reflecting council house sales in the latter decade) works through the age profile of the population. At present, owner-occupation is highest among 45-59 year olds (78%) and then falls to 58% among those age 80 years and older. But it is increasing most rapidly among the older age groups [Figure 5.12]. And looking forward to 2030, the profile of ownership shown in Figure 5.13 is possible, with 75% of people becoming homeowners by the age of 45 and remaining so throughout the rest of their life.

These very large housing assets could be relevant to pension adequacy in two ways; either via their liquidation during retirement or via a bequest of housing assets to inheritors who on average, will themselves own houses and who can therefore sell the inherited asset to fund retirement without selling their own house. At present, the liquidation route is of minimal importance. Mean housing wealth only falls with age after retirement because older age groups

[5]Note: The CML published some empirical research on this issue in September, which suggests a large proportion of people see housing equity as a source of finance in retirement (Smith, 2004)

[6]Note: MFS, 2003, GB

[7]Note: This calculation is based on an annuity rate of 5%.

Figure 5.11 Percentage of People Planning to Draw on Property Assets During Retirement, by Age and Private Pension Membership

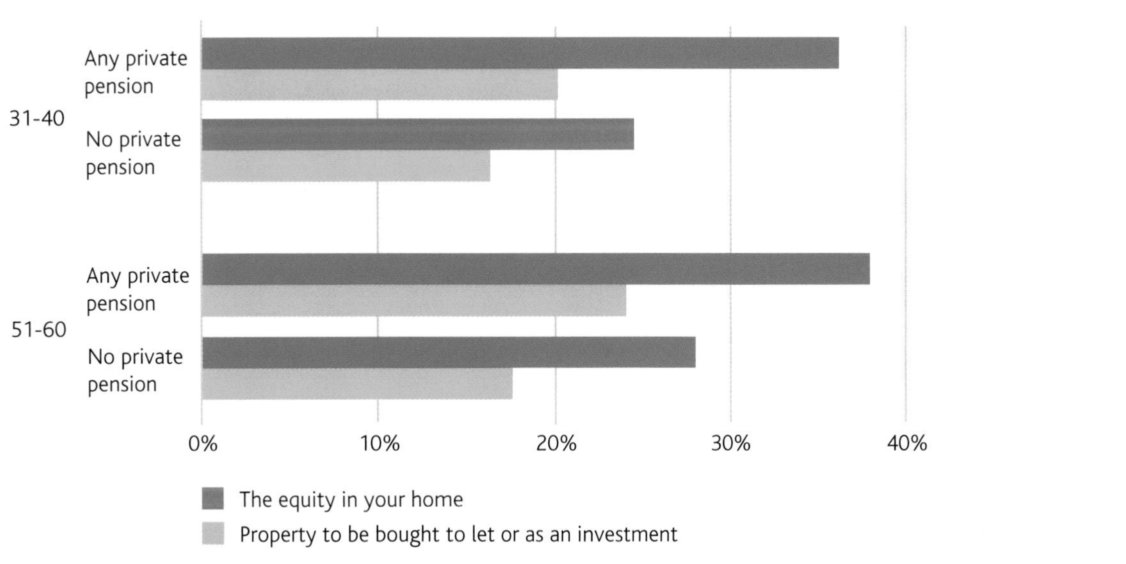

Source: NOPWorld Financial Research Survey, July 2003-May 2004

Note: Based on all non-retired population. The question asked is: We are interested in the financial plans people make for their retirement as well as or instead of pensions. Which of the following do you plan to use to provide for your retirement? A range of options is available.

Table 5.5 Net Housing Wealth of Homeowners Approaching Retirement, by Income

Net equivalised family income band	Median income (£)	Median net housing wealth (£)	Net housing wealth as a multiple of income
£0-£9,499	6,434	62,200	9.7
£9,500-£17,499	13,365	66,350	5.0
£17,500-£24,999	20,637	89,100	4.3
£25,000 and over	32,449	124,100	3.8

Source: Median income and median net housing wealth from Banks J, Emmerson C and Oldfield Z (2004)

Note: Data is shown for non-retired 55-59 year old homeowners.
The non-retired include all those in work and all not in work who do not describe themselves as retired even though some of these may never work again.

include a higher percentage of non-owners. Among those who are owner-occupiers, housing wealth does not fall during retirement, reflecting the fact that for most people the key benefit of housing wealth during retirement is the availability of rent-free living [Figure 5.14]. Thus while pension fund savings are legally required to be liquidated during retirement, and while non-pension financial assets are in fact largely liquidated except at high wealth levels, housing assets are largely kept till death and bequeathed. But these bequests could in turn be relevant to pension adequacy for the next generation.

The "house-as-pension" option cannot therefore be dismissed. To assess its validity and importance, we need to consider four issues:

- The macroeconomics of housing: are housing assets just like other assets as stores of value and as potential vehicles for inter-generational resource transfer, or are they in some sense unique?
- Methods of asset value realisation: is liquidation during retirement likely to become significant, or is inheritance of housing the key issue?
- Overall life-cycle issues: will other claims on housing assets during retirement (e.g. long-term care) or other changes in financial behaviour by age (e.g. the rise of student debt and later house purchase) offset the impact of higher home ownership among the elderly?
- Distributional issues: what is the correlation between pension asset and housing asset ownership?

Figure 5.12 Home Ownership by Age

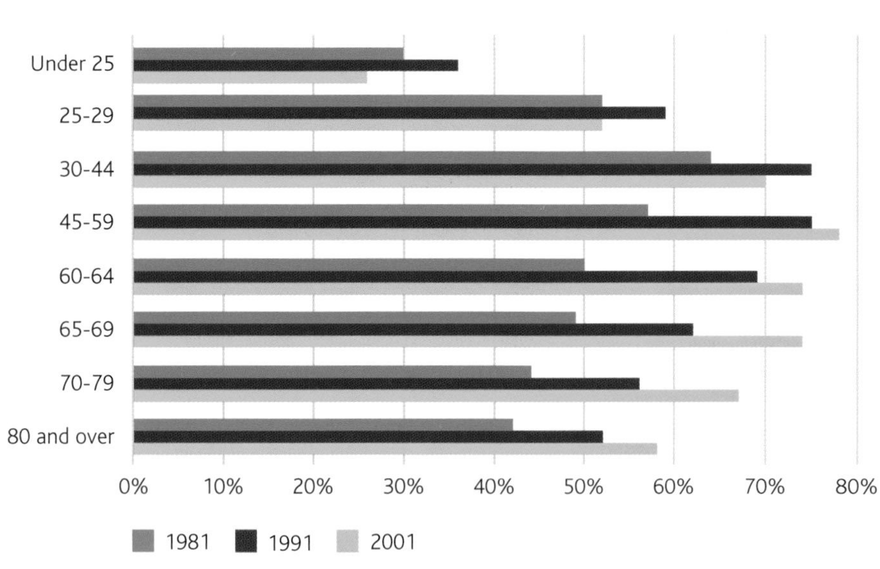

Source: Living in Britain, GHS, GB

Note: Age refers to the age of the household reference person. The household reference person is defined as follows: in households with a sole householder that person is the household reference person; in households with joint householders, the person with the highest income is taken as the household reference person; if both householders have exactly the same income, the older is taken as the household reference person.

Figure 5.13 Home Ownership, by Age: Possible Steady State 2030

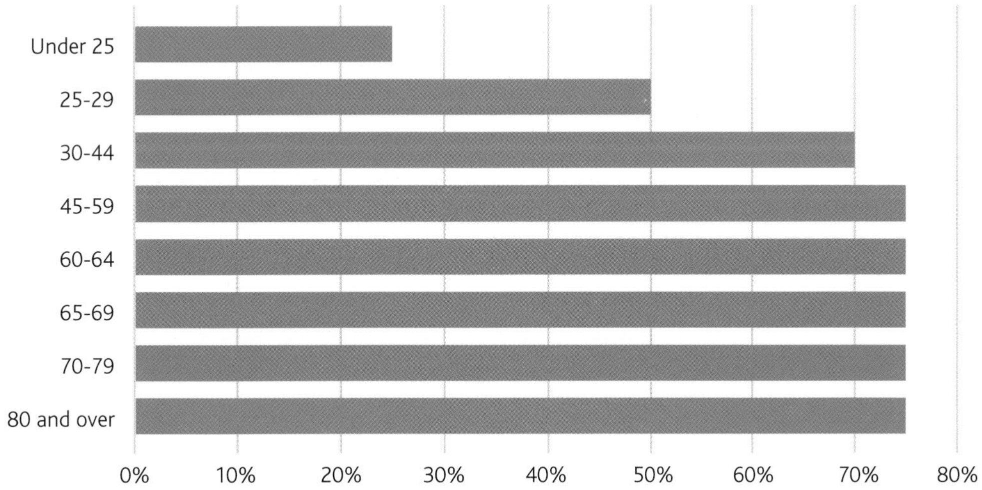

Under 25
25-29
30-44
45-59
60-64
65-69
70-79
80 and over
0%
10%
20%
30%
40%
50%
60%
70%
80%

Source: Pensions Commission estimate based on Living in Britain, 1981, 1991, 2001

Figure 5.14 Mean Net Housing Wealth, by Age

50-54
55-59
60-64
65-69
70-74
75-79
80 and over
£0
£20,000
£40,000
£60,000
£80,000
£100,000
£120,000
All individuals
Individuals with positive net housing wealth

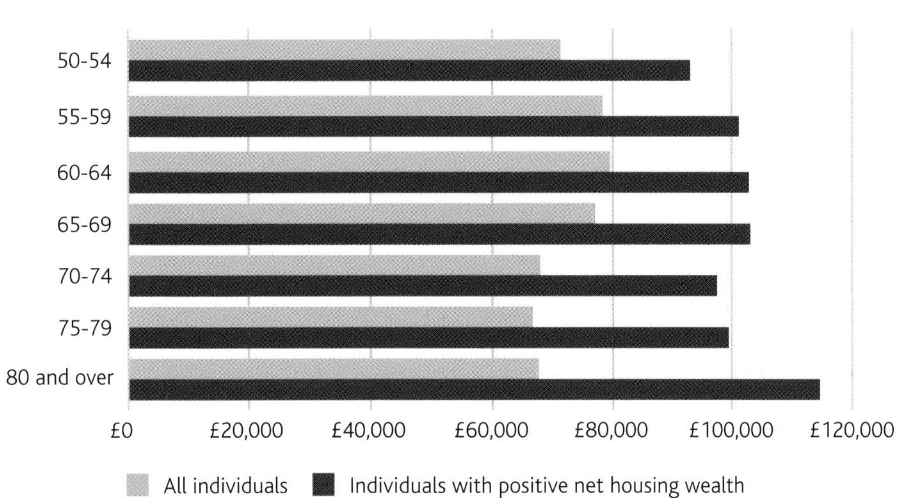

Source: ELSA, 2002, England

4. The macroeconomics of saving through housing assets

Appendix B discusses the macroeconomic theory of funded pension savings. It explains how the accumulation of assets by workers and decumulation by pensioners effects a transfer of consumption resources from workers to pensioners, and thus allows an individual moving through the life stages to smooth consumption over the life-cycle. It also discusses two ways of thinking about the price at which the assets will be bought and sold – as discounted present values of future streams of dividend or interest income, and as resulting from the balance of demand and supply, i.e. the relative number and resources of buyers and sellers. It explains how both ways of thinking are compatible, and their implications for how demographic change might impact future asset prices.

In essence, houses are no different from other categories of income-producing asset, and the theory discussed in Appendix B applies as much to housing as to productive business capital owned via equities and bonds. Houses are assets which produce a stream of income benefits (rents or the ability to live in them rent-free), and which in essence do so even if the person who owns the house also occupies it, so that the rent is notionally paid by the occupier to himself. Their value should in the long run therefore bear a logical relationship to the level of market rents, but is also determined by the balance of demand and supply, the number and the resources of buyers and sellers at any one time.

There is therefore no inherent reason why the purchase and sale of houses should not perform exactly the same role as funded savings via equities and bonds in effecting a resource transfer between generations. In principle, housing assets could be accumulated by one generation and then sold on to the next generation, providing the resources to finance consumption during retirement. There are however two important features specific to housing assets which carry implications for the risks involved in using houses to achieve inter-generational transfer.

- The first is that housing assets deliver one specific category of consumption, while the business assets which lie behind a diversified portfolio of bonds and equities support the delivery of the full range of all other categories of consumption. Therefore, while in the very long run a diversified portfolio of business assets should deliver a return and trade at a price linked somewhat to the growth and efficiency of the whole economy, irrespective of any change in relative demand for one or other category of consumption, housing assets should trade at prices linked specifically to the demand for accommodation. Over the last 50 years, these prices have moved in ways which have made housing a very attractive investment. While the increase in prices alone has not matched equity returns, the underlying return, after allowing for the rent-free accommodation enjoyed but also deducting the cost of maintenance, has compared well with equity returns and shown much lower variance over 20 year periods [Figures 5.15 and 5.16].[8]

[8]Note: The returns presented in Figure 5.16 may however be an overstatement of long-term returns if a significant element of house price appreciation is explained by capital investment to improve homes (e.g. new kitchens, central heating etc). Further work is required to identify the scale of such investments, which are not clear from available figures. [See Appendix C for further discussion of this issue.]

Figure 5.15 Distribution of Returns on Housing from Price Appreciation only, over 20 Year Periods: 1930-2003

40
30
20
10
0
Frequency
Mean 2.1
Median 2.0
0-2
2-4
4-6
6-8
8-10
10-12
12-14
Annualised real rates of return

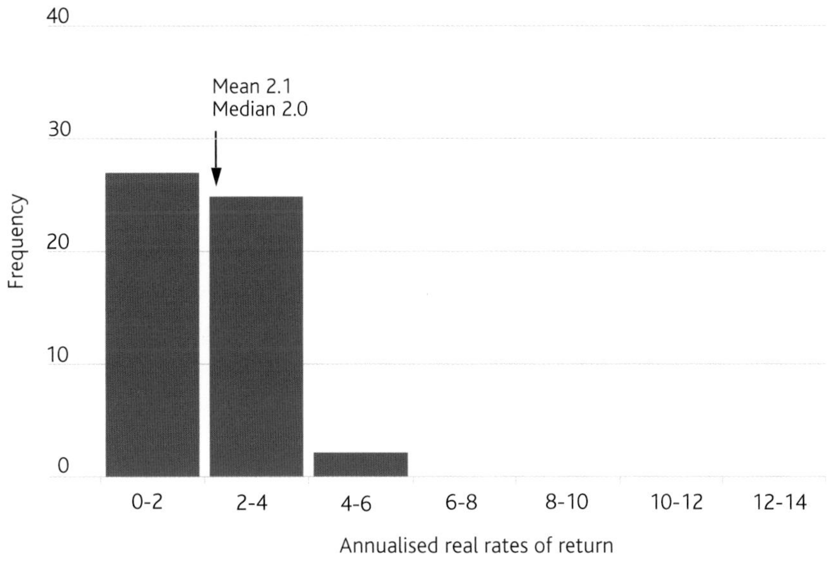

Source: Pensions Commission calculations based on ODPM house price series.

Figure 5.16 Comparison of Distribution of Adjusted Housing and Equity Returns over 20 Year Periods: 1930-2003

Mean 5.6
Median 5.5
40
30
20
10
0
Frequency
0-2
2-4
4-6
6-8
8-10
10-12
12-14
Annualised real rates of return
Mean 6.4
Median 6.0
Housing Returns adjusted for actual and implicit rents received minus cost of maintenance
Equities

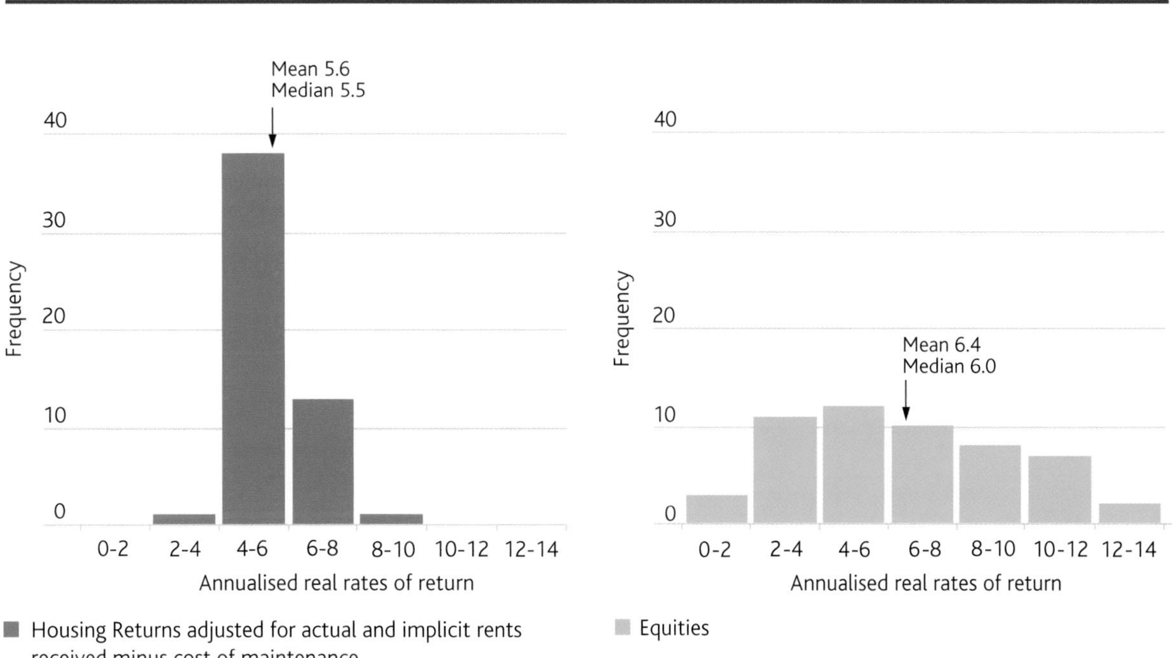

Source: Barclays Equity Gilt Study, Adjusted housing derived from Pensions Commission calculations based on ODPM house price series and ONS Blue Book

Note: See Appendix C for details of adjustments.

Such returns **may** continue in future, especially in areas where there is population growth and tight constraints on new housing supply.[9] But conversely, the logical impact of the demographic trends outlined in Chapter 2, with fertility rates below replacement levels, should be to depress house prices relative to a higher fertility alternative, suggesting the possibility of lower house prices as the baby boomers, or those who inherit from the baby boomers, seek to sell off houses to the next, smaller generation.[10] House prices are therefore as exposed to potential demographic effects as equity prices: indeed even more so since houses, far more than equities, are bought and sold in largely closed national markets, with only minimal overseas investment. Even absent the thorny issue of whether house prices today are at a cyclical and unsustainable peak, the long-term evolution of house prices is highly uncertain and debatable both nationally and even more so in specific regions or localities.

- The second distinctive feature of housing is that buying and then keeping a house, rather than liquidating it during retirement, provides protection against uncertainty over the future cost of housing. Demand for housing and market rents may go up or down, but owner-occupiers, notionally paying themselves an imputed rent, are protected, or in financial terms "hedged", either way. It is therefore economically rational for people who have accumulated net equity in a house by age of retirement, to maintain the right to rent-free retirement through continued ownership of a housing asset. Retirees gain benefits from owner-occupation via rent-free living, reducing the income replacement rate below what would otherwise be required. Economic rationality as well as emotional ties to the family home and a desire to bequeath therefore lie behind the observed phenomenon that housing equity, unlike non-pension financial assets, is not liquidated during retirement.

The implication of this is that if housing is to play a role in providing retirement income, it needs to do so in ways which do not require pensioners to give up their right to rent-free living, i.e. their hedge against volatility in house prices and rents.

5. Using housing assets to fund retirement

There are four ways in which housing assets could play a role in funding retirement without sacrificing the benefit of rent-free living: trading down; equity release; buy-to-let; and inheritance. The last of these seems likely to play the greatest role in supplementary pension provision.

[9]Note: Whether this is the case will depend partly on whether government plans to increase housing supply and ease development constraints are successful. See the Barker Review.

[10]Note: One factor which could offset the demographic effect of a smaller next generation is the steady fragmentation of average family size due to the increase in the number of single people living alone. This can increase the demand for units of housing, even if population is stable. But it is possible that this fragmentation effect will reach a limit, and that the overall demographic effect will dominate over the very long-term.

- **Trading down:** Complete liquidation of housing equity at time of retirement is unlikely to be appealing or economically rational for any but a very small minority of people. But many people enter retirement with larger houses or flats than they need for their own retirement living and in theory could trade down, releasing funds to support consumption in retirement. Some trading down does take place. The *Survey of English Housing* found that for 20% of people moving between un-mortgaged properties, the main reason to move was that they wanted a smaller or cheaper house, as did 19% of people moving from a mortgaged property to one which is owned outright. And the average number of rooms per house does fall slightly for age groups over 60, among owner-occupiers as well as among renters [Figure 5.17]. But the scale of funds releasable by trading down is limited by people's desire to live in local and familiar areas and in equally attractive areas, even if in a smaller house. Sixty-one percent of the English housing stock is semi-detached or terraced. The great majority of those with inadequate pension savings are likely to live in such houses. The value releasable by trading down from a semi-detached house to a terraced one varies by region, but on average would deliver assets equal to around only 30% of the implicit value of the state pension, even at today's perhaps overvalued property prices [Figure 5.18].

Figure 5.17 Mean Number of Rooms in Accommodation, by Tenure and Age: 2002-03

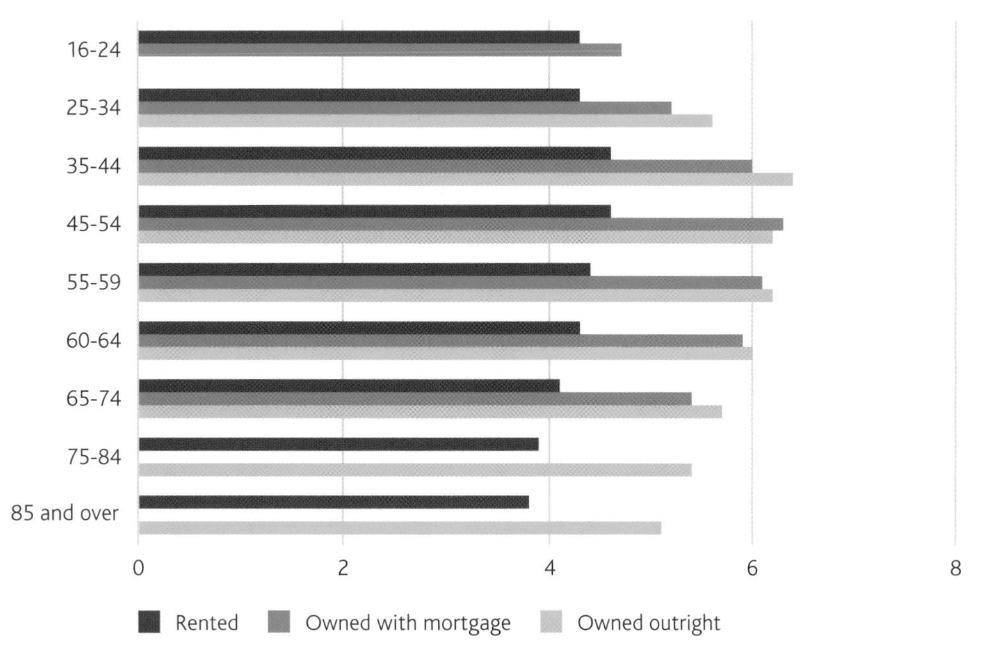

Source: FRS 2002-03

Note: Small sample sizes mean some results cannot be shown.

- **Equity release:** A number of products exist which enable people to remain in occupation of their house while borrowing against its value. The two main current variants are home reversion schemes and lifetime mortgages. Estimates of the size of the market vary, but in total it remains very small with only around 1% of pensioner households currently using these products, which amount to perhaps 0.5% of all outstanding mortgage debt [Table 5.6]. Typical interest rates in the lifetime mortgage product are significantly higher than for standard mortgages (e.g. around 7% in September 2004 compared with around 4.9% to 6.0% for best buy mortgages), reflecting the limited development of this market and the inherent risk of lending when the final maturity date of the loan is unknown. It is difficult to assess the scope for further development. Clearly for some people, including for instance the 10% of the population who are childless at retirement age (a figure likely to grow closer to 20% in the next 20 years), it could be an attractive option.[11] It is therefore important that regulation and consumer information are designed to ensure the best value to customers and appropriate selling. But qualitative survey evidence, for example by the Institute for Public Policy Research (IPPR), suggests that homeowners wish to bequeath at least some housing assets to their children. This makes it likely that for many owner-occupiers, equity release will be seen as a distress option rather than as part of their pre-planned approach to retirement. And as long as equity release is a product for a small minority, who may be a self-selecting group of poorer credit risks, its unattractive interest rates are likely to continue. Equity release may therefore remain trapped in a small, high-price sub-sector of the market.

- **Buy-to-let**: The buy-to-let market has soared in the last five years. Figures from the Council of Mortgage lenders suggest that the number of buy-to-let mortgages has risen from 29,000 at the end of 1998 to 475,000 in June 2004, with related mortgage debt outstanding rising from £2 billion at the end of 1998 to £47 billion in June 2004.[12] On some estimates, buy-to-let mortgages now account for almost 8% of all new mortgage advances.

  The vast majority of buy-to-let investors are also owner-occupiers of other properties, and thus have no need to retain the buy-to-let property to provide rent-free living in retirement. Their investments therefore represent savings available to meet retirement needs, savings which could be placed within the tax wrapper of a Self Invested Pension Plan (SIPP) from April 2006.

[11]Note: Though this group of people are also those most likely to have to finance residential care, and thus perhaps have to make other claims on housing equity.

[12]Note: This increase may be slightly overstated because some investors previously financed buy-to-let with general commercial loans rather than explicitly named "buy-to-let mortgages". But the impact of this overstatement is likely to be small.

Figure 5.18 Difference in Average Price of Semi-detached and Terraced House, by Region: Jan-Mar 2004

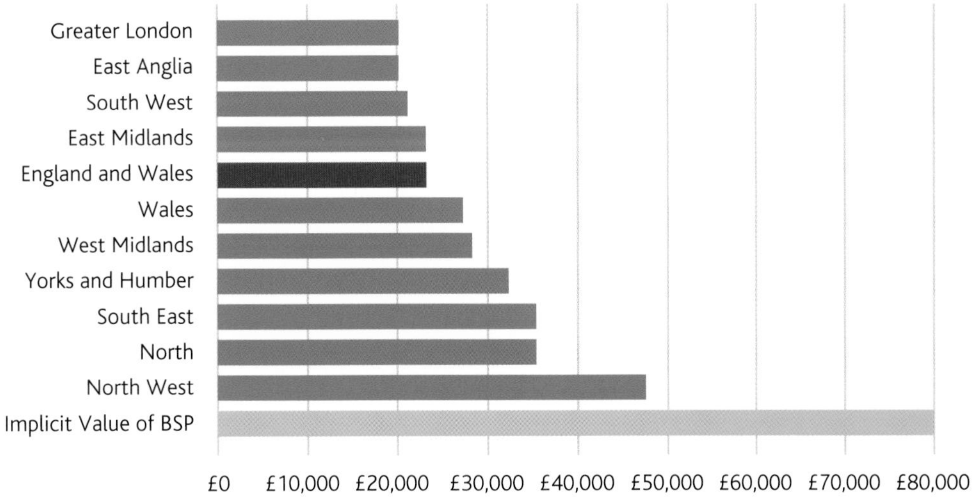

Greater London
East Anglia
South West
East Midlands
England and Wales
Wales
West Midlands
Yorks and Humber
South East
North
North West
Implicit Value of BSP

£0 £10,000 £20,000 £30,000 £40,000 £50,000 £60,000 £70,000 £80,000

Source: Land Registry
Annuity Bureau, current rates, 2 August 2004

Note: The implicit value of the BSP is calculated using a single life index-linked annuity rate of 5% for a 65 year old man.

Table 5.6 Scale of Market For Equity Release Products

	Lifetime mortgages		Home Reversions
	CML estimate	SHIP estimate	SHIP estimate
Number outstanding	71,500	70,000	10,000
Total value (£m)	3,300	1,000	55
Average value (new loans) (£)	46,000	44,000	46,000

Product Definitions

Lifetime mortgage – mortgage part of capital value of the home, but no repayments of capital are required. The interest is added to the original loan amount and repaid when the property is sold.

Home reversion scheme – sell all or part of the house to a company. On death, the provider receives the full value of the part of the property sold.

Source: Council of Mortgage Lenders (CML) data for 2004, Q2.
Key Retirement Solutions/Safe Home Income Plans (SHIP) data for first half of 2004.

Note: Total value data from SHIP is the total value released in the 12 months ending June 2004.

Buy-to-let investment therefore represents simply a specific asset class decision, an alternative to investment in equities and bonds. Specific investment risks arise from this asset class decision. The investment is often highly geared, increasing both upside and downside potential. And the running rental yield is driven by the specifics of the rental market and indeed usually by one very localised market, rather than by wider economic and market trends. It is therefore likely that buy-to-let investments will generate both exceptionally high and exceptionally low or indeed negative returns for different individuals. But despite this volatility, it will prove an attractive alternative to other forms of pension saving for some adept or lucky investors.

But buy-to-let is likely to remain relevant to only a minority of those who lack good pension provision. While there are 475,000 buy-to-let mortgages, the number of investors is lower, with an estimated 46% of investors owning more than one rental property. And at the macroeconomic level, buy-to-let investment cannot transform the adequacy of saving for retirement. For every buy-to-let investor, there needs to be a renter, i.e. someone who is not an owner-occupier. Only to the extent that buy-to-let represents a transfer to private ownership of social housing stock does it increase the total wealth held in private hands. In the long-term therefore, the buy-to-let market cannot grow significantly unless there is a considerable increase in the number of people who rent rather than own a home, perhaps through later entry into the housing market. But later entry into the housing market means a later date at which mortgages are repaid, reducing the average net housing equity with which all of those who are not buy-to-let investors enter retirement. Buy-to-let on a really large scale would therefore imply a major move away from the relatively even distribution of housing equity, relative to income, which currently distinguishes houses from non-pension financial assets. Buy-to-let can only become a major savings asset for some people if housing equity becomes a less significant asset for others.

Finally, however, it is worth noting one variant of renting-out which could play a minor but still useful role for some homeowners: the renting out of individual rooms to lodgers. With many homeowners entering retirement with surplus rooms and a proliferation of single person households among younger people, it would be a logical and useful development. Sociological and house design barriers however seem likely to limit this to a small minority of homeowners.

- **Inheritance**: The Commission's judgement is that the three options considered above are likely to play only a limited role in providing resources to fund income in retirement. The vast majority of houses are likely to remain owned by owner-occupiers, and most owner-occupiers will continue to hold on to housing equity throughout retirement, though with an element of trading down. But the implication of this is that the great majority of housing assets will be bequeathed, usually free of mortgages, and will be inherited by people the great majority of whom already own the housing asset needed to deliver rent-free living in retirement. If the future steady state model envisaged in Figure 5.13 is correct, 75% of retirees will enter retirement with a housing asset, and at least 75% of these (and probably a considerably higher percentage due to the positive correlation of owner-occupation between generations) will inherit a share of a house. Given average longevity and average ages of child bearing, this inheritance will on average occur in the decade before or after retirement, and in the long term, with an average family size of two or less, the average couple approaching retirement will inherit two halves of two different homes. This will give on average, investable assets worth, at present house price levels, about £180,000. Even when converted to annual pension income at an index-linked annuity rate of say 5%, this will make a significant contribution to income replacement rates for the average person.

However this long-term and "on average" model clearly does not apply today. While the average home in 2001-02 was worth about £130,000, only 38% of estates in that year were valued at £60,000 or more, with 47% either trivial (and therefore excluded from the probate process) or less than £10,000 in value [Figure 5.19]. But this reflects the fact that the big increases in home ownership of the 1970s and 1980s are yet to work through to older age groups. Home ownership among 80+ year olds is currently 58%, but could be about 75% by 2030.

The Commission's current belief is therefore that, over the long term, the inheritance of housing equity may play a significant role in funding retirement for many people. During the consultation period we would welcome comments on this general proposition. We have already identified however some factors which might offset this general proposition, and we are clear that even if the proposition holds in general, it cannot be treated as a universal or sufficient answer to the problem of pension adequacy.

Figure 5.19 Estimate of Distribution of Estates, by Value: 2001-2002

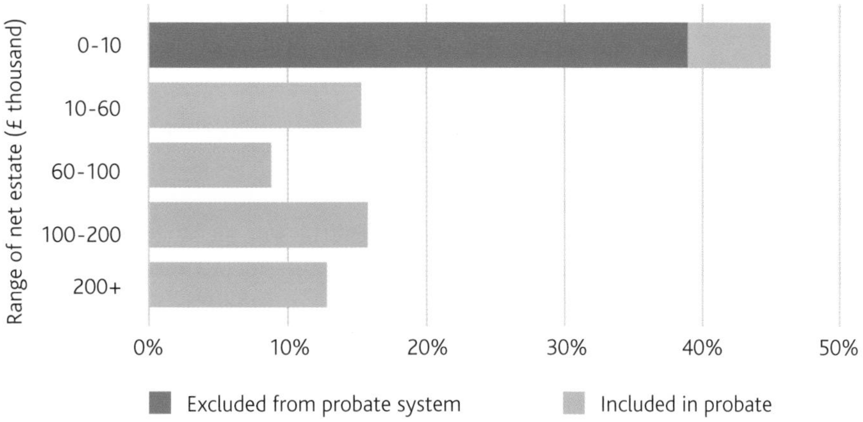

Range of net estate (£ thousand)
0-10
10-60
60-100
100-200
200+
0%
10%
20%
30%
40%
50%
Excluded from probate system
Included in probate

Source: Inland Revenue and Pensions Commission estimate.

Note: Includes an estimate for the small estates excluded from probate.

6. Life-cycle issues and other potentially offsetting factors

We have already identified a demographic effect on house prices as one factor which might undermine housing as a source of retirement income. Inheritance per person will tend to increase over the next 50 years, everything else being equal, because average family size has fallen: there will therefore be fewer inheritors per bequeather. But if the next generation of workers is smaller than the current one, house prices will, everything else equal, tend to fall. If the birth rate is below replacement levels, future inheritors cannot assume that they will inherit houses as valuable (relative to earnings) as today, except in the case where there is large scale immigration of people who wish to buy houses but have no right to inherit them.

In addition however, there are a complex set of issues relating to the inter-relationship between different changes in the pattern of savings and consumption over people's life-cycles.

- The most obvious is that housing wealth may not be available to fund pensions, or to deliver inherited assets to the next generation, if it is used to pay for long-term care. The scale of likely housing equity realisation for this purpose is unclear.

- A more complex effect relates to the age of entering into work and into the housing market. Increasing numbers of people will likely hold housing assets till death, and bequeath them typically to people in their fifties and sixties. But these people may increasingly over time have entered into the housing market at a slightly later age, either because of the high price of housing or because of student debts. Figure 5.12, which sets out house ownership by age group, shows that house ownership is now falling slightly among age groups under 44 years. Future inheritors in their fifties and sixties may therefore be more likely than current 50 and 60 year olds to owe substantial mortgage debt, especially if a low inflation environment is maintained, and may therefore need to devote some of their inheritance to paying this off. Or they may feel the need to support their children in the repayment of student debts, or via gifts to fund initial house deposits: a recent Joseph Rowntree Foundation report found that a significant number would be willing or able to provide this support.[13]

The overall themes are that we cannot plan to spend the same money twice, and that house ownership offers no magic escape route from the demographic challenge outlined in Chapter 1. The Commission therefore intends over the next year to investigate whether an integrated consideration of all of the factors influencing life-cycle saving and consumption patterns would revise or limit our belief that inheritance of housing assets might on average play a significant role.

[13]Note: Homeowners with adult children who were not owner-occupiers were asked whether they would be willing and able to give financial support to a child buying a house in the next 10 years. Fifty-five per cent thought they would be able to give financial support to the child. And nearly three-quarters thought it was likely that they would be willing to give financial support.

Even however if "in general" and "on average" inheritance of housing equity will play a significant role in funding retirement, it is clear that it cannot be a sufficient or universal solution, because of the distribution of housing assets and of inheritance. Even a random correlation between marriage patterns, family sizes and house values would leave many people enjoying substantial inheritances while others received none. Inheritance would thus solve a randomly selected subset of the pension saving gap. But marriage patterns will tend to exacerbate the inequality of the distribution, since children of better-off parents tend to marry children of other better-off parents. The future will thus see many couples inheriting significant housing assets, but other couples inheriting none. Inheritance moreover is positively correlated with the wealth of the inheritor: people who have accumulated more wealth by the age of 50-59 expect to inherit more [Figure 5.20]. Inheritance of housing assets is likely therefore to be either not correlated or negatively correlated to the existence of severe pension gaps [Figure 5.21]. This is the present pattern of house ownership, to which we now turn.

Figure 5.20 Expected Chances of Receiving Inheritance among those approaching Retirement, by Wealth Quintile

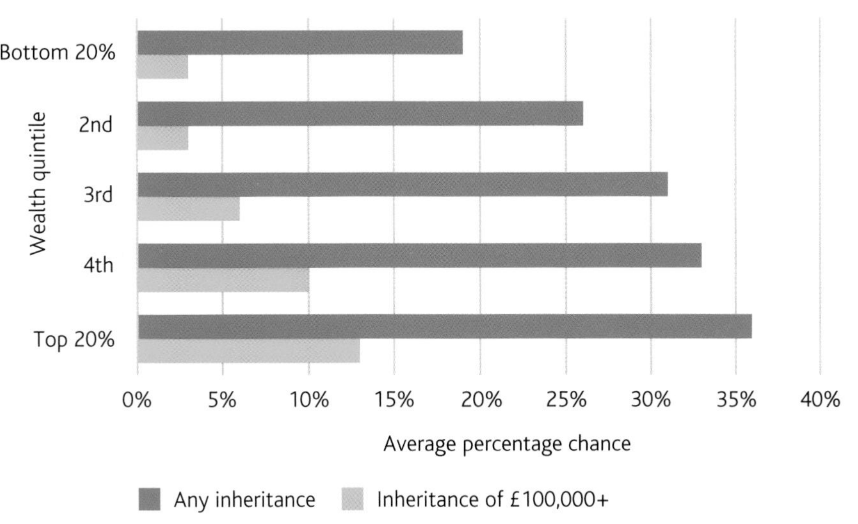

Source: ELSA, 2002, England

Note: Data is shown for 50-59 year olds.

7. The distribution of home ownership and pensions assets

As discussed in sections 2 and 3 above, ownership of housing equity is more evenly distributed than ownership of non-pension financial wealth. It also appears to be more evenly distributed than pension rights. Table 5.7 sets out the estimated net housing equity owned by 55-59 year olds expecting to retire on different levels of private pension income, and the implicit capital value of those pension expectations. The value of housing owned increases in line with expected pension income, but not nearly as dramatically.

It is not the case, however, that home ownership is concentrated among those who are least likely to have pension rights. Indeed the opposite is true, especially at lower incomes. Among non-retired people aged 40-49 with an annual income from £9,500-£17,499, 80% of those who have private pensions are owner-occupiers compared to 64% of those with no pension. In the £17,500-£24,999 income band the distinction is less extreme; 89% of those with a pension own a home compared to 79% with no pension. A similar pattern is found among 50-59 year olds [Figure 5.22]. The relationship would need to be the other way round (i.e. higher home ownership among those without pensions) for us to assume that housing equity is being accumulated as an alternative to pension rights.

Figure 5.21 Mean Chance of Receiving an Inheritance of Greater than £10,000 when approaching Retirement, by Private Pension Status

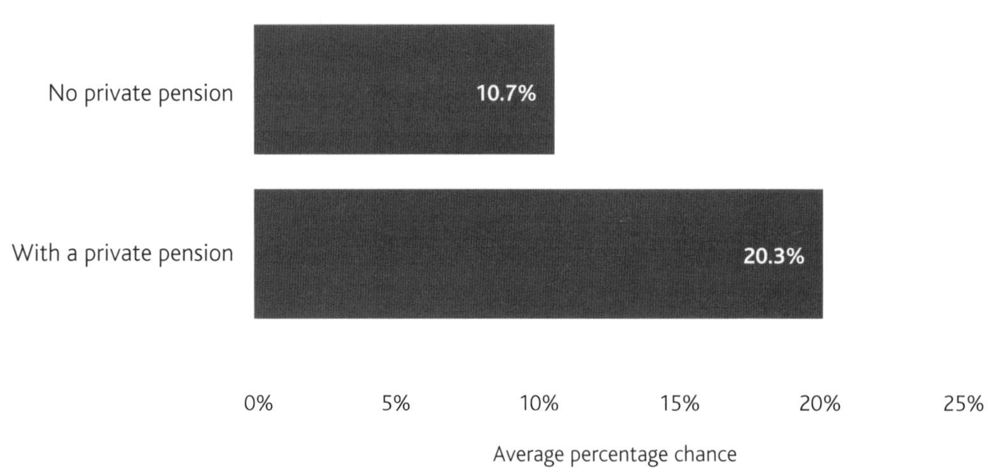

Source: Banks J, Emmerson C and Oldfield Z (2004)

Note: Data is shown for non-retired 50-59 year olds.
The non-retired include both those in work and those not in work, who do not describe themselves as retired, although some of these people may never work again.

Table 5.7 Housing wealth and Pension Expectations among those approaching Retirement

Expected private pension income	Median expected pension income (£)	Implicit capital value of median expected pension income (£)	Median net housing wealth (£)
£0	0	0	20,000
£1-2,500	1,200	24,000	50,000
£2,501-6,000	4,000	80,000	74,550
£6,001-12,500	8,750	175,000	71,500
£12,501 and over	20,833	416,660	100,000

Source: Banks J, Emmerson C and Oldfield Z (2004)

Note: Data is shown for non-retired 55-59 year olds.
The non-retired include both those in work and those not in work, who do not describe themselves as retired, although some of these may never work again.
Expected pension income is from private pensions on a family basis and adjusted for family size.
A single life indexed annuity for a 65 year old man was assumed in the calculation of the implicit capital value.
Net housing wealth is on a family basis.

Figure 5.22 Percentage of Home Ownership among the Non-Retired, by Pension Participation, Age and Income

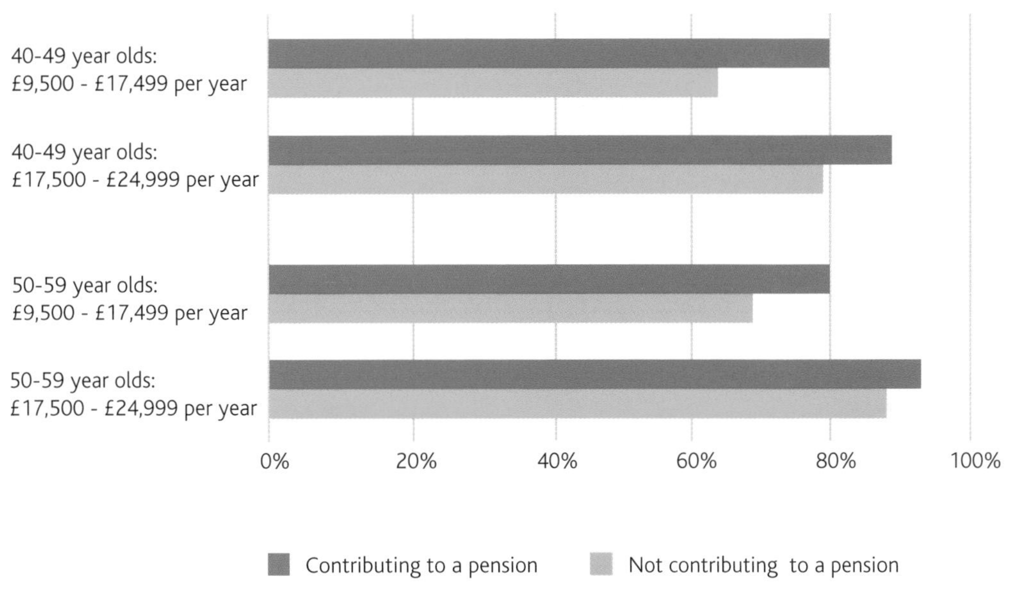

Source: MFS, GB, 2003

Note: The non-retired include both those in work and those not in work who do not describe themselves as retired, although some of these may never work again. Income is on a gross household basis but has been adjusted for family size. Home ownership is either individual or joint.

Nor is it the case that those who have no private pension, but are owner-occupiers, tend to own much more valuable houses. Within the same income and age band, and looking only at those who are owner-occupiers, median net housing equity seems to be very similar or slightly lower for those without pensions, though mean net housing equity is slightly higher [Figure 5.23]. This might be explained by a small minority of people with no pension arrangement but significant wealth, but may simply reflect the imperfections of the data. The most reasonable conclusion from the data is that the housing wealth of owner-occupiers is uncorrelated to pension scheme membership. It would need to be inversely correlated to pension scheme membership to be a clear alternative. Home ownership will help many non-pension savers, but not all.

Again we find therefore that while housing assets, either via equity release techniques or via inheritance, will clearly be an important source of retirement income for some people, they cannot be considered as providing a general and sufficient solution to the problem of deficient pension provision.

Figure 5.23 Net Housing Equity of Non-Retired Homeowners, by Age and Income

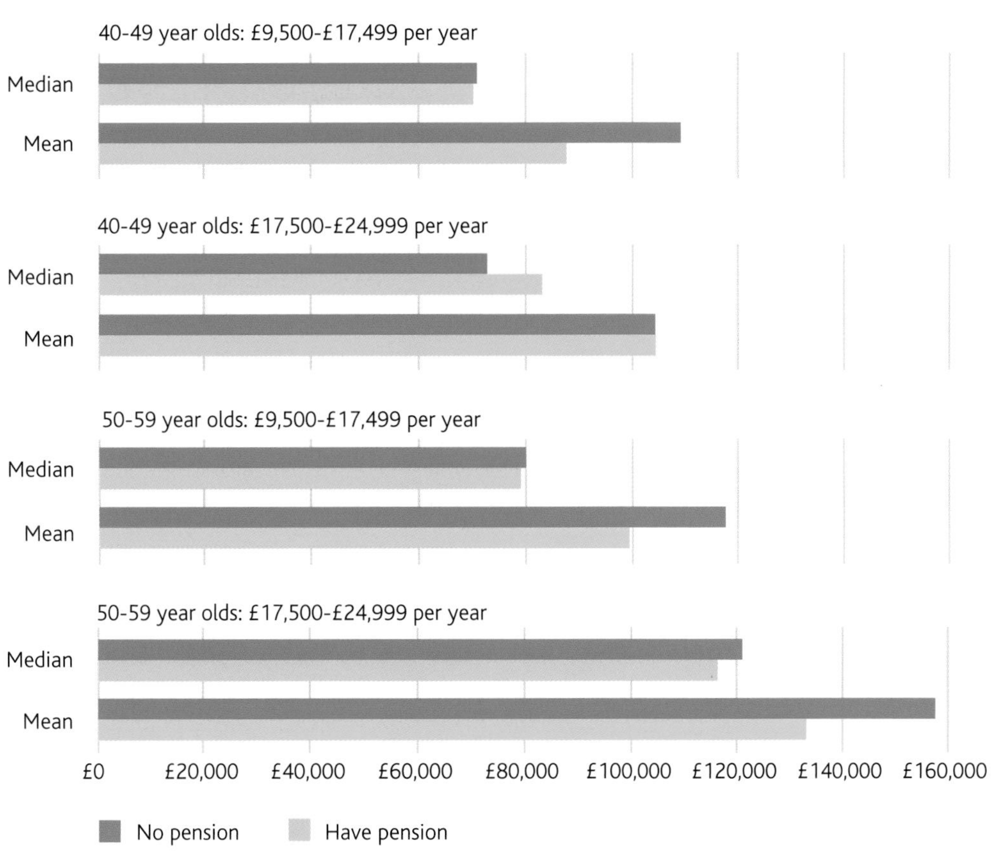

Source: MFS, 2003, GB

Note: The non-retired include both those in work and those not in work, who do not describe themselves as retired, although some of these may never work again. Income is on a household basis, adjusted for family size. Some of the differences at the mean may not be significant due to smaller numbers of individuals who own houses but have no pension.

8. Privately owned business assets

Business assets sold at or during retirement will for some people be a significant source of retirement income. ONS figures suggest that the value of unquoted equity (i.e equity in private companies) held by the household sector was about £118 billion at the end of 2003. But this wealth-holding is heavily concentrated. Only a very small minority of self-employed people and business owners have significant realisable business assets.

- Small Business Service (SBS) data suggests that there are 4.0 million business enterprises in the UK, 2.5 million organised as sole proprietorships, 0.5 million as partnerships and 1.0 million as companies. But 2.9 million of these businesses have no employees other than the self-employed company owner. In the vast majority of these businesses the individual is essentially selling his or her labour services, and in only a very small percentage of the 2.9 million will there be significant business assets which can be sold when the business owner ceases work. Of the 1.2 million businesses which do have employees, moreover, 0.8 million have between one and four. While some of these businesses (e.g. small partnerships) may have realisable equity value, the proportion is likely to be small. Only among the 0.4 million businesses with more than five employees is there likely to be a significant proportion where the sale of the business is likely to provide a significant source of wealth.

- Research for the SBS (2002) meanwhile gives us a feel for how many of these businesses may deliver really significant sources of retirement wealth.[14] The researchers' estimates, from interviews with businesses and accountants, suggest that there are around 3,000 small and medium sized enterprises sold each year with a price in the range £250,000-£3 million. With the annunitised value of £250,000 being about £10,000-£12,000 per year, and with around 60,000 self-employed people retiring each year, it seems likely that only a very small proportion of the self-employed have business assets sufficient to fund the equivalent of a fully paid-up final salary scheme for the average earner.

The expansion of the self-employment during the 1990s has not therefore been accompanied by the emergence of a new category of retirement provision for other than a small minority. The fact that pension saving among the self-employed is not increasing (see Chapter 3) therefore remains a concern.

[14]Note: SME Ownership and Succession – Business Support and Policy Implications, University of Central England (2002)

Barriers to a voluntarist solution

6

As Chapters 4 and 5 described, the present level of pension right accrual, private and state combined, will leave many with inadequate pensions. And as Chapter 2 described, there are likely to be limits to solving the problem solely via increased retirement ages. If state system plans are taken as given, a higher level of private saving is required.

There are however big barriers to the success of a voluntary pension saving system, some inherent to any pension system, some specific to the UK. Most people do not make rational decisions about long-term savings without encouragement and advice. But the cost of advice, and of regulating to ensure that it is good advice, in itself significantly reduces the return on saving, particularly for low earners. Reductions in Yield arising from providers' charges can absorb 20-30% of an individual's pension saving, even though they have fallen to a level where provision to lower income groups is unprofitable. This poses a fundamental question: in principle can a voluntary market for pensions work for low income, low premium customers?

But both the behavioural barriers to savings and the costs of provision have been made worse by the bewildering complexity of the UK pension system, state and private combined. This complexity reflects the impact of multiple decisions made over the last several decades, each of which appeared to make sense at the time, but the cumulative effect of which has been to create confusion and mistrust. Means-testing within the state system both increases complexity and reduces, and in some cases reverses, the incentives to save via pensions which the tax system creates. The scope of this means-testing would grow over time if current indexation approaches were continued indefinitely.

Unless therefore new government initiatives can make a major difference to behaviours it is unlikely that the present voluntary private system combined with the present state system will solve the problem of inadequate pension savings.

A free market voluntarist approach to pension savings would work if individuals made rational choices based on good understanding of attractive incentives to save. These conditions do not apply in the UK today, partly for reasons inherent to pensions savings, partly for reasons specific to the UK.

This chapter explores these barriers to a voluntary solution under five headings:

1 Inherent barriers to effective pension markets.

2 Specific UK barriers: complexity and lack of trust.

3 Specific UK barriers: the impact of high selling and administration costs.

4 Specific UK barriers: the impact of means-testing.

5 Incentives to save facing different groups of people.

1. Inherent barriers to effective pension markets

The theory of rational economics assumes that people make utility maximising choices between different products thinking through the consequences of purchase for both present and future standards of living and shopping around to find the best value. But there is an increasing body of academic work, known as behavioural economics, which demonstrates that very few individuals actually operate in this rational and well-informed fashion. The consequences of this for the efficiency of markets are greatest when dealing with complex products and decisions with long-term consequences, such as those involved in pension saving. The panel on the following pages explains some of the key findings of this behavioural economics work. The relevant findings for the pensions market are that:

- People faced with complex financial decisions which have long-term consequences will often put off the decision unless some external agent (the state, employer, or salesperson) pushes them over the decision-making threshold.

- Individual decisions are heavily influenced by the way that questions are framed, and by inertia. Employer pension schemes with automatic enrolment but the right to opt-out produce much higher participation rates than those which require individuals to opt-in [Figure 6.1].

Figure 6.1 Percentage of Employees Participating in a 401(k) Pension Scheme With and Without Automatic Enrolment

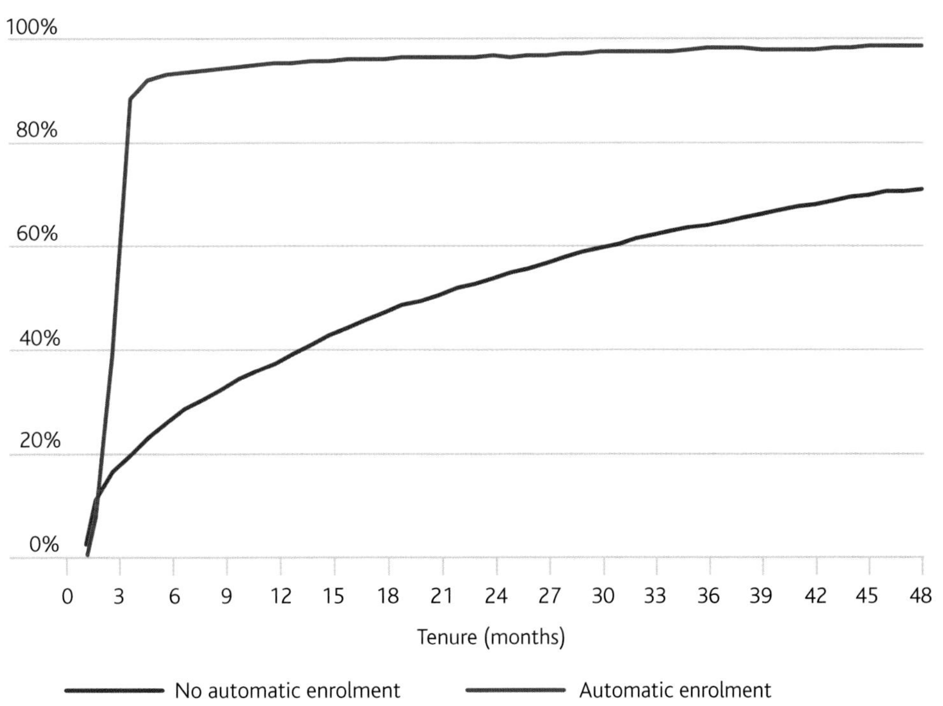

Source: Madrian and Shea, (2001)

Note: This shows the participation rate for two cohorts of employees within the same firm. The automatic enrolment cohort were employees who had to make a specific decision to opt-out of the 401(k) plan, the no automatic enrolment cohort had to make a specific decision to join the 401(k) plan.

Insights from behavioural economics

Economics traditionally works on the simplifying assumption that people make rational decisions, optimising their welfare on the basis of all available information logically assessed. Behavioural economics uses insights from psychology and experiments to understand how people actually behave in real life. People still try to maximise their welfare, but they use short cuts in information-gathering and decision-making, and the actions they choose are often not those predicted by the rational agent assumption.

Primarily in the USA behavioural economists have undertaken research which gives insights into how people make financial decisions, especially on pension savings. The main insights relate to the decision to save, asset allocation decisions and the annuity decision.

The decision to save

The research identifies barriers that prevent people from saving, even when they recognise that it is in their best interest to do so. Researchers find extensive evidence of **procrastination**: a high proportion of people are persuaded by information and advice that saving is desirable but delay implementation often indefinitely. Thus for example:

- Following a seminar for potential participants in a 401(k) pension plan, 100% of non-members said that they would join the plan after the seminar, but six months later only 14% had done so, not much higher than the 7% join-up rate among non-members who had not attended the seminar [Choi et al, 2001].

- Another survey found that 68 out of 100 employees in a US company believed they were not saving enough, 24 of the 68 said they would start saving more within three months, but only three of the 24 actually did so. [Choi et al, 2001].

The fact that people procrastinate, putting off important actions, is unsurprising: a confirmation of common-sense observation. But it challenges a key assumption in traditional economics, since the formal economic interpretation of this procrastination is that individuals do not discount consumption over time with equal discount rates between all time periods, but apply "hyperbolic discount rates". This means that in trading-off consumption today versus consumption in the near future, they use a far higher discount rate than when trading-off consumption today versus in, say, 20 years time. Over a 20 year period they are willing to sacrifice current consumption (i.e. to save), but as between this year and next they strongly prefer consumption today. Therefore the decision is always to start saving 'next year', but when next year arrives, the preference is to start the year thereafter. Pension saving is therefore put off indefinitely via a continual series of 'next year' delays. But if the same people could be faced with the choice, "start saving this year, or you won't get another opportunity", they would start.

Another key finding is the **power of inertia.** People often accept the situation as it is or choose the course of action which requires least decision-making. People who start saving usually keep saving, often at the same contribution rate. People who are not saving usually keep not saving. And pension schemes in which the default option for new employees is to join, produce much higher pension participation than if an active decision to join has to be registered. Thus:

- Figure 6.1 shows the difference in participation rates in a 401(k) pension saving scheme for two different cohorts of new employees in an American firm. When the scheme enrolled people automatically unless they registered a deliberate opt-out the participation rate was 30% higher, even after 48 months, than when enrolment required an employee to opt-in.

- But opt-out and opt-in choices influence not only participation rates but also contribution rates. Employees opted-in were given a default contribution rate of 3%, and Figure 6.2 shows that almost all of them accepted this. By comparison, the cohort which consciously decided to opt-in chose higher average contribution rates, clustering around 6% because that maximised the employer's matching contribution.

'Save More Tomorrow' plans exploit insights from both hyperbolic discount rates and inertia to encourage increased savings. Under these plans, individuals are offered two choices:

1. To increase their pension contributions immediately.

2. To 'Save More Tomorrow' by delaying the increase until after the next pay-rise.

Those who opt to save more tomorrow will have their contributions increased at each pay rise until they decide to stop. As Figure 6.3 shows, Save More Tomorrow plans generate greater impact than the provision of advice.

Asset allocation decisions

Traditional finance theory assumes that people make rational investment decisions, choosing between different asset classes in the light of prospective risk/return trade-offs, and thinking logically about overall risk/return objectives. Even for financial industry experts this would be an immensely challenging task, requiring in theory both detailed analysis of the past risk/return performance for different asset classes, and a robust theoretical approach to deciding whether past performance carried information relevant to the assessment of future risks and returns. For the vast majority of non-professionals it is simply an impossible task. As a result, people's decisions are hugely influenced by the range of options with which they are presented, and by emotional considerations such as familiarity. Thus for instance:

- People's choices are influenced by the options available. TWA pilots offered five equity funds and one fixed income fund, chose on average to invest 75% in equities. University of California employees offered one equity fund and four fixed income funds chose 34% equity investment [Benartzi and Thaler, 2001].
- People invest in things that they understand. This seems to be the explanation of heavy investment in own company stock, even where there is no company pressure, and even when, post-Enron, the extreme dangers of this strategy should be clear.
- People shy away from complexity. As a result more choice can produce more procrastination. Iyengar et al (2003) investigated how 401(k) participation varied with the number of funds from which employees can choose. When only two funds were offered the participation rate was 75%, falling to 60% if over 50 alternatives were available.
- And people chase the market and follow fashions. In the technology boom, people invested more in technology the higher the price went i.e. the more that prices diverged above rational valuation. But equally, individuals are very loath to admit mistakes, with very little re-balancing of portfolios out of poor performing assets. While this can sometimes be rational (if prices have moved from irrational highs to irrational lows) the evidence suggests that inertia is the dominant force. Once people have made asset allocation decisions, they tend to leave them unchanged.

Pension income: annuitisation decision

Another insight from empirical research is that people are generally not good at estimating probabilities or understanding the consequences of risk. Annuities are unpopular with consumers because they have difficulty in estimating and understanding the risks against which an annuity protects. Lump sums are therefore preferred even when the income stream is much smaller on an actuarially comparable present value basis.

Thus, for example, the US Defence Department offered an early retirement deal where people could choose between a lump sum or an annuity. The annuities had an internal rate of return between 17.5% and 19.8% when government bonds were yielding 7%.

Economists estimated that all officers and half of the enlisted personnel would opt for the annuity. But 52% of officers and 92% of enlisted personnel opted for the lump sum [Mitchell and Utkus, 2003].

Figure 6.2 Pension Contribution Rates With and Without Automatic Enrolment

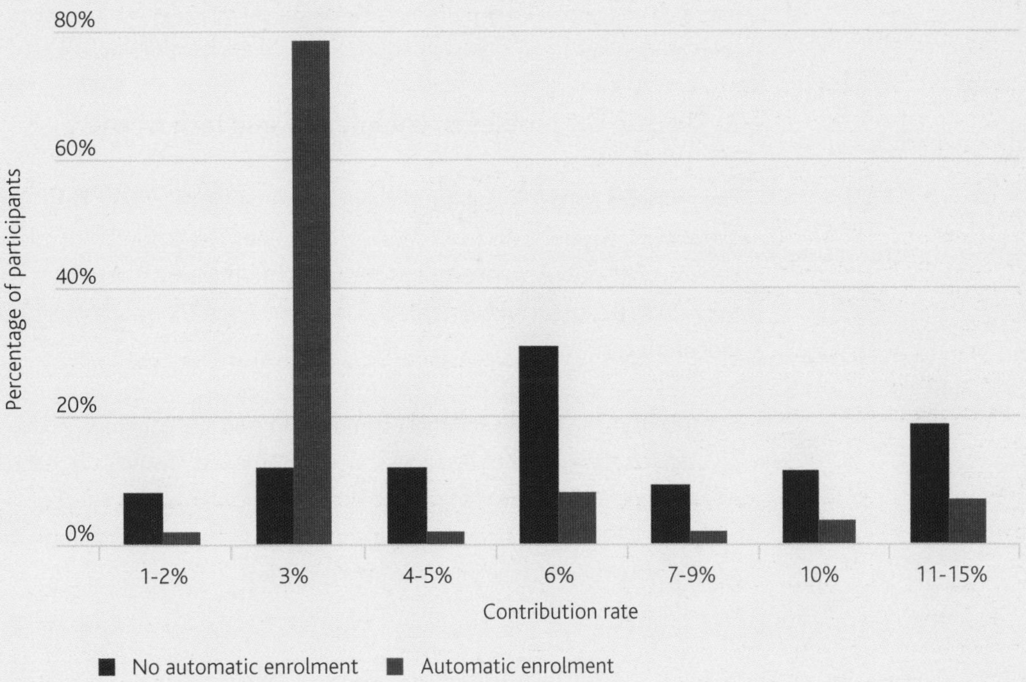

80%
60%
40%
20%
0%
Percentage of participants
1-2%
3%
4-5%
6%
7-9%
10%
11-15%
Contribution rate
No automatic enrolment
Automatic enrolment

Source: Madrain and Shea, 2001

- Question framing and inertia are indeed more powerful influences on decisions than information and advice. As explained in the panel, "Save More Tomorrow" schemes, which commit individuals to devote future pay rises to savings, have more effect than seminars or sales literature [Figure 6.3].

- Asset allocation decisions are hugely influenced by the choices presented. If a financial adviser or scheme trustee asks individuals to choose freely between four equity funds and two bond funds, the choice made will be more equity focused than if two equity funds and four bond funds were on the available list.

- And too much choice makes people avoid a decision. Many savers faced with 20 product or fund choices will be less likely to make a saving decision than if presented with only three choices.

The implication of these findings is that external influences are hugely important in saving decisions. Many people will only save if some trusted institution, such as the government or their employer, instructs or encourages them to save, or facilitates saving via automatic enrolment. Or they will only save if a financial adviser persuades them to. The findings of behavioural economics indeed provide theoretical support for the life insurance industry's long-held belief that pension products are sold not bought, with only a tiny proportion of people confident enough to buy pension products via a "direct execution" route [Figure 6.4]. But the need actively to sell products, and to, persuade people to save, makes the individual sale of pension products inherently expensive, particularly for people with low incomes and low savings levels, since most of the costs are fixed and do not vary with the size of the premium paid. And products which have to be actively sold to imperfectly informed and unconfident customers can easily be mis-sold. As a result, the sales process has to be regulated, which increases the cost yet further.

2. Specific UK problems: complexity and lack of trust

The problems set out above are inherent to any pension system. They help explain why governments in all developed societies play a significant role in pension policy, either as direct providers, or as incentivisers, encouragers and regulators. But these problems are made worse in the UK by complexity and lack of trust.

Complexity: The UK has the most complex pension system in the world. This reflects the impact of decisions made over the last few decades, each of which appeared to make sense at the time, but the cumulative effect of which has been to create bewildering complexity in the state system, in the private system, and in the interface between them.

Figure 6.3 Impact of Save More Tomorrow on Contributions to 401(k) Plans

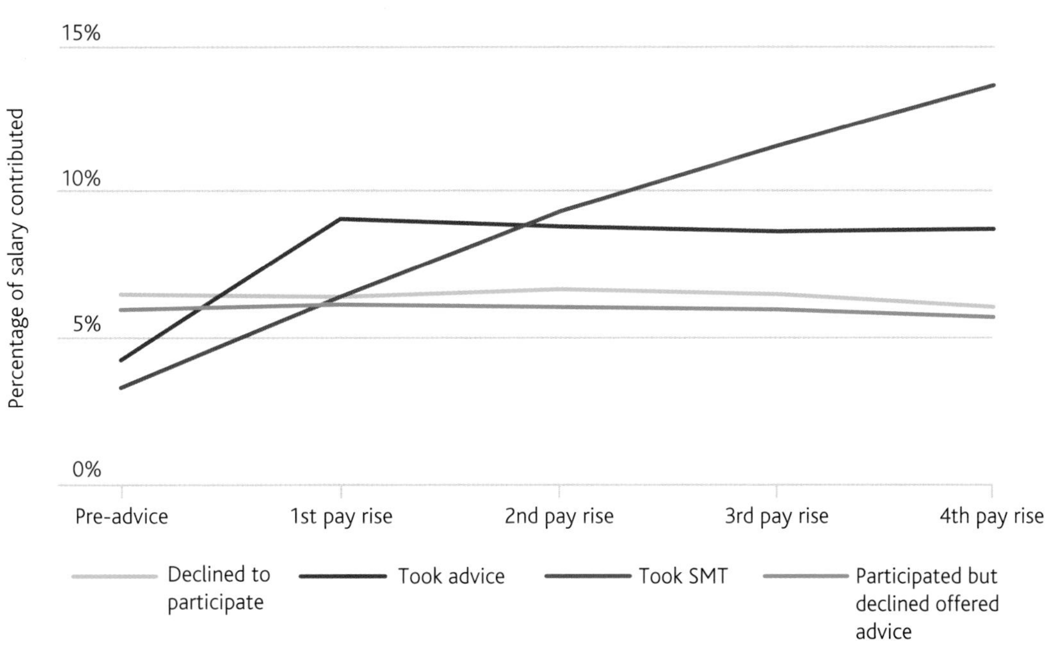

Source: Thaler and Benartzi (2001)

Note: This compares the contributions to 401(k) plans depending on whether individuals took financial advice or participated in the Save More Tomorrow plan.

Figure 6.4 Individual Pension Sales by Channel: 2003

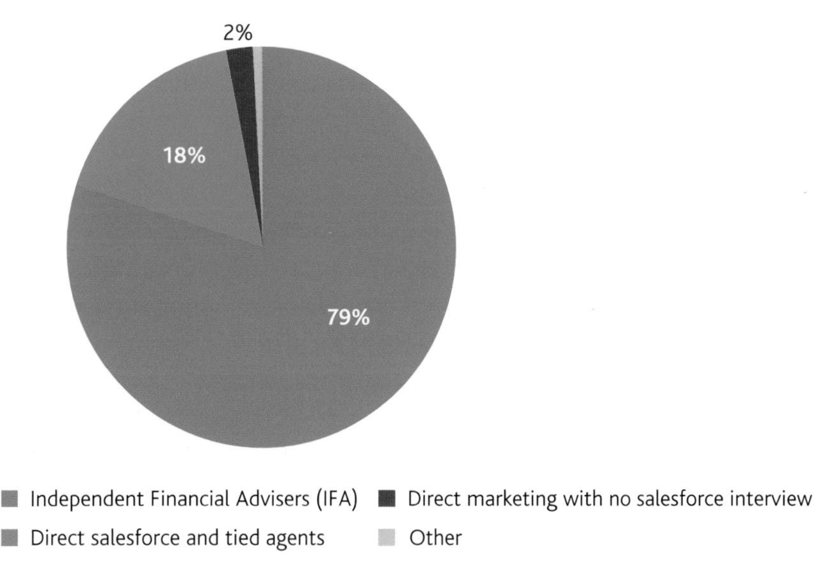

Source: ABI new business statistics, 2003

Note: Data includes all Stakeholders, GPPs and FSAVCs.

- The state system is a complex combination of a relatively ungenerous contributory Basic State Pension (BSP), a means-tested Pension Credit, withdrawn as income rises, and a second tier earnings-related system (SERPS/S2P), the terms of which have been changed many times in the last 25 years, creating multiple different cohorts of individuals with rights accrued on different bases. Both the complexity and frequency of change contrasts dramatically with, for instance, the US system, where the key features of the Social Security system have been remarkably stable over 70 years, or with the main continental systems. Looking forward, any individual's state pension entitlement will depend crucially on the indexation applied to multiple values and thresholds (the UEL, the LEL, the LET, the Guarantee Credit, and the BSP). These indexation policies are announced only one Parliament ahead, do not command cross-party consensus, and have been changed frequently in the past. As a result, it is close to impossible for individuals to have a clear idea of what they can in future expect from the state system, and survey evidence shows that this is indeed the case [Figure 6.5].[1]

- The private system meanwhile has developed, for a set of historical reasons, a complex set of legal and tax forms (COSR, COMP, GPP, APP, Stakeholder, AVC, FSAVC etc). These multiple legal forms make it extremely difficult for many people to combine different pots of pension savings, which in turn increases costs. They also generate confusion among customers, and indeed among industry and government statisticians. [Appendix A explains how confusion about the distinction between GPP and Defined Contribution (DC) occupational pensions is one of the factors which has led to problems in National Statistics estimates.] While the Government's tax simplification proposals will be a useful step away from this complexity, legal differences between trustee and contract-based forms will remain as barriers to pension pot combination and to customer understanding. And while the government provides significant tax incentives to private pension saving, the majority of people do not know what tax relief rate they receive on pension contributions [Figure 6.6].

- Finally, the UK has introduced a unique complexity at the interface between the state and private systems: the contracting-out option. The terms of this option have been changed several times, creating incentives for the rational individual to first contract-out and then contract back in, further proliferating the number of small pension pots, some but not all of which are subject to complex annuity indexation requirements. [See the panel in Chapter 3 for a description of contracting-out.] The overall effect of this complexity has been to increase costs and create customer confusion, and thus to make it less likely that a voluntary solution can work. Only 44% of people claim good or reasonable understanding of pension issues, and this percentage seems to be falling rather than increasing [Figure 6.7].

[1]Note: The potential impact of new government initiatives to change this situation, e.g. via pension forecasts, is considered under the heading "Revitalised voluntarism" in Chapter 7.

Figure 6.5 Do you have a clear idea of how much state pension you can expect in retirement?

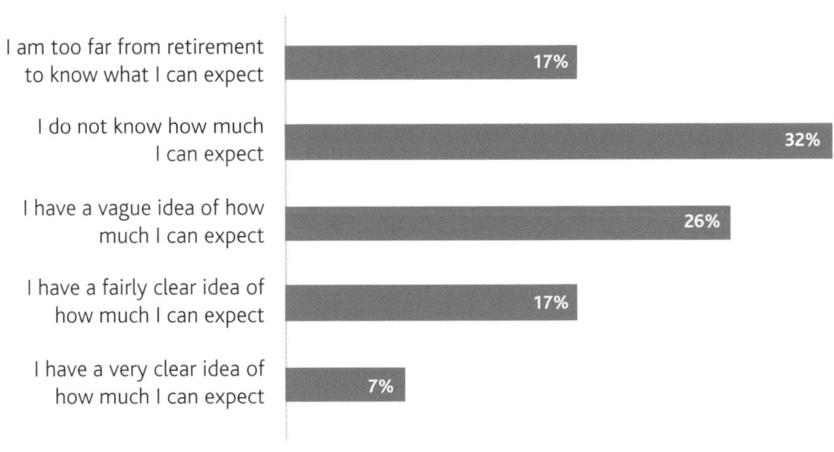

Source: Pensions and Savings Index, Survey 1 (Sept 2003), by YouGov for the ABI

Figure 6.6 What do you think is the level of tax relief you are personally entitled to receive on your pension contributions?

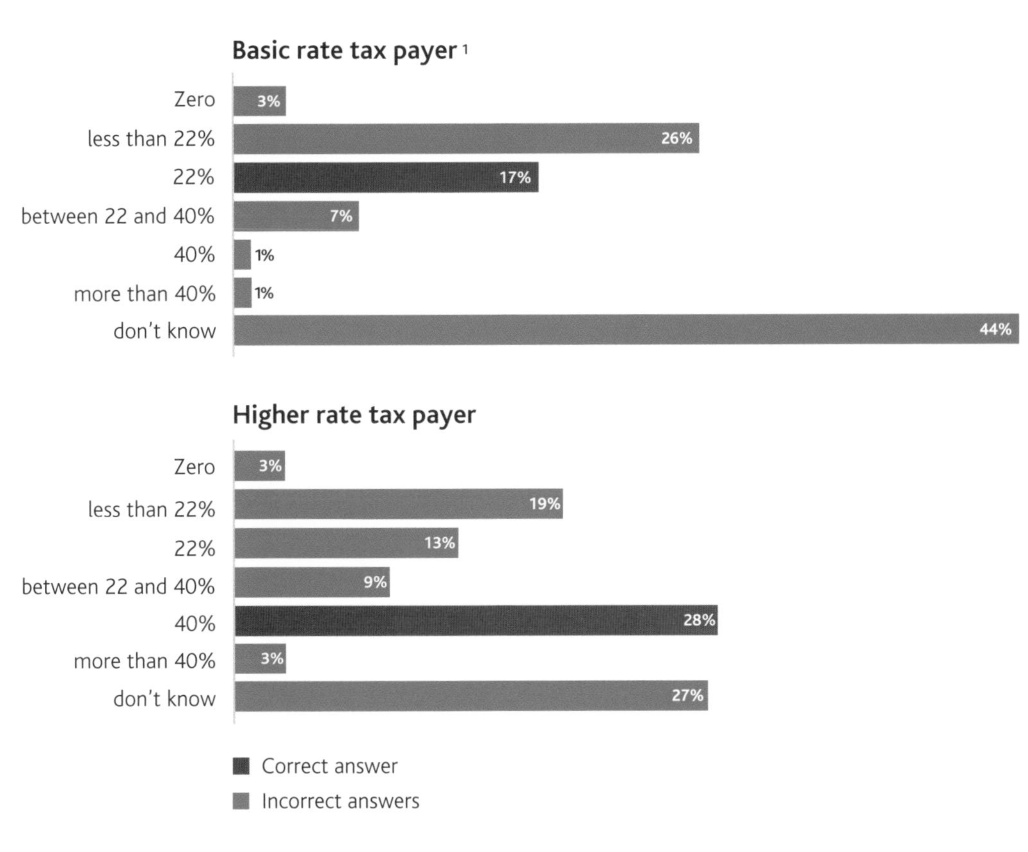

Source: Pensions and Savings Index, Survey 1 (Sept 2003), by YouGov for the ABI.

Note: Results are percentages of the relevant population.

[1] In fact basic rate taxpayers who are receiving Working Tax Credit or Child Tax Credit, could, at least over some range of income, be receiving an effective rate of tax relief of 59%. These survey results suggest, however, that almost none of them know this.

Trust: Most individuals lack confidence about their ability to make rational decisions when thinking about pension saving. They are therefore heavily reliant on advisers whom they trust. But in the UK today two of the key potential sources of advice are not trusted. The retail financial services industry has lost the trust of customers as a result of a sequence of mis-selling scandals and problems (such as pension mis-selling, endowment mis-selling, Equitable Life, split capital trusts). And the government is not trusted either, probably because of the frequency with which governments over the years have changed state pension promises. Only employers still show up in surveys as trusted on pension matters at least by those who are actually members of occupational pension schemes. While this may seem surprising in the light of the major, highly publicised, and tragic cases of pension fund insolvency, it may reflect understanding of the reality that the vast majority of employer Defined Benefit (DB) promises have been met [Figure 6.8]. Trust in DB schemes may also grow in future to reflect the insurance provided by the Pension Protection Fund.

3. Selling and administration costs

Both the inherent and the UK specific barriers increase the costs of selling and processing pension products, particularly when sold on an individual basis. The only way to deliver private pension products at low cost is via economy of scale intermediaries, such as large companies. But trends in pension provision (in particular the declining participation of employers) are reducing the role of bulk purchasers. And the Sandler product measures to reduce the cost of individual sale seem unlikely to transform the situation.

- It is important to identify all the costs that stand between the rate of return in the wholesale markets (which we presented in Figures 3.52-3.54 Chapter 3), and the return which the individual saver receives. These come in two forms:

  - Explicit costs charged by the pension provider or overtly paid by the scheme trustee/administrator in an occupational scheme. These cover the costs of sales and administration, as well as fund management fees. For personal pension contracts, regulation requires that these are explicitly revealed.

  - The implicit costs (the cost of dealing incurred by fund managers) which reduces total return, but which is not explicitly revealed.

Figure 6.7 Self-Reported Knowledge on Pensions

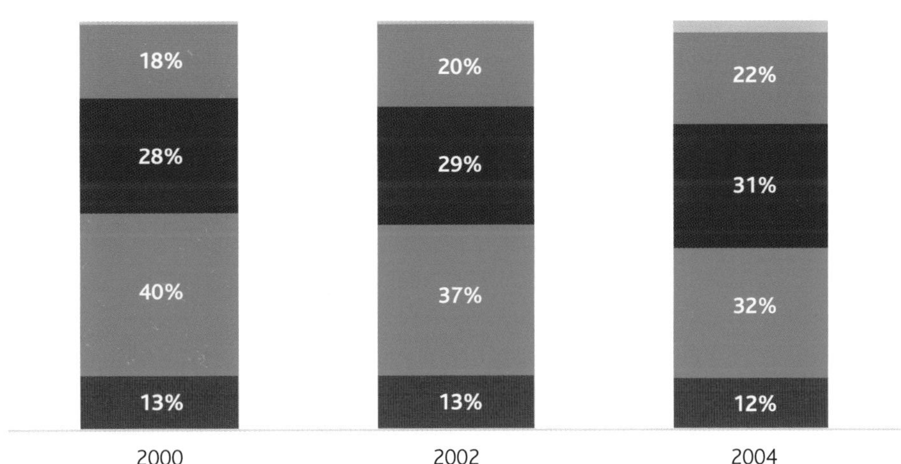

- I have a good knowledge of pensions issues
- I have a reasonable, basic knowledge of pensions
- My knowledge of pensions is patchy
- I know little or nothing about pensions issues
- Don't know

Source: 2000 figures taken from Mayhew, V (2001) Pensions 2000: Public Attitudes to Pensions and Planning for Retirement; 2002 figures taken from Mayhew, V (2003) Pensions 2002: Public attitudes to Pensions and Saving for Retirement; 2004 figures taken from National Statistics Omnibus Survey for Pensions Commission.

Note: Results are percentages of the population.

Figure 6.8 Who People Trust to Deliver on Pension Promises

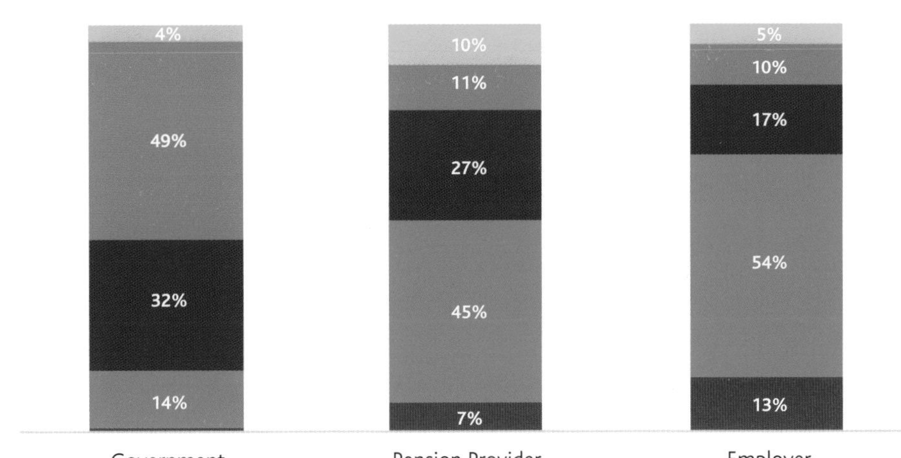

How much do you trust the following to not let you down on your pension?

- I trust a great deal
- I tend to trust
- I tend to distrust
- I do not trust at all
- Don't know

Source: Pensions and Savings Index, Survey 1 (Sept 2003), by YouGov for the ABI.

Note: The sample for the questions about trust in the government and pension providers were all individuals who were members of at least one pension scheme. The sample for the question about trust in their employers was all those who had an occupational pension scheme. The results are percentages of the relevant population.

- Explicit costs vary hugely by size and type of scheme. Large scale occupational schemes, whether DB or DC, can have explicit costs as low as 0.2% of fund value each year, while small occupational schemes can have an explicit cost up to 0.5%. According to the GAD Survey of Occupational Pensions Schemes in 2000, the overall average administration cost of private sector schemes was 0.4%. But individually purchased pensions typically have a Reduction in Yield (RIY) of 1% or more. Estimates of the cost of GPPs are less readily available but discussions with industry providers suggest that they range from 0.5%-1% for companies with between 50 and 1,000 employees. GPPs tend to be more expensive to administer than occupational schemes, both because they are typically sold to smaller firms than those with occupational schemes, and because while the terms of GPPs are bulk negotiated by employers, the legal contract is with the individual employee, generating individual-specific sales and administration costs [Figure 6.9].

- Estimates of implicit costs vary, but one major study published by the FSA in 2000 suggests that they could be as high as 1.3% for actively managed equity funds, and 0.5-1.3% even for equity trackers. Some of these results, particularly for index trackers, look surprisingly high, and the Pensions Commission will conduct more work over the next year to validate results, and to extend the work to cover bonds, where implicit cost ought to be significantly less. But it is clear that implicit costs add significantly to the overall costs, with implications for post-cost return. In our modelling we have assumed implicit costs of about 0.4%-0.5% on average across all asset classes. [See the panel on the following pages for discussion of the FSA study, other data on implicit costs and the basis of our assumptions.]

Figure 6.9 An Estimate of the Overall Cost Curve: Reduction in Yield

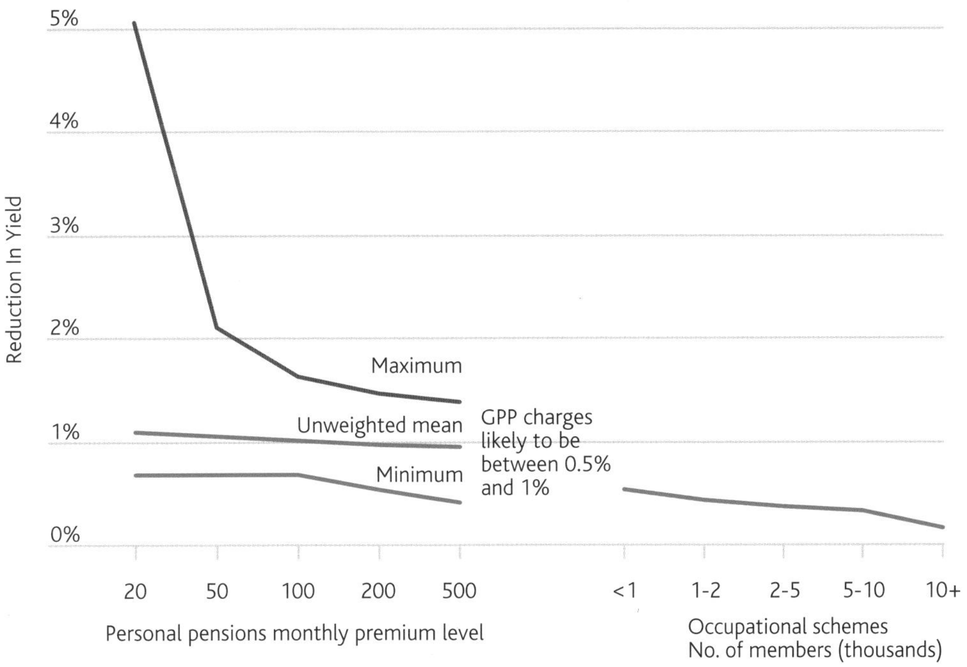

Reduction In Yield
5%
4%
3%
2%
1%
0%
Maximum
Unweighted mean
Minimum
GPP charges likely to be between 0.5% and 1%
20 50 100 200 500
Personal pensions monthly premium level
<1 1-2 2-5 5-10 10+
Occupational schemes
No. of members (thousands)

Source: Personal pension data from FSA comparative tables.
Occupational pensions from GAD survey 1998.
GPP estimates based on discussion with the industry.

Estimating implicit costs of investing

Some of the costs involved in investing are fairly clear, and indeed some are required to be by regulation. Personal pension products are required by regulation to reveal the Reduction in Yield (RIY) which results from the price charged by the provider to cover costs of selling, administration and fund management. The estimates of the costs of occupational pensions presented in Figure 6.9 also cover all these explicit costs.

But even if these explicit costs were zero, investors would not receive the full market return calculated (as in, for instance, Figures 3.52 and 3.54) from market prices and dividend yields. This is because there are, in addition, trading costs, which are sometimes called implicit costs because their impact is not explicitly revealed, but rather reduces the return on investment before explicit costs are deducted.

Estimating the implicit costs is difficult but vital, if as seems likely, the implicit costs are for some investors as significant as explicit costs.

In February 2000, the Financial Services Authority published an occasional paper authored by Kevin James, which is believed to be one of the most detailed studies of implicit cost.[1] The paper is not specifically focused on pensions, but on retail investments such as unit trusts, but its findings are likely to be broadly applicable to pension investment as well.

James considers two issues:

- What are the inherent implicit costs of each specific trade, and what therefore are the annual costs of trading for any given fund turnover in a year?
- What is the observed difference between gross returns in the market and net returns to investments (but before explicit costs)? This difference is the actual implicit cost given actual levels of fund turnover.

Implicit costs per trade

James estimates the cost of a two-way trade, i.e. the cost of buying one equity and selling another. In the London equity market he estimates the elements of this to be

Broker Commission	30 b.p.[2]	(i.e.15 b.p. on both buy and sell side)
Bid-offer spread (The difference between the quoted price to buyers and to sellers.)	75 b.p.	(i.e. 37.5 b.p. on each side)
Price impact (Reflecting the fact that buying can move the price up and selling move the price down.)	25 b.p.	(i.e. 12.5 b.p. on each side)
Stamp Duty	50 b.p.	(only charged on the buy side)
TOTAL	180 b.p.	

These costs per trade, multiplied by the turnover of a fund, would give the total annual reduction in yield. Thus if a fund turned over 200% (i.e. 100% sold plus 100% bought) in the London market, a RIY from implicit costs of 1.8% would be expected.

These estimates do not feed into James' estimates of actual observed implicit costs (explained below). But it is useful to compare them with recent estimates of cost per trade to gauge whether costs may have changed since James' analysis.

Pensions Commission discussions with industry experts suggest present day estimates of 28 b.p. commission for a round trip trade (close to James' figures) but 70 b.p. for the cost of trading (combining the bid-offer spread and price-impact) compared with James' 100 b.p. This may reflect the fact that bid-offer spreads have come down, slightly for FTSE 100 stocks and significantly for FTSE 250 stocks, partly as a result of changes in the London Stock Exchange system for the matching of buy and sell orders.

Including the 50 b.p. for stamp duty these alternative estimates would suggest a round trip cost of 148 b.p. versus James's 180 b.p. These suggest that estimates of implicit costs drawn from late 1990s data might somewhat overstate present costs, but not dramatically so.

[1]Note: The price of retail investing in the UK, FSA occasional paper 6 (February 2000)

[2]Note: A Basis Point (b.p.) is one-one hundredth of a percentage point i.e. 0.01%

Estimates of actual implicit costs

James' estimates of what implicit costs actually were is derived by looking at the difference between market returns and the returns actually achieved by funds before explicit costs were charged. He draws on a large sample of funds from the Micropal database, and makes some complex econometric adjustments to allow for the different investment style of different funds.

His estimates are shown in Figure 6.10, with UK active funds showing an implicit cost of 1.3% per year, UK trackers 0.88% per year, USA actives 0.9% per year, and US trackers 0.4% per year. The lower levels for the US can largely be explained by the absence of stamp duty, which if turnover were, say 100% (combining buy and sell orders), adds 0.25% per year costs.

Assessment and assumption for modelling

The paper's analysis of costs as they were in the late 1990s appears methodologically robust and it is clear that implicit costs can be high, particularly for actively managed funds. The results, however, appear to some industry experts to be surprisingly high for UK trackers, and may not reflect the recent growth in importance of the tracker funds, which along with the decline in the bid-offer spread, may have resulted in reduced costs. And an alternative check can be made by looking at the actual level of stamp duty paid and then grossing up for other costs. In 2002/03 UK stamp duty paid on shares was £2.5 billion, equivalent to 22 b.p. on the stock market value at the end of 2002. Our latest industry estimates suggest that stamp duty accounts for 50 b.p. out of 148 b.p. for a combined sale and buy round trip i.e. for about 33% of all trading costs. This implies total trading costs of 66 b.p. of fund values.

Balancing these different considerations the Pensions Commission has decided to assume 65 b.p. implicit costs for equity investment on average (consistent with a lower rate for tracker funds and a higher one for active). Implicit costs for bond funds should be much less, but the Commission has not discovered an existing analysis of this issue. For now we use 25 b.p. for corporate bonds and 10 b.p. for government bonds in our modelling.

Combining these two assumptions would suggest about 40-50 b.p. for a balanced bond and equity portfolio. This compares well with an estimate of about 50 b.p. given to us by a major pension fund manager for total implicit costs across all their funds under management.

During the consultation period we would like to hear views on whether our current assumptions appear too high or too low. We intend to conduct further research and to request information from fund managers on this issue.

Figure 6.10 Estimated Annual Percentage Reduction in Yield resulting from Implicit Costs: from Kevin James' paper

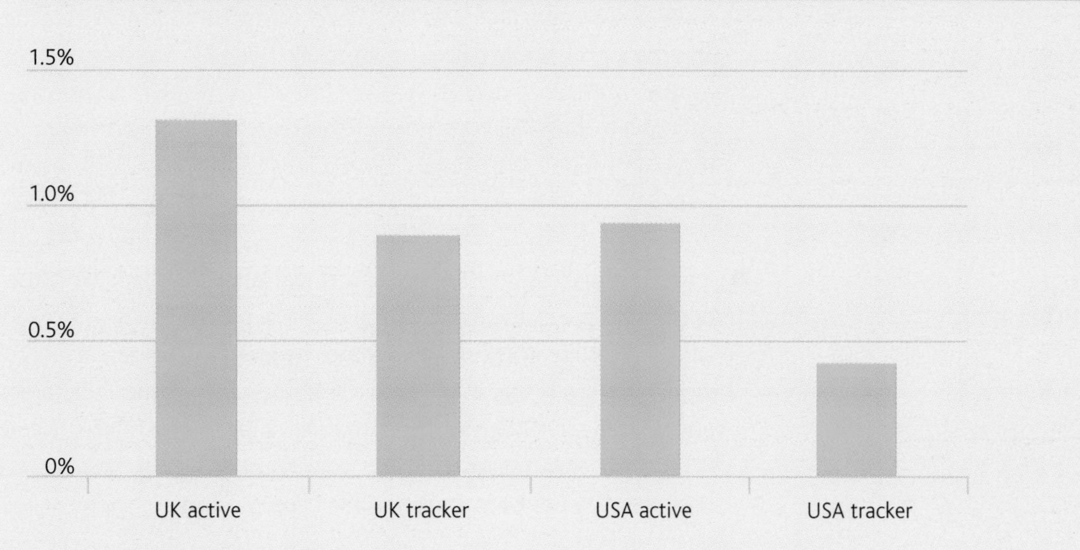

Source: FSA, Occasional Paper 6 (February 2000)

- Explicit prices for individual pensions have come down significantly from those seen in the early 1990s, with the Stakeholder Pension price cap of 1% Annual Management Charge (AMC) having a major impact on industry pricing [Figure 6.11]. But it is likely that at present price levels the financial services industry cannot sell profitably to lower income, small premium savers. At least 75% of the total explicit cost of providing a pension under the current sales regime is incurred upfront in the selling and set-up process, is independent of the size of the premium, and is to a significant extent determined by the regulations governing the sales process, which exist to prevent mis-selling. Unless these costs are covered by the price charged, Independent Financial Advisers (who as Figure 6.4 showed form the dominant sales channel for personal pensions) will not sell pensions, but focus on other more profitable products. It is clear from industry statistics and interviews that most IFAs now see personal pension sales as a low priority and are instead focused on protection products (e.g. term insurance), single premium bonds, income draw-down and other annuity related products, and in particular over the last year, mortgages.

- Concerns about the profitability of pension sales under the current Conduct of Business regulations, lay behind Ron Sandler's recommendations that a new lower cost sales regime should be designed for the sale of standardised savings products, including a pension product, which would be subject to a price cap. The FSA proposed in June (see 2004 CP 04/11) that a "lighter touch" sales regime should be allowed, permitting the use of lower cost, less highly trained advisers, and a shorter interview process. HM Treasury published its proposals in June, accepting the industry argument (which was supported by a number of detailed cost models) that a 1% price cap would be too stringent. It agreed that a price cap of 1.5% for the initial ten years of a pension falling to 1% for the remainder of the contract would be required to make pension sales profitable even under the lighter touch sales regime. This cap regime would be equivalent to a RIY of 1.2% for a pension contract maintained over 20 years. In fact at the moment, for reasons discussed in the panel in Chapter 7 ("Can costs of low persistency be reduced?"), the typical pension contract lasts less than ten years. For a contract lasting 10 years, the RIY under the new price cap will be 1.6%.

- It is hoped that the combination of the new sales regime and the looser price cap will revitalise industry interest in the personal pension market and, in particular, in selling to lower income low premium savers. Estimates suggest that as the allowable charge cap increases it becomes profitable to serve a significantly larger percentage of the market [Figure 6.12]. There are however three reasons why the impact of these measures may not be as great as some hope.

Figure 6.11 Reduction in Yield for the Average Personal Pension Contract Held for 25 Years

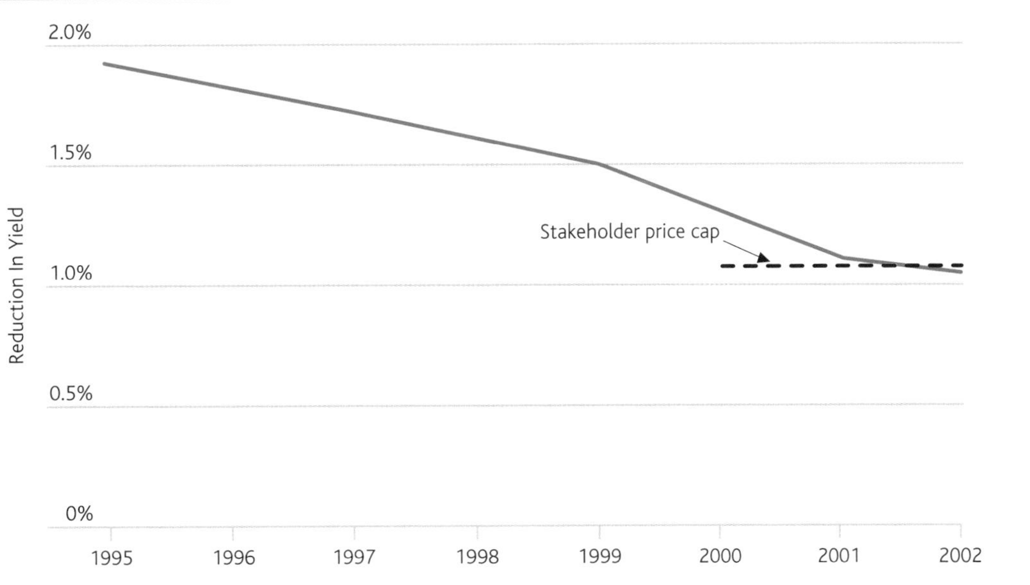

Source: FSA disclosure surveys

Note: Stakeholder pensions were introduced in April 2000. The annual management charge is capped at 1% per year which is equivalent to a 1.1% RIY over 25 years.

Figure 6.12 Profitable Premium Levels and Policy Length: Estimates from the ABI model

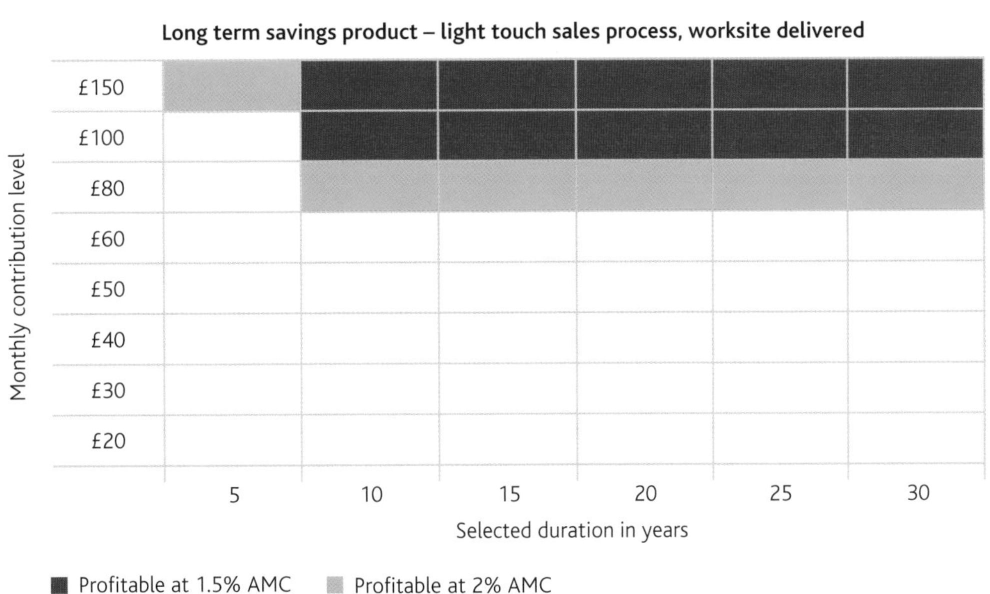

Source: ABI submission to the consultation on the charge cap for Sandler products

Note: Results based on ABI cost model produced prior to the decision on the Sandler price cap and sales regime

1. While it may now in theory be profitable to serve lower income savers, most of the cost models suggest that profitability will be only marginal and only under certain assumptions:

   - The Deloitte model commissioned by HM Treasury[2], for instance, explicitly assumes that lower income customers buying individual personal pensions will only be profitable as part of a bundle of both high and low income customers, with an implicit cross-subsidy between them. But cross-subsidy does not occur in fully competitive and informed markets and will not be available if providers either deliver pensions to high-income customers at below the price cap, or if they aim for high profitability by targeting high income customers alone.

   - The Aegon[3] model which concentrates on the GPP market, suggests that a 26 employee firm can be profitably served within a price cap of 5% contribution charge plus 1% AMC (equivalent to an RIY of 1.3% if someone saves for 30 years) assuming that the light touch sales regime allows a reduction in costs of 25%. But this still implies a large unservable market of firms of less than about 20 employees. And the model makes the explicit assumption that GPPs can only be profitable if employers make a contribution, and that the total contribution is £123 per month, i.e. a contribution rate of 7% on median earnings), since only with an employer contribution will employee participation rates rise to profitable levels.

2. The economics assume the training, accreditation, and deployment of an entire new basic advice sales force, which does not yet exist. It is unclear if the industry will actually develop and deploy this sales force in large numbers. Discussions with major players in the IFA market have revealed considerable doubts as to whether the option of using the new basic advice salesforce will make a significant difference to the attractiveness of pension sales to lower income, small premium customers.

3. Most fundamentally, however, if the industry does require a 1.5% AMC to sell to low income customers or employees of small firms, that cost is itself a major disincentive to saving and has implications for the level of saving required to deliver adequate pensions. For a pension saver contributing over 30 years and achieving a 4% gross return, an AMC of 1.5% means that 24% of the accumulated savings and investment return is absorbed in operating expenses by the time of retirement. Once implicit costs of say 0.5% are also taken into account, the combined annual reduction in return of 2% would absorb 30% of the fund. The RIY this implies of 2.1% is high relative to reasonable expectations of rates of return. Such RIYs and indeed higher ones appeared acceptable in the 1980s and 1990s because of the very high real returns achieved in those decades on equities, and in the 1990s on

[2] Note: The Deloitte model is published in HM Treasury and DWP (July 2003) *Assessing the likely market impacts of charge caps on retail investment policies.*

[3] Note: The Aegon model was a confidential annex in Aegon (2003) *Aegon UK response to HM Treasury and DWP Pensions Consultation document: process product specification for Sandler "stakeholder" products.*

Figure 6.13 Distribution of Real Annualised Rates of Return on UK equities Over ten Year Periods Since 1899

Frequency – numbers of periods
20
15
10
5
0
Whole period
mean 5.5
median 5.2
After 1977
mean 10.5
median 11.1
-14 – -12
-10 – -8
-6 – -4
-2 –0
2–4
6–8
10–12
14–16
18–20
Annualised real rates of return
1977 onwards
Whole period

Source: Barclays Equity Gilt Study 2004

Figure 6.14 Distribution of Real Annualised Rates of Return on UK Gilts Over ten Year Periods Since 1899

Frequency – numbers of periods
20
15
10
5
0
Whole period
median 0.1
Whole period
mean 1.1
After 1977
mean 6.9
median 6.9
-14– -12
-10– -8
-6– -4
-2–0
2–4
6–8
10–12
14–16
18–20
Annualised real rates of return
1977 onwards
Whole period

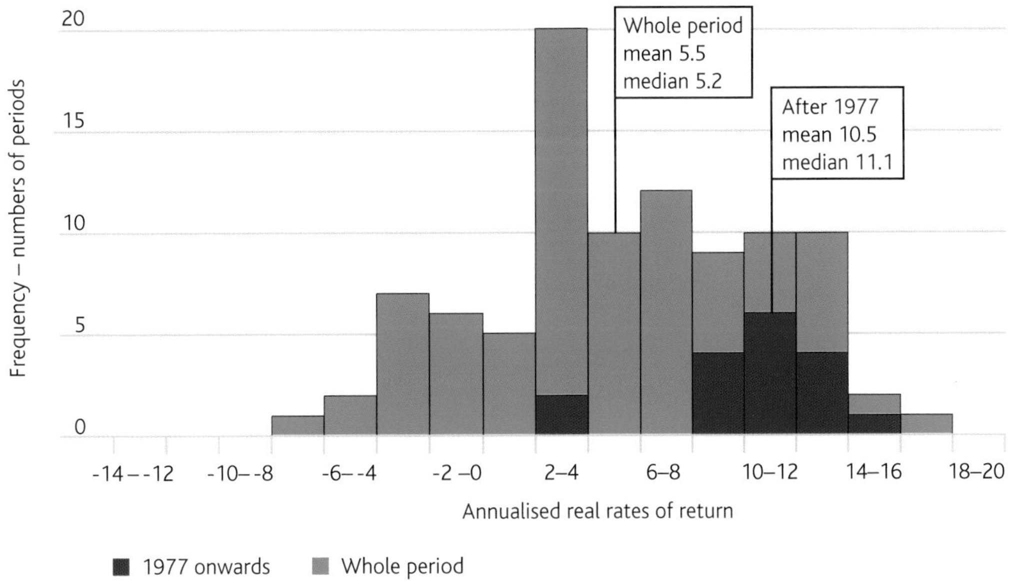

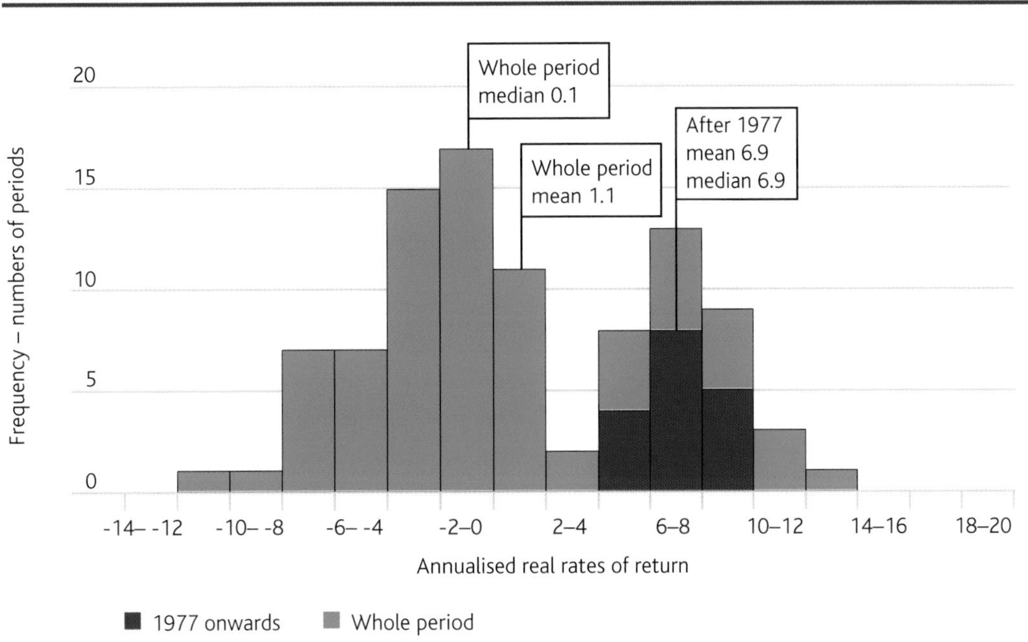

Source: Barclays Equity Gilt Study 2004

nominal bonds. But these returns were exceptional in historical context and cannot be expected to apply in the future [Figure 6.13 and 6.14]. Looking forward, reasonable expectations of real rates of return are more likely to be about 6% for equities, 2% for gilts and 2.7% for corporate bonds, implying overall pre-cost returns of about 4.1% for a balanced portfolio. [See Appendix C for the precise assumptions used in the modelling.] Against such returns, a RIY of 2.1% represents a major reduction in the return on saving and thus incentive to save. It may still be rational for people to save at very low or indeed negative real rates of return but RIYs at this level also increase substantially the contribution rate required to achieve adequate pension income.[4]

The issue which therefore needs to be debated, and on which the Pensions Commission invites views during our consultation process, is whether this implies that there is a segment of the pension market, comprised of lower income savers and people working for small firms, to which a free market will never be able to sell pension products profitably except at RIYs which make saving unattractive.

4. The impact of means testing

The total impact of all tax, NI contributions and benefit policies which impact the return on saving are extremely complex, as the panel at the end of this chapter explains. The vast majority of people are better off saving via pension contributions than out of post-tax earnings. But for some people the economic incentives to save are reduced by the impact of means-testing within the UK state system, an impact which would increase over time if current indexation approaches were continued over the long-term.

- Means-testing has grown as the by-product of government policies for which there was a clear logic. The present Government believed in 1997 that the biggest immediate problem with the UK pension system was high levels of pensioner poverty. It aimed to fix this problem but within tight public expenditure constraints. The way chosen to do this was to target resources via means-tested benefits to ensure that all pensioners can receive at least the Guarantee Credit currently £105.45. The only way then to avoid 100% withdrawal rates over the first £25.85 of private pension income (the difference between the Guarantee Credit and the BSP), was to apply a lower withdrawal rate over a wider band of income. The combination chosen, via the Pension Credit arrangements, was a 40% withdrawal rate over about £60 of income. As a result of the introduction of the Pension Credit therefore, a smaller proportion of pensioners face very high withdrawal rates, but 40% of all pensioners face combined tax and benefit withdrawal rates of over 50% [Figure 6.15].

[4] Note: It may make rational sense to invest even at a negative real rate of return because people need to support consumption in retirement, and therefore need to use savings to transfer income from working life to retirement even if it gives a poor return. Simple economic theory tends to assume that people need to be enticed into consumption deferral by positive real returns, but this assumption breaks down if there is no option of simply storing consumption goods for future use, and given the need for future consumption. For this reason, savings rates can rise in periods of negative real return (e.g. the mid-1970s).

- The number of people covered by means-testing would grow further if current indexation approaches were continued indefinitely. The Government wishes to avoid pensioner poverty, and has therefore been increasing the Guarantee Credit in line with average earnings. But it also wishes to contain public expenditure on pensions and has therefore been increasing the BSP in line with prices. While indicative long-term public spending forecasts reflect the continuation of this, the Government has no long-term commitment to any particular indexation approach. But if it and future governments did continue indefinitely a policy of Pension Credit indexation to average earnings but combined with a BSP linked to prices, by 2050 over 60% of pensioners would face the 40% withdrawal rate implicit in the Pension Credit, and many would face higher rates still due to the additional impact of tax. [See the panel on the following pages for a description of the Pension Credit system and why its coverage would increase over time if current indexation approaches were continued indefinitely.]

Figure 6.15 Distribution of Marginal Deduction Rates for Pensioners Before and After the Introduction of the Pension Credit

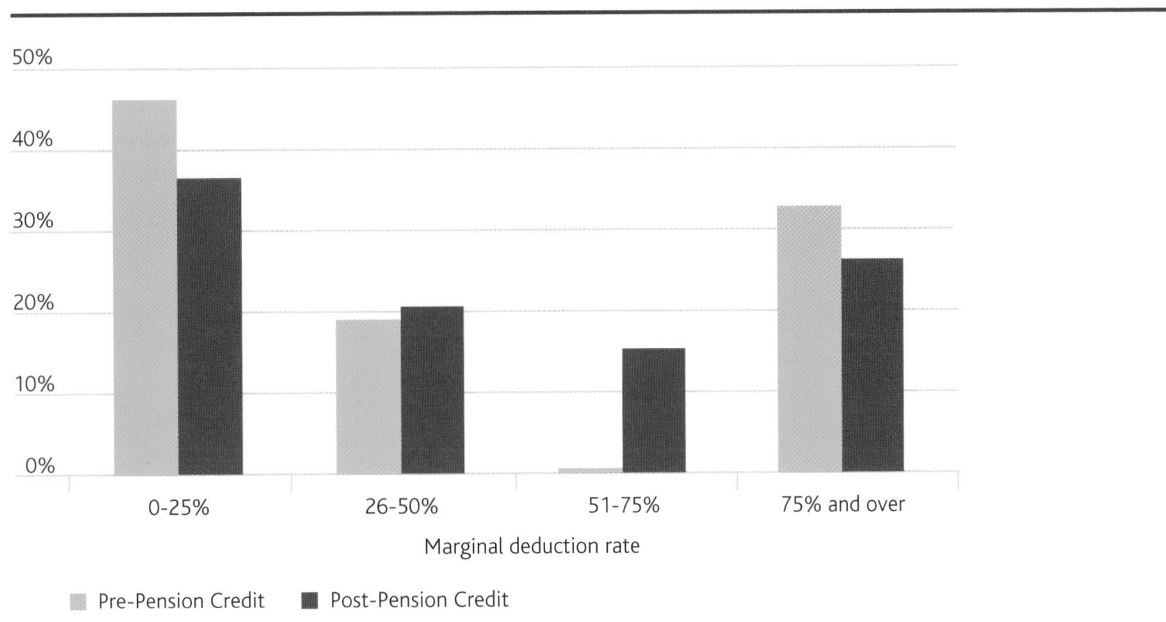

Source: DWP Policy Simulation Model 2004-05

Pension Credit

Pension Credit is a means-tested benefit available to people over 60. It has two elements: the 'Guarantee Credit' and a 'Savings Credit' which is only available to people aged 65 plus. These two components add up to a benefit which tops people's income up to a level of income and then is tapered away at 40p for every extra pound of pre-benefit income above a particular level. The impact of the Pension Credit is therefore to make many people better off, but to reduce the incentive to save for some of them.

Structure of the Pension Credit

The impact of the Guarantee Credit is shown in Figure 6.16. It simply tops people's income up to a particular level (£105.45 per week for a single person in 2003/4) with a pound for pound withdrawal rate for any pre-benefit income. For example, someone with £90 pre-benefit income (including BSP, SERPS/S2P and private pension income) ends up with £105.45 post-benefit income, as does someone with £100 in pre-benefit income. Since people aged 60-64 can receive the Guarantee Credit but not the Savings Credit, this is the situation they face. This was also roughly the situation faced by all people over 60 before Pension Credit was introduced in 2003, that is under what was then called the Minimum Income Guarantee (MIG).

The Savings Credit is an additional means-tested benefit relating to income above the level of the BSP. Its value is calculated in such a way as to mean that the effective withdrawal rate of the Pension Credit (Guarantee Credit and Savings Credit) is 40% if pre-benefit income is above the BSP (while withdrawing 100% if income is below the level of the BSP) [Figure 6.17].

Future Evolution of the Pension Credit

If current indexation approaches continued indefinitely, the Pension Credit would become more generous. This is because of the way the different thresholds used to calculate it would be uprated. The key thresholds are the level of the Guarantee Credit, which under current policy is uprated in line with average earnings, and the start point of the Savings Credit, uprated in line with price inflation (it is actually the level of the BSP). This would mean that over time the gap between the Guarantee Credit and the start of the Savings Credit would widen.

Figure 6.18 illustrates this by showing the possible shape of the Pension Credit at different points in time on this basis. All figures are in constant earnings terms. Over time the starting point of the Savings Credit would fall in earnings terms, whilst the level of the Guarantee Credit is constant. As a result, the Savings Credit would extend over a wider range, which means more people would be entitled to it and many people would be entitled to more. Clearly this would represent a boost to people's income and would mean more people's net income kept pace with average earnings. However, it also would mean more people seeing a reduced benefit to their net income from private saving.

Incentive effects of Pension Credit

Pension Credit affects people's incentives to save in a private pension because it changes the benefit to them of receiving this income as well as the need for it. However different groups of people are affected differently. Figure 6.19 and Tables 6.1 and 6.2 show the impact on incentives to save for the four different groups affected by the Pension Credit. The groups relate to different levels of income, as illustrated in Figure 6.19.

The tables demonstrate that, compared with the Minimum Income Guarantee, the Pension Credit improves incentives for some people (group B) but worsens them for others (group C). The evolution of the Pension Credit on the basis of current indicative plans would mean that over time these groups would become larger.

However, a change in incentives does not necessarily lead to a change in behaviour, particularly as incentive effects are complex, vary from person to person and depend on the decision they face.

The impact of the Pension Credit on incentives, moreover, depends on whether we are comparing the Pension Credit with the MIG system, or with the system as it existed before the MIG. Thus for example:

- Someone in group C who was considering saving a little extra into their pension has seen their gain from doing so reduced by the Pension Credit.
- However, if they were considering whether to save or not save, their gain from doing so has been improved by the Pension Credit, that is by the addition of the Saving Credit to the Minimum Income Guarantee.
- Compared with the situation in which there were no means-tested benefits at all, however, the introduction of the Pension Credit (the Savings Credit and the Guarantee Credit) has reduced incentives for individuals to save whatever decision they are making.

Figure 6.16 Guarantee Component of the Pension Credit

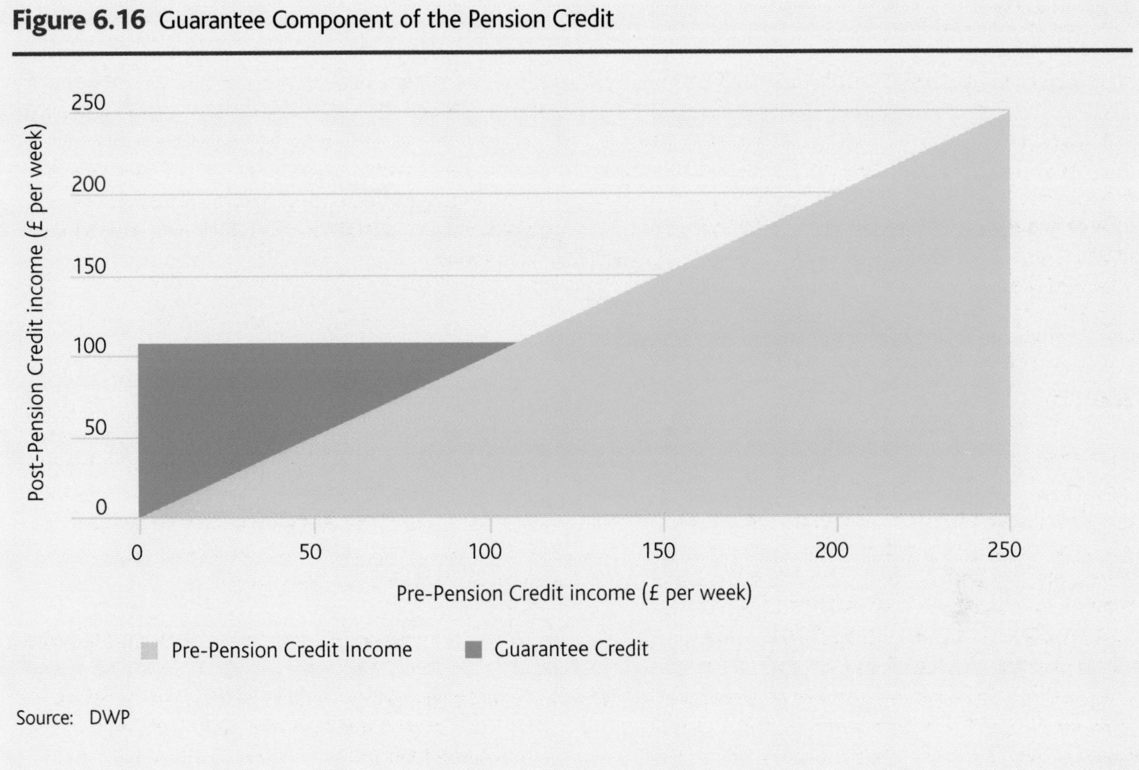

Source: DWP

Figure 6.17 Guarantee and Savings Credit Components of the Pension Credit

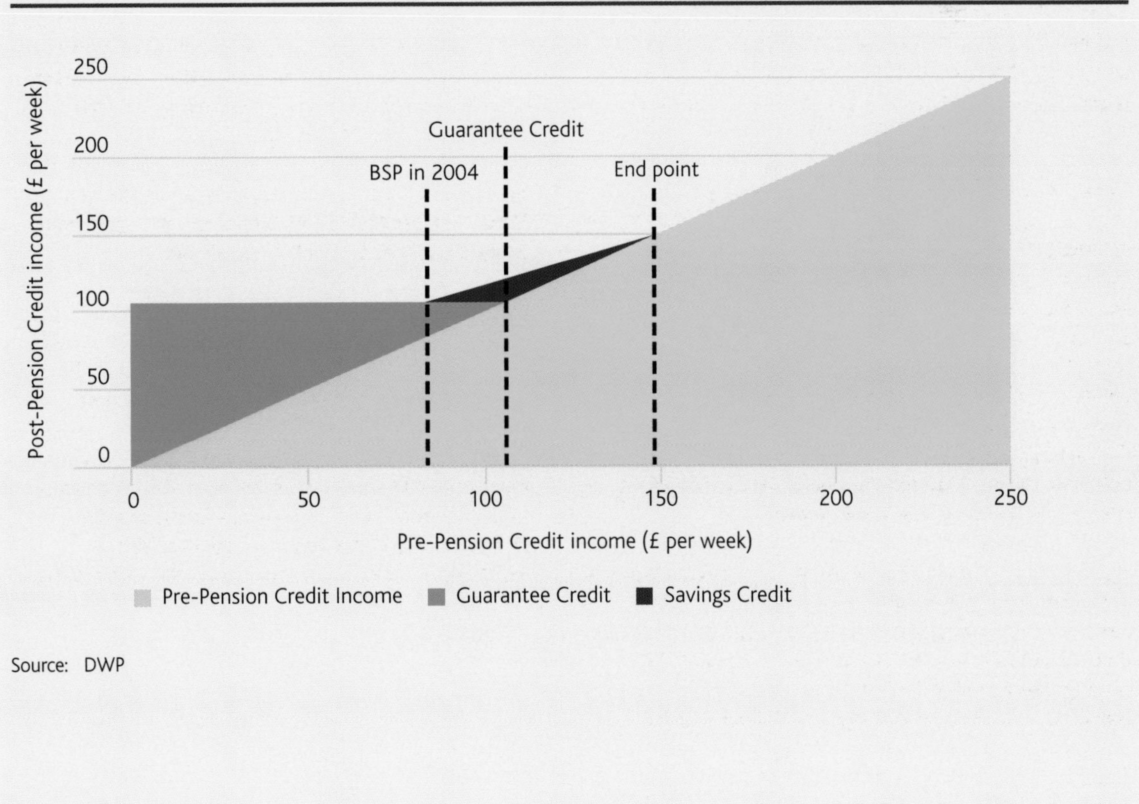

Source: DWP

Figure 6.18 Evolution of the Pension Credit

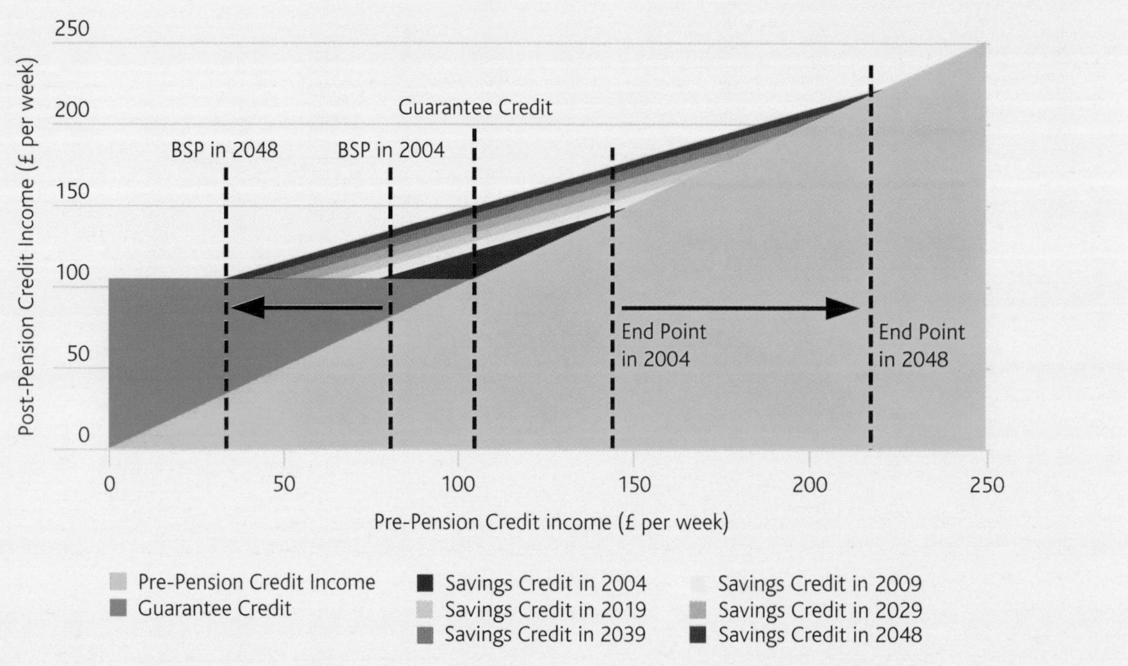

Source: DWP

Figure 6.19 Incentive Effects of the Pension Credit in 2019

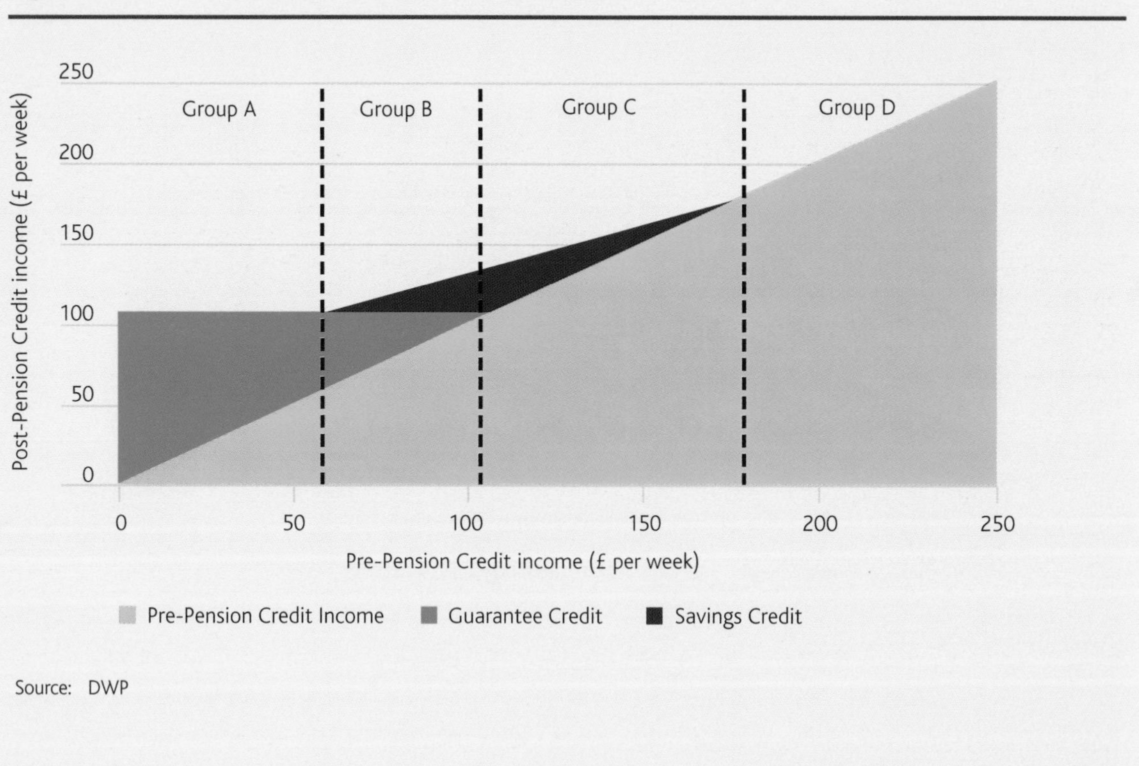

Source: DWP

Table 6.1 The Impact of the Pension Credit on the Gain From Saving Privately: £1 of saving

Counterfactual	Measure	Group A	Group B	Group C	Group D
Compared with Minimum Income Guarantee	Marginal gain	Unaffected (remains 0)	Increased from 0 to 60p	Reduced from £1 to 60p	Unaffected (remains £1)
	Average gain	Unaffected (remains 0)	Increased from 0 to 0-26p	Increased from 0 to 39p to 26-39p	Unaffected (remains 39p-£1)
Compared with no means-tested benefits	Marginal gain	Reduced from £1 to 0	Reduced from £1 to 60p	Reduced from £1 to 60p	Unaffected (remains £1)
	Average gain	Reduced from £1 to 0	Reduced from £1 to 0-26p	Reduced from £1 to 26-39p	Reduced from £1 to 39p-£1

Note: The marginal gain is the increase in post-benefit income from an increase in pre-benefit income of £1. The average gain is the average gain in post-benefit income from every £1 of pre benefit income. The average gain from voluntary saving would vary according to the amount of existing provision (e.g. from BSP and SERPS) a person has and this is explored in more detail in the rates of return appendix.

Table 6.2 The Impact of the Pension Credit on the Need to Save Privately

Counterfactual	Measure	Group A	Group B	Group C	Group D
Compared with MIG	Overall income	Unaffected	Reduced	Reduced	Unaffected
Compared with no means-tested benefits	Overall income	Would depend on policies			Unaffected

- These withdrawal rates can under some circumstances have a significant impact on the rational incentives to save. The overall impact of tax, NI and benefit policies on incentives to save is extremely complex. Some complexities to note are:

  - Most (but not all) people who can secure an employer's contribution are better off saving via pension contributions than being paid a higher salary at equivalent cost to their employers and saving out of post-tax earnings. This results from the combined impact of tax relief and the fact that additional pension contributions (up to certain limits) are not liable to employer's NI contributions. [See Table 6.4 within the panel, "Pension tax relief and the potential to save via pensions: the full complexity" at the end of the chapter.]

  - Some people on low to median earnings receive a high effective rate of tax relief on pension contributions, (up to 59%) since pension contributions reduce the calculated income used in determining Child Tax Credit and Working Tax Credits, and thus increase the tax credits received. For some people therefore higher effective tax relief on contributions will offset means-testing effects on pension income in retirement. However for those on incomes low enough to receive the maximum Child Credit (i.e. below the earnings limit to which withdrawal begins) this increase in the effective rate of tax relief will not apply.

  - While the Pension Credit reduces incentives to save relative to those which would pertain if there were no means-tested benefits, it has increased them for some people, though reduced them for others, when its impact is compared to that of the Minimum Income Guarantee. [See Table 6.1].

- Despite the complexities however, there are clearly many people for whom means-tested benefits do create a significant disincentive to save individually: and these will tend to be people least likely to gain the benefit of the NI efficiencies of employers' contributions. And it is clear that the sheer complexity of the current pattern of incentives is a problem. As Figure 6.6 has shown very few people understand even the simple income tax relief effects. The number of people who understand the myriad variants illustrated in Table 6.1 and Table 6.4 is still less.

- If therefore current indexation arrangements were continued indefinitely savings by low income individuals (and eventually by middle income individuals) would likely be depressed by the impact of means-testing. This would be for three reasons.

  (i) Because means-testing makes savings rationally less attractive for some people.

  (ii) Because IFAs and other pension sellers, for whom low income customers are in any case the least attractive segment of the market, will be wary of selling to people potentially affected by Pension Credit withdrawal for fear of future mis-selling accusations.

  (iii) Because the complexity can in itself be an impediment to rational savings decisions. Thus for instance, while many IFAs are aware of the negative impact of means-testing, very few people understood that for some people this is offset by the impact of Working Tax Credit and Child Tax Credit.

5. Incentives to save: rates of return for different categories of saver

Charges and means-testing can have significant influence on incentives to save for a pension. The other key influences are the degree of tax relief including the impact of Working Tax Credit and Child Tax Credit and the presence or absence of an employer contribution. Together these four factors result in hugely different incentives to save for different categories of saver.

Table 6.3 and Figures 6.20 to 6.23 on the following pages present results from the Pensions Commission's model of pension returns. These results are highly stylised, and rates of return achieved by specific individuals will reflect numerous complex factors not included here. [See Appendix C for details.] But the results here illustrate some of the key drivers of returns achieved. In each case we assume that return on saving after implicit costs but before all other costs, i.e. the return the saver would receive in a world of no taxes, no benefits, no explicit selling and administration costs, and no employer contributions, would be 3.2% real. This 3.2% real return would result from the combination of a 4% real return during the pension fund accumulation stage (after implicit costs but before explicit costs), and a 1.3% return during the annuity phase (the rate implicit in annuity pricing today).

Starting with this pre-everything return, Table 6.3 shows how the post-everything return varies for different categories of saver.

- The most typical case is probably someone who is a basic rate taxpayer at the margin in working life and retirement and who faces a 1% AMC on his pension fund. He contributes 7.5% of his salary into his pension and this is matched by his employer. His pre-everything return translates into a post-everything return of 5.2%. How this builds up is shown in Figure 6.20.

- Figure 6.21 shows the return on saving for someone who was a 40% taxpayer during working life, but a 22% payer in retirement, who is above the Pension Credit, who receives an employer contribution equal in size to his own contribution, and who enjoys, from membership of a large occupational DC scheme, explicit costs of only 0.3%. For this person a pre-everything return of 3.2% real on their own contributions alone becomes a 6.5% real return after all effects. The decision to participate in the employer's scheme should for this saver be an obvious one.

- Figure 6.22 shows the position for someone who pays 22% tax in working life and is on the Pension Credit in retirement but was not on Working Tax Credit during working life. He receives no employer contribution and faces a RIY from explicit costs of 1.5%. For this person a pre-everything return of 3.2% becomes 0.7% after all effects. A case can be made that this person should still save, given that the real value of contributions is, just, maintained and because people need to be able to defer income to cover consumption in retirement, even if the return is poor. But the incentives are hardly compelling, and look even worse once risk is taking into account. The example considered assumes a 50% equity weighting during the pension fund investment phase. But equity investment means that returns could diverge significantly, up or down, from the illustrated figures. Only 100% investment in real index-linked bonds would avoid that risk, but at the expense of a lower expected return of about 2.0% at the pre-everything level and -0.8% after all effects.

- Figure 6.23 however illustrates that if the person who was on Pension Credit during retirement [considered in Figure 6.22] had received Working Tax Credit throughout his working life, and if his earnings fell within the range at which the 37% withdrawal taper applies, his return could look significantly better. The 3.2% pre-everything return now becomes 4.1% after all effects. Someone who is on means-tested benefits in retirement, but did not receive Working Tax Credit, but did at some stage in their working life receive Child Tax Credit on the taper, would receive a return somewhere between that illustrated in Figure 6.22 and Figure 6.23. This reflects the fact the Child Tax Credit would only apply for a proportion of total working life reflecting the smaller number of years with the increased effective match rate. Finally it should be noted that some people with higher incomes in retirement may receive Child Tax Credit on the taper at some point during their working life and could therefore receive a better return than illustrated in Figure 6.20.

Table 6.3 Effective Rates of Return for Stylised Individuals with and without an Employer Contribution: Assuming a 3.2% return before all taxes and explicit cost

	No Employer Contributions	Employer Contributions
Higher tax payer in both working life and retirement. Not means-tested, 0.3% AMC.	3.9%	6.4%
Higher tax payer in working life, basic rate in retirement. Not means-tested, 0.3% AMC.	4.1%	6.5%
Basic rate tax payer in working life and retirement. Not means-tested, 1% AMC.	2.6%	5.2%
Basic rate tax payer on Working Tax Credit in working life, and on means-tested benefit in retirement. 1.5% AMC.	4.1%	5.2%
Basic rate tax payer in working life and on means-tested benefits in retirement, 1.5% AMC.	0.7%	3.2%

Note: The rate of return on individual saving across both accumulation and decumulation is 3.18%. We assume he starts saving at 35 and makes either an individual contribution of 15% or makes a 7.5% contribution with a 7.5% employer contribution. To simplfy the analysis we have assumed no earnings growth in real terms.

Figure 6.20 Effective Real Rate of Return for Stylised Individual Who Pays Basic Rate Tax in Working Life and Retirement

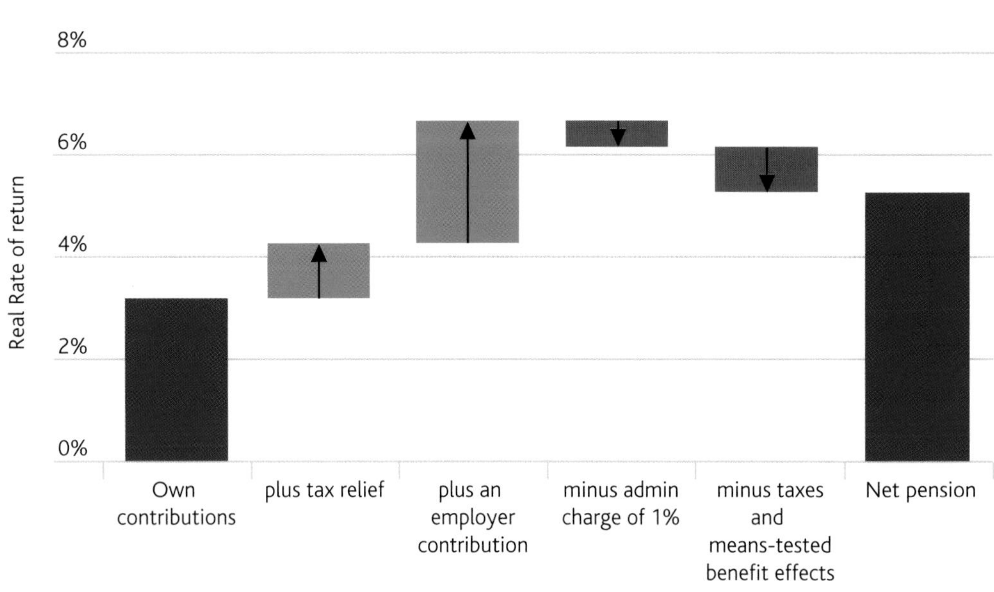

Note: The rate of return on individual saving across both accumulation and decumulation is 3.18%. We assume that he starts saving at 35 and makes a 7.5% contribution with a 7.5% employer contribution. To simplify the analysis we have assumed no earnings growth in real terms. He pays an annual management charge of 1%.

Figure 6.21 Effective Real Rate of Return for Stylised Individual Who Pays Higher Rate Tax in Working Life and Basic Rate Tax in Retirement

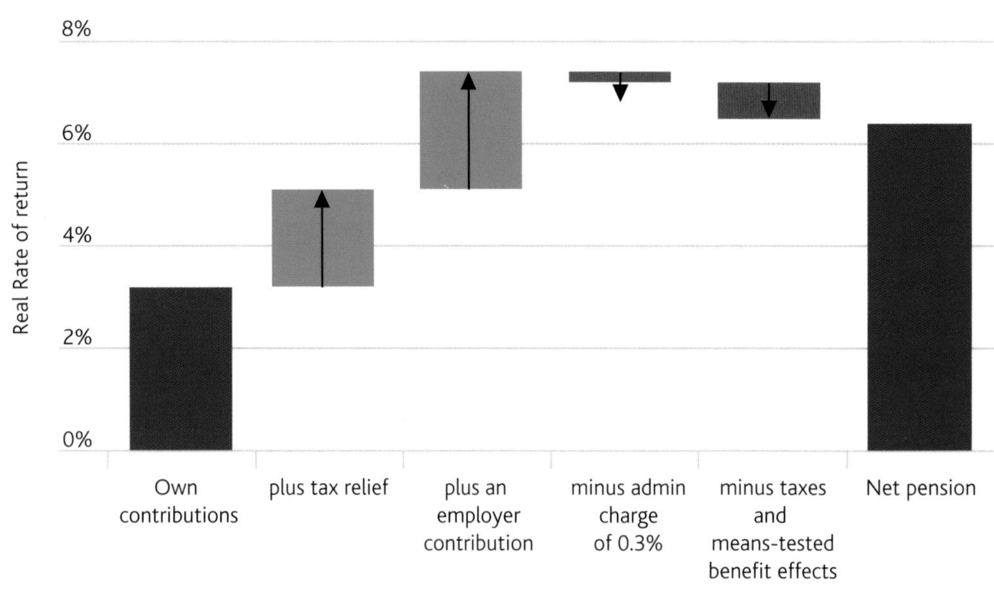

Note: The rate of return on individual saving across both accumulation and decumulation is 3.18%. We assume that he starts saving at 35 and makes a 7.5% contribution with a 7.5% employer contribution. To simplify the analysis we have assumed no earnings growth in real terms. He pays a annual management charge of 0.3%.

Figure 6.22 Effective Real Rate of Return for Stylised Individual Who Pays Basic Rate Tax in Working Life and Receives Means-tested Benefits in Retirement: not on Working Tax Credit during working life

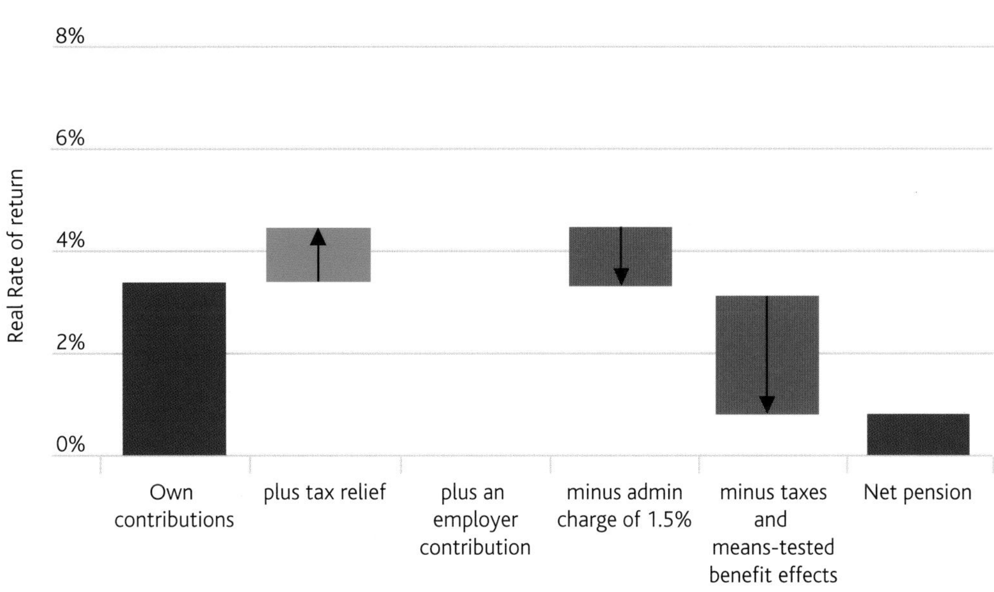

Note: The rate of return on individual saving across both accumulation and decumulation is 3.18%. We assume that he starts saving at 35 and makes an individual contribution of 15%. To simplify the analysis we have assumed no earnings growth in real terms. He pays an annual management charge of 1.5%.

Figure 6.23 Effective Real Rate of Return for Stylised Indivdidual who pays Basic Rate Tax and is on Working Tax Credit in Working Life and is on Means-tested Benefits in Retirement

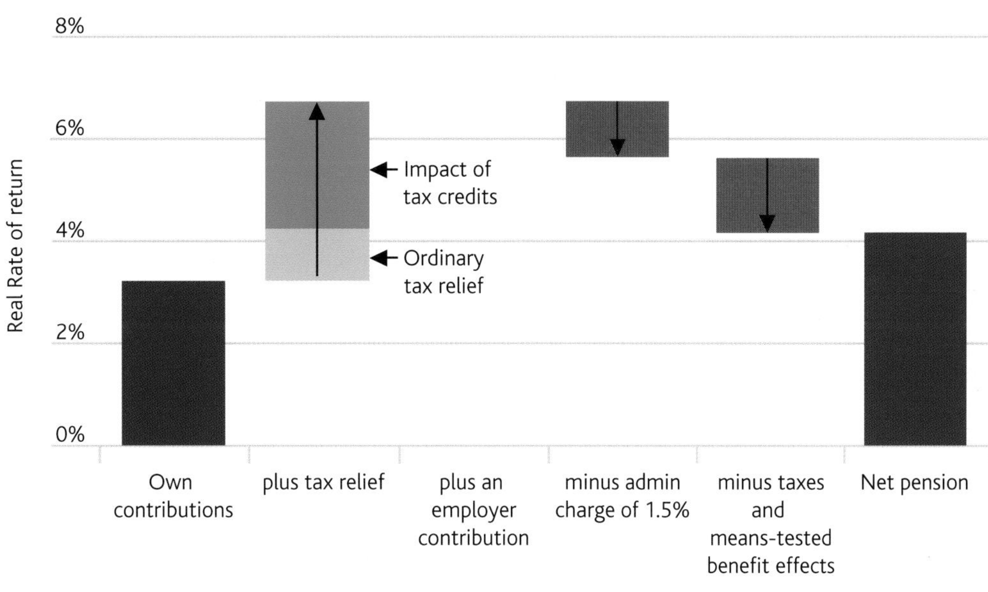

Note: The rate of return on individual saving across both accumulation and decumulation is 3.18%. We assume that he starts saving at 35 and makes an individual contribution of 15%. To simplify the analysis we have assumed no earnings growth in real terms. He pays an annual management charge of 1.5%.

Conclusion

The rational case for saving therefore varies hugely and few people understand the full complexity. Once behavioural barriers to rationalism are considered in addition, the barriers to solving Britain's savings gap through a voluntarist solution are clear. Unless new government initiatives make a major difference to behaviour, the current voluntary system, combined with the current state system, is unlikely to deliver a solution to the problem of inadequate pension saving. One of, or some mix of, three types of change is therefore required. Either:

(i) A revitalisation of the voluntary system.
(ii) Significant changes to the state system.
(iii) An increased level of compulsory savings.

The issues involved in choosing between these options are outlined in Chapter 7.

Pension tax reliefs and the incentive to save via pensions: the full complexity

The analysis illustrated in Figures 6.20 and 6.22 looks at the incentive to save through someone's own pension contributions, in terms of the rate of return which he or she would receive, taking the level of employer contributions on offer as given. This captures the impact of income tax treatment, the charges levied by providers, the potential value of employer contributions, and the reduction in return via means testing in retirement.

But this only captures part of the complexity of the impact of the state on the decision to save though a pension. This depends not just on the income tax system, but also on the way in which contributions of different kinds affect people's liability to National Insurance (NI) contributions (and in turn on any effect that those contributions have on later entitlements to state pensions).

Another way of looking at the incentives on offer is to look at the increase in the size of someone's 'pension pot' that results from contributions (after allowing for later taxation and benefit impacts) by comparison with what they could have accumulated if they had taken net pay and put it into another form of savings. In many cases, the value of this is **greater** than they could otherwise have added to their savings – the government is effectively 'matching' people's pension contributions with a top up, and the greater the rate of matching the bigger the incentive to save via a pension. In some others, the system reduces the accumulated savings.

How this works out depends on several factors:

- Whether the contributions made come from the employ**er** or the employ**ee**. If they come from the employer, they reduce the gross pay on which NI contributions (both employer and employee) and income tax are calculated. If they come from the employee, they do not affect NI contributions, but do reduce the amount that is subject to income tax.
- How high someone's income is when at work – if it is over the Upper Earnings Limit (UEL) for NI contributions, they are liable to employee NI contributions at only 1% on any extra pay they receive, otherwise they pay 11%.
- The income tax rate of the saver both when at work and in retirement. We consider two cases below. In one someone pays the basic rate when at work (so gets income tax relief at this 22% rate) and in retirement (apart from the quarter of the pension pot that can be withdrawn tax-free). In the other, someone pays the higher rate when at work (so gets income tax relief at 40%), but only pays the basic rate when in retirement (again apart from the tax-free lump sum).
- The value of any **additional** state pension they would receive if they pay more in NI contributions. For those on high incomes, above the UEL, this does not enter the equation. But for those on lower incomes, extra contributions do lead to a higher State Second Pension. However, the changes in the rules of the S2P mean that (as explained in Appendix F) the system is becoming more flat rate and less related to contributions than in the past, so this is becoming a less important consideration than it used to be.
- Whether someone ends up on the withdrawal schedule of Pension Credit, and so liable to means-testing.

The illustrations below look at how much someone could add to their pension or savings pot as a result of alternative ways in which their employer could remunerate them by an extra £113 per month. Of course, individuals cannot usually go to their employer and negotiate an individual deal to, say, increase, employer pension contributions on their behalf. But when employers are thinking of the overall remuneration package for their employees, and unions are negotiating with them over employment terms, it is precisely the total of wage costs that matters.

Saving out of net pay

If the £113 flows through to the employee as pay, the employer will pay £13 in employer NI contributions and £100 in gross pay. Then:

- For basic rate tax payers (if below the Lower Earnings Limit (LEL)), extra employee NI contributions will be £11, and extra income tax £22. This leaves £67 to go into the savings pot. In addition the extra NI contributions create additional state pension rights worth £4.18.[1]
- For higher rate tax payers, extra employee NI contributions will be only £1, but extra income tax £40, leaving £59 to go into the savings pot.

It is these amounts that the value of pension pots have to be compared with – remembering that capital can be withdrawn tax-free from normal savings, but the amounts coming out of pensions are liable to tax, whether they come from the capital itself or from accumulated returns on it.

[1]Note: This is the Net Present Value of the foregone S2P for a man aged 40, earning between the Lower & Upper Earnings Threshold of earning £100 less.

Saving through employer contributions

If the employer makes pension contributions on someone's behalf, the whole £113 can go into the pension scheme, as there would be no liability to NI contributions or income tax. When the money is eventually paid out, a quarter comes out as a tax free lump sum, but the rest will be subject to income tax, assumed here to be at the basic rate. Allowing for this means that the accumulated pension pot has a value equivalent to £94.36 of normal savings.

However, some people will end up affected by Pension Credit withdrawal on pensions in payment. If they are subject to Pension Credit withdrawal but are below the income tax threshold, they lose 40% of their (non-lump sum) pension. This means that their accumulated pension pot would be worth £79.10 of normal savings.[2]

However, some people will end up subject both to basic rate income tax and to Pension Credit withdrawal (at 40% on net income). This would mean that the value of their accumulated pension pot would only be £67.91 of normal savings.[2]

Saving via employee contributions

If, on the other hand, it is the employee who makes the contributions, there is no effect on the National Insurance contributions that have to be made – the employer has to pay £13, and then the employee NI contributions are either £11 (below the UEL) or £1 (above the UEL). This leaves either £89 or £99 of gross contributions to go into the pot. Allowing for the tax treatment of the money on the way out as above, this gives the following possible cases:

- For someone originally above the UEL, and paying basic rate income tax in retirement, the £99 of contributions generate a pot worth £82.67 in terms of normal savings.
- For someone originally below the UEL, and paying basic rate income tax in retirement, the £89 of contributions generate a pot worth £74.32.
- For someone originally below the UEL, facing PC withdrawal but not income tax in retirement, the £89 of contributions generate a pot worth £62.30.
- For someone originally below the UEL, and facing **both** Pension Credit withdrawal and basic rate income tax in retirement, the £89 of contributions generate a pot worth only £53.49.

Tax Credits

For people who are on the taper for Tax Credits the consequence of receiving an extra £100 in gross pay is that their Tax Credits are reduced by £37. This is taken into account in Table 6.4 for cases of this kind, but showing that the saving they could make out of net pay would only be £30. However if the additional wage costs are used either for employer or employee pension contributions, their Tax Credits will not be affected as contributions are deducted from gross income for calculating tax credit entitlements.

The overall balance

Table 6.4 below shows how these choices measure up for four different cases, and the "rate of matching" from the state system that they imply when one compares the effective value of the pensions pot someone ends up with, compared to the savings pot they could have had if accumulated out of net pay. In the case of employer pension contributions, they adjust for the lower value of state pension rights which would affect those with earnings below the Upper Earnings Threshold.

Implications

Putting this all together, and remembering the significant degree of simplification involved even in these calculations:[3]

- For most people, the state either significantly adds to their savings if they make them through a pension, or at worst leaves them in much the same position as they would have been in through other kinds of saving.
- Employer pension contributions are substantially more favoured than employee contributions. Even in the worst case (a basic rate saver who faces both basic rate tax and Pension Credit withdrawal in retirement), the treatment of employer contributions is no worse than that of other savings. In most cases, the state **adds** to what could otherwise have been saved out of net pay.
- The system offers the largest incentives to save via pensions to people who pay higher rate tax when at work, but basic rate tax in retirement [as Figure 6.21 also illustrates].
- However, where people are making employee pension contributions, and will end up facing both basic rate income tax and Pension Credit withdrawal in retirement, the rate of matching is significantly negative – the means-testing acts as a disincentive to pensions as a form of saving. For those who end up on other means-tested benefits, such as Housing Benefit, the effect is, of course, even greater.[4]

[2]Note: This does not allow for the effect that other savings, if high enough, would also have on Pension Credit entitlement.

[3]Note: They do not allow, for instance, for the tax treatment of pension fund income by comparison with other forms of investment income.

[4]Note: Although, it should be remembered that if savings are high enough, means-testing will also act as a disincentive to other forms of saving as well.

- But if someone is in a position that their tax credits would increase in reaction to the lower pay resulting from greater pension contributions, the effective rate of matching is significantly positive regardless of whether they face Pension Credit withdrawal in retirement.

- Because so much of the incentives come in this form of "matching", if they are converted into an annualised rate of return, their value is greatest for those who make their pension contributions latest.

All of this is, perhaps unsurprisingly, poorly understood. This means that the potentially positive impact of the incentives that actually exist for most people may not be affecting their behaviour (or that of people selling pensions to them). Some people may believe that the existence of Pension Credit withdrawal no longer makes saving via a pension worthwhile, even though, if the employer makes the contributions and they end up below the personal tax allowance, the state is actually still effectively adding to their pension pot. The table also shows that the state is giving some of the largest incentives to accumulate pensions to those who are most likely to be doing so already, and that **some** of those least likely to save receive the smallest incentive.

Table 6.4 Impact of the state system on accumulated savings resulting from different uses of an extra £113 of wage costs to the employer

Tax position (pre/post retirement)	Saving out of net pay	Equivalent pension pot		Total increase to pension saving	
		Employer contributions[5]	Employee contributions	Employer contributions	Employee contributions
Higher rate/ basic rate	£59	£94.36	£82.67	60%	40%
Basic rate/ basic rate	£67	£91.10	£74.32	36%	11%
Basic rate/ PC withdrawal	£67	£76.59	£62.30	14%	-7%
Basic rate/ PC and basic rate	£67	£65.95	£53.49	-2%	-20%
Basic rate and tax credit withdrawal/ Pension Credit withdrawal	£30[6]	£76.59	£62.30	155%	108%
Basic rate and tax credit withdrawal/ Pension Credit and basic rate	£30	£65.96	£53.49	120%	78%

[5]Note: Adjusts for loss of state pension rights for basic rate tax payers with gross value of £4.18, and so net value of £3.26 (basic rate in retirement), £2.51 (Pension Credit withdrawal in retirement), or £1.96 (both).

[6]Note: If someone is paying NI contributions, basic rate tax and on the taper for Tax Credits the net pay from £100 extra gross pay is £30.

7 Revitalised voluntarism, changes to the state system, or increased compulsion?

Chapter 6 concluded that unless new government initiatives can make a major difference to behaviour, the present voluntary system of pension savings, combined with the present state system, is unlikely to deliver adequate pension provision. To achieve adequacy, there are three possible ways forward:

(i) a major revitalisation of the voluntary system; and/or
(ii) significant changes to the state system; and/or
(iii) an increased level of compulsory private pension saving beyond that already implicit within the UK system.

This chapter considers possible change along these three dimensions, and the issues to be considered in choosing between them. Its purpose is solely to stimulate debate and to highlight the difficulties, as well as the advantages, of any way forward. Analysis of these issues, discussed only in outline here, will be the key focus of the Pensions Commission between now and the publication of the Second Report in autumn 2005.

The way forward must involve some mix of:

1 Successful revitalisation of the voluntary system;

2 Significant change to the state system;

3 Increased compulsion.

1. Revitalised voluntarism?

Chapter 6 identified reasons why the current voluntary system is unlikely to deliver adequate savings. Some of these are inherent to any system of voluntary private savings. But Chapter 6 also identified ways in which current features of the UK system reduce incentives to private savings, particularly for some low income savers. Figures 6.20 to 6.23 showed how a pre-cost, pre-means-testing return of 3.2% real can become over 6% for some categories of saver but can be reduced to 0.7% for others, with the differences driven by four levers: employer contributions, tax relief (including tax credit effects), administrative costs and means-testing.

In addition Chapter 6 identified that the effectiveness of the voluntary system was being undermined, and the inherent barriers made worse by complexity, lack of trust and understanding.

A revitalised voluntary system would therefore require some mix of action to address the four identified levers and a programme to improve customer understanding. This would imply:

- **A big increase in the percentage of firms making employer contributions:** By definition, however, this is a very difficult lever to influence within a voluntary system. Encouragement and codes of conduct (such as that suggested by the CBI) might have some effect. More widespread use of techniques such as automatic enrolment would be beneficial. And the restoration of the employer's rights to make membership of an occupational scheme a condition of employment (removed in 1988) could be considered. But such measures may be unlikely to transform behaviour, particularly in small firms.

- **Changes to the system of tax relief:** As Figures 6.20 to 6.23 make clear, the benefit of tax relief varies widely between different individuals, particularly when the indirect effects of the Working Tax Credit and Child Tax Credit are taken into account. And it is clear that many people have little understanding of the effective tax relief they could enjoy. A variety of options to make tax relief benefits more general and more easily understood (e.g. matching contributions) could be considered.

- **Major reductions in selling and administration costs:** The design of Sandler products and of the new sales regime have not delivered the dramatic reductions in costs hoped for in the Sandler Report, and HM Treasury has accepted that a 1.5% Annual Management Charge (AMC) for 10 years, reducing to 1% thereafter, is required to sell savings products to low premium customers. At this level, there is a real issue of whether personal pension saving by low earners is attractive. But the cost models used to inform this decision reveal the very large costs created by lack of persistence and by contract proliferation. Radical thinking on product design supported by simplification of the legal regimes might enable some of this cost to be eliminated, building on the potential created by the tax simplification changes. The panel at the end of this chapter describes the size and causes of non-persistency costs, and explores the possible features of product redesign which would be required if reduction were to be possible.

- **A reduction in the impact of state system means-testing on incentives to save for some lower and middle income people:** This issue is considered below.

- **A major increase in the level of customer understanding of pension related issues and of financial issues in general:** The Government's Informed Choice strategy aims to increase this understanding. Key elements to this approach are: [See Table 7.1 for details.]

  - Pilots of approaches such as automatic enrolment and "Save More Tomorrow" schemes which aim to overcome the problems of inertia and procrastination.

  - Schemes to improve the quality of information people receive about their pension rights.

  - Integrated pension forecasts, to help people to understand what pension income they are forecast to receive.

  - Programmes to help raise financial awareness and skills.

  In addition the FSA is putting further effort into its Building Financial Capability strategy. The open issue is whether such efforts can overcome the inherent barriers to customer understanding and psychology outlined in Chapter 6. The Pensions Commission will look more closely at this issue over the coming year.

The potential impact of changes along any of the five dimensions considered above is difficult to gauge. But the Commission's judgment is that radical rather than incremental change along some combination of these dimensions will be required if the voluntary system alone is to close the savings gap.

Table 7.1 Government Policies to Increase Understanding of Pensions

Informed Choice Projects / Initiatives **Behavioural economics**	**Progress**
Automatic enrolment Exploring a range of techniques aimed at increasing membership of workplace pension schemes to establish which are the most effective in delivering increased savings and to understand the implications for individuals, employers and pension providers.	Exploring and testing the different approaches, results due Autumn 2005.
Commitment to save more in the future Testing an approach to pension saving whereby employees can decide to commit some, or all of any future salary increases to their pension savings to improve overall pension contributions.	Plan to pilot during 2005.
Workplace information and advice	
Employer pilots Evaluating the effectiveness of four options providing information and advice in the workplace.	Currently piloting the different methods with 100+ employers. Evaluation results due Summer 2005.
Legislation requiring employers to offer information and/or advice Reserve power is being sought in the Pensions Bill to require employers with low levels of employer contribution and scheme membership to offer their employees access to pensions information and advice.	Subject to Royal Assent the shape of any regulations made under this power will be informed by the pilot evaluation results in Summer 2005.
Pensions information on pay slips To support and encourage employers to include details of employer pension contributions in pay slips.	Guidance for employers and payroll managers to be published in 2005.
Pensions information on job vacancies To encourage employment agencies to offer information about pensions on job vacancies as a matter of course.	Job Centre Plus will be collecting pensions information on all job vacancies from October 2004.
Pension Forecasting	
Combined Pension Forecasts A Combined Pension Forecast includes state pension information alongside information provided about occupational or private pension schemes	Issued over 1.9 million to date, plan to have issued 6.3 million by end of 2005/06.

Table 7.1 Government Policies to Increase Understanding of Pensions (continued)

Informed Choice Projects / Initiatives **Pension Forecasting** (continued)	**Progress**
Automatic Pension Forecasts Issued automatically by DWP to targeted customer groups starting with women over 50, on a cycle with a maximum of three years between forecasts.	Plan to have issued 2 million by end 2004/05 and 8 million by end of 2005/06.
Supporting Financial Decision Making	
Online retirement planner A web-based tool that will help people with their financial planning for retirement. It will include a forecast of their state and private pensions via on-line feeds where possible.	Due to be launched in Spring 2006.
Pension scheme tracing The Pensions Schemes Registry is a database holding details of all UK occupational and personal pension schemes with two or more members. Utilising this database, OPRA currently provides a tracing service, free of charge, for individuals to identify old or "lost" pensions.	Subject to Royal Assent for the Pensions Bill the DWP will take on responsibility for the service from April 2005
Financial education and awareness A programme of work with other government departments, the Financial Services Authority, employers, the voluntary sector and others to raise overall levels of financial education and awareness of the need to plan and provide for retirement.	The DWP is a member of the Schools group and is leading the Planning for Retirement Group
Building Financial Capability (FSA)	
Identified the seven priority areas 1. Schools: laying the foundations 2. Young adults (16-25): new responsibilities 3. Work: reaching people through the workplace 4. Families: being a parent 5. Borrowing: making informed decisions 6. Retirement: planning ahead 7. Advice: the role of 'generic' advice	Working groups have been set up for each work area, which have identified the priorities in each area. More detail is available in *Building financial capability in the UK* published by the FSA in May 2004.

2. Significant changes to the state system

The Pensions Commission's primary focus is on the private funded pension system, rather than the details of the state Pay As You Go (PAYG) system. But options for reforming the private system cannot be assessed without considering both the implications of the state system for private saving, and possible state system changes as an alternative or complement to private system reforms. Three considerations suggest a potential role for state system changes:

- Means-testing within the state system is already creating, and if current indexation approaches were continued indefinitely would increasingly create, disincentives to private saving, particularly for some low income savers.

- The complexity of the current state system is an impediment to clear consumer understanding of what the state will deliver, and therefore what individuals need to save themselves. This further confuses incentives to save.

- The contributory nature of the state system is a major driver of the inequality between men and women in pension provision, which is highlighted in Chapter 8.

Many proposals are therefore put forward for changes to the state system. Most of these involve a higher basic pension but less means-testing, aiming to reduce disincentive effects. But if these proposals are made, the potential consequences and disadvantages need to be faced alongside the potential benefits. Thus as an illustration:

- Under current Government projections, expenditure on pensioner benefits (BSP, S2P, Pension Credit, Winter Fuel Payments, over-75s TV Licences and Christmas Bonus) is expected to increase from around 5% of GDP in 2003/04 to around 5.7% of GDP in 2043/44.

- If the State Pension Age (SPA) is not raised, a non-contributory basic state pension set at the current level of the Guarantee Credit (i.e. at society's current definition of the minimum income required for a dignified retirement), and maintained at this level relative to average earnings, would imply expenditure on pensioners rising to around 8.2% in 2043/44 if S2P and the Savings Credit were abolished. If S2P were retained, expenditure on pensions would be around 9.5% of GDP in 2043/44.

- Alternatively, a basic non-contributory pension set at the current level of the Guarantee Credit (with no S2P or Savings Credit) but with public expenditure on pensions limited to today's 5% of GDP would require the state pension age to rise to 74 by 2043/44 or to 72 if the aim was to keep expenditure at the 5.7% of GDP envisaged under current plans for 2043/44. The implications of this for different socio-economic groups would need to be considered carefully, given the major differences in current life expectancy illustrated in Chapter 2.

A higher state pension would improve incentives to save for those on low incomes but would not in itself deliver pensions likely to be considered adequate for any except the bottom quartile of income earners. Even with radical changes to the Basic State Pension (BSP), therefore, two issues would remain: whether there should be government policies to ensure adequacy above the minimum level, and if so whether such adequacy should be achieved via a PAYG scheme or via funded savings. These issues are fundamental to any consideration of compulsory savings.

3. Earnings-related pensions: compulsory or voluntary: funded or unfunded?

One possible approach to pension policy is to limit the government's role to ensuring that all citizens have sufficient income for a dignified retirement via a generous but flat-rate pension, but with no government responsibility for providing pensions linked to earnings, nor for ensuring that private savings are sufficiently large to provide pensions in line with lifetime earnings. This is, for instance, the overt philosophy of New Zealand's citizenship pension. But it is not the approach traditionally taken in the majority of rich developed countries. And it is not the UK's starting point today.

The UK today has a system of mandatory, second tier pension provision covering all employees (but not the self-employed). All employees and their employers must either make National Insurance (NI) contributions to secure rights under the SERPS/S2P system, or invest the equivalent of these contributions in funded pensions. [See the panel in Chapter 3 for a description of the contracting-out system]. Compared with most other countries, this compulsory, earnings-related tier of the system is fairly limited and might become more so over time if current indexation approaches were continued indefinitely.

- As Figure 3.3 showed, the UK's second tier system still leaves total UK state pension provision for the median earner closer to that provided by flat-rate pension systems (e.g. Canada, Ireland, and New Zealand) than to the US, let alone continental European levels.

- Current plans moreover will make the system increasingly flat-rate over time, with everyone earning above 108% of average earnings receiving the same level of contributory benefits [see Figure 3.20].

- And this increasingly flat-rate nature of the benefit will be mirrored, if current indexation arrangements are maintained over the long-term, by a decreasing level of contributions at high income levels and eventually at average earnings levels, as the panel on the following pages explains.

- Essentially therefore, present indicative long-term plans entail a reduction in the level of mandatory earnings-related provision, and thus, if the percentage of people choosing the contracted-out option stays constant, a reduction in the level of "compulsory" funded savings.

Mandatory earnings-related pensions in the UK – Future declining compulsion?

The UK already has a mandatory earnings-related pension system for employees. All employees and the self-employed are compelled to pay National Insurance (NI) contributions to accrue the Basic State Pension (BSP). Employees however pay in at a higher rate than the self-employed, and in return either accrue S2P (previously SERPS) or contract-out, using National Insurance "rebates" to invest in a funded pension. If current indexation arrangements are continued indefinitely, the extent of this compulsion by income group would change: rising for low earners but falling for higher earnings. In the long-term the net effect may be a decline in "compulsory" funded savings as a percentage of GDP.

NI contributions do not relate exclusively to pensions nor even to social security expenditure in total. The removal of the Upper Earnings Limit (UEL) on employer's contributions (in 1985) made the link between contributions and pension accruals less clear; the introduction of the 1% uncapped employee contributions (in 2003) provides a source of general taxation revenues for the NHS; and it is difficult to identify precisely the element of NI contributions which specifically relates to SERPS/S2P. But possible future trends in the employee contributions can be used to illustrate possible changes in the level of compulsory funded saving, since contracted-out rebates are received on the same slice of earnings (between the Lower Earnings Limit (LEL) and the UEL) on which employee contributions (other than the 1% NHS levy) are payable [Figure 7.1].

Employees contribute based on their earnings between the Earnings Threshold, currently about 20% of average earnings, and the Upper Earnings Limit, currently about 130%. Present indicative forecasts imply the levels of both rising in line with prices. If this did occur then their value would fall relative to earnings. The Earnings Threshold would fall to about 10% of average earnings by 2050, and the UEL to about two thirds (with 1.5% annual real earnings growth). As a result, in relative earnings terms, the curve of Figure 7.1 would shift to the left. People on relatively low multiples of average earnings would pay an increasing proportion of income in S2P-related NI contributions, while at higher multiples of average earnings the proportion would fall [Figure 7.2].

This does not necessarily mean that the state pension system is becoming less redistributive, since the changing profile of contributions is accompanied by the changing profile of benefits, which as Figure 3.20 illustrated are becoming more flat rate. Rather, present plans for indexation, if continued over the long-term, simply reduce the level of mandated pension provision: with people on higher earnings and, after 2034 on average earnings, paying less in and getting less out.

The implication for the level of "compulsory" funded savings occurring are complex. For people who choose to stay contracted-in, Figure 7.2 represents changing levels of PAYG contributions, roughly matched by the changing profile of benefits in Figure 3.20. For those who contract-out, Figure 7.2 also implies a changing profile of compulsory funded savings. But since contracting-out is more common at higher earnings levels, the overall long-term effect of indexing of the LEL and the UEL to prices would likely be a declining level of "compulsory" funded savings.

Figure 7.1 Employee NI Contributions as a Percentage of Earnings Now and in the Future, if Current Indexation Plans are Continued Indefinitely

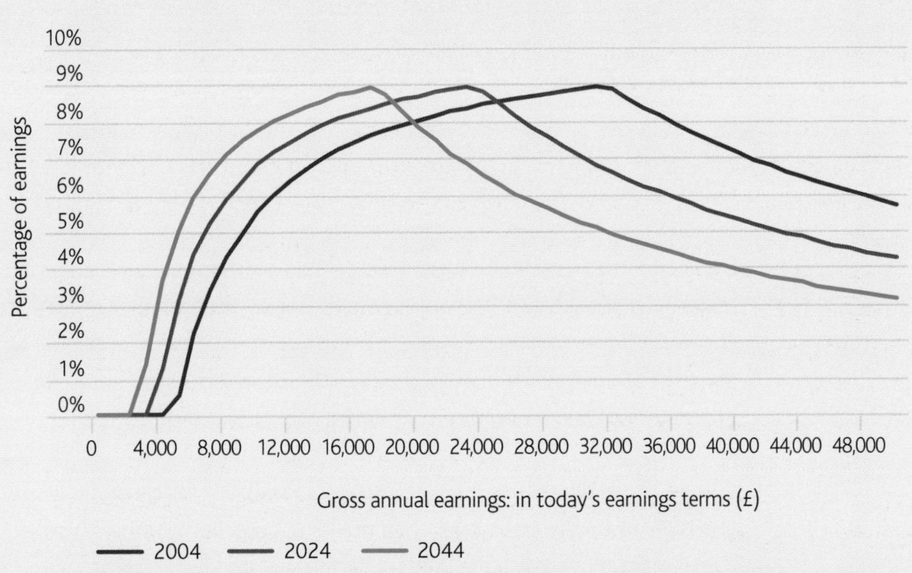

Source: Pensions Commission calculations based on present values of Earnings Threshold and Upper Earnings Limit, with 1.5% annual real earnings growth[1]. Assuming that both are indexed with prices.

Figure 7.2 How Employee NI Contributions would evolve for people on different earnings

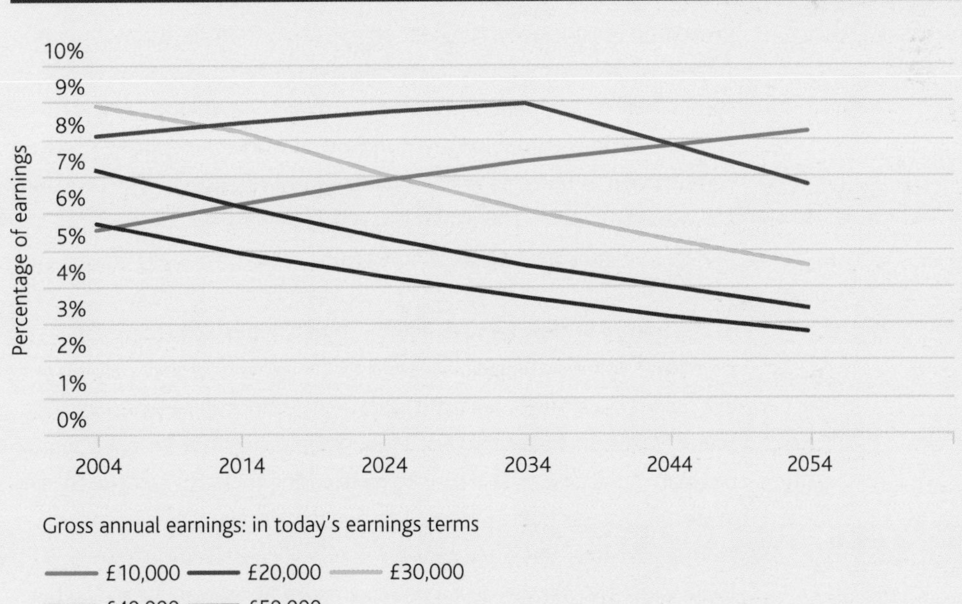

Source: Pensions Commission calculations based on present values of Earnings Threshold and Upper Earnings Limit, with 1.5% annual real earnings growth[1]. Assuming that both are indexed with prices.

[1]Note: The possible further fall in contributions forecast in the Government Actuary's Quinquennial Review of the National Insurance Fund is not taken into account.

But despite this erosion, the UK does have and will have for many years at least an element of compulsory earnings-related pension, which can, at the employer or individual's option, take the form of a state determined minimum savings level. Thus, while the Pensions Commission's terms of reference asked us to consider whether the UK should ever develop a tier of compulsory private saving, the question is rather whether that tier should be increased in scope.

The answer depends first on society's approach to the philosophical issue raised above and in Chapter 4: whether there should be any government responsibility to ensure "adequacy" above the basic level required for a dignified retirement. In Chapter 4 we defined the Commission's pragmatic response, arguing that there was a case for society to ensure or at least encourage some minimum level of earnings-related pension for people up to, say, the 75th percentile (currently £29,000) But we also highlighted the importance of debate on this issue during the consultation period.

If however we do assume a government responsibility for ensuring pension provision above the basic level, then the issue becomes whether this should be delivered through a state PAYG scheme (such as SERPS/S2P) or via compulsory private saving, or a mix of these two options. Consideration of the advantages and disadvantages of these two alternatives helps define the criteria for assessing the attractiveness of the compulsory funded option.

The difference between funded and unfunded options for pension delivery is often overstated. As Appendix B describes, in any pension system the current generation of pensioners is reliant on a resource transfer from some group of current workers. As a result, funded pension systems as well as PAYG systems will be put under pressure by demographic change. And if funded pension saving is compulsory, the individual worker is required to sacrifice consumption as much as under a tax-based PAYG system. The dividing line between compulsory saving and taxation is therefore a fine one. But there remain four important possible differences:

1. The nature of the claim: In a PAYG system, future pensioners are dependent on future political decisions for the delivery of their pension promise. In a funded system they are dependent on the future market value of their assets. Given the frequency with which governments have changed pension promises in the past, people may be more willing to accept compulsory savings in identified assets than increased taxation matched by a PAYG pension promise. Whether this is the case, however, will depend crucially on how risky those assets are, which is driven both by market price volatility and by the trustworthiness and financial strength of financial intermediaries.

2. The impact on the savings rate: Funded private savings only deliver an increase in GDP and thus in the resources available to make increased pensioner incomes affordable if they increase the national savings rate, either in the form of net claims on overseas assets, or via an increase in domestic investment. A key issue for compulsory savings schemes is whether this increase is actually achieved, or whether people who are compelled to save in pensions will simply offset this by reducing their savings in other asset categories or by higher borrowing.

3. The division of risk: In the traditional PAYG scheme, the government absorbs both the risk of future increases in life expectancy (by setting a pension age in advance) and implicitly promises a guaranteed return on pension contributions. In a compulsory savings scheme with Defined Benefit (DB) providers these risks are largely absorbed by employers. In compulsory Defined Contribution (DC) schemes these risks reside with the individual. Given the shift to DC now occurring, this would probably be the predominant pattern in any expanded compulsory system. Shifting the long-term (i.e. pre-retirement) longevity risk to individuals has the advantage of giving individuals the freedom to make their own trade-offs between retirement age and income in retirement, and of creating incentives to later retirement. [See the "Pensions and Risk" panel in Chapter 3 for more detailed discussion of this issue]. But handing investment risk to people with low income and limited other resources has disadvantages. Issues relating to risk management and to the provision of explicit or implicit advice therefore become particularly important in a system where people have been compelled to save.

4. Selling and administration costs: PAYG state-run pension systems typically achieve far lower running costs than systems of voluntary private savings. Figure 7.3 repeats Figure 6.9 from Chapter 6, but with the cost of the UK state pension system added. The UK's state system running costs are about 0.1% of the value of the pension liability, compared to 0.2% in large scale occupational schemes and well over 1% in most personal pensions. A crucial issue in compulsory savings schemes is therefore whether the elimination of the need to persuade the customer to save can lead to a major reduction in Reduction In Yield (RIY), bringing the operating costs of funded schemes closer to those of a PAYG scheme.

The impact on aggregate savings, the management of risk and costs of administration are therefore three specific issues to consider in drawing lessons from compulsory savings systems in other counties.

Compulsory savings: international experience

Many countries across the world have introduced a tier of compulsory private savings over the last 20 years. This experience is analysed in Appendix D, and summarised in Table 7.2.

The details of the schemes differ widely on many dimensions: for example, whether there are compulsory employer contributions or employee contributions or both; the level of savings required; the administration arrangements. But they can usefully be considered in three categories:

- The Netherlands and Switzerland: European countries which for a set of historical reasons and over a number of decades developed a "quasi-compulsory" funded approach to the delivery of the earnings-related element of the pension system.

- Developing or recently developed countries (e.g. Bolivia, Mexico, and Chile) which have decided to build second tier provision via the funded route, or which have switched from a PAYG system to a funded one, with the development of domestic capital markets often as one of the specific policy objectives.

- Australia, which developed compulsory private savings in the 1990s as a deliberate policy response to the perceived inadequacy of private pension savings, given the low level of state pension provision.

The Australian experience is clearly the most directly relevant to the UK as that of an already developed economy choosing to introduce a tier of compulsory savings in response to a perceived savings gap. It should also be noted however that the Australian model grew out of a condition specific to Australia and absent in the UK: the existence of a national collective bargaining system in which it was possible to manage the introduction of compulsory employer contributions as an explicit alternative to higher cash wages.

Detailed consideration of the advantages and disadvantages of compulsion in general and, if appropriate, of specific scheme design will be key aspects of the Commission's work over the next year, and is therefore not presented here. But as background to the debate which the Commission wishes to stimulate in the consultation period, preliminary findings on two of the key issues identified are noted here:

Figure 7.3 An Estimate of the Overall Cost Curve including the National Insurance System: Percentage RIY

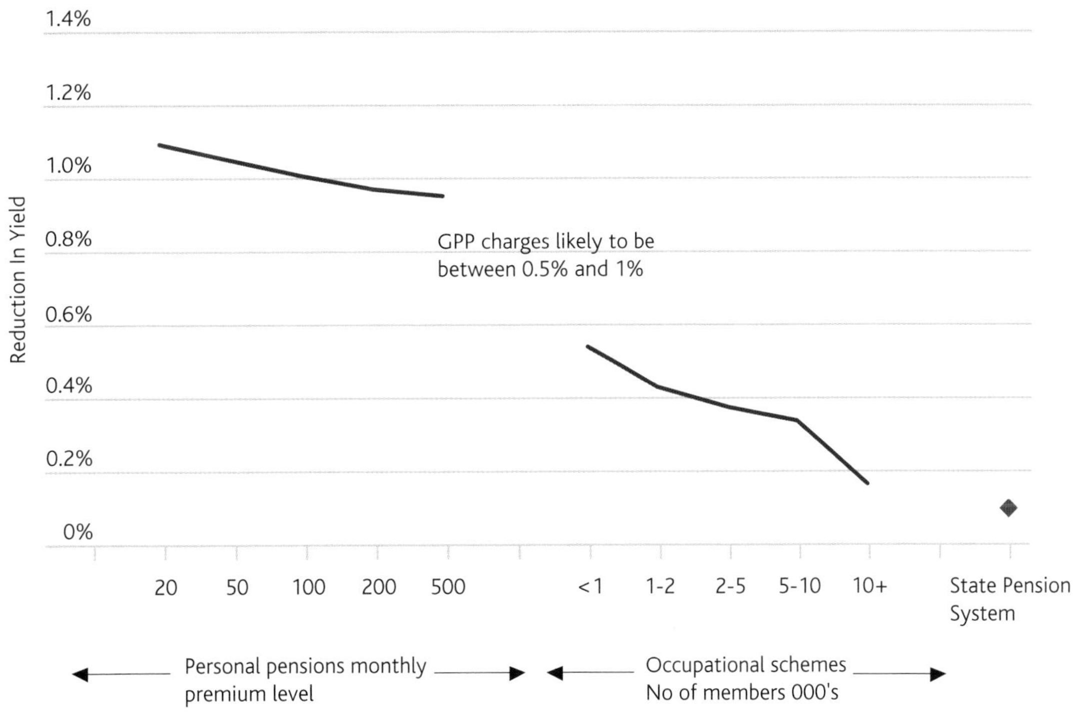

Reduction In Yield

1.4%
1.2%
1.0%
0.8%
0.6%
0.4%
0.2%
0%

GPP charges likely to be between 0.5% and 1%

20 50 100 200 500

< 1 1-2 2-5 5-10 10+

State Pension System

Personal pensions monthly premium level

Occupational schemes No of members 000's

Source: Personal pension data from FSA comparitive tables: the line shown is the unweighted mean.
Occupational pensions from GAD survey 1998.
GPP estimates based on discussion with the industry.

Note: National Insurance Fund estimate is based on the assumed total value of accrued state pension rights and the estimated administration cost of the National Insurance fund.

Table 7.2 Countries with mandatory funded second pension pillars

Country	Year of introduction of present system
Chile	1981
Switzerland, The Netherlands*	1985
Australia	1988
Denmark, Peru	1993
Argentina, Colombia	1994
Uruguay	1996
Bolivia, Hungary, Kazakhstan, Mexico	1997
El Salvador, Poland	1998
Sweden	1999
Hong Kong	2000
Latvia	2001
Dominican Republic	2003

Source: Bateman, Kingston and Piggott "Forced Savings" 2001

Note: *The origins of the Dutch system lie earlier.

- **The impact on aggregate savings:** There is no clear and well-supported consensus on the likely impact of compulsory savings on the aggregate savings rate of a developed economy. The introduction of the Dutch and Swiss compulsory saving systems occurred so gradually and so long ago that it is impossible to estimate their impact. The experience of developing countries, starting with undeveloped equity and bond markets, is not directly relevant to the UK. But the best study available for the nearest UK comparator, Australia, suggests that some positive impact on the aggregate savings rate may be achieved. The Australian household savings rate actually fell during the decade of introduction of compulsory savings and the specific features of the Australian scheme, with a 100% lump sum on retirement, made it easy for many Australians to offset the impact of compulsory saving by borrowing more against houses and using the lump sum to pay off their mortgage [Figure 7.4]. But a study by the Australian Reserve Bank suggests that relative to what would otherwise have occurred, compulsory savings did produce some increase in savings, particularly among lower earners. Their best estimates are that 38% of compulsory pension savings are offset by a reduction in other savings (or increased borrowing) but that 62% does represent incremental savings. The degree of this offset varies across the income distribution. Those with higher income are more likely to be able to reduce other savings or borrow more, but those with lower income are unlikely to be able to increase borrowing because of credit constraints.[2]

- **Administration costs:** While in theory it should be possible for a system of compulsory saving to produce a radical reduction in selling and administration costs given the large costs involved in the "persuasion to save" step of the selling process, in fact many compulsory savings schemes around the world do not achieve this [Figure 7.5]. The reasons for this failure, and the design features which would be required to achieve a cost-efficient compulsory system, will be considered in the next phase of the Commission's work.

Consultation on three possible ways forward

This chapter has set out the factors which need to be considered in deciding between the three possible ways forward: a radical revitalisation of the voluntary system; changes to the state system or increased compulsion. The Pensions Commission has reached no conclusion as to which of these should be the way forward, but is clear that one of these or some mix of these is required. The consultation process over the next three and a half months aims to gather views and evidence on this choice, to help inform the Commission's recommendations by autumn 2005. The consultation process and the issues for debate are described in Chapter 9.

[2]Note: Connolly and Kohler, 2004

Figure 7.4 The Australian Household Savings Rate as a Percentage of GDP: 1960-2002

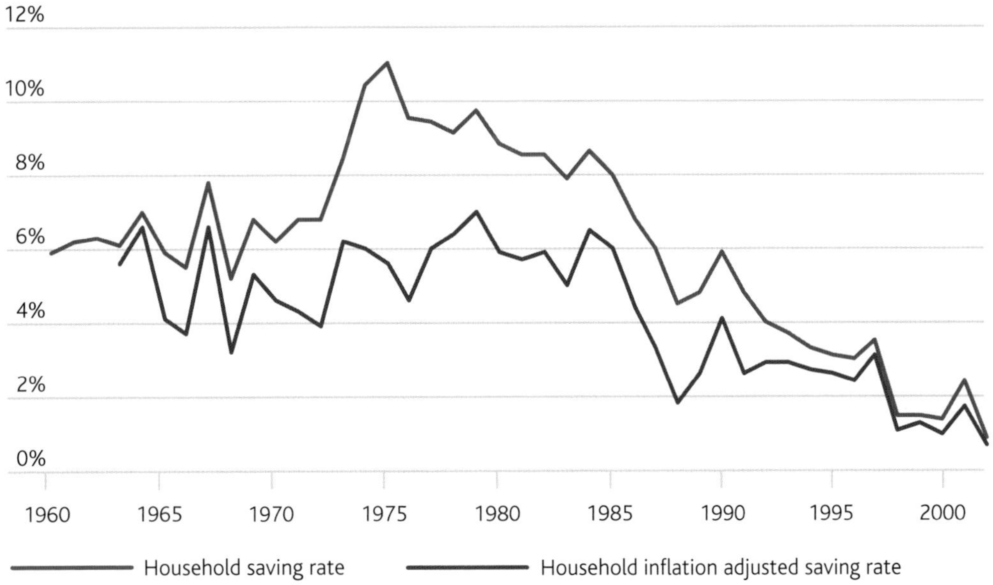

12%
10%
8%
6%
4%
2%
0%

1960 1965 1970 1975 1980 1985 1990 1995 2000

Household saving rate   Household inflation adjusted saving rate

Source: Reserve Bank of Australia

Figure 7.5 Charge ratio in Compulsory Savings Schemes: 2000.
Total percentage reduction in accumulated pension fund

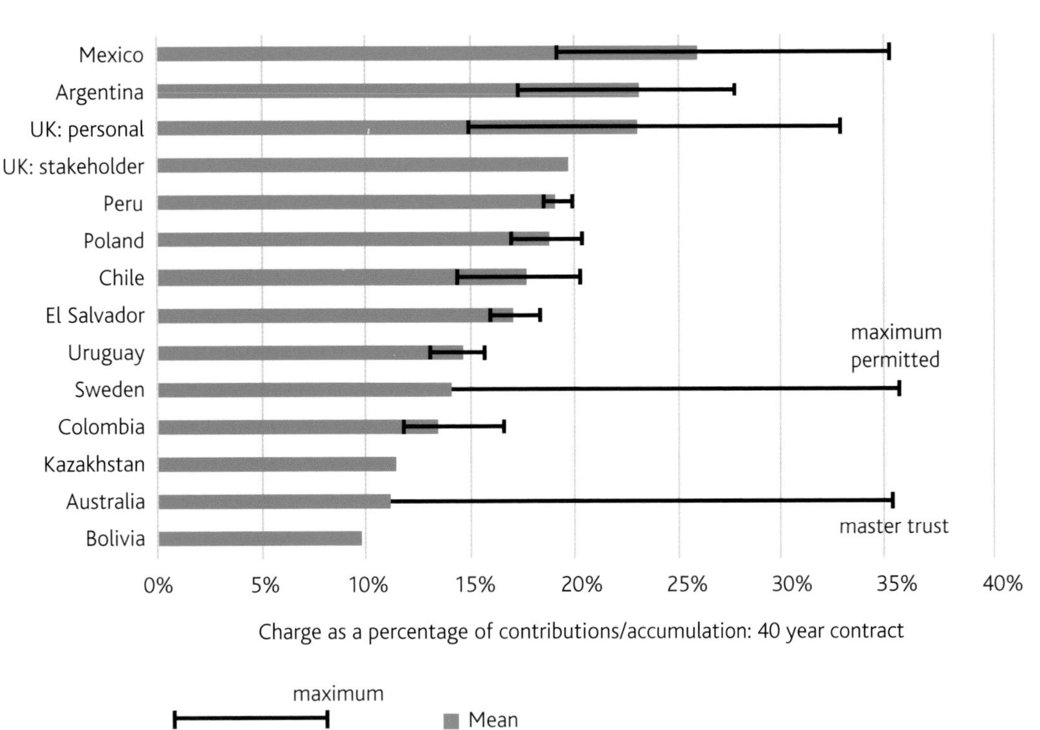

Source: Whitehouse, 2000

Notes: The charge ratio shows the total reduction in the value of the pension acculmulation resulting from annual charges over the entire contract length. For example, a RIY of 1% per year for a contract length of 25 years, and assuming gross returns of 6% per year, produces a charge ratio of 15%

Can costs of low persistency be radically reduced?

Analysis of the cost models presented by the life assurance industry as part of the Sandler products review process illustrates the very large costs created by lack of persistence and by contract proliferation in personal pensions. A key issue is whether product redesign could radically reduce these costs.

As Figure 7.6 illustrates, more than one third of all personal pension contracts lapse after four years (that is either no new contributions are made or the funds are transferred to another provider) and this percentage is increasing. As a result there are 22 million personal pension contracts in place according to the ABI, but only 10 million people receiving tax relief into personal pensions, many of whom also have other pension arrangements (e.g. occupational pensions).

Each new personal pension contract creates significant cost. From the insurance companies' point of view, the cost is usually the Independant Financial Adviser (IFA) commission, typically around 35% of initial year premiums. From a fundamental point of view, the key element of the upfront cost is the IFA (or direct sales force) interview involved in selling the product, an interview carefully controlled by regulation because of the dangers of misselling.

Until recently these set-up costs were recovered from non-persistent savers via high exit penalties, with the result that many people who were unable to continue pension payments throughout the full term of the contract faced very large Reductions in Yield and received hugely negative rates of return [Figure 7.7]. Exit penalties are restricted by the Stakeholder legislation (in order, among other things, to facilitate transfer to other lower cost competitors). But the costs created by lack of persistency and contract proliferation remain, and are therefore reflected in average prices and in industry assessments of the attractiveness of different market segments at different price levels. If costs could be reduced, more customers could be served profitably.

One of the cost models which the Pensions Commission has looked at suggests that the price (expressed in AMC terms) required profitably to provide a pension scheme to people on average earnings as part of a 26 member GPP could be reduced from 1.5% to 0.85% if persistency were 100%. While 100% persistency will never be achievable, the issue is whether significantly increased persistency and thus significant cost and price cuts are possible.

The reasons for lack of persistency are varied. They include switches to a new provider offering apparently better value, unemployment and other changes in economic circumstances, and changes in job. The latter factor may be the one potentially most susceptible to change via product and practice redesign, aiming to achieve either increased persistency or lower cost of change. At present people joining a new employer typically can only get access to employer contributions by joining the employer's scheme, rather than by asking for contributions to a pre-existing scheme.

During the consultation period, the Pensions Commission would therefore be interested in hearing ideas for product or practice redesign which could substantially reduce the costs created by low persistency, and proposals for any regulatory changes required to make that reduction possible.

Figure 7.6 Persistancy in Personal Pension Policies: Percentage of New Policy Holders Continuing to make Contributions after 1, 2, 3 or 4 years

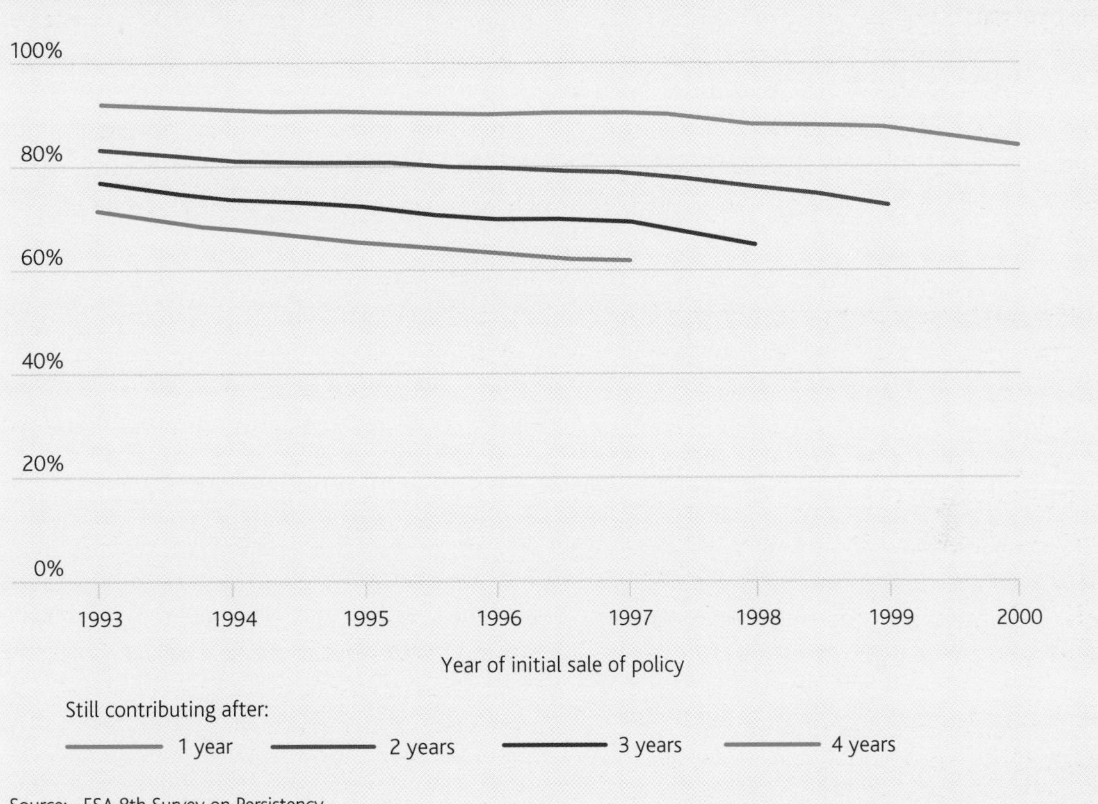

Source: FSA 8th Survey on Persistency

Note: Those ceasing contributions could be either ceasing pension saving or transferring the plan to another provider.

Figure 7.7 Impact of Exit Penalties Imposed in 1990: Percentage Reduction in Yield

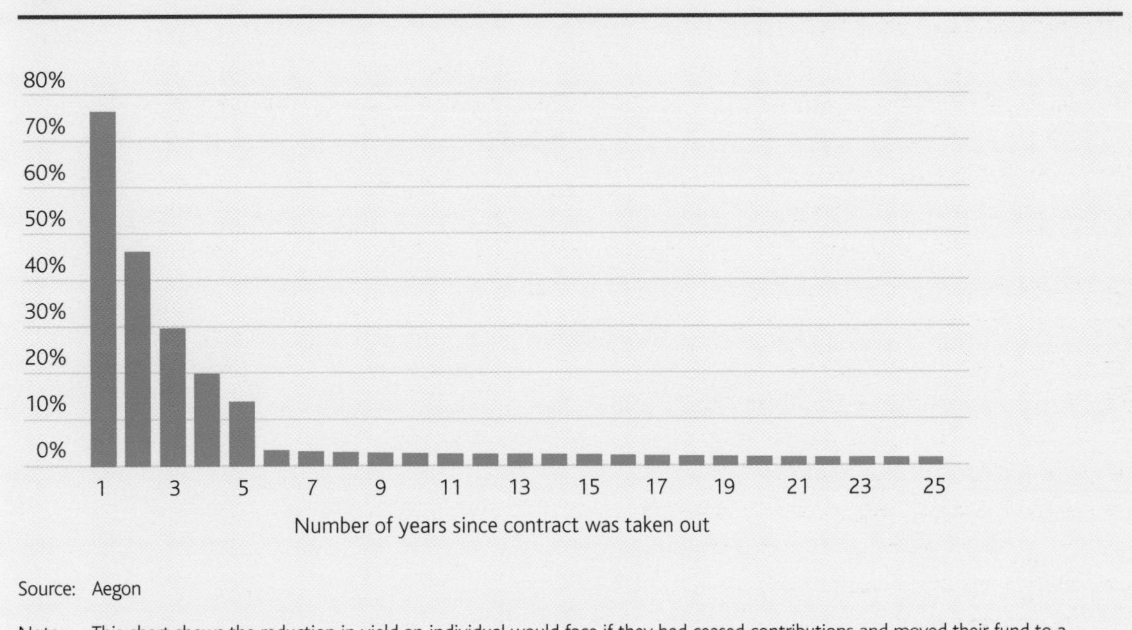

Source: Aegon

Note: This chart shows the reduction in yield an individual would face if they had ceased contributions and moved their fund to a new provider.

Women and pensions

8

Women pensioners in the UK today are significantly poorer than men. This reflects both labour market features (lower employment rates, lower average earnings, and more part-time work) and specific features of the UK's state pension system. These state system features have in the past entailed many women gaining pension income through their husband, and reflected assumptions about family structure which have ceased to be valid. An effective pension system for the future must be one in which the vast majority of women accrue pension entitlements, both state and private, in their own right.

Some progress towards that aim is now occurring, with some labour market trends favourable to women, and some changes in the state system which benefit women. But important issues remain relating to overall equality in the workforce, to state system design, and to low levels of pension provision and take-up in some service sectors in which women's employment is concentrated.

This chapter covers 6 topics.

1 The fact that female pensioners are on average poorer than male pensioners and the reasons for this.

2 Past and present labour market drivers of women's relative position.

3 Features of the UK state system which have disadvantaged women.

4 Social changes which make past reliance on spouses' pensions an invalid basis for future pension policy.

5 Recent and likely future trends in the labour market and in pension provision, several of which are favourable to women, but with significant problems remaining.

6 Gender specific issues in pension policy in both the state and private systems.

1. Current female pensioners are poorer than men

On average current female pensioners are significantly poorer than male pensioners. This is partly because women live longer, accounting for 67% of all over 80 year olds, and older pensioners (both men and women) tend to be poorer [Table 8.1 and Figure 8.1]. This in turn reflects the fact that pensions during retirement rise (at best) with inflation, while pensions at the point of retirement tend to rise in line with average earnings.

But even adjusting for this age effect, female pensioners at any given age tend to be poorer than male.

- As Figure 8.1 shows single female pensioners are poorer than single male pensioners of the same age. They receive a similar level of state benefit, though more of it is means-tested. But they receive a much lower level of occupational pension income [Figure 8.2].

- While within married pensioner couples, the predominant source of pension income is linked to the man, with independent sources of women's retirement income much lower [Figure 8.3].

This pattern reflects both past labour market experiences and specific features of the UK state pension system.

Figure 8.1 Average Gross Income of Single Pensioners, by Sex and Age: 2002/03

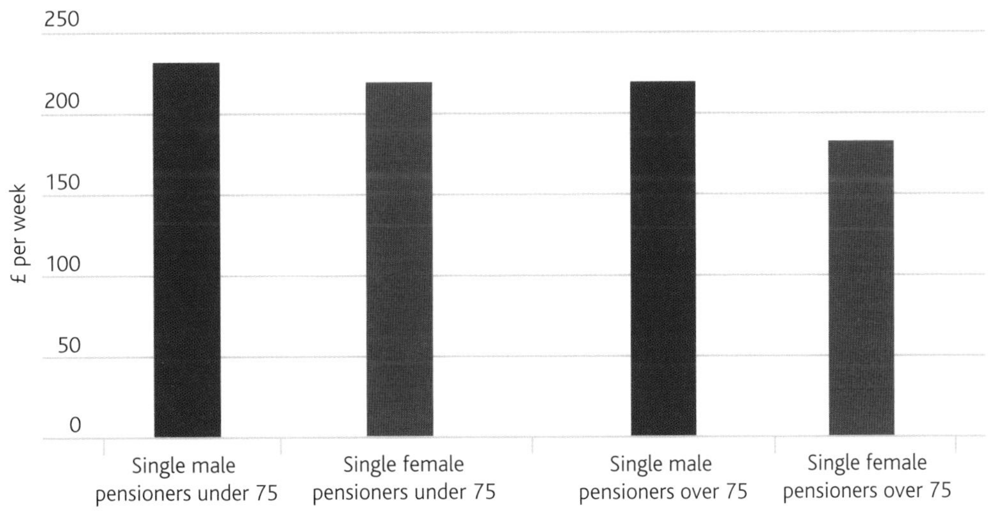

Source: The Pensioners' Incomes Series 2002/03

Table 8.1 Older Population, by Sex: Mid 2002, UK

Millions	Age 60-64	65-69	70-74	75-79	80+	All 60+
Men	1.4	1.3	1.1	0.8	0.8	5.4
Women	1.5	1.4	1.3	1.1	1.7	6.9
Total	2.9	2.6	2.3	1.9	2.5	12.3
Women as a percentage	51%	52%	54%	58%	67%	56%

Source: ONS, General Register Office for Scotland, Northern Ireland Statistics and Research Agency.

2. Labour market experience and consequences for private pensions

Current female pensioners receive much lower levels of occupational pension because during working life they had much lower levels of employment, a greater tendency to be in part-time work, lower average earnings, and a greater tendency to work in service sectors where pension provision was less prevalent.

- In 1984, for instance, when today's 65 year old pensioner was aged 45, the employment rate for 35-49 year old women was 65% versus 88% for men, and 55% of these women were employed as part-timers compared to 1% of men [Figure 8.4]. Lower overall employment meant fewer opportunities to accrue pension rights; and part-time employment, until the early 1990s, very rarely involved pension scheme membership.

- In 1980 as today, moreover, women's private sector employment was concentrated in service sectors which were less likely to provide Defined Benefit (DB) pension schemes, and more likely either to have low levels of membership of any pension scheme, or to provide less generous Defined Contribution (DC) schemes [Figures 8.5 and 8.6].

- And even when women were in DB schemes, the greater prevalence among women of interrupted careers meant that, in the period before leavers rights were introduced (the key changes were in 1975 and 1986) many women lost a significant proportion of their benefits.

The impact of this lower level of pension accrual has been offset by access to husband's pension rights for women who are married to men in DB schemes, which since 1978 have been required to provide widows benefits, in order to contract-out of SERPS/S2P.

But single women have lower retirement income as a result of lower pension accrual. And for women married to men with DC pensions, survivor spouse income has often been nil or minimal because the vast majority of annuities are purchased on a single life and non-indexed basis [Figure 8.7].

Figure 8.2 Components of Average Gross Income of Single Pensioners by Sex: 2002/03

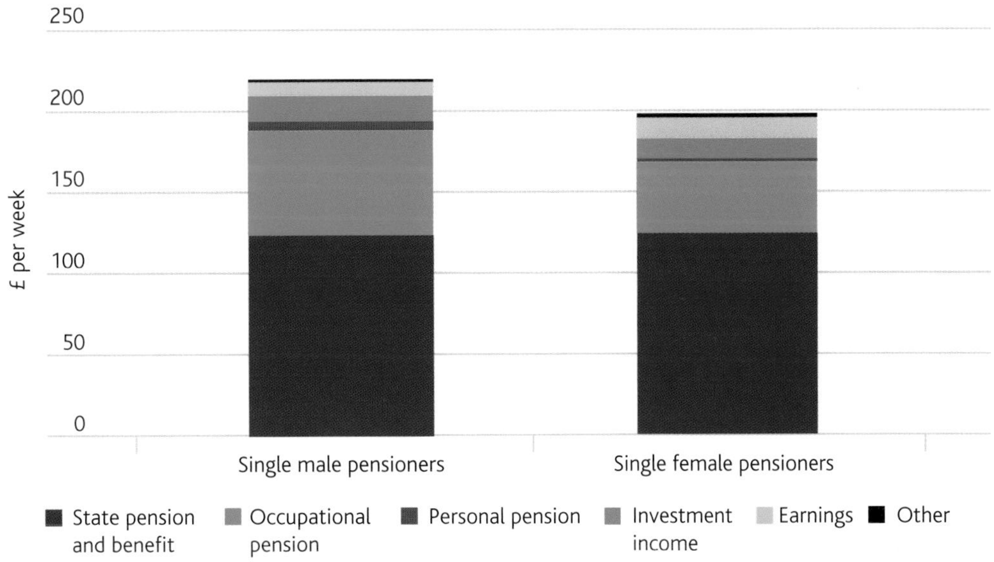

250
200
150
100
50
0
£ per week
Single male pensioners
Single female pensioners
State pension and benefit
Occupational pension
Personal pension
Investment income
Earnings
Other

Source: The Pensioners' Incomes Series 2002/03

Figure 8.3 Components of Average Income of Individual Pensioners Within a Couple: 2002/03

300
250
200
150
100
50
0
£ per week
Men
Women
State pension and benefit
Occupational and personal pension
Self-employment
Investment income
Earnings
Other

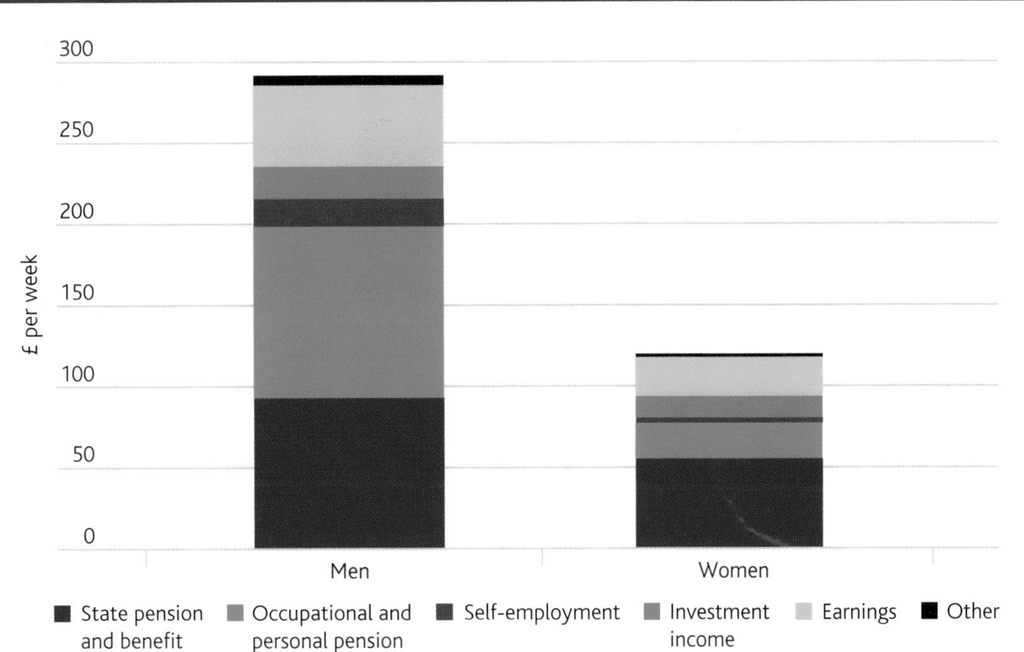

Source: Individual incomes of men and women 1996/97 to 2002/03: a summary, Women and Equality Unit

Note: A pensioner couple is defined as a couple where at least one member of the family unit is of state pension age or over.

Figure 8.4 Employment Rates for Men and Women aged 35-49:1984

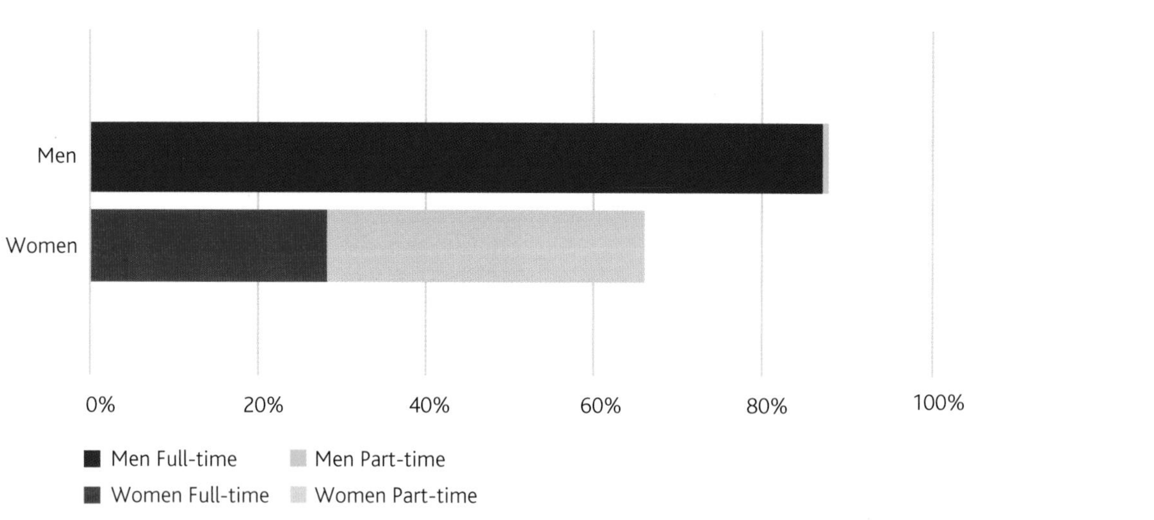

Source: LFS Spring 1984, ONS

Figure 8.5 Private Sector Employment, by Industry Sector and Sex: 1980 and 2003

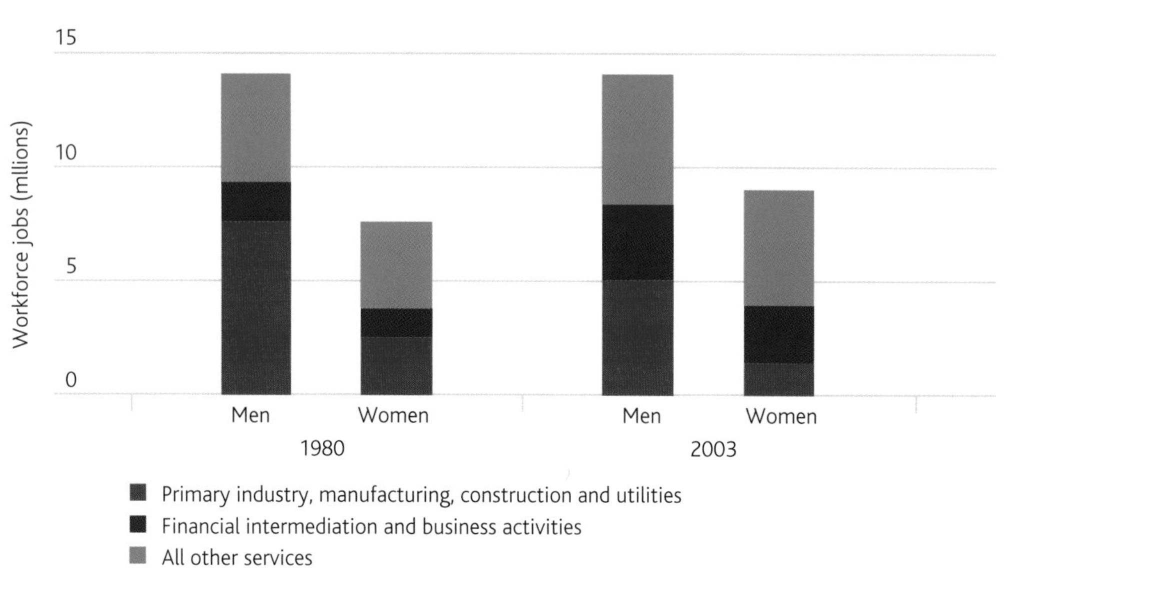

Source: Workforce jobs series, ONS

Notes: Excludes the public administration, health and education sectors as a proxy for the public sector. All other services includes: distribution, hotels and restaurants, transport and communication, and other services.

Figure 8.6 Private Sector Employer-Sponsored Pension Scheme Membership, by Industry: 2003

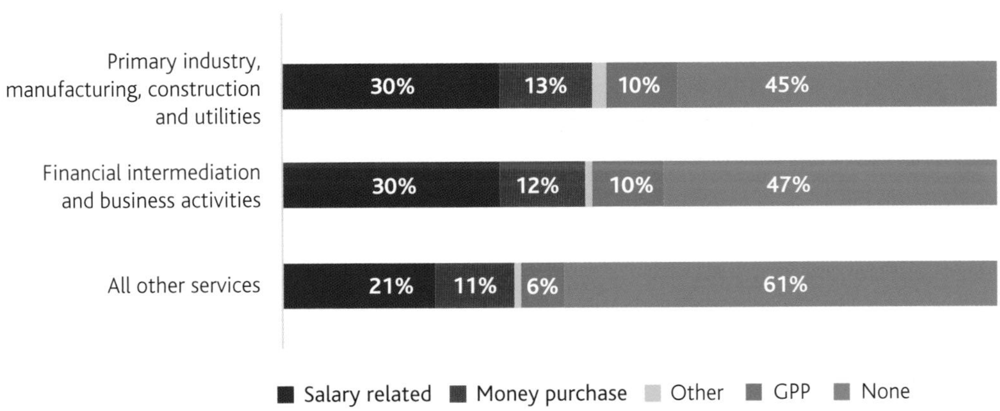

Source: Ungrossed NES, 2003

Notes: All other services includes: distribution, hotels and restaurants, transport and communication, and other services. Using ungrossed NES data may inflate the level of participation. For more information see Appendix A.

Figure 8.7 Breakdown of Annuity Type Purchased

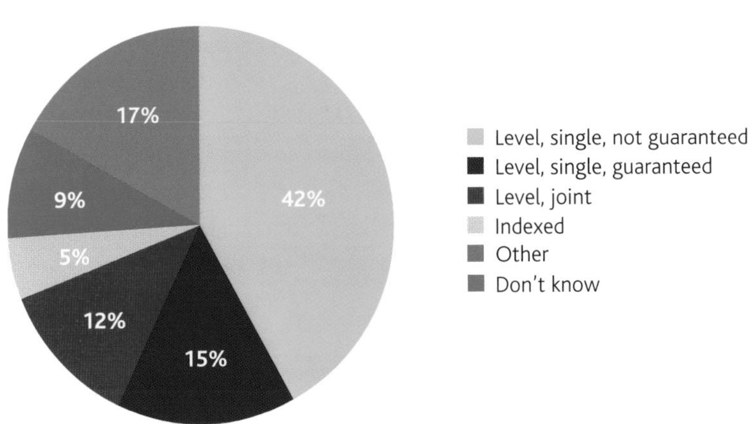

Source: Annuities: the Consumer Experience, 2002, ABI

Finally for women buying their own annuities out of maturing DC pension funds, annuity income has been lower both because of lower average retirement ages, and because of lower annuity rates at any given age, reflecting higher female longevity [Figure 8.8].

The DB-DC shift will therefore tend to worsen the situation for female private sector workers.[1]

3. State system design features.

Women have lower state pensions because the state system is contributory, has only partial mechanisms to compensate for caring responsibilities, and has several "cliff-edge" features, which mean that women who fall below particular earnings levels or who have a small number of years in employment not only accrue less pension benefits, but disproportionately less.

- The UK state pension system is described in Appendix F. The key characteristics relevant to the relative position to women are that (i) the Basic State Pension (BSP) and the Second State Pension (SERPS/S2P) are contributory systems, with the level of pension received dependent on the number of years of contributions made, and (ii) the accrual profile has a number of "cliff-edges" within it, the impact of which tends to affect women far more than men. Specific problems are that:

  - If someone has worked for less than 10 years during their working life, they would not on the basis of their contributions, receive any BSP [Figure 8.9]. Home Responsibilities Protection (HRP), provides a partial offset to this effect for people with caring responsibilities. But the details of how HRP is calculated (the fact that it does not act as an accrual of years of contributions itself but as a multiplier of contributions of the years accrued as a result of employment) means that this offset is less than total. As a result a woman with 20 years of home responsibilities and 10 years of employment would accrue only 50% of a BSP, while a man with a 30 year employment record would accrue 70%. HRP moreover works on **whole** years of caring, and therefore fails to accrue for many women taking partial year breaks to care.

  - Someone earning below the Lower Earnings Limit (LEL) (currently £79 per week i.e. £4,108 per year) in any one job, will accrue no state pension rights, even if they work in several such jobs with combined earnings above the LEL. While this is matched by the fact that such a person will also be making no National Insurance (NI) contributions, the net effect is that many women with several part-time jobs fail to accrue BSP rights.

[1]Note: Pensions Commission analysis also suggests that the DB-DC shift has a disproportionate effect on women because the impact of career breaks on pension accrual is now greater in DC schemes than in DB schemes (following improvements in leaver's rights).

Figure 8.8 Level Single Life Annuity Rates, by Age and Sex: August 2004

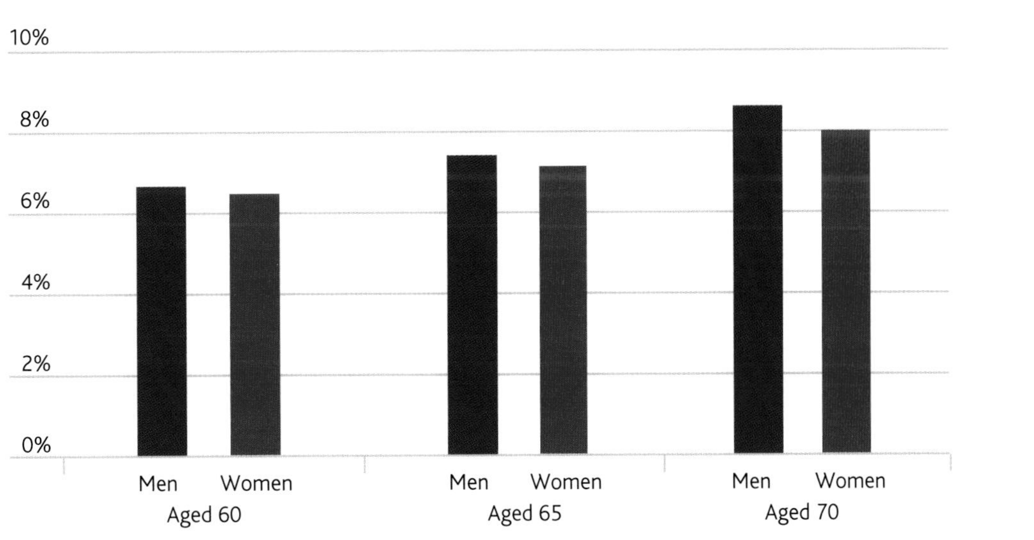

Source: The Annuity Bureau

Note: Based on the average of number 1 and 3 ranked providers.

Figure 8.9 Accrual of Basic State Pension

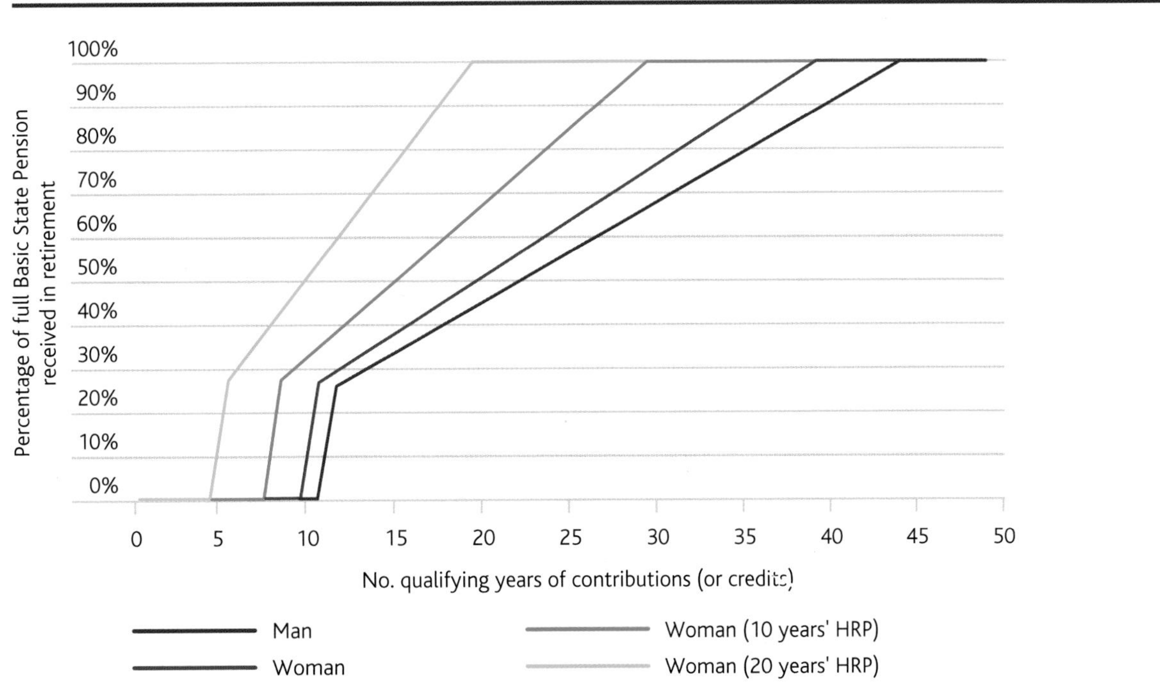

Source: Pensions Commission calculations based on state pension rules.

- A number of recent changes in the state system will improve the future position of female pensioners. The fact that rights can be accrued by someone earning above the LEL (£79 per week) but below the Primary Earning Threshhold (£91 per week) at which NI contributions begin, will help many low-paid women. So too will the improved treatment of the low paid under the increasingly flat-rate S2P.

- But the net effect of the historic shape of the UK state pension system, combined with women's past employment patterns, is that 69% of women aged 65-69 who receive BSP receive less than the full amount (compared with 15% of men). Forty percent of women who receive BSP based on their own contributions are entitled to less than 75% [Figure 8.10]. The impact of this on female pensioner poverty is more effectively offset following the introduction of Pension Credit than it was before. Two-thirds of Pension Credit beneficiaries are women. But the unavoidable consequence is that women's pension income from the state includes a larger means-tested element [Figure 8.11].

4. Social change making past assumptions invalid

The present distribution of pensioners' income reflects the state and private pension system which existed over several past decades. These reflected assumptions that many women would be able to rely in retirement on their husband's accrued pensions rights. But this assumption has become decreasingly valid as social habits and family structure have changed.

- The proportion of the female population that is married has been falling rapidly in the 35-44 year old age group and this effect will increasingly feed through to 55-64 year olds [Figures 8.12 and 8.13].

- As a result, GAD forecasts suggest that despite the continued rapid fall in widowhood before retirement, by 2021 38% of women aged 55-64 will not be part of an ongoing marriage, largely because they never married or because of divorce.

An effective pension system for the future must therefore be one in which the majority of women are accruing pension entitlements **in their own right.**

Figure 8.10 Percentage of BSP Received by 65-69 Year Olds: 2003

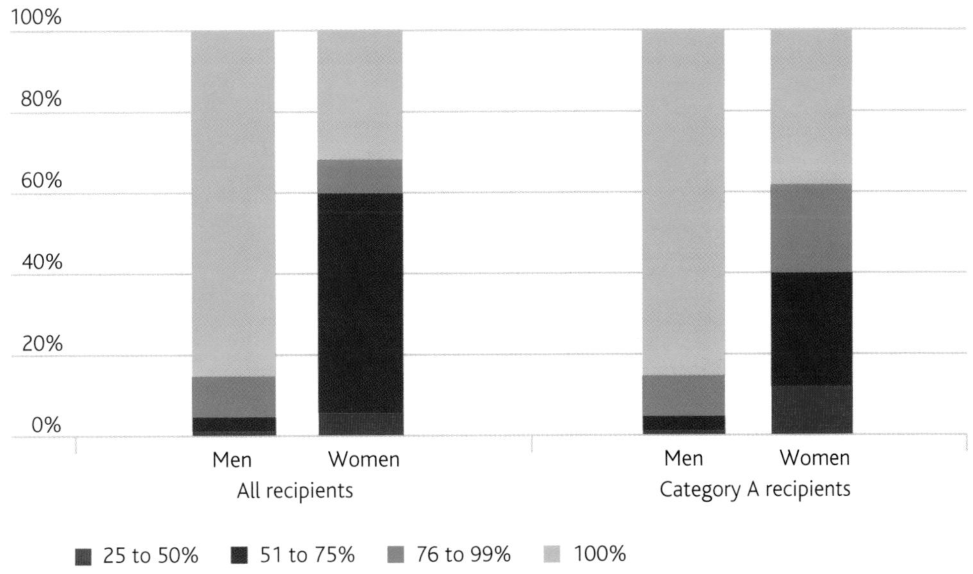

100%
80%
60%
40%
20%
0%

Men Women
All recipients

Men Women
Category A recipients

■ 25 to 50% ■ 51 to 75% ■ 76 to 99% ■ 100%

Source: Retirement Pension and Widows Benefit Administrative Data, 30 September 2003, DWP

Note: Category A entitlement is based only on the individual's contributions.

The figures for all women recipients show a much higher percentage of receipts because many women will receive 51-75% of the BSP as wives of fully paid-up men, and some will receive 100% as widows.

Figure 8.11 Components of Average State Pension and Benefit Income: 2002/03

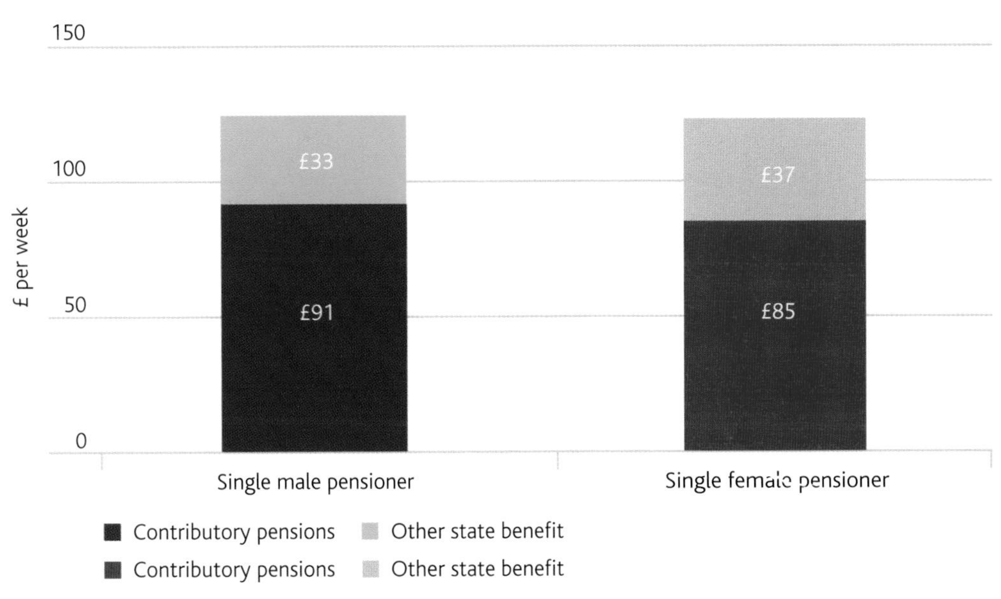

Contributory pensions
Other state benefit

Source: The Pensioners' Incomes Series 2002/03

Note: Other state benefit includes means-tested benefits and disability benefits.

Figure 8.12 Legal Marital Status of Women Aged 35-44

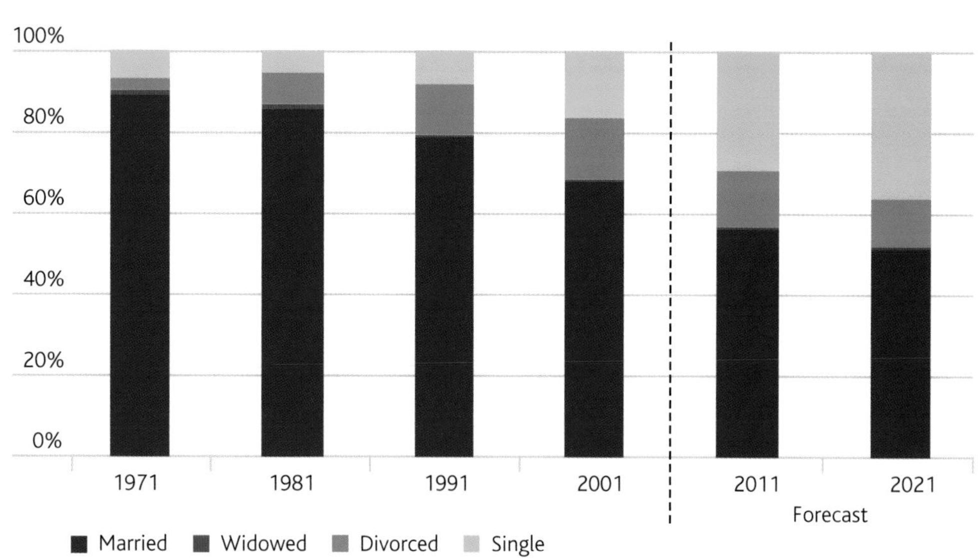

Source: Population statistics, ONS and 1996 based legal marital status projections, England and Wales, GAD

Note: Population estimates by marital status for 1971 are based on the 1971 Census; those for 1981 are based on the 1981 Census and have not been rebased using the 2001 Census. Estimates for 1986 onwards are based on the 2001 Census. Estimates for 1991 and 2001 are based on the 2001 Census.

Figure 8.13 Legal Marital Status of Women Aged 55-64

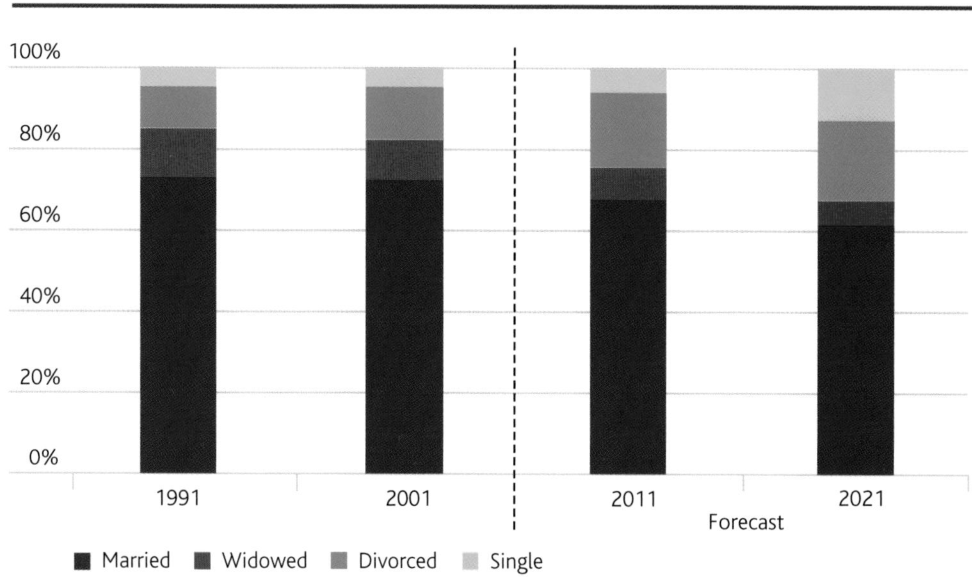

Source: Population statistics, ONS and 1996-based legal marital status projections, England and Wales, GAD

Note: Population estimates for 1991 and 2001 are based on the 2001 Census

Figure 8.14 Employment Rates for Men and Women, by age: 16-60

100%
80%
60%
40%
20%
0%
16
21
26
31
36
41
46
51
56
Age
Men 1985
Women 1985
Men 2004
Women 2004

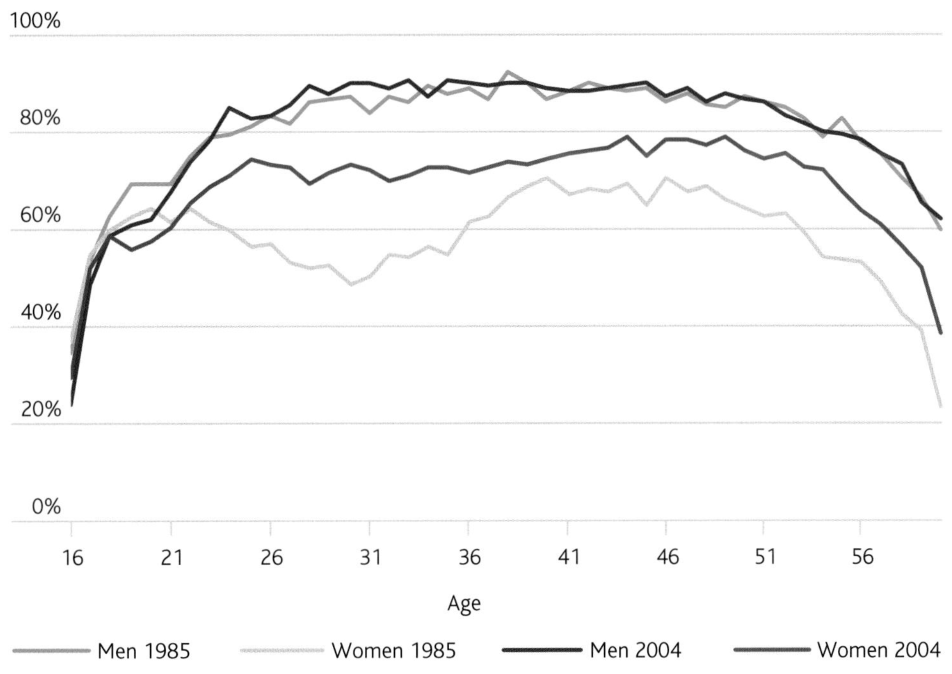

Source: LFS, Spring 1985 and 2004

Figure 8.15 Comparison of Full and Part-time Working for Men and Women, by age: 16-60

Percentage of men and women working
100%
80%
60%
40%
20%
0%
16
21
26
31
36
41
46
51
56
Age
Men full-time
Men part-time
Women full-time
Women part-time

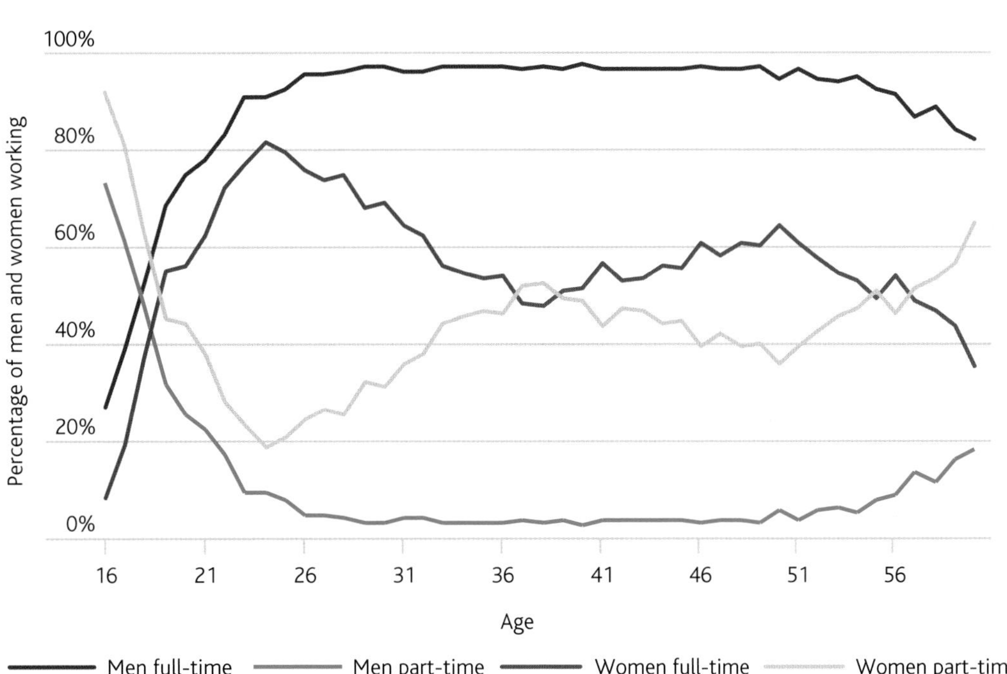

Source: LFS, Spring 2004, ONS

5. Several trends favourable to women but problems remain

Several of the factors which have led women to accrue less pension rights than men, in both the state and private system, are changing in women's relative favour, partly because the position of women is getting better, partly because the position of men is getting worse.

Several labour market trends are favourable to the relative position of women, but with significant problems, particularly for part-time female workers, still remaining.

- Women's employment rates have risen significantly at all ages, while men's are stable, though women's are still lower and still contain a much larger part-time element [Figures 8.14 and 8.15].

- The gap between the earnings per hour of full-time female workers and men has narrowed over the last 7 years, and significantly so among low paid women, perhaps reflecting the impact of the National Minimum Wage [Figure 8.16]. Notably, however, the gap between the earnings of part-time female workers and full-time male earnings is not narrowing except among the lowest paid [Figure 8.17].

- Female educational achievements, at GCSE and in terms of degree level study, have overtaken men's [Figures 8.18 and 8.19]. This may over time have consequences for pay convergence further up the income distribution, though evidence that within 5 years of graduation women earn less than men with the same qualifications illustrates that there may be other factors at work.[2]

Trends in pension rights accrual (in both the state and private systems) are also favourable.

- Despite the inflexibilities of "cliff-edges" referred to above, women below the age of 40 are now as likely to be accruing BSP rights as men, and more likely to be accruing S2P rights. This latter finding reflects the fact that men are far more likely to be self-employed and therefore to be outside the SERPS/S2P system [Figure 8.20].

[2]Note: Equal Opportunities Commission Working Paper Series No.1, 2002

Figure 8.16 Women's Full-time Hourly Pay as a Percentage of Men's Full-time Hourly Pay

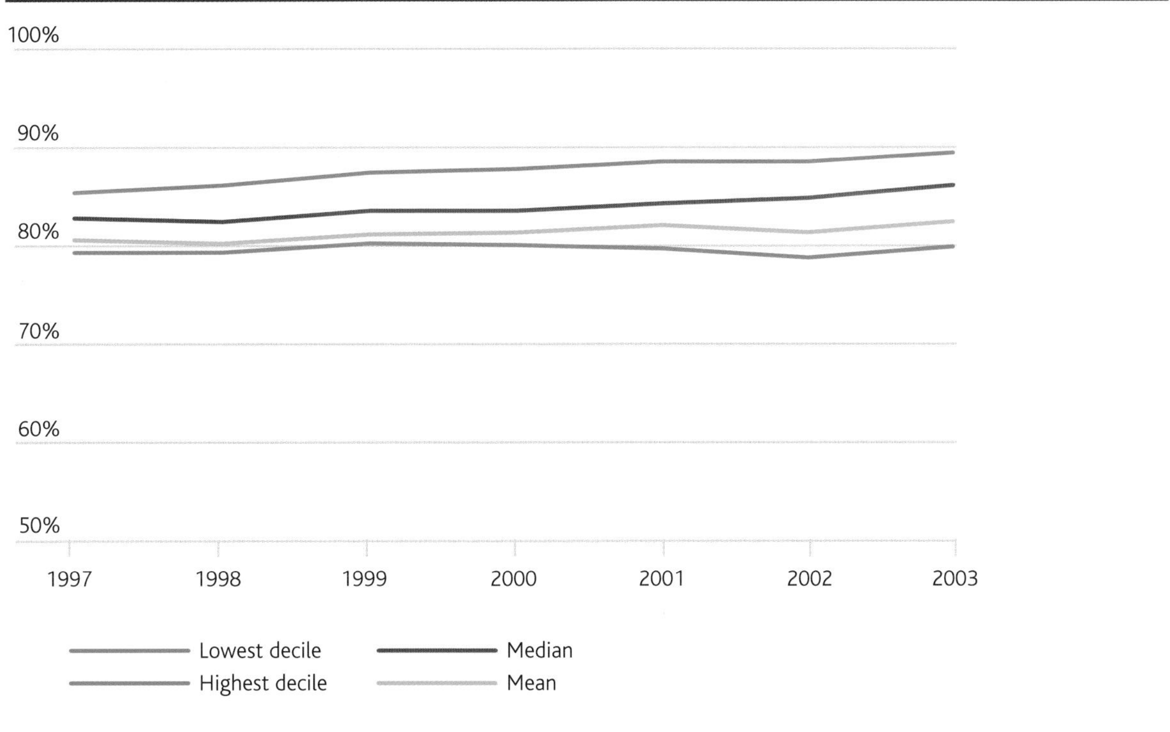

Source: Ungrossed NES.

Figure 8.17 Women's Part-time Hourly Pay as a Percentage of Men's Full-time Hourly Pay

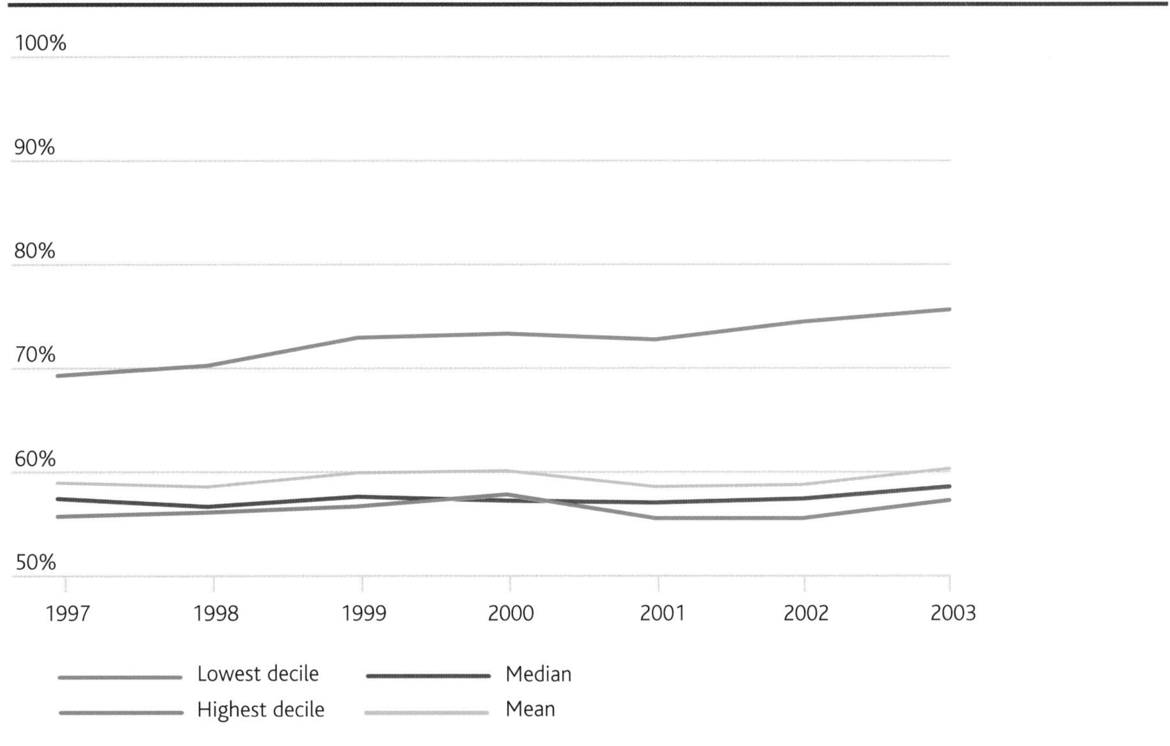

Source: Ungrossed NES.

Note: The survey excludes significant numbers of part-time employees with low weekly earnings.

Figure 8.18 Percentage of Pupils Achieving Five or More O Level/CSE/GCSE Grades A*-C

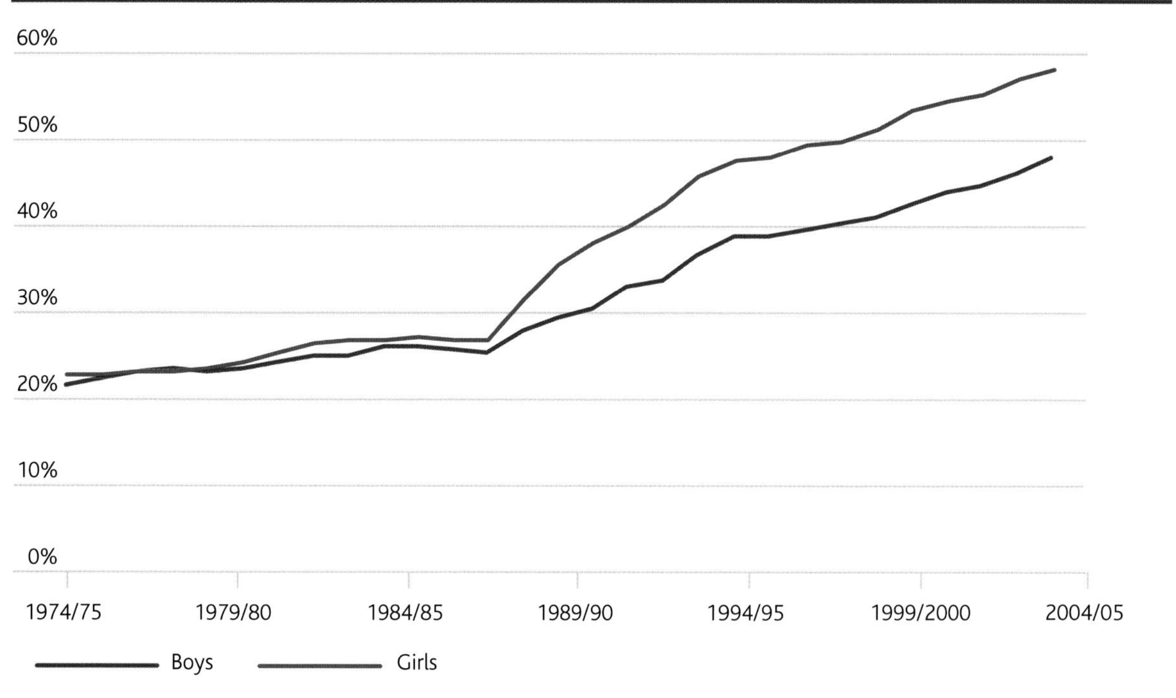

Source: Department for Education and Skills

Notes: Data for England.

Figure 8.19 Participation in University Education, by Sex

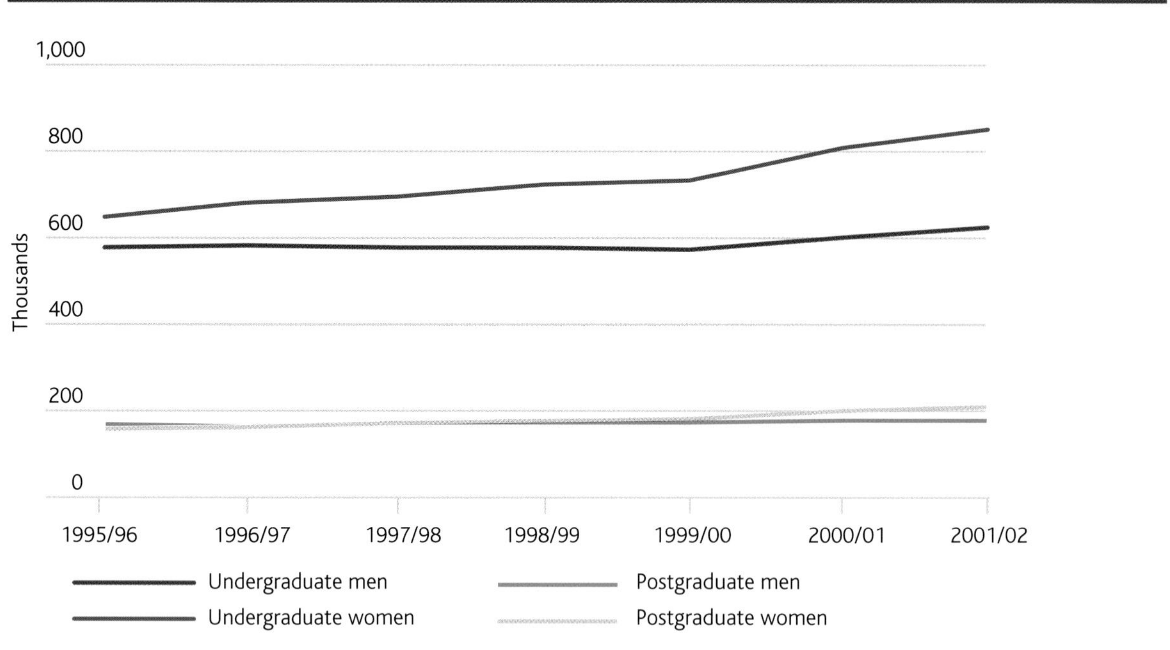

Source: Higher Education Statistics Agency

Figure 8.20 Accrual of State Pension Rights by Age and Sex: Percentage accruing rights in 2002/03

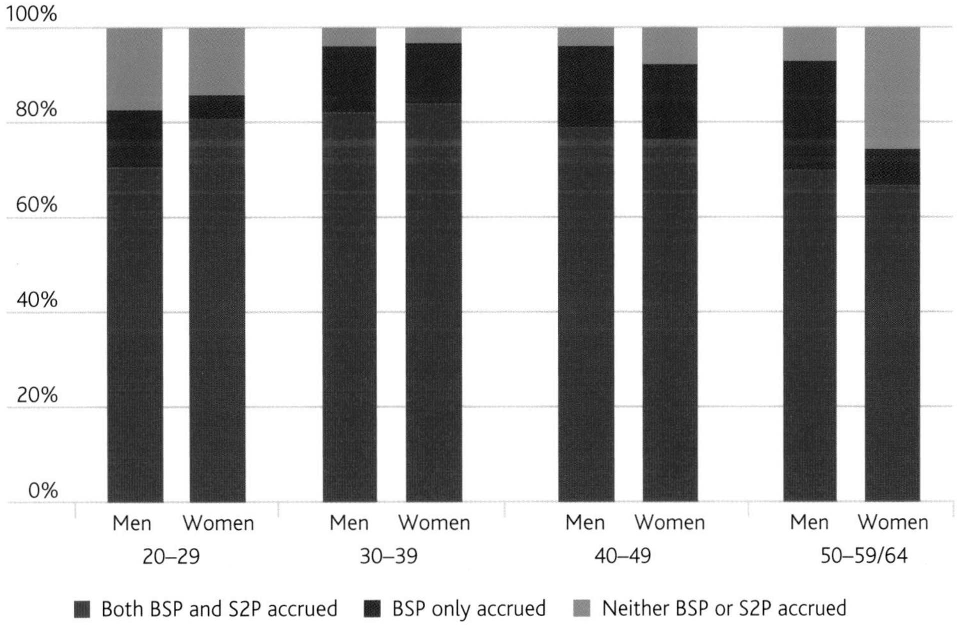

100%
80%
60%
40%
20%
0%
Men Women
20–29
Men Women
30–39
Men Women
40–49
Men Women
50–59/64

■ Both BSP and S2P accrued ■ BSP only accrued ■ Neither BSP or S2P accrued

Source: FRS 2002/03

Note: This analysis refers to an individual's accruals during 2002/03 only. It does not consider cumulative rights.

- Women in full-time employment have now become **more** likely to be a member of an occupational pension scheme than men and the percentage of part-time women in pension schemes has grown dramatically over the last 15 years [Figure 8.21]. Taking full-time and part-time employees together, female employees are still less likely to be in a pension scheme, but the gap is closing [Figure 8.22].

- At any given earnings level moreover, women are now more likely to be members of an employer sponsored pension scheme than men, and more likely to be members of DB schemes [Figures 8.23 and 8.24].

- This reflects trends in employment and pension provision by sector which are favourable to women and unfavourable to men.

  - The greater concentration of women in the public sector has meant that women are less affected by the rapid erosion of DB provision in the private sector [Figure 8.25].

  - The erosion of manufacturing employment, and the closure of DB schemes in the manufacturing sector (where they have been more prevalent than in the service sector), is eroding the advantage that men have gained from their greater concentration in manufacturing. The relative disadvantage that women have suffered from concentration in private sector services is thus declining, but because of a decline in men's pension provision rather than an improvement in women's [Figure 8.26].

Figure 8.21 Membership of Current Employer's Pension Scheme, by Sex and Full-time/Part-time Status

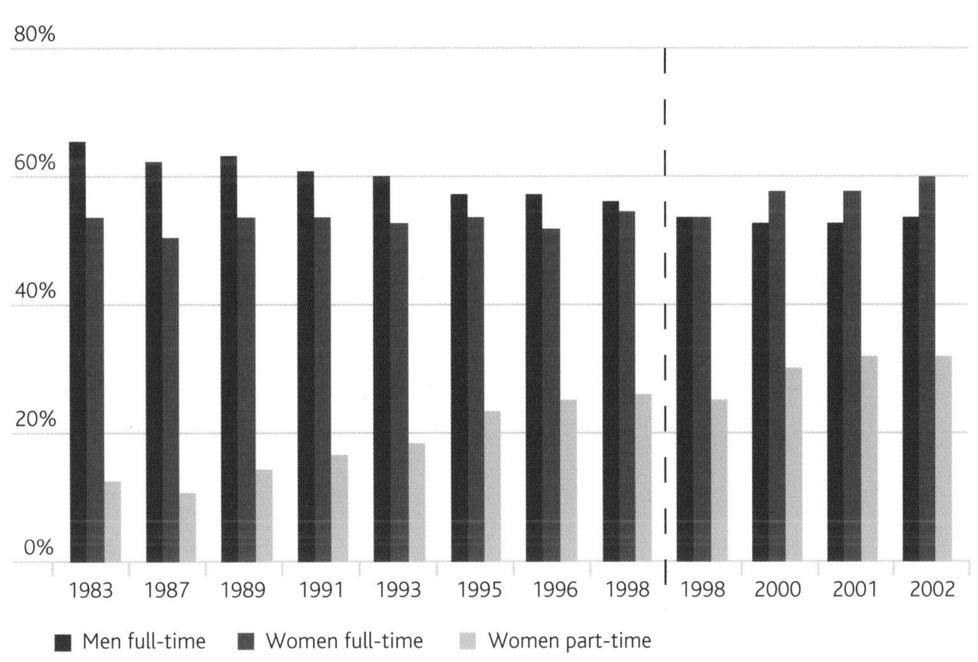

Source: Living in Britain, GHS 2002

Note: Trend data show unweighted and weighted figures for 1998 to give an indication of the effect of the weighting introduced in 1998.

Figure 8.22 Membership of Current Employer's Pension Scheme, by Sex: Percentage of Employees who are Members

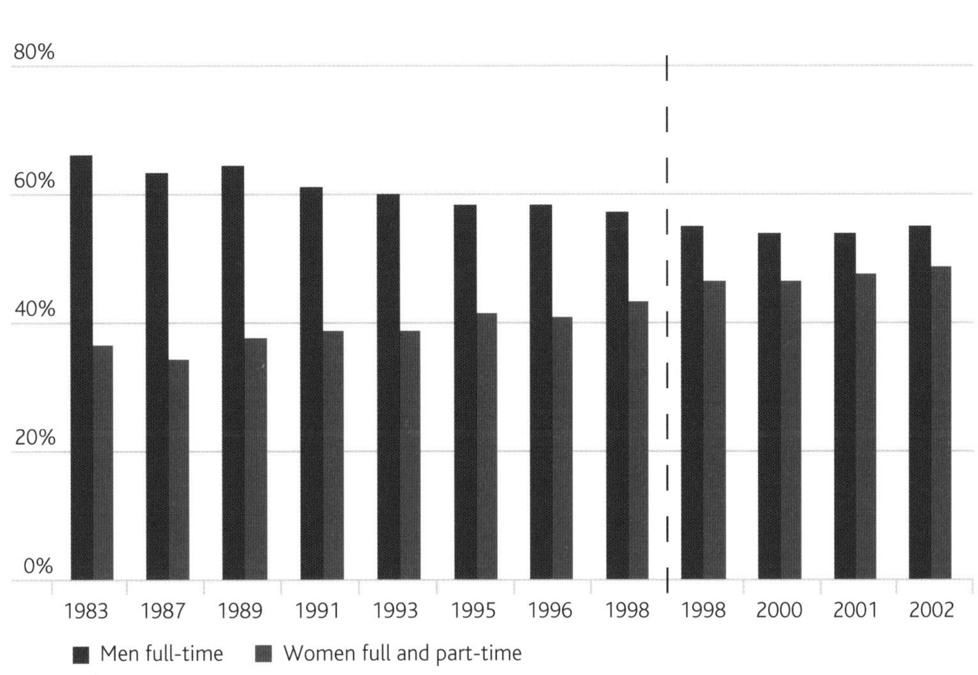

Source: Living in Britain, GHS 2002
LFS

Note: Trend data show unweighted and weighted figures for 1998 to give an indication of the effect of the weighting introduced in 1998. Participation for women estimated using LFS employment data.

Figure 8.23 Participation in Employer-Sponsored Pension Schemes, by Earnings Quintile

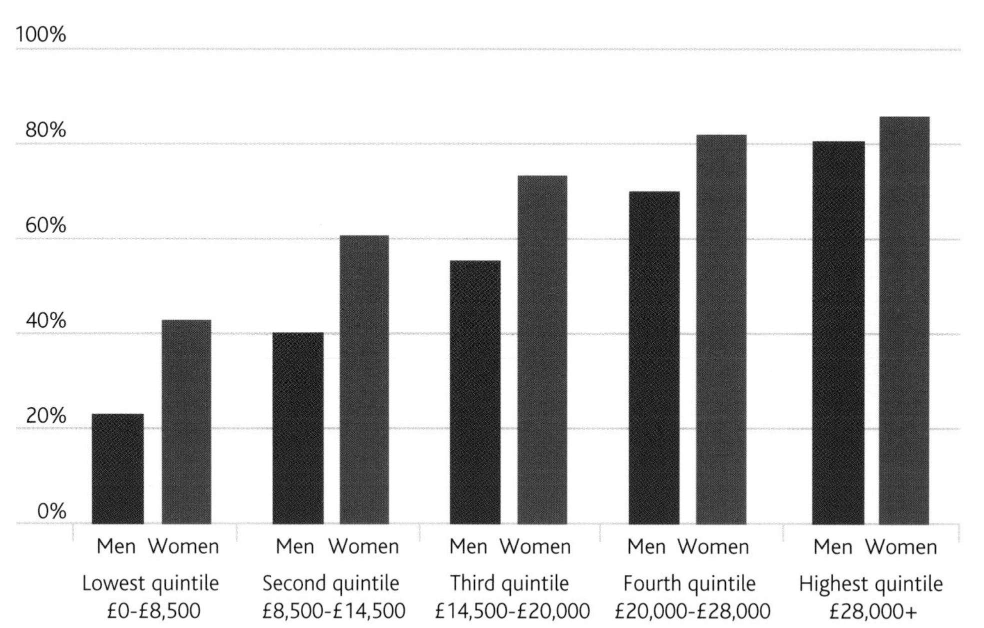

Source: Ungrossed NES, 2003

Note: Using ungrossed NES data may inflate the level of participation. For more information see Appendix A. Earnings quintiles based on annual earnings for all employees who have been in post for 12 months or more.

Figure 8.24 Participation in Salary-Related Employer-Sponsored Pension Scheme, by Earnings Quintile

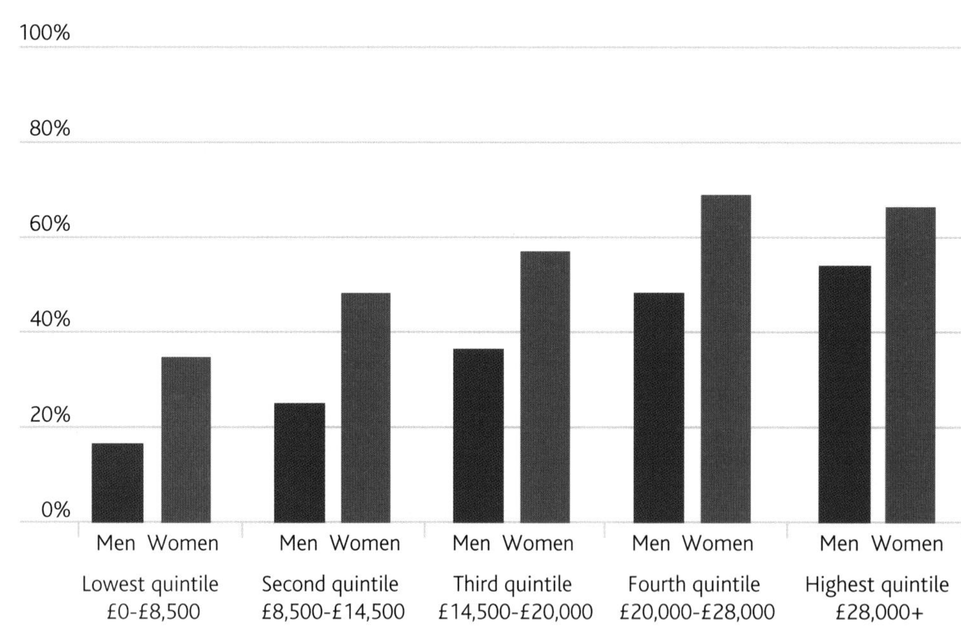

Source: Ungrossed NES, 2003

Note: Using ungrossed NES data may inflate the level of participation. For more information see Appendix A. Earnings quintiles based on annual earnings for all employees who have been in post for 12 months or more.

Figure 8.25 Employment by Sector, by Sex: 2003

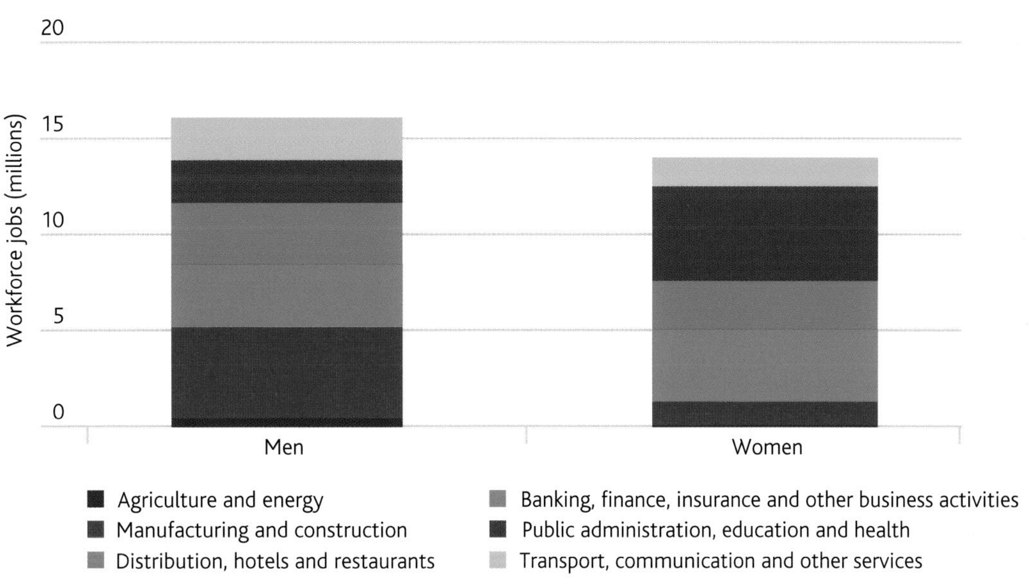

Source: Workforce jobs series, ONS

Figure 8.26 Trend in Workforce Jobs for Selected Industry Sectors

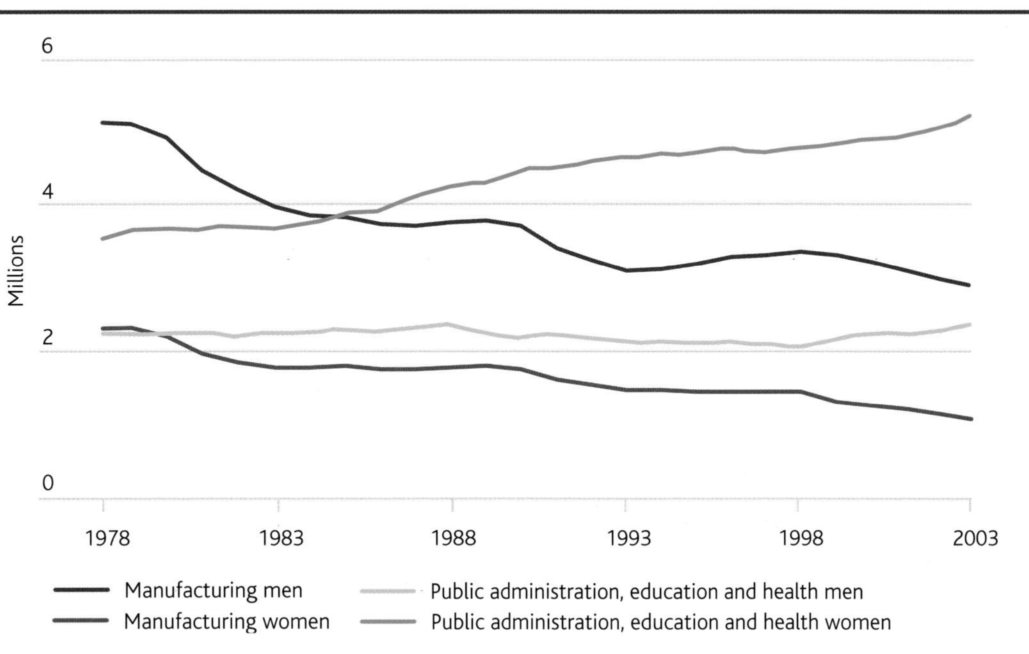

Source: Workforce jobs series, ONS

Note: Public administration, education and health will include some private sector employees in education and health.

- Finally the impact of lower annuity rates on the relative position of women retiring with DC pensions is likely to reduce. The equalisation of the State Pension Age at 65 is likely to encourage further convergence of average male and female retirement ages. And annuity rates at any given age are converging significantly as male life expectancy at 65 increases faster than female, a trend which GAD expects to continue [Figure 8.27].

Taken together, these trends are likely over the next 30 years to lead to a narrowing of the gender gap in pensioner income, a trend which indeed is already visible, with women now on average receiving 72% as much occupational pension income as men, compared to 61% in 1994/5 [Figure 8.28].

This does not mean that the position of future women pensioners will be adequate, since the male position to which women are converging is itself getting worse. And many women will continue to accrue inadequate pensions because of lower earnings than men, and because of lower number of years in employment. Even though female employees are as likely to be pension scheme members as men, women's lower overall employment rate will depress pension right accrual. But it does mean that gender specific issues of pension system design, while important, may be less vital to the position of future women pensioners than either (i) more general issues relating to equality while in work; or (ii) issues of pension system adequacy which apply equally to men and women.

6. Gender specific issues in pension policy

There are two ways in which changes in pension policy could have a disproportionate impact on the position of women: changes to the state system and the introduction of compulsion.

- While the specific design of the state pension system is not within the Pensions Commission's remit, it clearly has consequences for the overall adequacy of pensions and for the context of any Commission recommendations on the private system. And for lower paid women, there are issues of pension adequacy where the state system design will be of primary importance. Addressing the "cliff-edges" within the state system, (the 10 year rule, the impact of the LEL both in relation to single and multiple jobs, and the inflexibilities in HRP) would have an impact on the adequacy of pensions for lower paid women which could not be achieved by any change in policy towards private pensions which the Commission might recommend.

- If compulsory private pensions were introduced, the impact would be greatest among people not presently covered by an employer-sponsored pension scheme. While among full-time employees this would actually benefit more men than women, overall the benefit would be greatest for women, given the still low level of participation by part-time female employees.

Figure 8.27 Convergence of Annuity Rates

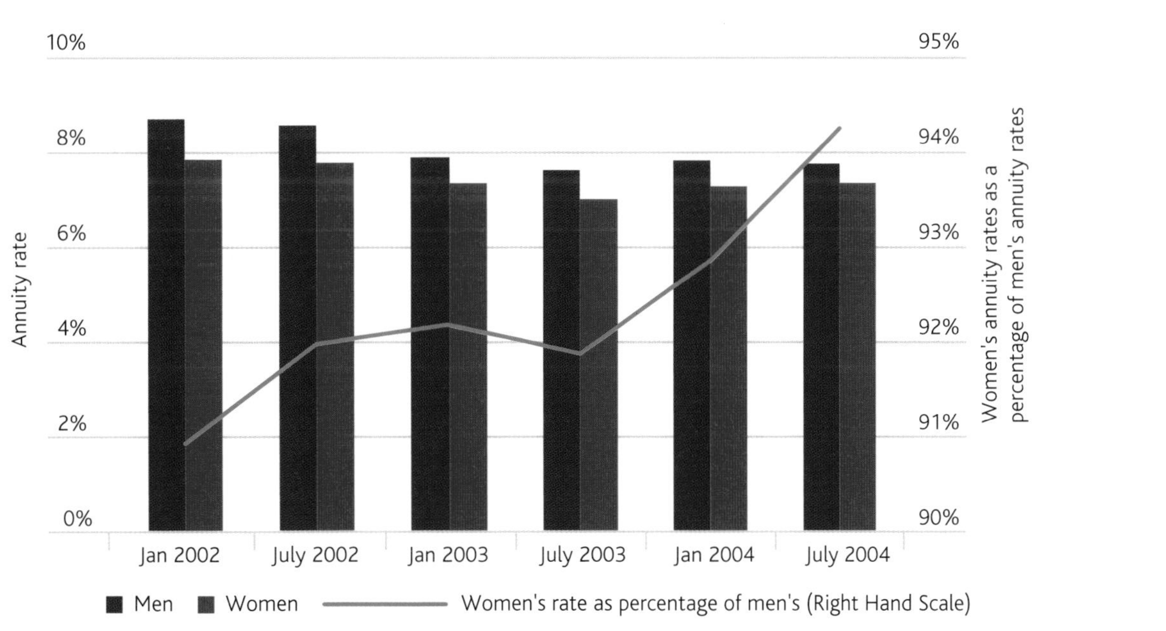

Source: The Annuity Bureau

Note: Rates are shown for 65 year olds purchasing £30,000 level, single life annuity: average of top three rates.

Figure 8.28 Average Occupational Pension Income of 65-69 Year Olds: 1994/5 and 2002/3: Women's income as a percentage of mens

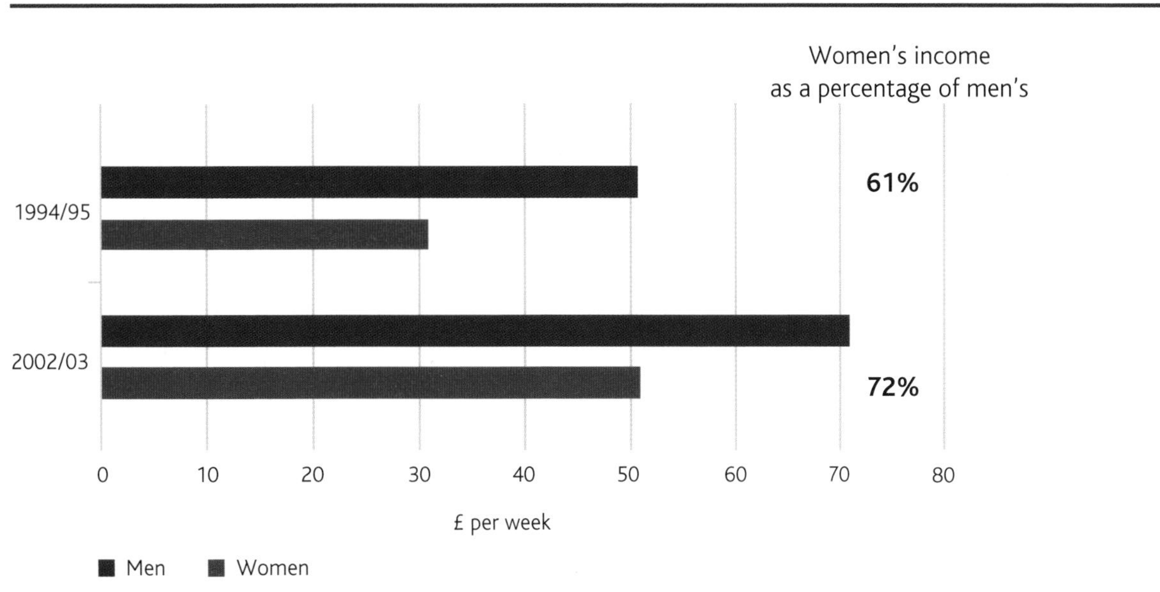

Source: FRS 1994-95 and 2002-03

9 Issues and consultation process

The Pensions Commission's Second Report is planned for Autumn 2005. That report will include the Commission's conclusions on the effectiveness of the existing UK pension system, in particular its private elements, and recommendations for change. It will present the Commission's conclusions on whether there is a need to expand the role of compulsion beyond that which is already implicit in the State Second Pension and the contracting-out options.

In its deliberations over the next year, the Commission would like to hear the views of interested and informed parties, and to get their reactions to this First descriptive report. It would be helpful if in setting out those reactions, organisations or individuals could separately and explicitly identify:

- Any areas where they believe that the First Report is factually wrong, or where we have failed to take into account relevant information sources.
- Any areas where we have made judgements about key variables (e.g. rates of return) which look too optimistic or too pessimistic.
- The organisation's proposed approach to the philosophical issue set out at the beginning of Chapter 4: What should be the role of government in pensions? Should it be limited to poverty prevention and to making well-informed choice possible? Or should government seek to ensure that people up to some level of income have made provision which they will consider adequate: and if so what level?

This chapter sets out specific issues on which we would particularly like to hear views.

Views on the following issues are sought:

- What should be the balance of responses to the demographic challenge described in Chapters 1 and 2?

  - What mix of the 4 possible options: pensioners becoming poorer relative to the rest of society; higher taxes/NI contributions devoted to pensions; higher savings or higher average retirement ages, should be pursued?

  - How far should government or society in general have a point of view on this trade-off versus leaving it to individuals to make their own choice?

- Is there broad agreement with the description of trends in the UK pension system set out in Chapter 3?

  - Is our assessment of the DB-DC shift and its implications for the future level of total contributions reasonable?

  - What is the appropriate risk-sharing balance between the state, employers, the financial services industry and individuals? Is the large shift of risk to individuals which is currently occurring acceptable, and if not is it avoidable?

- Is Chapter 4's assessment of the adequacy of existing and likely future pension provision reasonable?

  - Is our benchmark definition of "adequate" income replacement sensible?

  - Is our macro-model of likely future pension contributions and pension incomes too pessimistic or too optimistic?

  - Have we correctly defined the groups of people likely to be inadequately provided for and those likely to well be provided for?

- Are the conclusions of Chapter 5 reasonable?

  - Is it agreed that non-pension financial assets will play a non-trivial but modest role in pension provision? Could they play a bigger role in future?

  - Is it agreed that housing wealth, especially via inheritance, could play a significant role in pension provision, on average and overall, but that it does not provide a sufficient solution because of the pattern of distribution of pension rights and housing assets?

- Is there agreement that the current voluntarist system, combined with the current state system, is unlikely to deliver an acceptable solution to the problems for the reasons set out in Chapter 6?
  - In principle, can a voluntary system work at lower income levels?
  - Is there a segment of the market comprising lower income, lower premium savers, which cannot be served profitably by the financial services industry on a voluntary basis except at Reduction In Yields which make saving unattractive to the saver?
  - How important an impediment to save, or to advise people to save, is the impact of means-testing?
- Is our Chapter 8 analysis of the position of women pensioners and of how it is likely to evolve, reasonable? And what follows for pension policy?
  - Do people accept the principle that we need to aim for a system in which all individuals, men and women, accrue pensions in their own right?
  - Are there important private pension policy issues specifically affecting women or do the key issues affecting women relate primarily to the contributory nature of the state pension?
- What solutions to present problems should be proposed?
  - Can the voluntarist system be made to work, and if so by what means? How effective can financial education and informed choice be? Is a significant reduction in the extent of means-testing within the state system required to make voluntarism possible? Can the cost of provision (RIY) be reduced to more acceptable levels within a voluntarist system?
  - Do organisations believe that changes to the state system are required in order for a voluntary system to work effectively, or as a necessary complement to an increase in compulsion? And if they propose higher and less means-tested state pensions, what mix of the two inevitable alternatives (higher taxes/NI contributions or a higher SPA) do they propose?

- Is there a case for compulsory private savings and if so what form should it take? Should employers be compelled, or employees, or both?

- If compulsion was introduced, what design features would be required to ensure an appropriate balance between individual choice, guidance on sensible investment approaches, and low costs of administration?

The Commission would like to receive written submissions on these issues by end-January 2005.

Arrangements for written submissions

Please send written responses to:

pensions.commission@dwp.gsi.gov.uk

or

Pensions Commission Consultation
4th Floor, The Adelphi
1-11 John Adam Street
London WC2N 6HT

Tel No: 020 7962 8641

If you are responding on behalf of a representative group or organisation it would be helpful if you could make this clear and include brief background information on that group or organisation.

The information you send to us may need to be shared within the Pensions Commission and/or published in a summary of responses received as part of this consultation. We will assume that you are content for us to do this, and that if you are replying by email, your consent overrides any confidentiality disclaimer that is generated by your organisation's IT system, unless you specifically include a request to the contrary in the main text of your response to us.

Annex: Summary of findings and recommendations on data adequacy

The Pensions Commission's terms of reference asked us to comment on the adequacy of available data to support evidence-based pension policy: "To keep under review the regime for UK private pensions and long-term savings, taking into account the proposals in the Green Paper, *assessing the information needed to monitor progress*."

Appendix A responds to that request. Its overall conclusion is that present data sources are significantly deficient as a basis for some aspects of evidence-based policy. This is in part because they have not been designed to answer the questions we now need to consider and in part (in the case of aggregate national data) because of significant errors in past data gathering and analytical approaches. Some improvements will come on stream over the next year, but these will not transform data availability in the key areas where information is currently deficient. Recommendations on policy in the Pensions Commission's 2005 Report will therefore necessarily be based on the judgements from imperfect data which we present in this year's report.

The Appendix expands on this summary conclusion and goes on to make specific recommendations. These are reproduced below, along with one recommendation made in Appendix E.

Summary of recommendations on data improvements

This section summarises both likely developments already in hand which the Pensions Commission welcomes, and recommendations on further improvements which should be considered.

We welcome in particular:

- The work of the Pension Statistics Task Force to improve aggregate data.

- Piloting in the New Earnings Survey of new questions on employer and employee contributions.

- The plans of the new Pensions Regulator to develop a regular detailed analysis of scheme returns.

- The better information likely to emerge from data sharing between the Department for Work and Pensions (DWP) and Inland Revenue made possible by the current Pensions Bill.

- Office for National Statistics (ONS) plans to include equivalised income analyses within the Expenditure and Food Survey.

We make the following recommendations on priorities:

- The ONS Wealth and Assets Survey should be a major priority, and should aim to support:
  - Effective longitudinal analysis
  - Analysis of pension rights accumulation among all age groups
  - Analysis of the impact of inheritance on asset accumulation
  - Linkage to administrative records to allow a complete pension picture, including state pension rights
  - Some analysis of expectations and attitudes that influence savings behaviour
- Completion of the development of Pensim2, and its availability for Pensions Commission analysis, is important. We hope to be able to use its modelling capability during the next year of our work: this requires that it is available for use by, or on behalf of, the Pensions Commission by the end of February 2005 to help us develop and inform our conclusions for the Second Report.

We make the following proposals for consideration:

- It would be preferable for the Employers' Pension Provision (EPP) survey to be undertaken every two years.
- Adequate information needs to be gathered on Group Personal Pension schemes as well as on trustee based occupational schemes. The Government Actuary's Department, the new Pensions Regulator and others should give consideration to how such data can be gathered, and to the co-ordination of their data gathering efforts.
- DWP and the Department of Health should consider how best to share insights and coordinate research into the healthy/unhealthy ageing debate, which the relevant research councils (Medical Research Council and Economic and Social Research Council) should also note as a key issue for society.
- HM Treasury, DWP, ONS and Inland Revenue should consider whether there are wider lessons to be learnt from the severe problems that have occurred in aggregate pension statistics, looking in particular at (i) cross-departmental coordination; (ii) high-level credibility checks; and (iii) resource adequacy within ONS.

Recommendation on communication of demographic trends

Appendix E considers demographic trends. It explains that there are two different definitions of life expectancy used in published figures. The correct figure (i.e. the one that actually tells a 65 year old in 2004 the best estimate of how long he or she will live) is the "cohort life expectancy". The "period life expectancy" consistently underestimates true life expectancy if life expectancy is on an upward trend. Unfortunately, since period life expectancy figures are easier to produce, they are the most commonly used figures in Government publications and press reports.

- We recommend that official publications where possible use the cohort approach when describing current and future trends in longevity.

Glossary

Active membership	Active members are current employees who are contributing (or having contributions made on their behalf) to an organisation's occupational pension scheme. The scheme may be open or closed but cannot be frozen.
Additional Voluntary Contribution (AVC)	These are personal pension contributions made by someone who is also a member of an occupational scheme as a top-up to their occupational entitlement. Additional Voluntary Contributions can be made into the occupational scheme or to a stand-alone product called a **Free-Standing Additional Voluntary Contribution plan**.
Annual Management Charge (AMC)	This is the charge generally applied to personal pension plans where the fee is levied as an annual charge on the value of the fund. This charge covers the sales, administration and fund management costs of the fund.
Approved Personal Pension (APP)	This is a **personal pension** which meets certain regulatory requirements, so that it can receive **minimum contributions** (contracted-out rebates from NI payments) enabling an individual to **contract-out** of **S2P**.
Attendance allowance	A non-**means-tested benefit** payable to pensioners if they have additional needs because of illness or disability. For more details see Appendix F.
Automatic enrolment	A pension scheme where an individual is made a member by default, and has to actively decide to leave the scheme.
Average earnings terms	Figures have been adjusted to remove the effect of increases in average earnings over time. Thus if something shown in average earnings terms increases then it is rising faster than average earnings, whereas if it is constant, it rises at exactly the same pace as average earnings.

Average salary scheme	A **Defined Benefit** scheme that gives individuals a pension based on a percentage of the salary earned in each year of their working life (rather than the final year).
Basic State Pension (BSP)	Non-earnings-related pension based on an individuals' **National Insurance** contribution record. For more details see Appendix F.
Behavioural economics	A class of economic theories using insights from psychology to understand how individuals make economic decisions.
Cohort life expectancy	See life expectancy
Conduct Of Business (COB) regulations	The Financial Services Authority rules on how financial sales persons must sell financial **products**.
Contracting-out	The system by which individuals can choose to opt-out of **S2P** and use a proportion of their **National Insurance** contributions to build up a **funded** pension. For more details see Appendix F.
Contribution holidays	Temporary breaks in contributions by either the employer or employees taken because of a surplus in a **Defined Benefit** pension fund.
Council Tax Benefit (CTB)	A **means-tested** benefit through which the UK government helps qualifying individuals meet their Council Tax payments. Qualification criteria include income, savings and personal circumstances.
Defined Benefit (DB) Pension Scheme	A pension scheme where the pension is related to the members' salary or some other value fixed in advance.
Defined Contribution (DC) Pension Scheme	A scheme where the individual receives a pension based on the contributions made and the investment return that they have produced. These are sometimes referred to as money purchase schemes.
Direct execution	Where individuals buy a financial product directly from the provider without using a financial adviser.
Disability living allowance	A non-**means-tested benefit** which is mainly paid to people under **State Pension Age** if they have additional needs because of illness or disability. For more details see Appendix F.

Earnings threshold	The point at which employers and employees become liable for **National Insurance** contributions. In 2004-05 the threshold is £91 per week or £4,745 per year. Also known as the primary earnings threshold or secondary earnings threshold, since all are the same rate.
Economically inactive	People who are neither employed nor **unemployed**, e.g. those who are not doing paid work but caring for children.
Employer-sponsored scheme	A pension scheme which is organised through the employer, enabling pension contributions to be made through the payroll. Often the employer will also make a contribution. An employer-sponsored scheme can either be **occupational** or **group personal** in nature.
Executive pension scheme	A **Defined Contribution** pension scheme arranged through an insurance company for the benefit of a senior employee.
Final salary scheme	A **Defined Benefit** scheme that gives individuals a pension based on the number of years of pensionable service, the accrual rate and final earnings as defined by the scheme.
Free-Standing Additional Voluntary Contribution (FSAVC)	An **Additional Voluntary Contribution** plan which is separate from the individual's **occupational** pension fund.
Funded	Pension schemes in which pension contributions are paid into a fund which is invested and pensions are paid out of this pot.
Gilts	An abbreviation for 'gilt-edged securities'. These are bonds, loans etc issued by the UK government. They are often similar in structure to corporate bonds, paying a fixed amount to the owner following a given schedule. Gilts are generally considered to be one of the safer forms of investment so generate a correspondingly lower return than some more risky assets such as corporate bonds or equities. Some gilts make payments which are fixed in cash terms, whereas others make payments which go up in line with inflation (**indexed-linked gilts**).
Graduated retirement pension	A **National Insurance** pension scheme which ran from 1961-1975, providing earnings-related benefits based on contributions. For more details see Appendix F.

Group Personal Pension (GPP)	A **personal pension** scheme which is organised through the employer, but still takes the form of individual contracts between the employee and the pension provider.
Guarantee Credit	A **means-tested benefit** which is part of the Pension Credit and provides pensioners with a minimum level of income. In 2004-05 the level of the Guarantee Credit for a single person is £105.45 per week.
Guaranteed Minimum Pension (GMP)	The minimum pension that must be provided by a **contracted-out** salary-related scheme for pensions accrued between 1978 and 1997. The GMP is roughly equivalent to the **SERPS** foregone by **contracting-out**.
Healthy life expectancy	An index that combines measures of mortality and health to indicate expected years of life in good health.
Higher participation scenario	A "stretching but feasible" scenario of how employment rates might develop in the UK developed by the Pensions Commission for use in analysis. For more details see the panel in Chapter 2.
Home Responsibilities Protection (HRP)	This helps protect the **National Insurance** record of people who have caring responsibilities and are eligible for certain benefits. For more details on how this works see Appendix F.
Home reversion schemes	An equity release scheme where the individual sells all or part of their house to a company. On death the provider receives the value of the part of the property sold.
Housing Benefit (HB)	A **means-tested benefit** through which the UK government helps qualifying individuals to meet rental payments. Qualification criteria include income, savings and personal circumstances.
Implicit costs	The costs of trading which reduce the return achieved on an invested fund prior to applying explicitly identified management charges.
Income draw-down or income withdrawal	Where an individual takes the tax-free lump sum but does not convert the remaining pension fund to an annuity but draws income directly from the fund.

Independent Financial Adviser (IFA)	An independent financial adviser is someone who is authorised to provide advice and sell a wide range of financial products. They are distinguished from tied financial advisers, who can only give advice on investment products offered by a specific company.
Index trackers	A type of investment fund which is designed to follow a particular published index of the performance of **securities**, e.g. the UK all-share-index.
Indexing regimes	Policy on the up-rating of thresholds used in the calculation of tax or benefits. Typically these thresholds increase each year in line with inflation or average earnings. Over the long-term, indexing regimes can dramatically change the impact of taxes and benefits.
Index-linked gilts	**Gilts** which pay an income which increases in line with inflation and the capital values of which increase in line with inflation.
Individual Savings Account (ISA)	ISAs are accounts which can be used to hold many types of savings and investment products including cash, life insurance and stocks and shares. They are available to most UK residents and there are strict rules regarding the maximum amount allowed for each component and the overall amount you can invest in any one tax year. The returns earned in an ISA (capital growth and income) are tax free.
Insurance-managed occupational pension schemes	**Occupational pension** schemes where an insurance company is responsible for the administration of the fund and may also provide some guarantees relating to investment performance.
Large firm	For statistical purposes, the Department of Trade and Industry usually defines a large firm as one with 250 or more employees.

Life expectancy	Life expectancy (or the expectation of life) at a given age, x, is the average number of years that a male or female aged x will live thereafter, and is calculated using age and gender-specific mortality rates at ages x, x+1, x+2 etc. Period life expectancy is calculated using age-specific mortality rates for the period under consideration and makes no allowance for changes in age-specific mortality rates after that period. Cohort life expectancy is calculated allowing for subsequent known or projected changes in age and gender-specific mortality rates after that period as he or she gets older. For example, a period life expectancy calculation for a male aged 50 in calendar year 2000 would use male mortality rates for age 50 in 2000, age 51 in 2000, age 52 in 2000 (and so on). The cohort life expectancy would be calculated using male mortality rates for age 50 in 2000, age 51 in 2001, age 52 in 2002 (and so on). The cohort definition is the better measure of true life expectancy.
Life-cycle consumption model	An economic theory which suggests that people aim to smooth consumption from year to year over their lives. Since their income tends to vary, they use saving and dis-saving to meet this aim, for example, building up a pension pot while in work and running it down during retirement.
Lighter touch sales regime	A common financial services industry term referring to the new sales regime for financial advisers which will be simpler and quicker and hence cheaper to comply with than the current **Conduct of Business** rules. See the FSA's CP04/11, published in June 2004, for details.
Limiting longstanding illness	An illness, disability or infirmity that has troubled an individual over a period of time or that is likely to affect them over a period of time and limits their activities in some way. Survey respondents are asked to assess their own health according to these criteria. The responses are used as measures of chronic sickness.
Long-dated bond yield	The return received by owners of **long-dated gilts**.
Long-dated gilts	**Gilts** with many years (e.g. 20) left until maturity.
Longevity	Length of life.

Longitudinal	A research study which follows a group of individuals over a period of time.
Lower Earnings Limit (LEL)	The level of earnings at which an individual is treated as if they have made **National Insurance** contributions. In 2004-05 the limit is £79 per week or £4,108 per year.
Lower Earnings Threshold (LET), also referred to as the underpin	For the purposes of calculation of **S2P** anyone earning less than the Lower Earnings Threshold (£11,600 in 2004-05) and above the **LEL** is treated as if they had earnings at the Lower Earnings Threshold.
Matching contributions	An arrangement common in **employer-sponsored Defined Contribution** pension schemes by which a contribution made by an individual is added to by their employer. A pound of individual contributions might be added to by 50p or £1 up to a limit.
Mean	The average value of a group, calculated as the total of all the values in a group and dividing by the number of values.
Means-tested benefits	State benefits where the amount paid depends on the level of income, capital and other personal circumstances.
Median	The median of a distribution divides it into two halves. Therefore half the group are above the median value and half below.
Medium-size firms	For statistical purposes, the Department of Trade and Industry usually defines a medium firm as one with 50-249 employees.
Minimum contributions	Contributions paid into a **contracted-out personal pension** scheme from the **National Insurance** scheme in place of building up rights to **S2P**.
Minimum Income Guarantee (MIG)	The forerunner of the **Guarantee Credit**.
National Insurance (NI)	The national system of benefits paid in specific situations, such as retirement, based on compulsory earnings-related contributions by employers and employees. Self-employed people make contributions on a different basis.

New Deal 50 plus	A programme of help provided by DWP for people aged 50 and over who want to work.
Nominal gilts	**Gilts** which pay an income which is constant in cash terms (i.e. is not **index-linked**)
Normal age pensioners or normal age retirees	Used by the Pensions Commission to refer to people who are aged at or above the **State Pension Age** and who are retired.
Notionally funded	A form of **unfunded** pension scheme in the public sector, where pension contributions are theoretically paid from the relevant department to HM Treasury to purchase **gilts** but where the future cost still has to be met out of future tax revenue.
Occupational pension	A pension which is provided via the employer, but the pension scheme takes the form of a trust arrangement and is legally separate from the employer.
Old-age dependency ratio	Used by the Pensions Commission to measure the number of people above 65 to the number of people aged 18 or 20 to 64 in the population.
Pay As You Go (PAYG)	A pension system where the pension is paid out of current revenue and no funds are accumulated to pay future pensions. The **National Insurance** system is a Pay As You Go system.
Pensim2	A model being developed by DWP that simulates the future life course of a current population sample to estimate their future pension income. It will enable aggregate and distributional analysis of alternative policy, demographic and economic scenarios.
Pension accrual	The build up of pension rights. In a **Defined Benefit** scheme this may be based on the number of years of contributions.
Pension Credit	The main **means-tested benefit** for pensioners, which combines the Guarantee Credit and the Savings Credit. For more details see Appendix F.
Pensioner Benefit Unit (PBU)	A single (non-cohabiting) person aged over **State Pension Age** (SPA) or a couple (married or cohabiting) where the man, defined as the head, is over SPA.
Period life expectancy	See life expectancy.

Persistence	Where someone continues to make contributions to a pension scheme over time.
Personal pension	A pension which is provided through a contract between an individual and the pension provider. The pension produced will be based on the level of contributions, investment returns and annuity rates. A personal pension can either be employer provided (a **Group Personal Pension**) or purchased individually.
Price-indexed	Increasing each year in line with inflation.
Primary earnings threshold	See Earnings threshold.
Private equity	Ownership claims on companies which are not listed on a public exchange.
Protection products	Financial products which provide insurance against specific events, such as unemployment or illness.
Quartile	The quartiles of a distribution divide it into four parts.
Quintiles	The quintiles of a distribution divide it into five parts.
Quoted equities or bonds	Are listed on a public exchange. They therefore tend to be more easily traded than **unquoted equities** (i.e. **private equity**) or bonds.
Real terms	Figures have been adjusted to remove the effect of increases in prices over time (i.e. inflation), usually measured by the **Retail Price Index**. Thus if something shown in real terms increases then it is rising faster than prices, whereas if it is constant, it rises at exactly the same pace as prices.
Reduction In Yield (RIY)	This measures the effect of all charges (whether **Annual Management Charges** or **implicit costs**) on the return an individual achieves on investment. If the rate of return before charges was 6% but the individual receives a rate of return of only 4% after charges, then the Reduction In Yield is 2%.
Replacement rate	This measures income in retirement as a proportion of income before retirement.

Retail Prices Index (RPI)	This is an average measure of the change in the prices of goods and services bought for consumption by the vast majority of households in the UK.
Retirement annuity contract	The forerunner of modern **personal pensions**.
Sandler product	New savings products which are relatively simple and can be sold using a simplified sales process. For more details see HM Treasury's consultation paper *"Consultation on 'stakeholder' saving and investment products regulations"*.
Savings Credit	Part of the **Pension Credit**. It is a means-tested benefit for people aged 65 and over, which is withdrawn at the rate of 40p for each £1 of pre-Pension Credit income above the level of the **Basic State Pension**.
Secondary earnings threshold	See Earnings threshold.
Security	General term for equities, bonds and other investments.
Self-Invested Pension Plan (SIPP)	A **personal pension** where the individual chooses where to invest their funds instead of giving their funds to a financial services company to manage.
Self-administered schemes	An **occupational pension** scheme where the administration is carried out directly on behalf of the trustees and not handed over to an insurance company.
Small and Medium Enterprises (SME)	For statistical purposes, the Department of Trade and Industry usually defines a SME as a firm with 249 or fewer employees.
Small firm	For statistical purposes, the Department of Trade and Industry usually defines a small firm as one with 49 or fewer employees.
Social housing	Social housing is housing of an adequate standard which is provided to rent (or on a shared ownership basis) at below market cost for households in need by Local Authorities or Registered Social Landlords.

Socio-economic class — Classification of individuals based on occupation. The Registrar General's Social Class based on Occupation has been used in this Report:

Class	Description	Examples of Occupations
Non-manual		
I	Professional	Doctors, chartered accountants, professionally qualified engineers
II	Managerial & technical/intermediate	Managers, school teachers, journalists
IIINM	Skilled non-manual	Clerks, cashiers, retail staff
Manual		
IIIM	Skilled manual	Supervisor of manual workers, plumbers, electricians, goods vehicle drivers
IV	Partly skilled	Warehousemen, security guards, machine tool operators, care assistants, waiting staff
V	Unskilled	Labourers, cleaners and messengers

Stakeholder pension — A **personal pension** product which complies with regulations which limit charges and allow individuals flexibility about contributions.

State Earnings Related Pension Scheme (SERPS) — The forerunner of the **State Second Pension**, which provides an earnings-related **National Insurance** pension based on contributions. For more details see Appendix F.

State Pension Age (SPA) — The age at which an individual can claim their state pension. It is currently 65 for men and 60 for women. The State Pension Age for women will gradually increase to 65 between 2010 and 2020.

State Second Pension (S2P) — The **National Insurance** pension which gives benefits based on an individual's earnings and contributions. For more details see Appendix F.

Term insurance	Life insurance which covers a specific length of time, for example to cover a mortgage.
Third party information	An administrative data source generated from returns to the Inland Revenue by personal pension providers for each individual **personal pension** plan. The data are used for the publication of National Statistics and compliance checking purposes.
Total Fertility Rate (TFR) or Total Period Fertility Rate (TPFR)	The average number of children that a woman would bear if the female population experienced the age-specific fertility rates occurring in a particular year throughout their childbearing lifespan. It provides a measure of fertility that is comparable over time and geography as it controls for the underlying age distribution of the population.
Trading down	Buying a home that is less expensive than one's current home.
Underpin	Another name for the **Lower Earnings Threshold**.
Unemployment	The number of unemployed people in the UK is measured through the Labour Force Survey following the internationally agreed definition recommended by the International Labour Organisation, an agency of the United Nations. Unemployed people are: without a job, want a job, have actively sought work in the last four weeks and are available to start work in the next two weeks, or: out of work, have found a job and are waiting to start it in the next two weeks. For some of the ELSA analysis unemployment is not so strictly defined.
Unfunded	Pension schemes which are not backed by a pension fund. Instead current contributions are used to pay current pensions along with other funds provided by the employer.
Unquoted equity	See private equity.
Upper Earnings Limit (UEL)	The upper limit on earnings for the purposes of calculating entitlement to **S2P**. Also the upper limit for most employee **National Insurance** contributions. In 2004-05 it is £31,720 per year or £610 per week. For more details see Appendix F.

Upper Earnings Threshold (UET)	An intermediate point prior to the **Upper Earnings Limit**, which affects the accrual of **S2P**. For more details see Appendix F.
US treasuries	These are bonds, loans etc issued by the US government. They have very similar characteristics to **gilts**.
Withdrawal rate	The rate at which a **means-tested benefit** is reduced for an additional pound of pre-benefit income. For more details see Appendix F.
Working age population	Generally defined as those aged 16-59 for women and 16-64 for men. However in some of our analysis we have used a starting age of 20.

List of abbreviations

Abbreviations	Description
ABI	Association of British Insurers
ACA	Association of Consulting Actuaries
AMC	Annual Management Charge
APP	Approved Personal Pension
AVC	Additional Voluntary Contribution
BHPS	British Household Panel Survey
BSP	Basic State Pension
COB	Conduct of Business
COMP	Contracted Out Money Purchase scheme
COSR	Contracted Out Salary Related scheme
CTB	Council Tax Benefit
DB	Defined Benefit
DC	Defined Contribution
DWP	Department for Work and Pensions
ECHP – UDB	European Community Household Panel Users' Database
ELSA	English Longitudinal Study of Ageing
EPC	Economic Policy Committee
EPP	Employers' Pension Provision survey
ESRC	Economic and Social Research Council
EU	European Union
EU15	European Union 15 Member States
FRS	Family Resources Survey
FSA	Financial Services Authority
FSAVC	Free-Standing Additional Voluntary Contribution
GAD	Government Actuary's Department

GDP	Gross Domestic Product
GNP	Gross National Product
GPP	Group Personal Pension
HB	Housing Benefit
HRP	Home Responsibilities Protection
IFA	Independent Financial Advisers
IFS	Institute for Fiscal Studies
ISA	Individual Savings Account
IPPR	Institute for Public Policy Research
LEL	Lower Earnings Limit
LET	Lower Earnings Threshold
LFS	Labour Force Survey
LLMDB2	Lifetime Labour Market Database
MIG	Minimum Income Guarantee
NAPF	National Association of Pension Funds
NES	New Earnings Survey
NI	National Insurance
NINO	National Insurance Number
NIRS2	National Insurance Recording System
OECD	Organisation for Economic Co-operation and Development
ONS	Office for National Statistics
PAYG	Pay As You Go
PPF	Pension Protection Fund
RIY	Reduction in Yield
RPI	Retail Prices Index
SBS	Small Business Service
S2P	State Second Pension
SERPS	State Earnings Related Pension Scheme
SIPP	Self Invested Pension Plan
SPA	State Pension Age

SPI	Survey of Personal Incomes
TFR	Total Fertility Rate
UEL	Upper Earnings Limit
UET	Upper Earnings Threshold

Bibliography

ABI, (October 2003), *The State of the Nation's Savings*

ABI, (September 2003), *The Future of the Pension Annuity Market – summary report*

ABI, (2003), *ABI response to HMT consultation on Sandler products*

ACA, (May 2004), *2004 Smaller Firms Pensions Survey: A Divided Nation*

ACA, (March 2003), *Occupational Pensions 2003 Pensions Reform: too little, too late?*

Aegon, (May 2003), *AEGON UK Response to HM Treasury and Department for Work and Pensions Consultation Document: Proposed product specification for Sandler 'stakeholder' products*

Bajekal, M. *Healthy life expectancy by area deprivation: estimates for England, 1994-1999,* National Centre for Social Research, submitted for publication Journal of Epidemiology and Public Health

Balchin, S and Shah, D (May 2004), *The Pensioners' Income Series 2002/3,* DWP

Banks, J., Emmerson, C., Oldfield, Z. (forthcoming), *Prepared for Retirement? The pension arrangements and retirement expectations of older workers in England,* Institute for Fiscal Studies

Barclays Capital, (2004), *Barclays Equity Gilt Study*

Bardasi, E., Jenkins, S. and Rigg, J. (2002), *Retirement and the income of older people: a British perspective,* Ageing and Society Vol. 22, pp131-159

Barker, K. (March 2004), *Review of Housing Supply Delivering Stability: Securing our Future Housing Needs Final Report – Recommendations,* HMSO

Bateman, H., Kingston, G. and Piggott, J. (2001), *Forced Savings Mandating Private Retirement Incomes,* Cambridge University Press

Black, O., Richardson, I. and Herbert, R. (July 2004), *Jobs in the public sector mid-2003,* ONS, Labour Market Trends, Vol. 112, No. 7, pp271-281

Blake, D. and Burrows, W. (October 2001), *Survivor Bonds: Helping to Hedge Mortality Risk,* The Pensions Institute, The Journal of Risk and Insurance, 2001, Vol. 68, No. 2, pp339-348

Blöndal, S., and Scarpetta, S. (February 1999), *The Retirement Decision in OECD Countries,* OECD, Economics Department, Working Papers No. 202

Blundell, R. and Tanner, S. (December 1999) *Labour force participation and retirement in the UK,* IFS

Bobak, M., Kristenson, M., Pikhart, H. and Marmot, M. *A comparison of Russian and Swedish community – based data,* International Centre for Health and Society, University College London, UK and Department of Health and Society, University of Linkoping, Sweden

Breeze, E., Fletcher, A., Leon, D., Marmot, M. and Shipley, M. (2001), *Do Socioeconomic Disadvantages Persist Into Old Age? Self-Reported Morbidity in 29-Year Follow-Up of the Whitehall Study,* American Journal of Public Health, February 2001, Vol. 91, No. 2 pp277-283

Bridgwood, A. (2000), *People Aged 65 and over: Results of an independent study carried out on behalf of the Department of Health as part of the 1998 General Household Survey,* ONS

Brown, J. (1990), *Social Security for Retirement,* Joseph Rowntree Foundation, York

CBI, (June 2004), *Raising the bar. Benchmarking pension provision,* CBI Pension Strategy Group

CBI/Mercer Human Resource Consulting, (2004), *A view from the top: A survey of business leaders' views on UK pension provision*

Cebulla, A. and Reyes De-Bearman, S. (2004), *Employers' Pension Provision Survey 2003,* DWP, Research Report No. 207

Choi, J., Laibson, D., Madrian, B. and Metrick, A. (November 2001), *Defined Contribution Pensions: Plan Rules, Participant Decisions, and the Path of Least Resistance,* NBER Working Paper No. W8655

Connolly, E. and Kohler, M. (March 2004), *The Impact of Superannuation on Household Saving, Reserve Bank of Australia,* Research Discussion Paper 2004-01

Craggs, A. (ed), (June 2004), *Family Spending: A report on the 2002-2003 Expenditure and Food Survey,* ONS

Donkin, A., Goldblatt, P. and Lynch, K. (Autumn 2002), *Inequalities in life expectancy by social class 1972-1999.* Health Statistics Quarterly 15, pp5-15, ONS

DSS, (December 1998), *A new contract for welfare: Partnership in Pensions* Cm 4179, TSO

DWP, (February 2004), *Simplicity, security and choice: Informed choices for working and saving*

DWP, (2004), *Family Resources Survey 2002-03*

Economic Policy Committee, (2001), *Budgetary challenges posed by ageing populations,* ECFIN/655/01-EN final

Edwards, L., Regan, S. and Brooks, R. (2001), *Age old attitudes? Planning for retirement, means-testing, inheritance and informal care,* Institute for Public Policy Research

ESRC, (2004), *Seven Ages of Man and Woman: A look at the Life Britain in the Second Elizabethan era*

Feldstein, M. and Horioka, C. (1980), *Domestic Savings and International Capital Flows,* Economic Journal 90, pp314-329

Fries, J. (December 2002), *Reducing Disability in Older Age,* Journal of the American Medical Association, Vol. 288 No. 24

FSA, (July 2004), *Building Financial Capability in the UK*

FSA, (June 2004), *A basic advice regime for the sale of stakeholder products,* CP04/11

FSA, (December 2002), *Persistency of life and pensions policies Eighth survey*

GAD, (2004), *National Population Projections 2002-based Report giving population projections by age and sex for the United Kingdom, Great Britain and constituent countries,* TSO

GAD, (October 2003), *Government Actuary's Quinquennial Review of the National Insurance Fund as at April 2000*

GAD, (April 2003), *Occupational pensions schemes 2000: Eleventh survey by the Government Actuary* and previous editions

GAD, (1998), *Government Actuary's Department Survey of Expenses of Occupational Pension Schemes*

HM Treasury, (June 2004), *Consultation on 'stakeholder' saving and investment products regulations*

HM Treasury, (December 2003), *Long-term public finance report: fiscal sustainability with an ageing population*

HM Treasury and DWP, (July 2003), *Assessing the likely market impacts of charge caps on retail investment products*

HM Treasury, (July 2002), *Sandler Review: Medium and Long-term Retail Savings in the UK*

IDS, (2004), *Pensions in Practice 2004/05*

Iyengar, S., Jiang, W. and Huberman, G. (2003), *How Much Choice is Too Much?: Contributions to 401(k) Retirement Plans,* Pension Research Council, Working Paper 2003-10

James, K. (February 2000), *The Price of Retail Investing in the UK,* FSA, Occasional Paper Series 6

Joseph Rowntree Foundation, (2004), *Homeowners: Sons and Daughters*

Lunnon, M. (October 1998), *New Earnings Survey data on occupational pension provision,* Labour Market Trends, pp499-505

Madrian, B. and Shea, D. (2001), *The power of suggestion: inertia in 401(k) participation and savings behaviour,* Quarterly Journal of Economics, Vol. CXVI, Issue 4, pp1149-1187

Manton, K.G. and Gu, X. (May 2001), *Changes in the prevalence of chronic disability in the United States black and nonblack population above age 65 from 1982 to 1999,* Centre for Demographic Studies, Duke University, Durham, Proceedings of the National Academy of Sciences of the Unit

Marmot, M., Banks, J., Blundell, R., Lessof, C. and Nazroo, J. (ed), (December 2003), *Health, wealth and lifestyles of the older population in England: The 2002 English Longitudinal Study of Ageing,* UCL, IFS and National Centre for Social Research

Martin, C., Martin, L., and Mabbett, A. (April 2002), *SME Ownership Succession – Business Support and Policy Implications,* Knowledge Management Centre, Business School, University of Central England

Mayhew, V. (2003), *Pensions 2002: Public Attitudes to Pensions and Planning for Retirement,* DWP Research Report No. 193

Mayhew, V. (2001), *Pensions 2000: Public Attitudes to Pensions and Planning for Retirement,* DSS Research Report No.130

Mehra, R. and Prescott, E. (1985), *The Equity Premium: A Puzzle,* Journal of Monetary Economics, March 1985, pp145-161

Miles, D. (1999), *Modelling the impact of demographic change upon the economy,* Economic Journal, Vol. 109, No. 452, pp1-37

Mitchell, O. and Utkus, S. (2003), *Lessons from Behavioural Finance for Retirement Plan design,* Pension Research Council, Working Paper 2003-6

National Association of Pension Funds, (2003), *Twenty-ninth Annual Survey of Occupational Pension Schemes*

OECD, (October 2003), *Monitoring the Future Social Implication of Today's Pension Policies*

OECD, (October 2003), *Monitoring Pension Policies Annex: Country Chapters*

ONS, (October 2003), *New Earnings Survey 2003*

ONS, (2003), *United Kingdom National Accounts The Blue Book 2003,* TSO

Poterba, J. (August 2004), *Population Aging and Financial Markets,* Federal Reserve Bank of Kansas, Jackson Hole Economic Symposium

PPI, (July 2003), *State Pension Models*

Purcell, K. (Summer 2002), *Qualifications and Careers Equal Opportunities and Earnings Among Graduates,* University of the West of England, Equal Opportunities Commission, Working Paper Series No. 1

Rickards, L., Fox, K., Roberts, C., Fletcher, L., and Goddard, E. (2004), *Living in Britain, No 31, Results from the 2002 General Household Survey,* ONS, TSO, London

Samuelson, P. (1958), *An Exact Consumption Loan Model of Interest with or without the Social Contrivance of Money,* Journal of Political Economy 66, pp467-482

Sefton, J. and van de Ven, J. (2004), *Does Means Testing Exacerbate Early Retirement?* National Institute of Economic and Social Research, London, Working Paper 244

Shaw, C. (Spring 1999), *1996-based population projections by legal marital status for England and Wales,* ONS, Population Trends 95, pp23-32

Small Business Service, (August 2004), *Small and Medium-sized Enterprise (SME) Statistics for the UK 2003,* DTI

Smith, J. (Autumn 2004), *Exploring attitudes to housing wealth and retirement,* CML Housing Finance, Autumn 2004, pp22-33

Stark, J. (2002), Annuities – *The Consumer Experience,* ABI

Thaler, R. H. and Benartzi, S. (2004), *Save More Tomorrow: Using Behavioural Economics to Increase Employee Saving,* Journal of Political Economy, Vol. 112, No 1, Pt. 2, pp164-187

Thaler, R. H. and Benartzi, S. (2001), *Naïve Diversification Strategies in Defined Contribution Saving Plans,* The American Economic Review, March 2001, Vol. 91. No. 1, pp79-98

Thomas, M., Walker, A., Wilmot, A. and Bennet, N. (1998), *Living in Britain. Results from the 1996 General Household Survey,* ONS, TSO, London

Tily, G., Penneck, P. and Forest, C. (August 2004), *Private Pensions Estimates and the National Accounts,* Economic Trends No. 609

Towers Perrin, (June 2004), *Survey of Defined Contribution Pension Arrangements*

Tudela, M. and Young, G. (Winter 2003), *The distribution of unsecured debt in the United Kingdom: survey evidence*, Bank of England Quarterly Bulletin, pp417-427

Turner, A. (September 2003), *The Macro-Economics of Pensions,* Lecture to the Actuarial Profession

Watson Wyatt LLP, (January 2003), *Administration Cost Survey 2003*

Whitehouse, E. (June 2000), *Administrative Charges for Funded Pensions: An International Comparison and Assessment,* Pension Reform Primer Series, Social Protection Discussion Paper 0016

Willets, D. (July 2004), *The Pension Crisis: What it Means and What to do About it,* Speech to Politeia

Women and Equality Unit, *Individual incomes of men and women 1996/97 to 2002/03,* DTI

World Economic Forum, (2004), *Living Happily Ever After: The Economic Implications of Ageing Societies*

Yoo, P. (1994), *Age Distributions and Returns to Financial Assets,* Federal Reserve Bank of St. Louis, Working Paper 94-002B

Young, G. (2002), *The implications of an ageing population for the UK economy,* Bank of England Working Paper

WITHDRAWN
FROM STOCK
QMUL LIBRARY